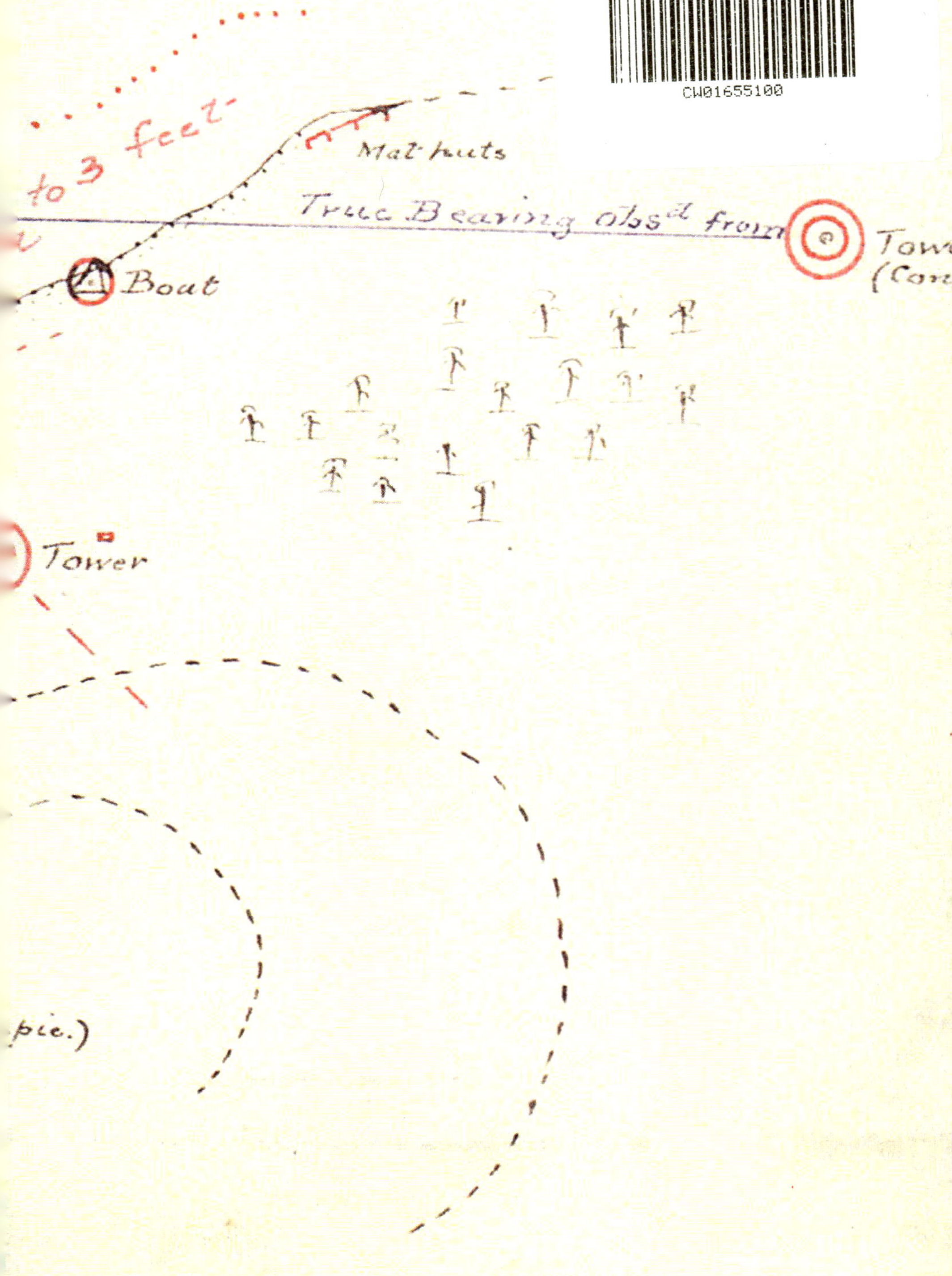
to 3 feet
Mat huts
True Bearing obsd from
Tow
(Con
Boat
Tower
pie.)

CW01655100

Copyright © Uncommon Ltd and individual contributors. 2018

This book is sold subject to the condition that it shall not, by way of trade or otherwise, be lent, resold, hired out, or otherwise circulated without the publisher's prior consent in any form of binding or cover other than that in which it is published and without a similar condition, including this condition, being imposed on the subsequent purchaser.

All images are copyright of the authors unless otherwise credited.

The opinions expressed in this book are those of the authors. Facts are deemed correct at time of going to print; some may be subject to change.

ISBN 978-99957-872-2-6

Publisher: Dora Bouhara
Collection Design: Jon Banthorpe
Editor & Art Director: Sharmeen Inayat
Copy Editors: Chloé Roubert, Frances Marks

Printed and bound in Italy by Graphicom srl.

Uncommon Ltd
Finance House, First Floor
Princess Elisabeth Street
XBX 1102
Ta Xbiex, Malta
www.uncommonguidebooks.com

UNCOMMON DUBAI +

EDITED BY
SHARMEEN INAYAT

The road is a sign of happiness

Because it is an eternal crossing.

—Adonis

CONTENTS

3. RECREATE

4. REROUTE

PREFACE

We do not know for certain why she is called Dubai, but a superfluity of stories make equally sound/unsound assertions: A woman called Dubaa who lived in the area; the crawling motion of an insect; to creep—in the way the creek creeps into the land; the personification of the bays of Deira and Bur Dubai as "two brothers"; baby locusts or a land devastated by a plague locusts; mastigure, a desert-roaming lizard; bees. There are even multiple readings of an old Arabic proverb: "they came with Daba Dubai". It has been suggested that it could mean 'they came with a swarm of locusts' or 'they came with a lot of money'. In a 2007 *Gulf News* article speculating on the etymological origins, one interviewee remarked that "the mind is comfortable with certain stories while other narratives seem very unlikely".[i]

The earliest known reference to a place called Dubai is to be found in the travelogue of Gasparo Balbi, a Venetian state jeweler and merchant. *Viaggio dell'Indie Orientali*, printed in 1590, includes 'Debai' in a list of areas and islands important to the pearling industry of the time, along with three other emirates: Abu Dhabi, Ajman and Ras Al Khaimah. Balbi records his journeys and observations to produce what must have been a resourceful guide for merchants, with information such as exchange rates, duties and travel routes.

The history of how mercantile port towns, languid fishing villages and tribal inland settlements coalesced into the interconnected network of city-states we understand the Emirates as today alludes to the area's intrinsic reliance on population mobility of the wider region and continual renewal and expansion. It is a useful premise for this miscellany and to understand the phenomenon of Dubai today. Tribal encroachment from the desert, economic growth of port towns, and exposure to classical, mercantile and settler empires resulted in shifting, negotiated, and often contested boundaries between settlements of sedentary, agricultural, maritime, and nomadic populations.

Dubai entered the 20th century as an imperial protectorate and a seemingly natural harbor with links to a mobile workforce and immigrant populations, most of which in turn maintained strong ties with their states of origin, notably India, Iran and others within the Arabian Peninsula. Perhaps in part by cause of its demographic flux, even during the thirty years of poverty between the decline of the pearl industry—after the Japanese advent of cultured pearls—and the start of the production of oil in the 1960s, the port gave the impression of a thriving market.

Since the era of the petrodollar boom, the population and consequently the urban footprint of Dubai are estimated to have doubled four times. There is little mystery in the correlation of these waves to those of regional instability and increasingly global forces coupled with local economic determinism. The city has regenerated herself, at the rate of a phoenix-a-decade in response to equally fluid and burgeoning ambitions.

Economic shifts have spawned local discourses on identity, place-making and belonging. Beyond projections of Dubai as an ersatz destination, these voices begin to identify the distinct rhythms of a differentiated and dynamic experience. They reveal narratives that can at once be comfortable and unlikely or, uncomfortable and likely.

The intent for this volume is two-fold: to collate reflections on change and exchange in the communal and private realms; and to offer anomalous narratives that are enmeshed in the urban realm. Assembled as a guide, insights are presented in four acts. *Relate* considers the wider context of the UAE to trace continental traversal and cultural currency. *Review* focuses on urban artifacts and the changing city as the vessel of collective aspirations for its past, present and futures. *Recreate* invites the reader into more intimate and private landscapes through poetry, fiction, and memoirs. And finally, *Reroute* trails residents into neighboring emirates and towns to explore paces, participants, and terrains of flux.

This is admittedly a subjective constellation of conversations, investigations, and memories meant to engage with, rather than attempt to resolve, the contradictions that suffuse the city.

Thank you Omie, for infinite joy, knowledge, support, and the fragile notion of being at home.

SHARMEEN INAYAT

---

i Alafrangi, Manal and Siham Al Najami. "The Secret Lives of Names" *Gulf News: Weekend Review*. March 28, 2007.

1. RELATE

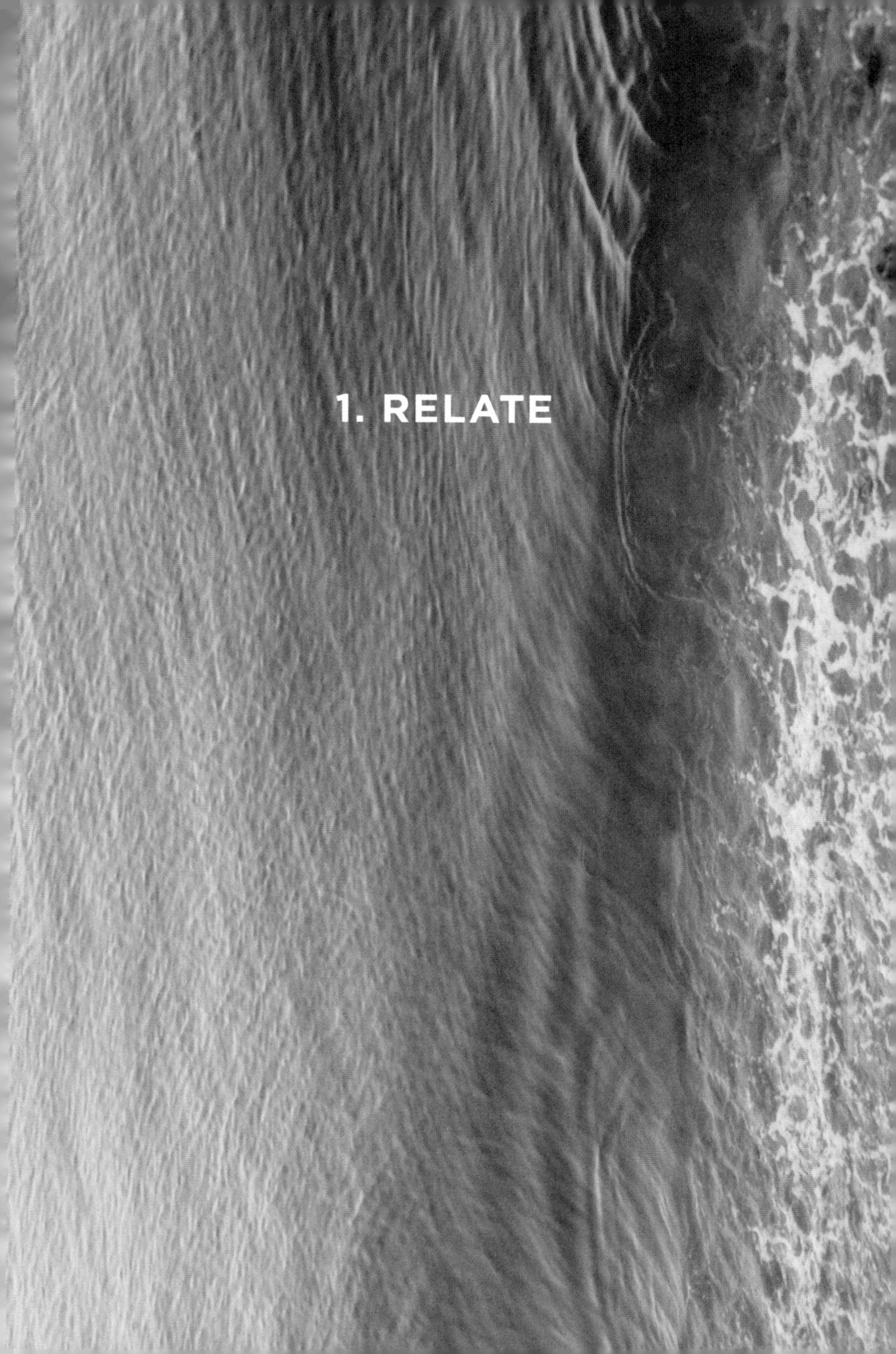

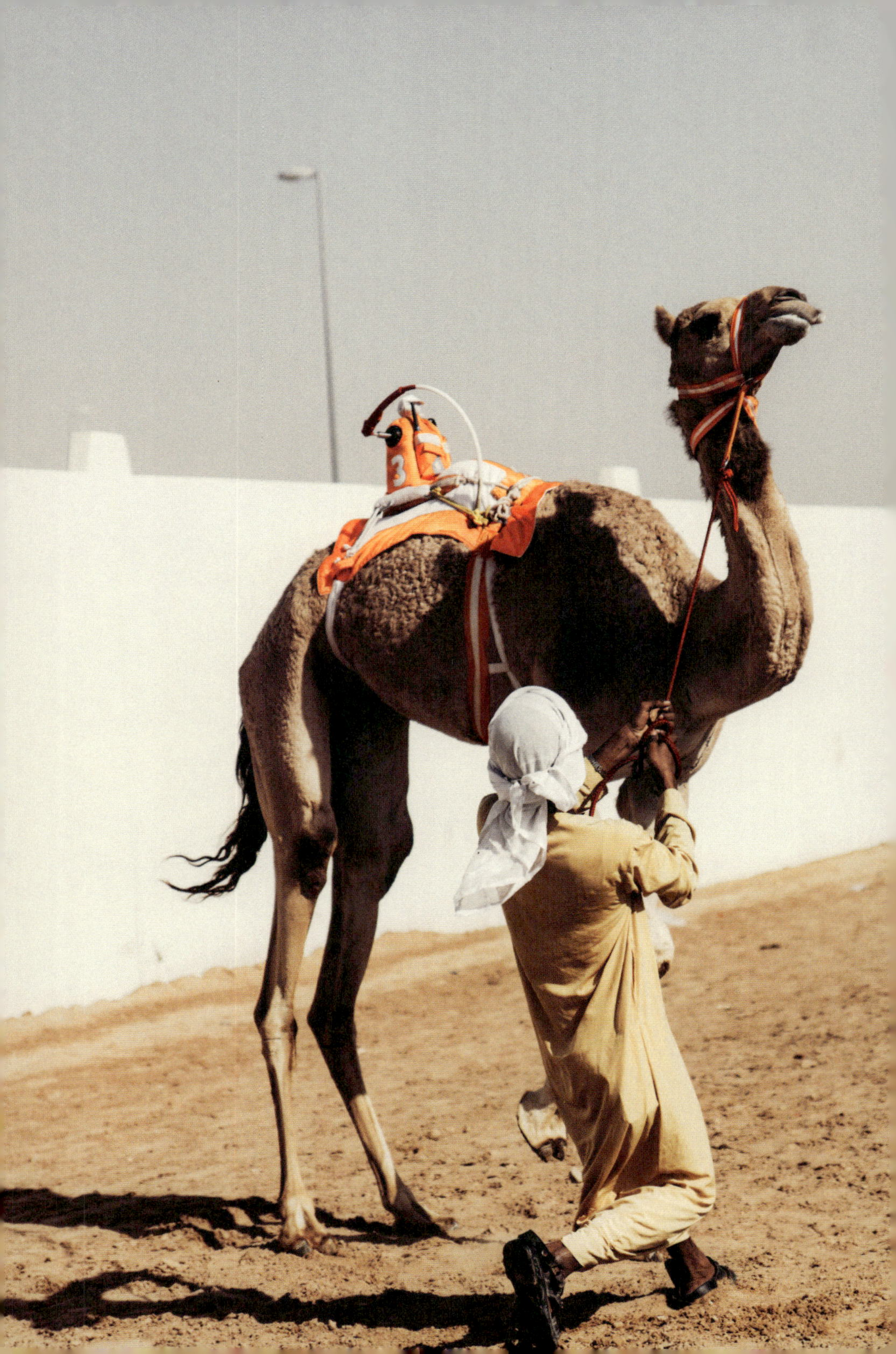
3

POETICS & POLITICS OF NEWLY INVENTED TRADITIONS: CAMEL RACING IN THE UAE

SULAYMAN KHALAF
PHOTOGRAPHS: ANNA NIELSEN

In the UAE, during the long racing season from October to April, the slender, tall, greyhound-like *hejin* (race camel) become the center of attention for locals and expatriates. The UAE as an imagined community rests on certain cultural, heritage-related foundations among which camel culture occupies a central position – it provides links to the historical past of the Emirates' pastoral way of life that has been swept away by oil-triggered modernization. Annual races also provide the Emirates' political community with a ritually constructed theater to celebrate its own specific political ideology, cultural traditions, and values by invoking nationalist themes, symbols, metaphors, and language. Framing these cultural celebrations with *Badu* (bedouin) poetics and cultural aesthetics gives greater credence to the idea of *asala* (cultural authenticity) for the Emirati national community, which currently perceives itself as seriously threatened by shifting and powerful global forces. Inventing such traditions aims at safeguarding cultural heritage and national identity, as well as the traditional dynastic political structure of the UAE as a modernizing nation-state.

Badu of Arabia used the camel as a significant cultural reference through which they constructed their worldview and assessed the fortunes and misfortunes of their desert life. This fact stems from the particularities of their ecology, economy, and political life that led them to construct a universe revolving around the camel. It is no exaggeration to say that the rhythm of their days and seasons was seen through the eyes of their camels. This ancient tradition of celebrating the camel and nomadic life was seriously undermined by the advent of oil wealth and the settled, affluent life it created for the Badu. Badu complaints about the loss of their traditional camel wealth and skills are balanced by the timely insights and realization of the national leaders that the preservation and revival (*ihya'*) of camel traditions are perfect cultural material for building the state's ideological and political identity.

* * *

With the oil economy came a shift in the use of camels from an economic to a cultural domain. With oil affluence and rapid social change came a quest to preserve national identity, and for this the camel has become a significant cultural currency. For the Badu, the camel is good to think about, good to romanticize, good to poeticize, and good to essentialize. With heritage revival gaining unprecedented importance it has been easy for the Badu, and their poets in particular, to carry on the tradition of using their camels as cultural references.

* * *

The Badu, like their Yemeni kin, compose their poems in response to real events and sociopolitical issues. Therefore, it is not surprising that camel racing has become the focus for the Badu to express their aesthetics in poetic communicative forms. These poems, with television imaging and commentary, constitute a politico-cultural universe that is meaningful to all. The cultural production is not confined to the spectacle of swift camels running, or the carefully crafted television images of royal rituals; it is also found in its most delicate form in the poetic language delivered during such events. The media's systematic projection of the Badu poetic tradition has become an integral part of camel racing. The ability to compose poetry, enjoy its beauty, or be moved by its force are all ingredients of Badu culture.

* * *

Poets, as they aestheticize, romanticize, and essentialize the pedigree of camels, become cultural agents operating against the forces of commoditization that are now prevalent in UAE society at large. The revival of their camel traditions is meant to support a sense of cultural continuity and conservatism in a society threatened by its own wealth and fast pace of change.

This contribution is an abridged version of an essay by Dr. Sulayman Khalaf entitled 'Poetics and Politics of Newly Invented Traditions in the Gulf: Camel Racing in the United Arab Emirates'. The full version was first published in *Ethnology*, Vol. 39, No. 3 (Summer, 2000), pp. 243-261.

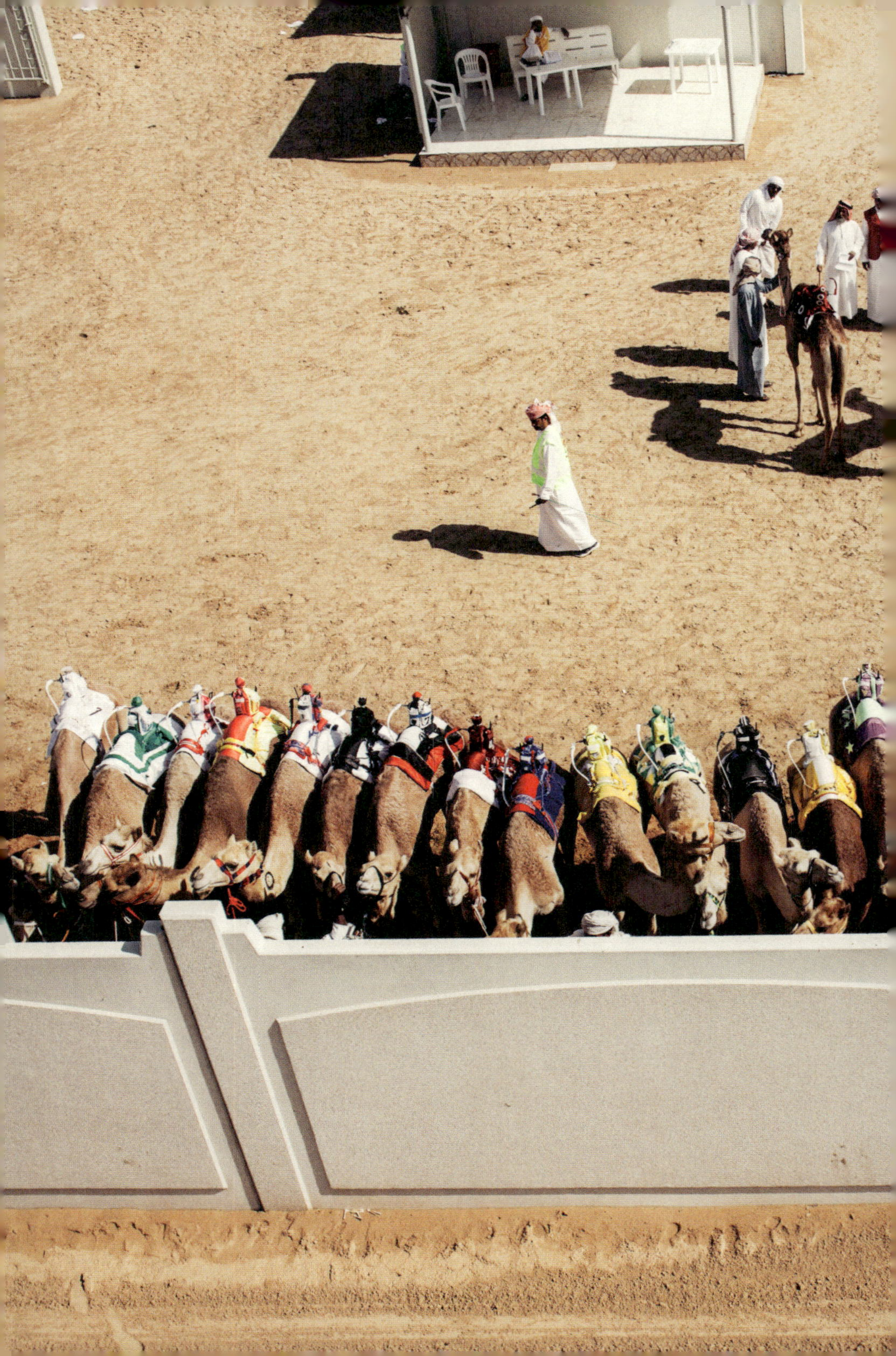

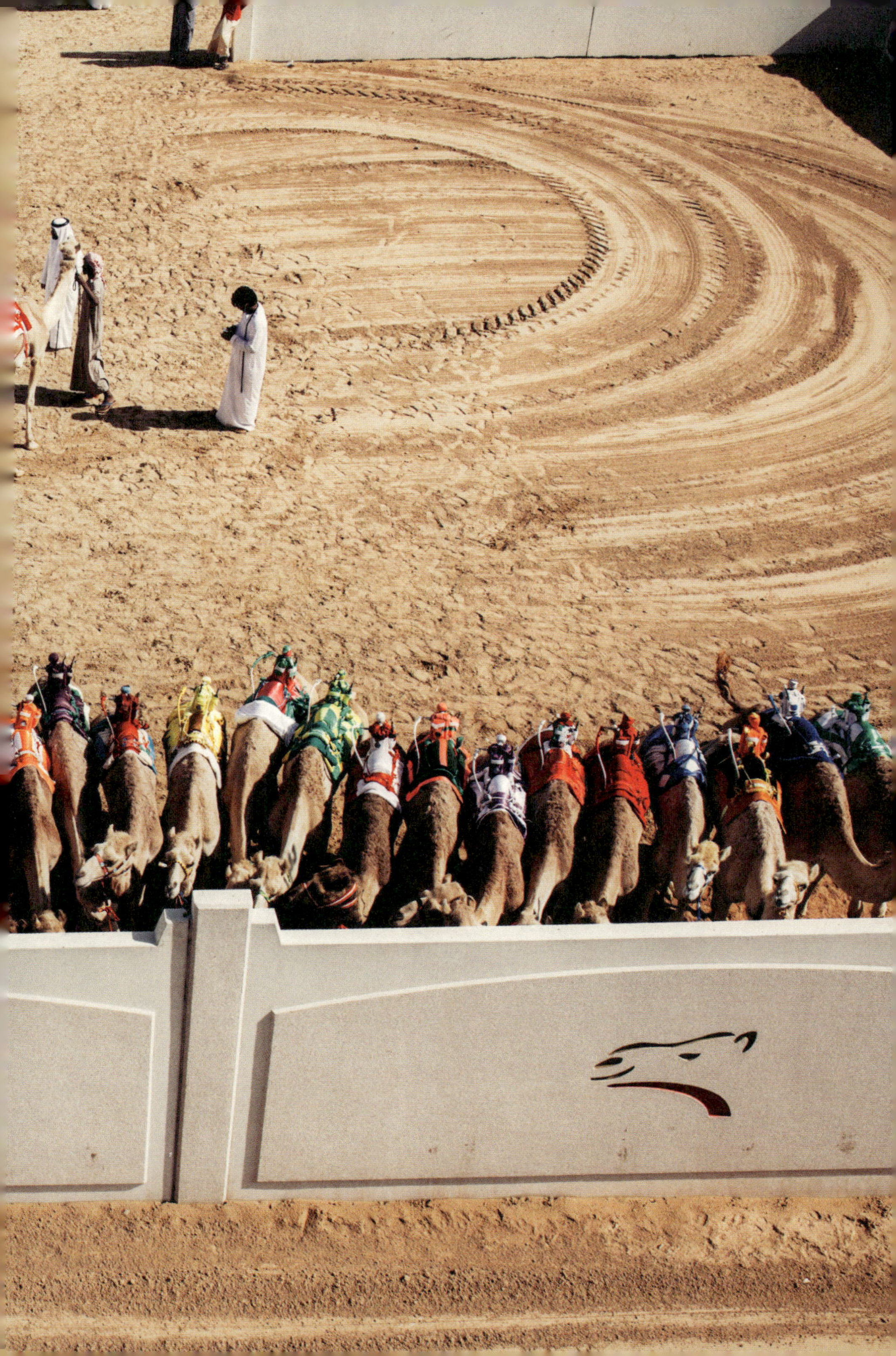

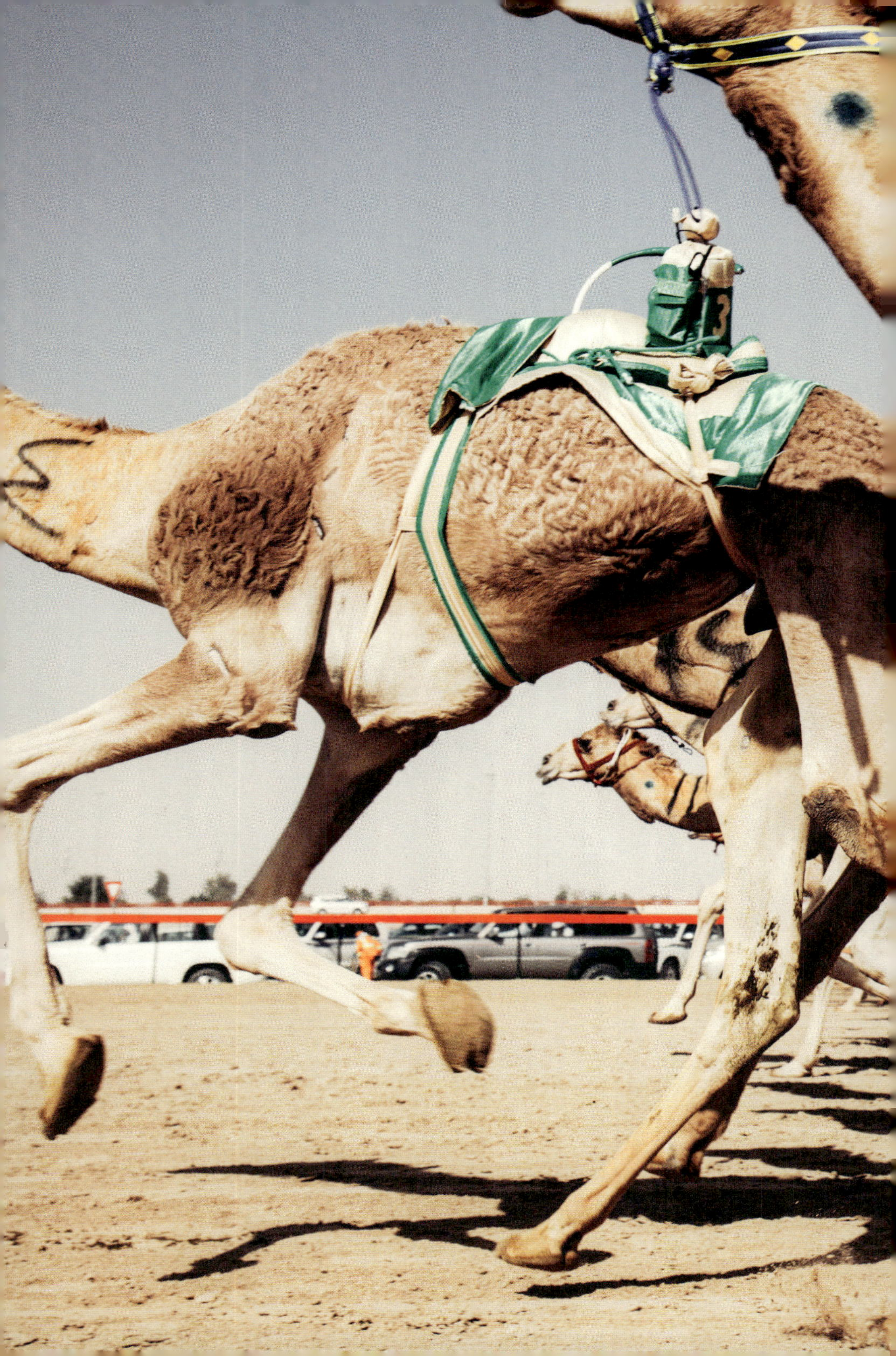

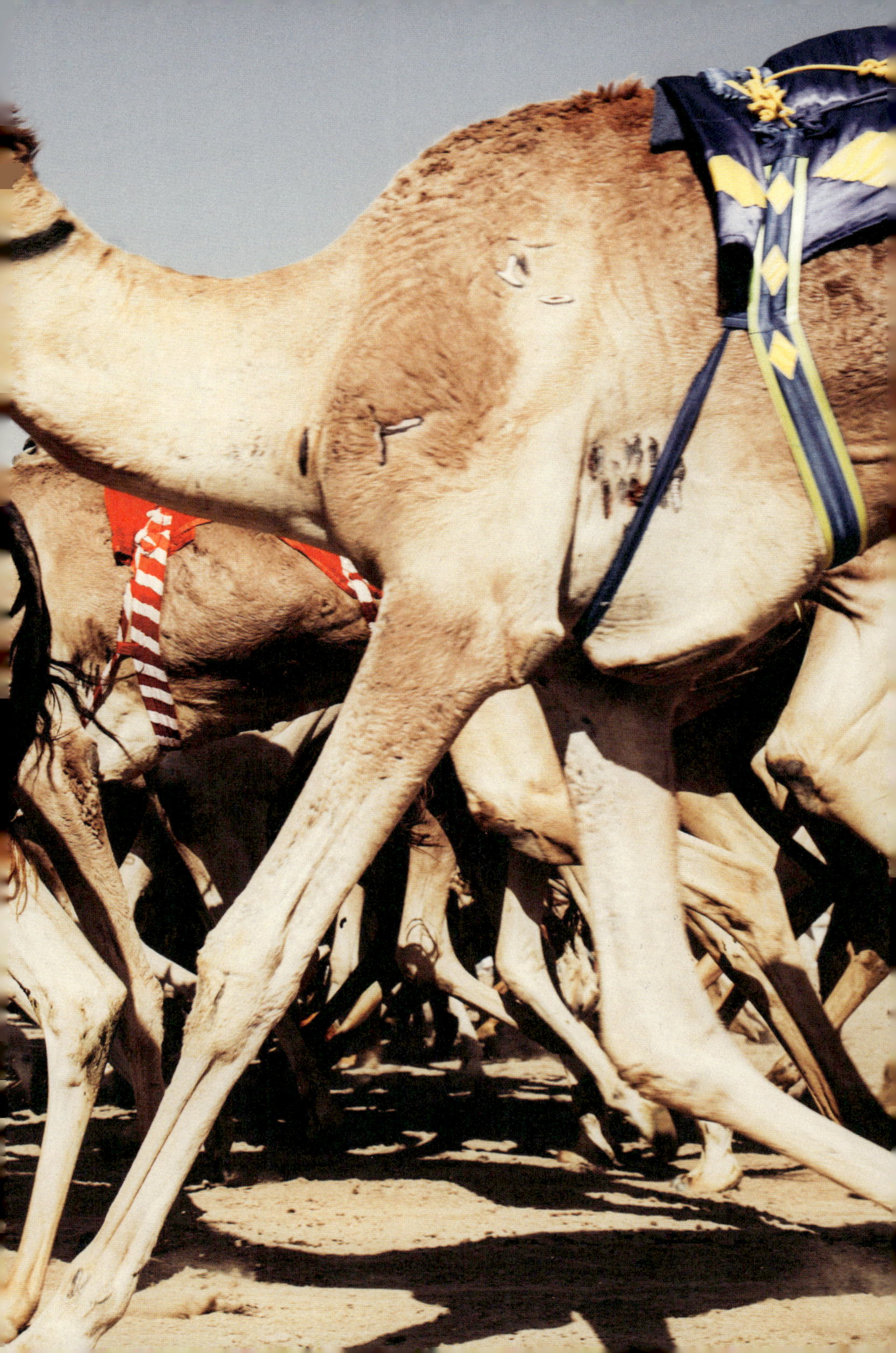

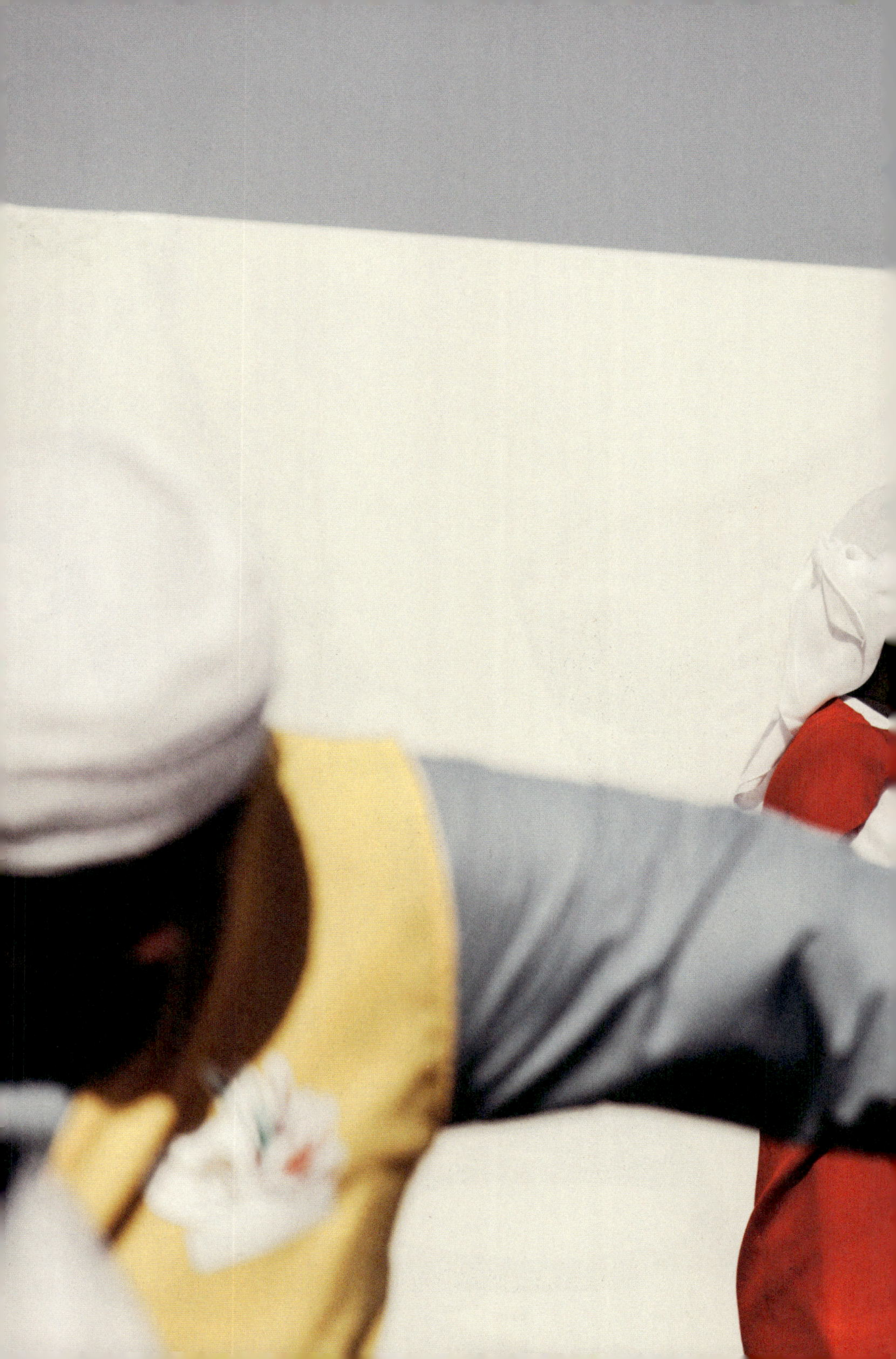

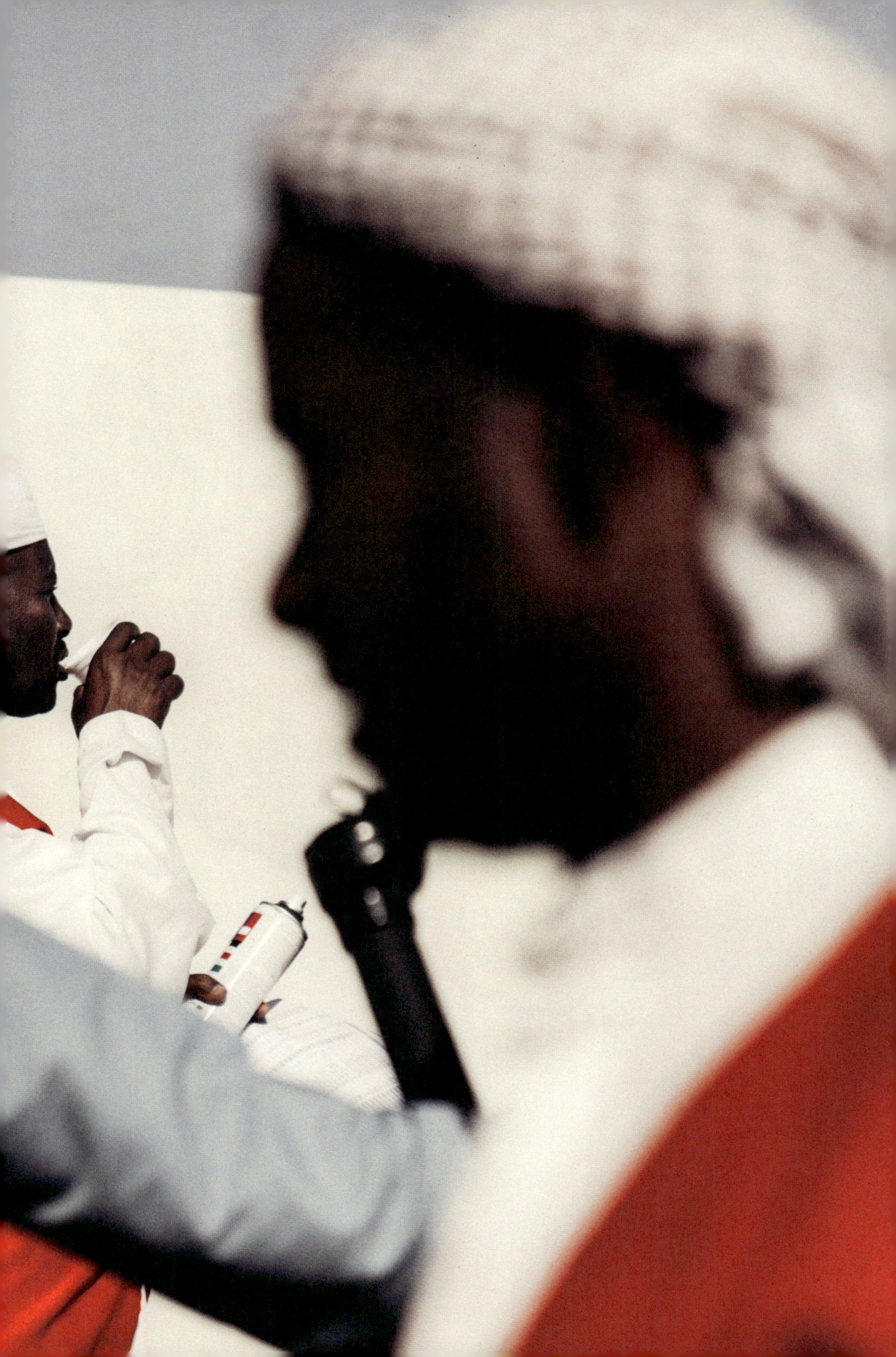

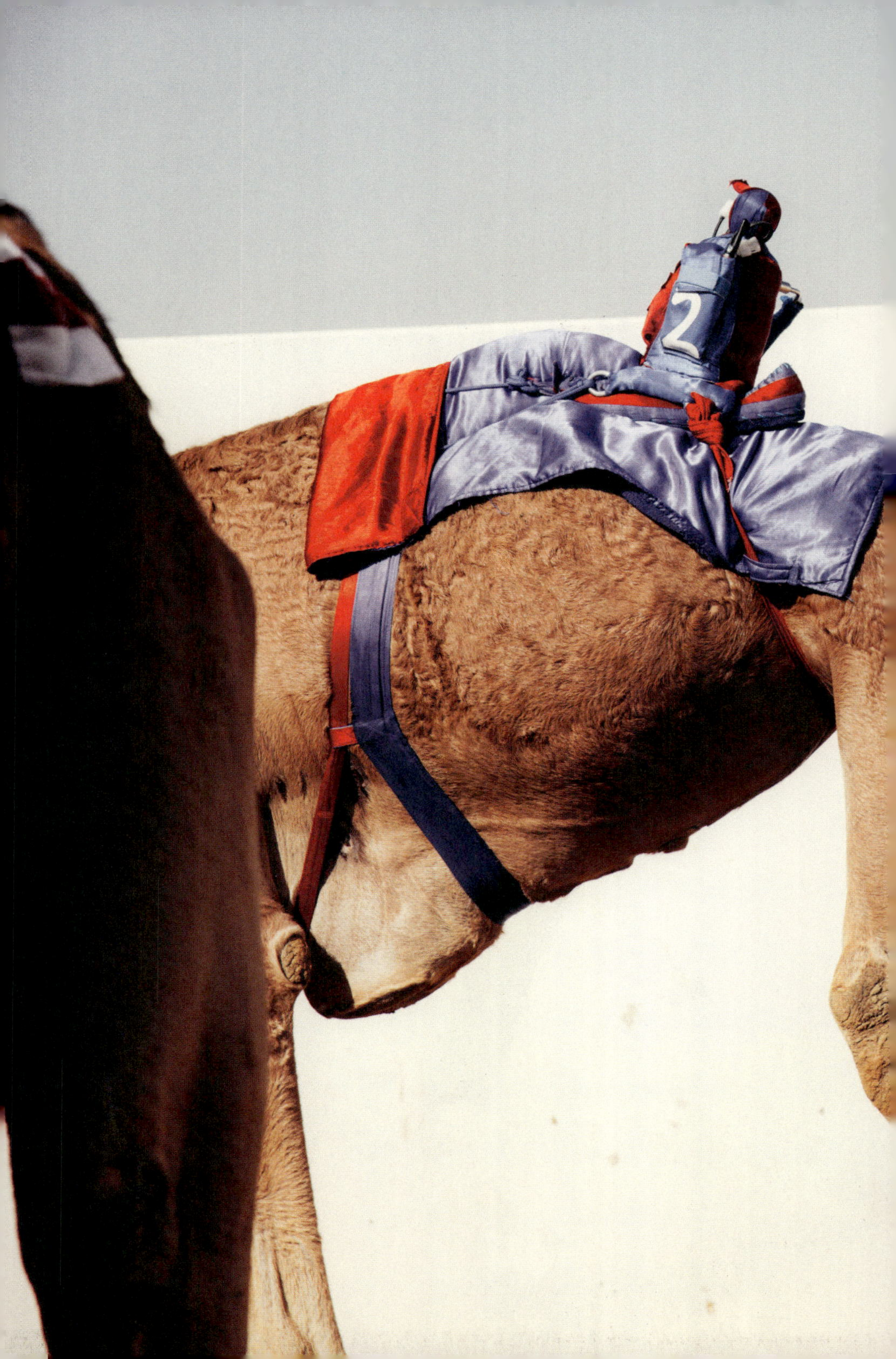

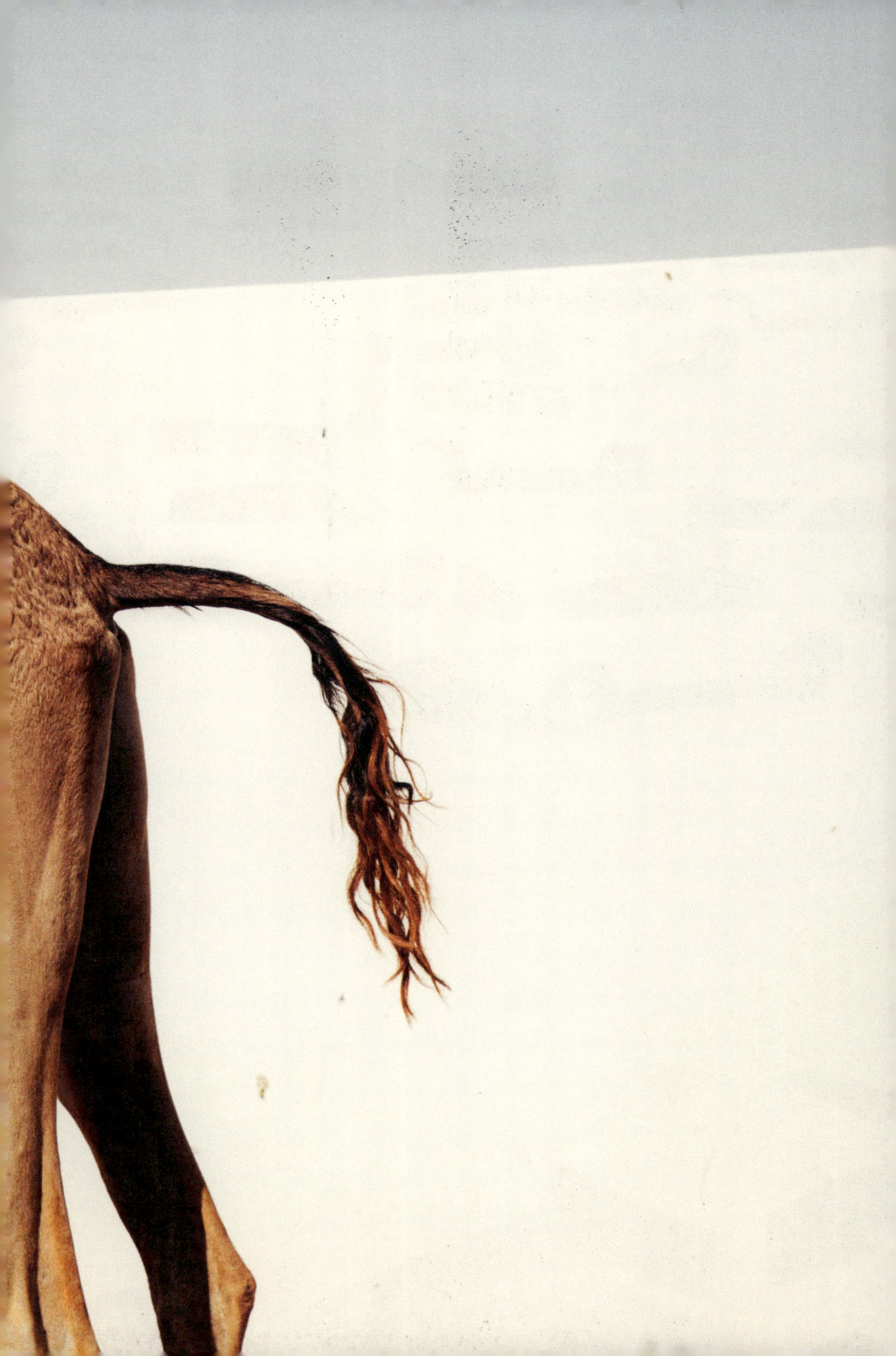

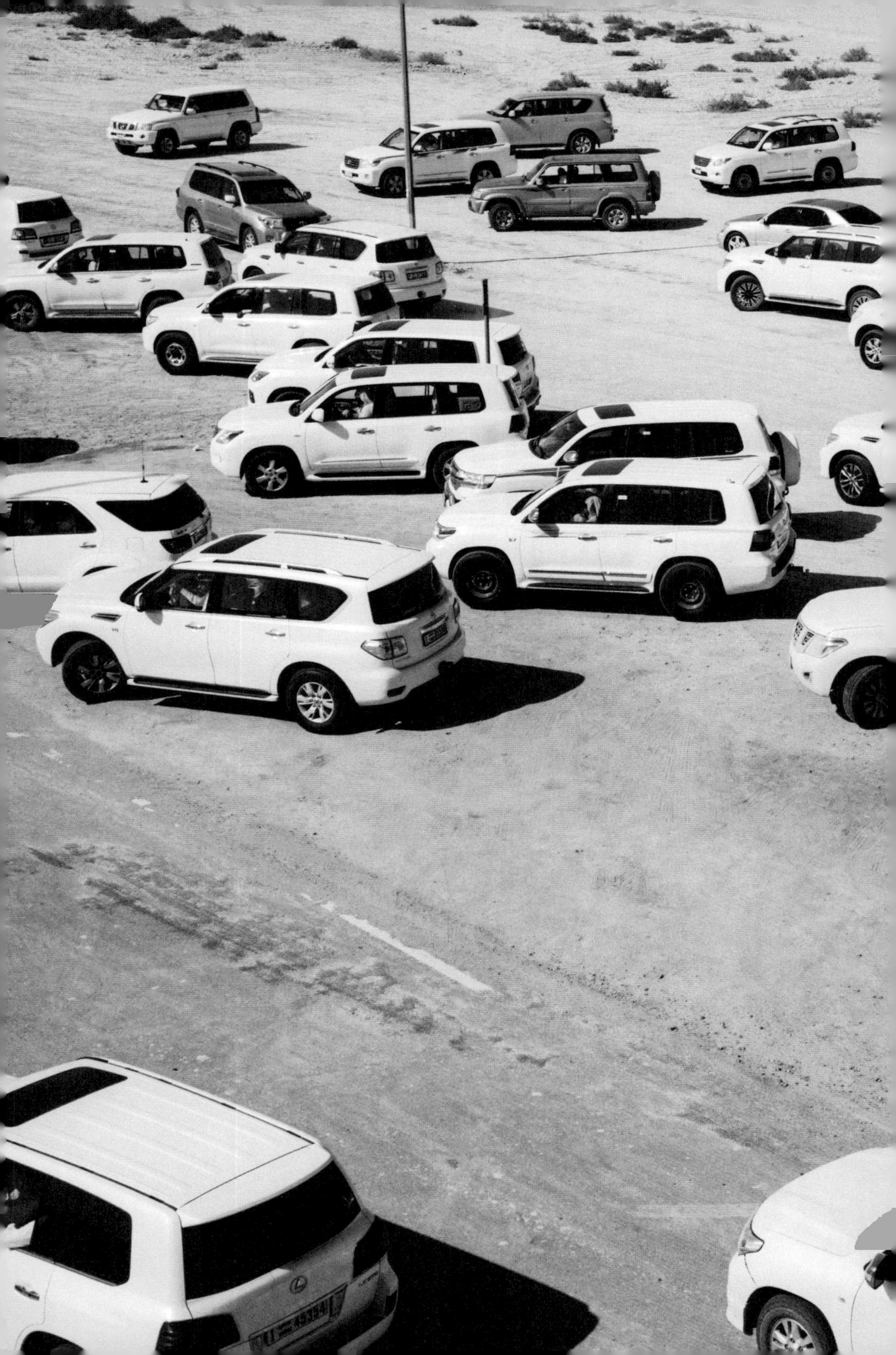

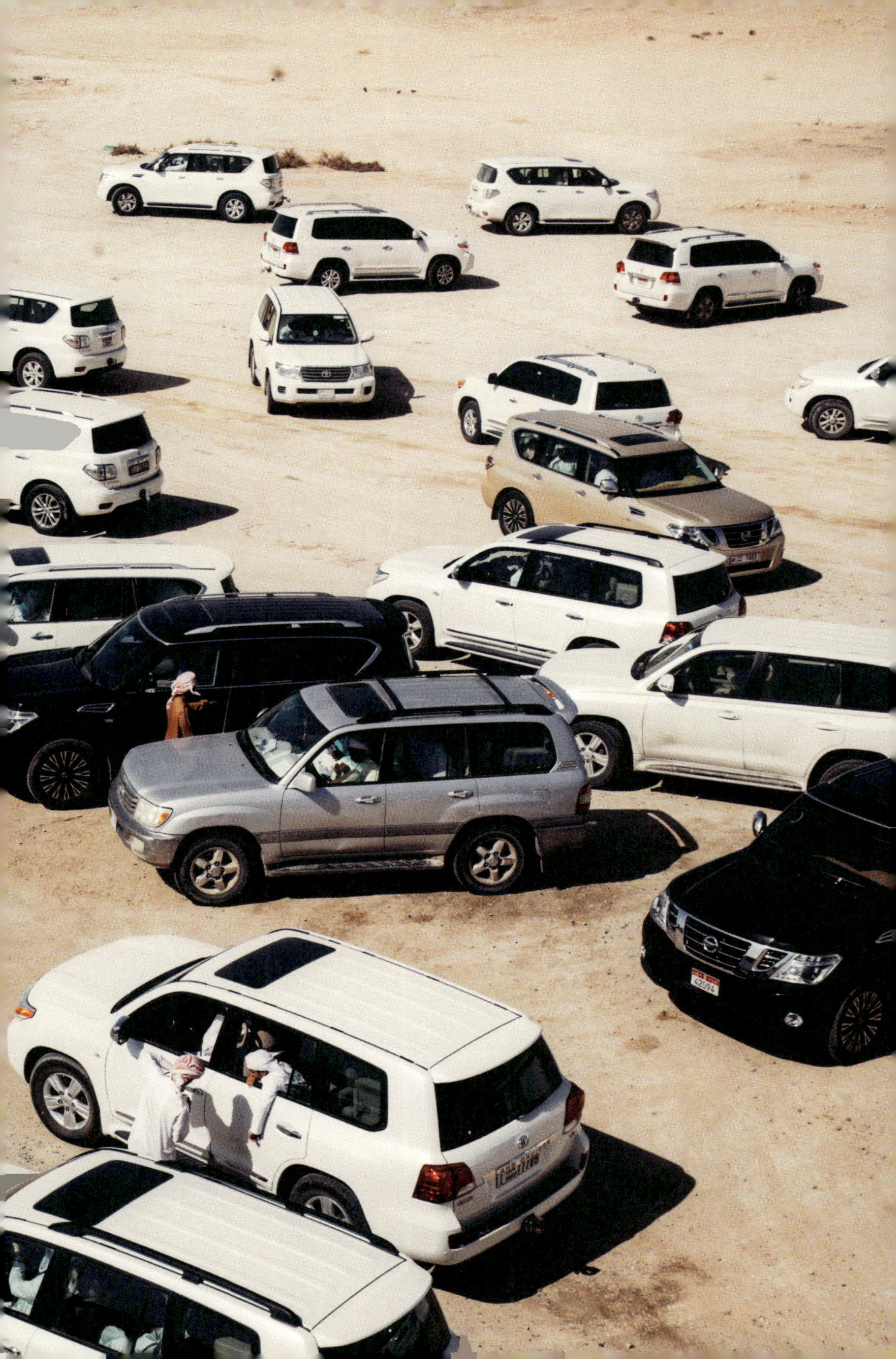

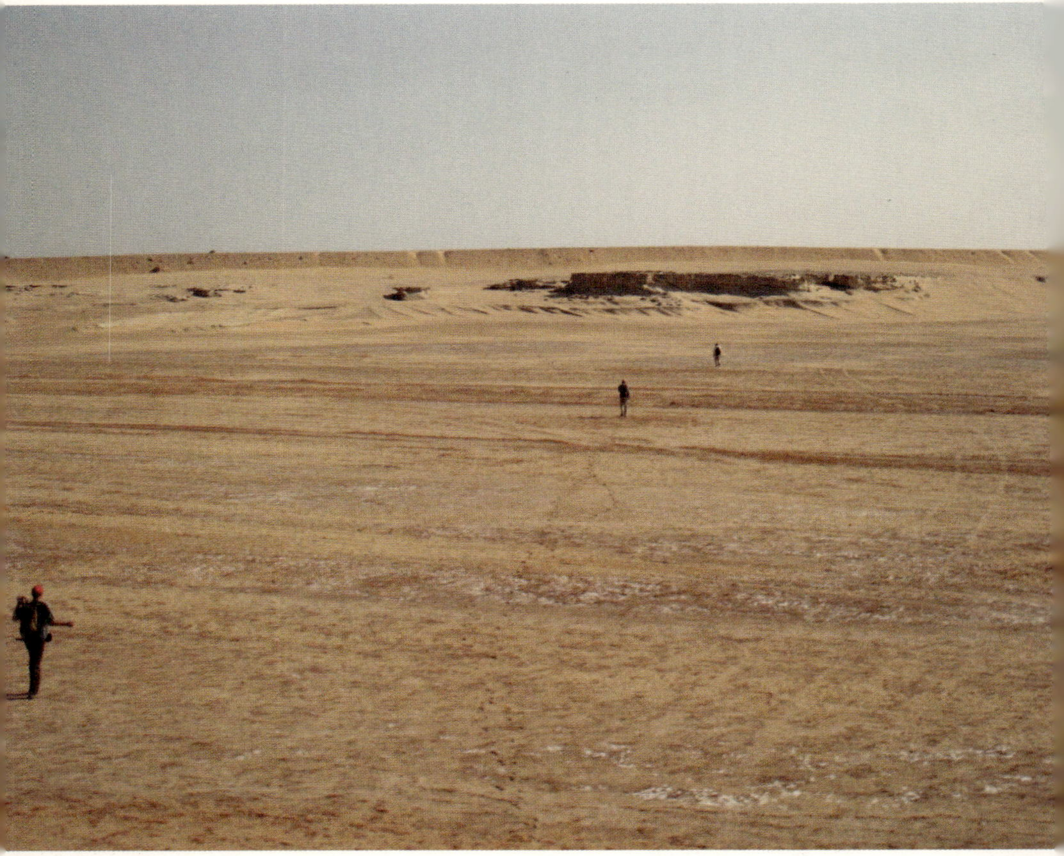

CROCODILES IN THE DESERT

FAYSAL BIBI

A few hours west, past Abu Dhabi city, the color of the sand changes from yellow to red. The flatness of the landscape gives way to topography, gently at first around Tarif, then more pronouncedly as one approaches Al Mirfa. Flat-topped *jebels* (mountains or hills) loom above the coastal *sabkhas* to the north and the white desert plain to the south. The jebels are layered, and each red, green, white, and brown stripe represents a brief geological interval, a time capsule. Each jebel is a layer-cake of prehistory.

Everywhere one looks in the Al Gharbia region, there are signs of ancient water. The individual grains in any handful of fresh red sand here are rounded—the result of water action and transport in river currents for hundreds or thousands of kilometers. All over these outcrops are fossils of plant roots. Some are cement-like, greyish-white, and lying on the surface. Others are more delicate networks, gently weathering out of the sands in a coating of salt and gypsum. The ground is littered in white flecks. Let your eyes adjust and the image will come into focus: fossil bones are everywhere. Catfish spines, reflective shards of elephant and hippopotamus teeth, and powdery bones of animals large and small. Unlike fresh bones, these are heavy and hard to the touch, the result of millions of years of mineralization underground.

These sands and the fossil animals they contain have been named the Baynunah Formation, in honor of an area in the Al Gharbia region of Abu Dhabi Emirate. These sediments were deposited some seven million years ago by a large extinct river system that we call the Baynunah River and are exposed today along more than 200 kilometers of coastline and extending over 30 kilometers inland.

We still know very little about the Baynunah River. Current directions measured in fossil sand ripples indicate that these waters originated from the west or northwest, probably in what is today Saudi Arabia or Iraq. These would have flowed through the western Emirates and into the trough where the Gulf sea sits today (it is a relatively young sea), eventually spilling into the Indian Ocean. The Baynunah River may have existed for only a few hundred thousand years, but during this time, this water source fed vegetation and sustained a diversity of animals that lived along its banks. Yearly floods deposited layer after layer of gravels, sands, and clays, rapidly burying any animal and plant remains that happened to be lying on the floodplain, and preserving these underground. Over thousands of years, groundwater movement drove minerals into tiny pores within the bones, and replaced subterranean spaces left behind by decomposed plant roots. Today, the Arabian Peninsula is a dry place, and the erosive action of wind and rain slowly carves down the old Baynunah sands, gradually revealing the fossils it had carefully entombed for millions of years.

Fossils have been collected here by archaeological and paleontological teams since the early ‘80s, including an expedition I co-led from 2003 to 2014. Many kinds of fossil animals have been discovered here. The most common—not surprising for a river—are fish. Among these are several species of catfish, a type of fish that today is known to prefer large, slow-moving rivers. A couple of freshwater turtles are also known from fragments of their shells, including a species of soft-shelled turtle. Fragments of a small species of hippopotamus are also quite common.

Studies of its skeletal remains showed it to be a new form that we recently named Archaeopotamus qeshta, after the Egyptian Arabic name for the living hippopotamus *sid qashta*.

More careful searching along the Baynunah outcrops reveals the remains of rarer animals. Fossilized teeth and jaws of a small, three-toed horse, several species of antelopes and short-necked giraffes, and a small monkey related to the guenons that today inhabit much of sub-Saharan Africa. A saber-toothed cat and hyenas were the main predators in residence. Also trudging around the landscape were no less than three species of elephants, one of these even larger than the living African elephant. Not only are its bones known from a couple of nice skulls and a skeleton, but one site even preserves a unique glimpse into how ancient elephants may have behaved and interacted. The site of Mleisa 1—deep inland and now almost entirely cutoff by a pipeline and railway construction—preserves the trackways of over a dozen elephants as they crossed what was then a muddy plain. The calcium-rich mud they walked through dried, hardened into rock, and was buried. Today, natural erosion has so perfectly exposed the site that one can walk alongside the fossilized footprints of the ancient elephant herd for over 100 meters, imagining that perhaps it was just yesterday that they crossed the landscape of Abu Dhabi, and not millions of years ago.

We also sieved the fossil sands with fine metal screens and recovered remains of tiny animals: individual teeth of several rodent species, including a jumping rat, Abudhabia baynunensis, which was named after the region. Another species, closely related to living cane rats of Africa, was a new discovery. Its teeth were stained yellow, and relatively large for a rodent—about the size of a hummus bean. We named it Protohummus dango (*dango* is an Emirati variety of the dish and *mus* is also conveniently Latin for a mouse). We even found vertebrae of a frog and several species of snakes and lizards, including a python.

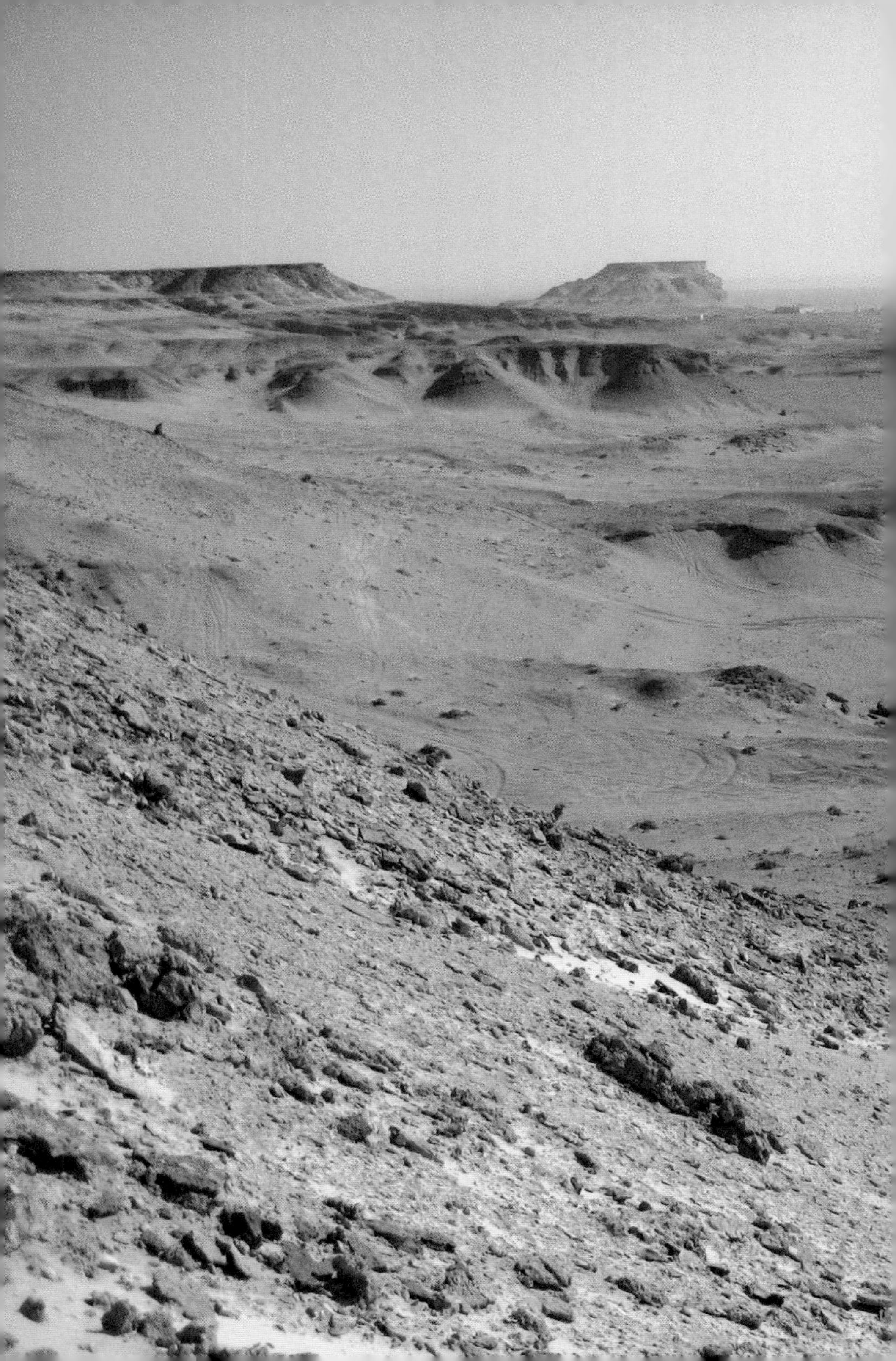

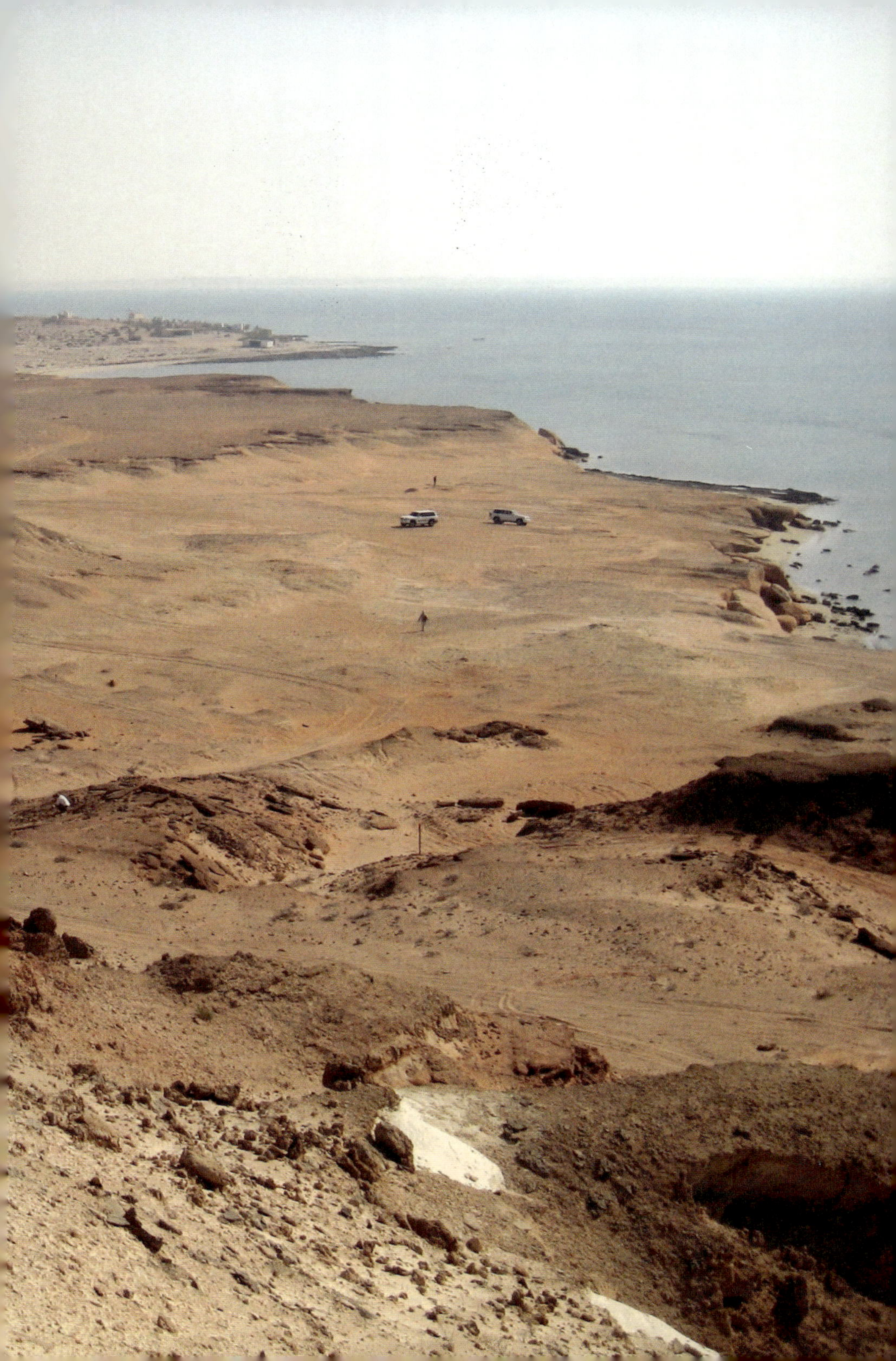

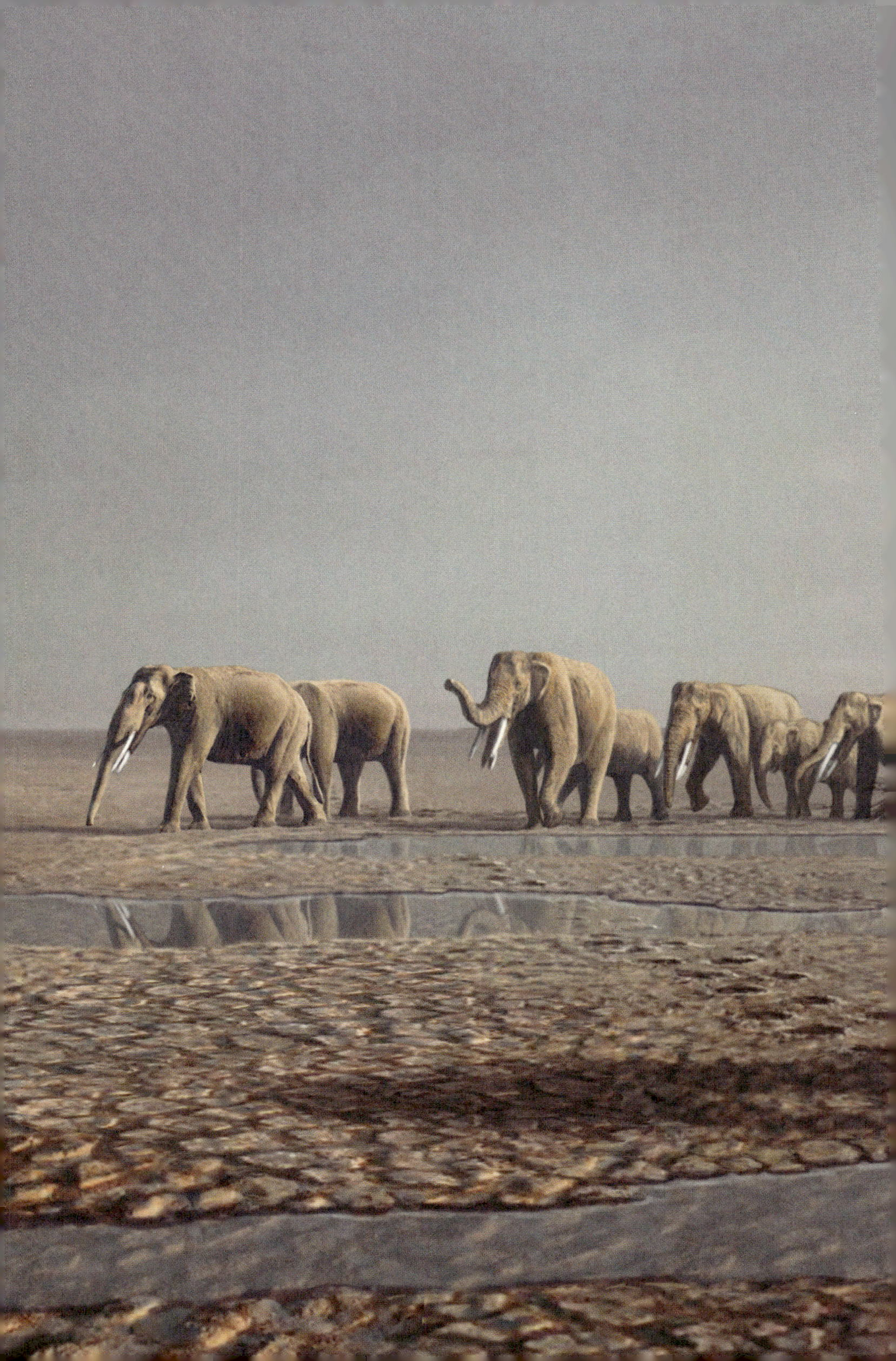

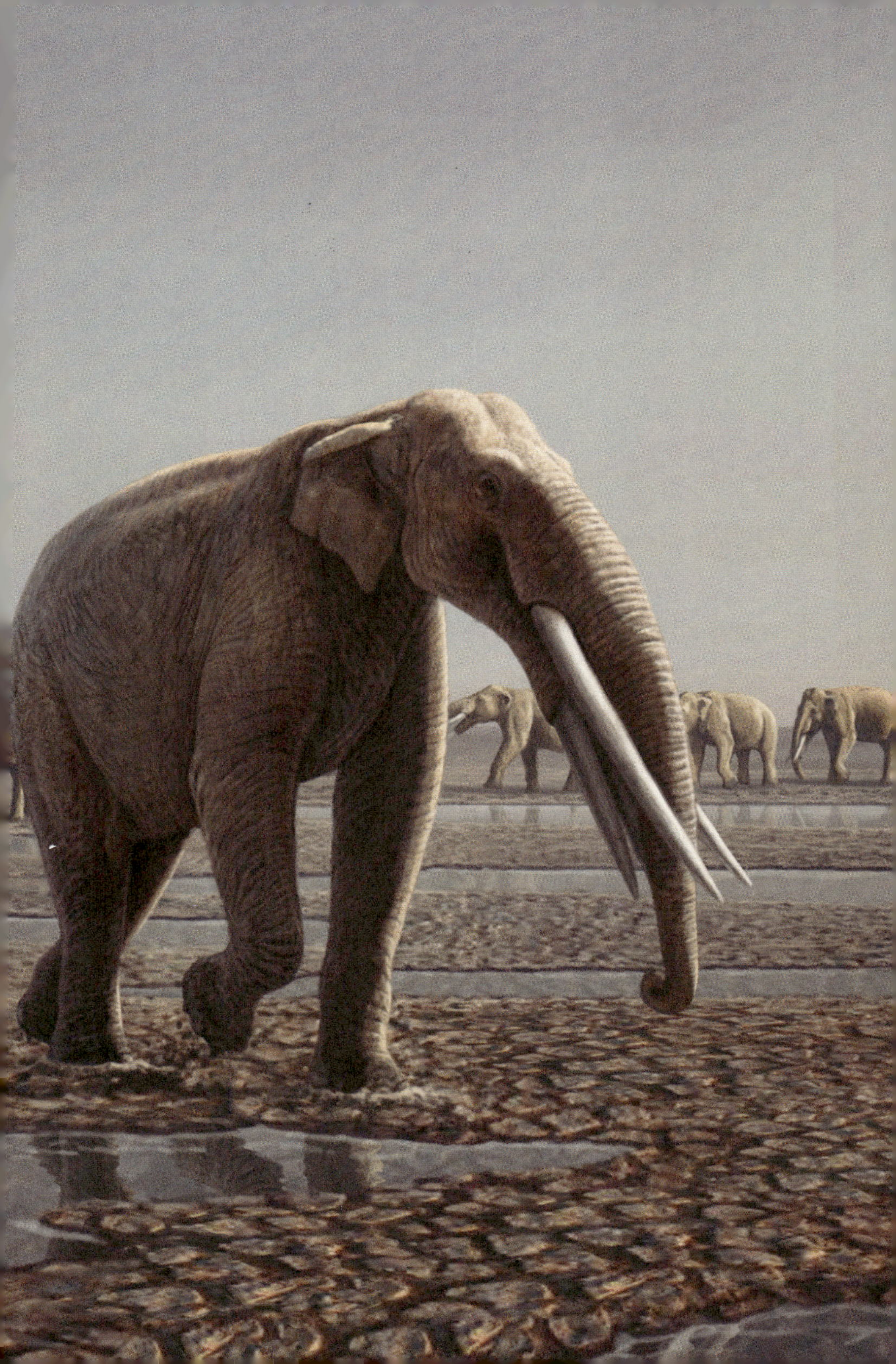

One of the most impressive finds we made happened in early 2010 after we were given special permission to survey some outcrops that lay within private grounds at Gerain Al Aysh. Climbing up a hill onto a ledge, I saw a tell-tale surface of white weathered fossil bone rising slightly above the sandy ground. Careful removal of the sand on all sides revealed this to be the surface of a complete crocodile skull that was lying horizontal, as it would have been if alive. Even seeing it in pictures still gives the impression of a crocodile in the water, lying motionless but watching, attentive to the first sign of an easy meal. One needn't be an anatomist to recognize it for what it is: a crocodile in the desert. Clearly out of place today, it is also a clear indication that the Arabian desert was not always as it seems.

To recover these fragments of prehistory, one inevitably confronts the challenges of the modern age. Fences, pipelines, ditches, plantations, junk heaps, firing ranges, refineries, and private grounds. Between one year and the next, several of our sites had been driven over by bulldozers. One of the main sites, Jebel Barakah, was designated a no-go military zone a few years ago.

The 13th century Arab writer Mohammed Kazwini tells an allegory in which he returns to the same place millennium after millennium and observes seas giving way to dry land, and entire cities and civilizations come and go over the same spot. Each time upon asking the inhabitants about changes and upheavals that have passed over their lands, they respond "Never—this place has always been as you see it now."

At the site of Hamra, not far from the Jebel Dhanna hotel, there is a chunk of fossil elephant tooth that sits on the side of a jebel. It was dislodged from its original resting place by a bulldozer perhaps twenty years ago or more, and piled on a mound of rubble on a steep slope. It is fractured and beyond any hope of repair. Its value lies in remaining exactly where it is, overlooking its sandy grave to one side, and a highway strung with power lines to the other; a silent witness to the unyielding progress of cement, steel, and asphalt, into whose bases it will finally crumble and meld. The fossils of Abu Dhabi are the embodiment of Kazwini's allegorical traveler, and, if we decipher their stories, they reveal a fascinating history of life on earth that is far beyond the capacity of any single human lifetime.

Image credits: Mauricio Anton, "Paleoart elephants," pp. 34-35; Mark Beech, pp. 38-39.

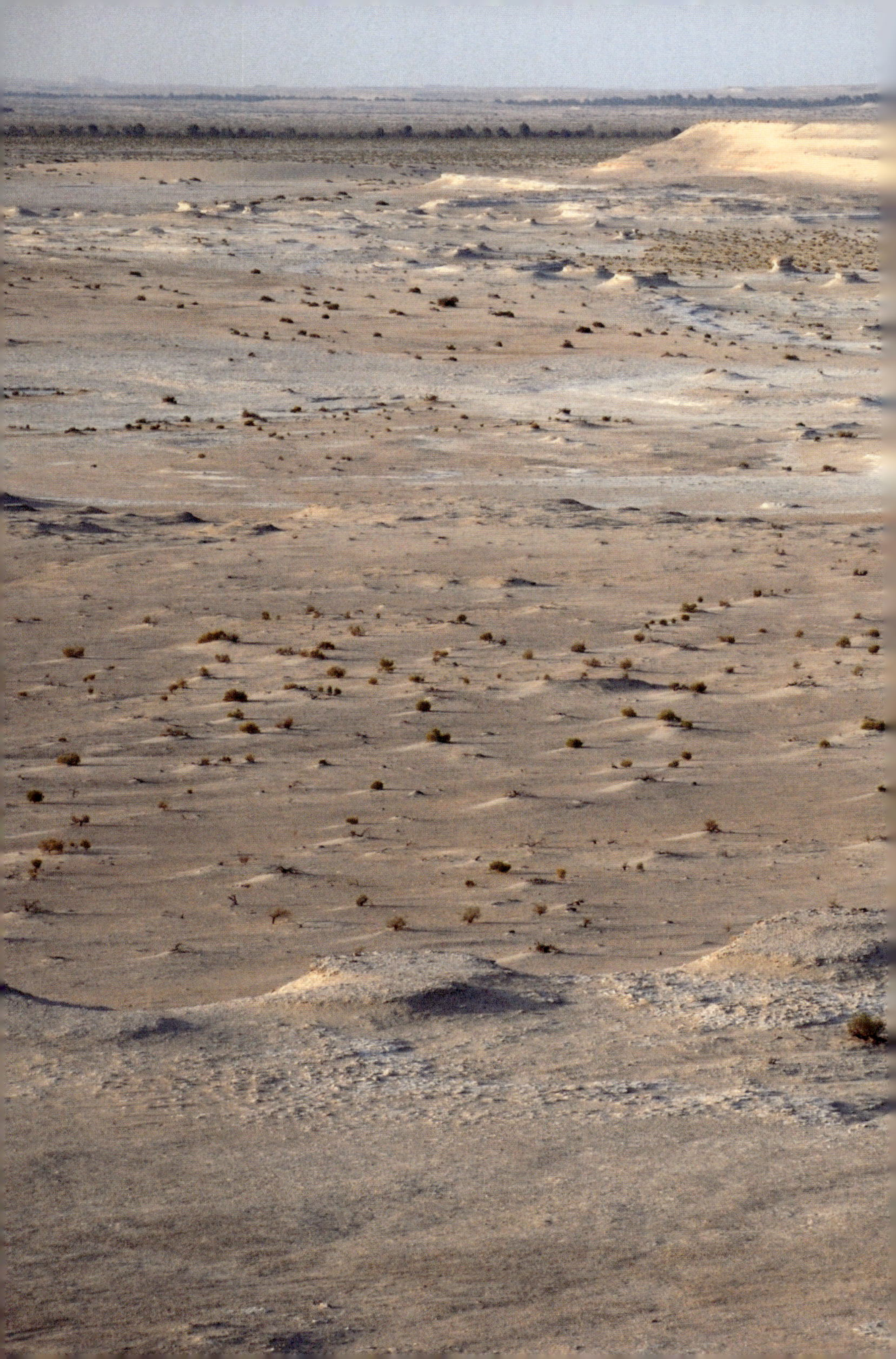

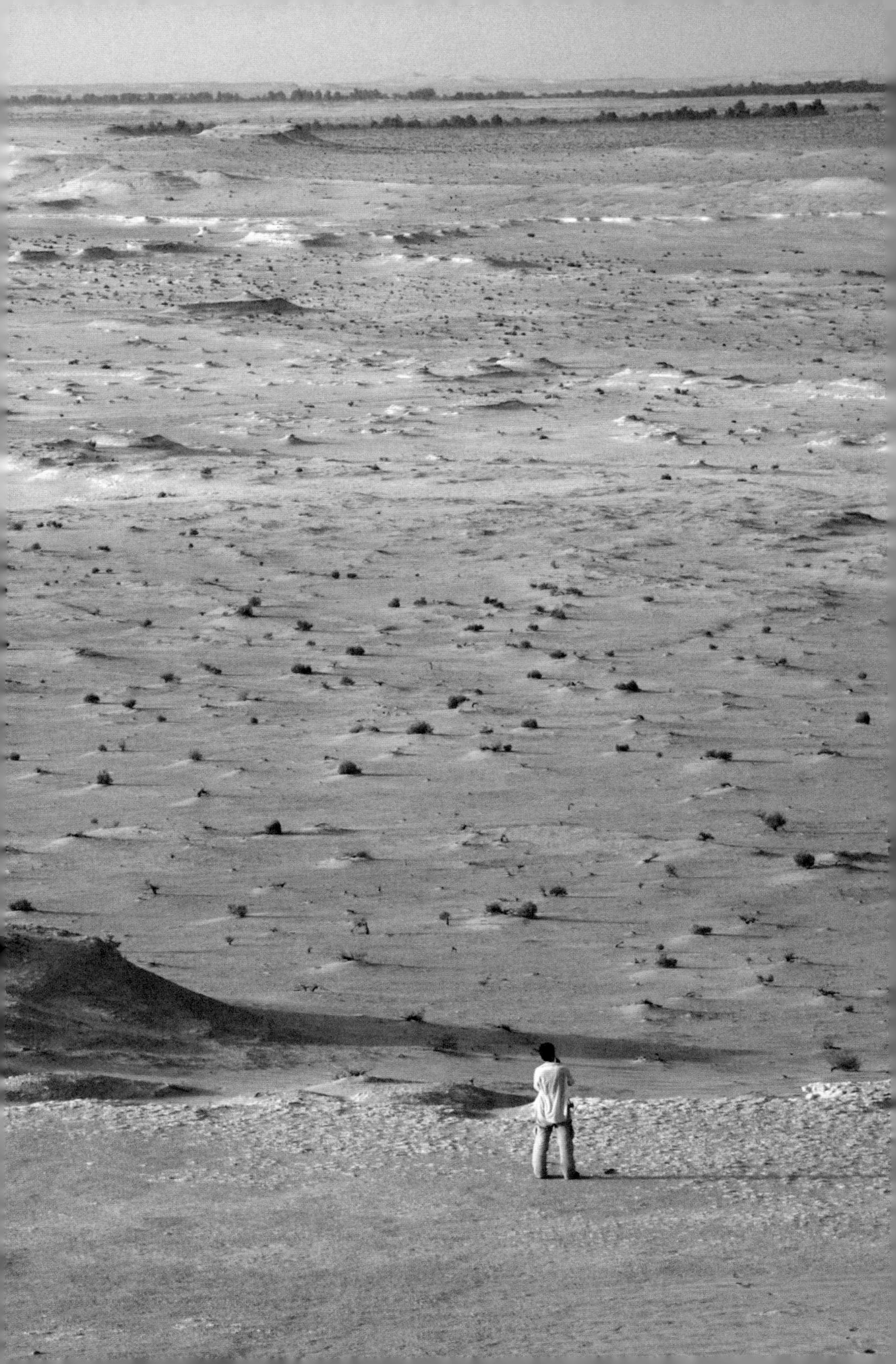

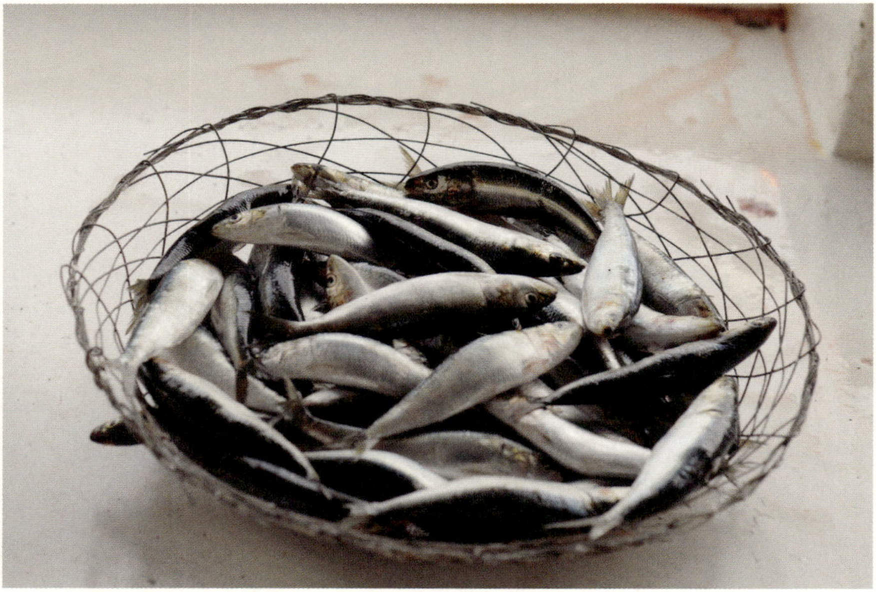

A SHOAL OF STORIES

SALLY PROSSER

I'm overwhelmed by the quantity of fish, the lines of tables manned by men all dressed alike in blue overalls. The catch is delivered at one end and buyers swoop on the new arrivals, some so fresh they're alive, gills still heaving. The shapes and sizes of these creatures across concrete slicked with murky moisture has me wide-eyed. Small sharks, pale, limp and white in a row; vast, bloody, dark tuna, portioned into monstrous pieces; prawns of all sizes. Since that first visit I have returned many times of the year, but the visual assault never diminishes.

It was here that I was introduced to Hussein, an Emirati who went to sea as a tea boy and rose to captain in a sailing career of over forty years. People also call him Nokhoda, which is the word for captain and in Persian translates to 'god of the boat'. His bartering was severe and when a less than pristine fish was slid onto the scales he went berserk. However, he was kind and gentle when cooking us lunch, and when we all sat on the floor to eat the charcoal grilled fish from a communal platter, he slid extra portions onto my plate when I wasn't looking. Once we would have eaten *hammour*, a type of firm, white-fleshed, spotted grouper, but stocks of these are so diminished by over-fishing that they are now endangered.

The old market is soon to be swept away as well, to make way for a new, modern facility. Smaller markets have been built further up the coast in the new areas of Dubai; their architecture echoes the past, with ornamental wind towers and barred windows. The impact of more and better markets on fish stocks is unknown, despite the 'choose wisely' campaign set up to protect them.

The changing state of fishery is not confined to the UAE nor to overfishing. Across the Gulf in Iraq, families would meet every Friday on the banks of the River Tigris to cook and eat a type of carp called *barbel* which was abundant. The ritual of *masgouf*, a way of cooking it suspended upright by the fire on sticks of fruit wood, was centuries old. The land by the river was appropriated by Sadam Hussein during his regime. Consequently, the river diminished, was polluted and fenced off. People fleeing the regime talked of 'the flavour of freedom' and one such family brought that flavour to Dubai, where you could marvel at the sight of slender carp on sticks by roaring flames and savour the smoky, creamy flesh. It kept the flavour alive here for years while it disappeared in its homeland. Sadly, the original Bait Al Baghdadi burned down recently but others have continued the tradition in Dubai.

In a small, smart square in Deira you can plunge your hands into another fish tale. Our order is delivered to the long table covered in paper. Scattered over it in a heap: crab, prawns, clams, squid and rice make a mound of plenty. We pour sauce over it, don plastic gloves and dig in, tearing each morsel apart with our hands to extract the sweet meat. A seafood boodle fight is thought to have originated on islands in the Philippines during the Second World War among soldiers in the military. When food was scarce it was a way of fighting for your share. Now it's a fun night out in this part of town.

Fish swimming lazily along the coast, in the clear turquoise waters of the Gulf, might now take an unexpected right turn and end up on a detour. Dubai has recently split itself further. A shiny canal, as broad as the River

Thames, makes a path from the natural inlet of the Creek to a new breach carved by man, turning the old district of Bur Dubai and much of the new heart of the city into an island, circling it like a beltfish. Walking along the banks early morning, I witness paddle-boarders snaking over its shimmering surface, a police rescue boat cruising leisurely and jet-skiers making waves. All this in the shadow of the huddle of Downtown Dubai buildings, where the towers gleam like the shiny scales of a mackerel.

The sea and its bounty has shaped and moulded Dubai's growth and direction as much as the revenue from 'black gold' that was drilled until pretty much exhausted. Livelihoods were earned (and lives lost) by fishing and diving for pearls until the Japanese worked out how to culture identical, perfect replicas. Dredging the sand from the Creek to make it more navigable by boat sustained its role as a trading hub. It soared from a few sleepy huts by the ocean to the worldwide brand it is today in less than quarter of a century. It's understandable that the Emirate might look to its position on the coast to secure its future; to attract investment, tourism and a setting for more prime real estate. Balancing the flavour of the past with the demands of the new is a fishy tale to be continued.

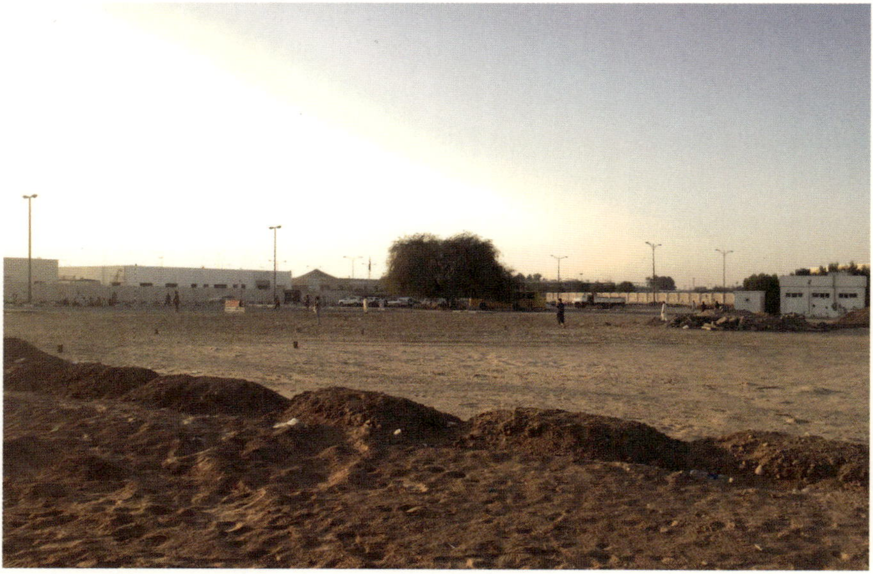

01. CRICKET GAME IN THE STREET, SHEIKH KHALIFA STREET.
SHARJAH. 2017.

CRICKET FIELDS: INSTRUMENTS OF PLACE-MAKING AND MEMORY IN THE UAE

BEATRIZ ITZEL CRUZ MEGCHUN & JUAN ROLDÁN MARTÍN

"The wispy nickel cables and the magnets upheld in space by their own magnetism—marking the gaps in continuity—lay bare a hidden force and suggest unresolved possibilities, by suturing the cavities to reveal the horror vacui."

Olivier Debroise, *Memory City*

Over the past 46 years, the UAE has undergone a remarkable and rapid transition that has encompassed a wide spectrum of change—social, urban, economical—achieved without serious dislocation. In its construction remains the original motives, but with time each emirate has solidified and modified the motives of its very development.

Trying to define the UAE's urban dimension, or to adequately discuss it, requires a laborious and extensive research. We will limit ourselves here to specific aspects that we believe enter into the consideration of the subject: the appropriation of urban voids. We want to shine a light on the continuous process of influences, of exchanges, often of contrapositions between the urban facts and the ideal proposals of people inhabiting it. We aim to understand the city in a more holistic manner, balancing the fixed urban fabric and the elements open to interpretation (Sennet, 2013) where people discuss, collide and reinvent the city.

The emirates can be studied as the product of the functional systems that generate its architecture—and therefore of urban spaces—and as a spatial structure. Indeed, they go beyond urban designs that host built environments, since they are also part of the recollection of human behaviours that reshape spaces lodged with history, cultural and social meaning.

Each emirate's nuances and characteristics cannot be explained without understanding the conformations and aspirations that correspond to an almost predestined individuality. Their urban fabric has changed through time, their neighborhoods are never complete, never at rest due to the thousands of witting and unwitting acts in every day. Every building, alley, empty land—space—is a place that carries intentions that are more or less noble, more or less conscious, and more or less aesthetically expressed. These inanimate spaces are the scenarios that give life to the memory of the city, within these structures comes the knowledge of the city. These spaces are the ones that we consider relevant, as they become instruments of social discourse for those living in the UAE.

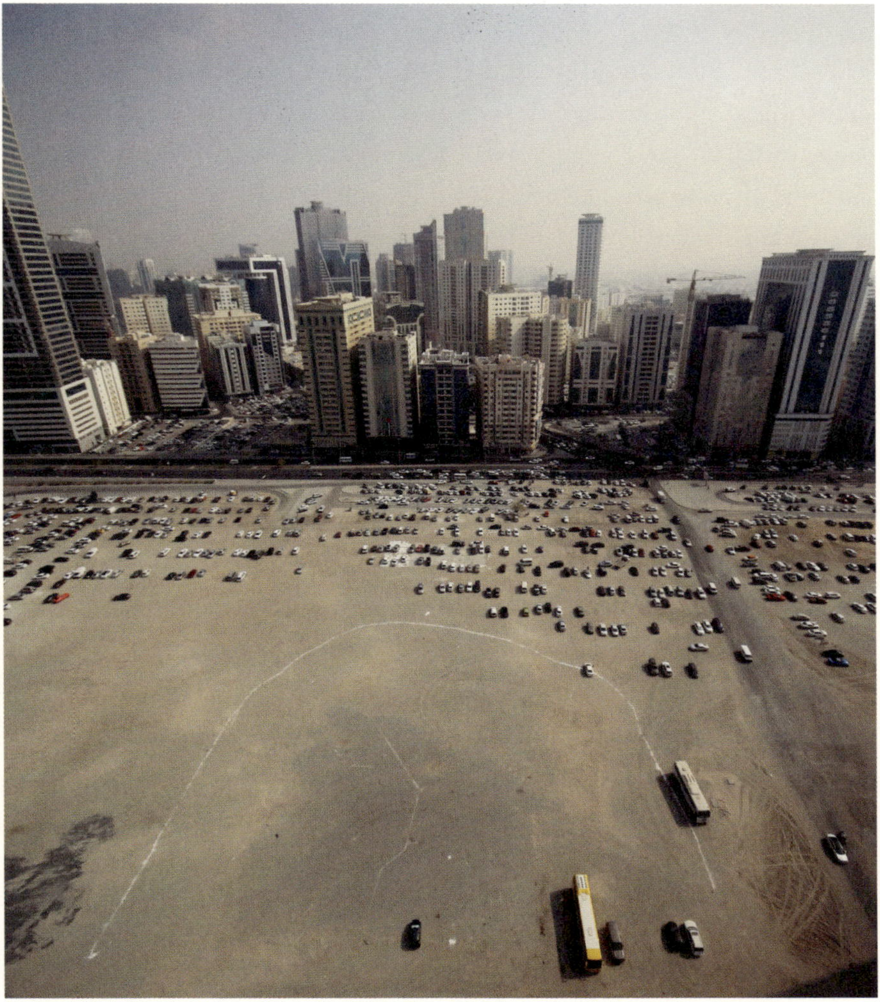

02. TEMPORARY MARKINGS OF A CRICKET FIELD IN A PARKING LOT, AL-QASBA. SHARJAH. 2017.

CITIES AND VOIDS

The city has been studied from different angles, analysing diverse factors, including social values and actions, that are so abstract they fail to reflect their reality. Academics and researchers use frames to explore and discuss patterns and elements of urban process and urban form that provide a historical perspective of how these are made—and subsequently how they evolve.

Urban processes concern with laws, institutions, and people, as they are quintessential to defining the urban form. They involve ownership of urban land, regulatory measures such as construction codes, instruments for funding urban change—taxes and bond issues—and administrative structure of cities. The urban form is reflected in every building, as each one is a place with intentions that have been worn down by time, vicissitudes of his history or tectonic, or other phenomena. Metaphors of cities are important as they provide accurate images of the reality lived by inhabitants; for this reason we are going to discuss the term 'liminal space'.

Liminality is a term borrowed from social anthropology that architects use to describe the transitional threshold between two dissimilar spaces. The word has its origins from the Latin word līmen, limin meaning 'threshold, doorway, limit'. The idea of liminal first appears in the field of anthropology in 1909 with Arnold Van Gennep in his seminal work Les Rites de Passage. The term evolved and expanded through the work of Victor Turner, as he propagated its usage into other fields. His work focuses entirely on the middle stage of the rites of passage—the transitional or liminal stage, which draws analogies with the transformative space in architecture. Turner (1969) suggested that liminal space is "the ritual passing through a period and area of ambiguity, a sort of social limbo which has few—though sometimes these are most crucial—of the attributes of either the proceeding or subsequent profane statuses or cultural states". For example, some of the characteristics that define this type of space include layering, dissolution, blurring, ambiguity, among others, as they have the ability to be transformed by occupants. This means that these spaces are experienced, and thus pose questions to their occupants about their surroundings, leading to heightened awareness of the space as a transformative threshold between distinct spaces (Zimmerman, 2008).

Empty spaces, alleys, corridors, parking lots, are for example associated with rituals carried by inhabitants, especially by expats, in the UAE. These spaces are the vehicles for the exploration of liminal spaces since they are heightened with ritualistic acts that go from undertaking recreational activities to social activities. They are a representation of transformative threshold since they exhibit a nexus between vulnerability and power, as they are a locus of potential. They are a release from structural limitations that occupants use to their advantage, transforming them into places full of meaning for their rituals. Immigrants living in Sharjah converge on these interstices where tacit knowledge, processes, problems and purposes are dynamically negotiated and worked out.

These temporary spaces, perceived as liminal space, become the place par excellence for the communal negotiation and resolution of an array of complexities, such as parking, exercising, socialising, inherent in how different intentionalities intersect with the uncertain trajectories of access to social and recreational resources. According to Ledema et al. (2005), these types of unique sites are where decisions can be held in abeyance and where uncertainties and provisional decisions can co-exist; a space where social hierarchy can be attenuated if not suspended, and a space where people can agree to work around rules and regulations. In other words, a space where rituals become sufficiently flexible and negotiable to enable their appropriation for specific practices.

CASES

"In Ersilia, to establish the relationships that sustain the city's life, the inhabitants stretch strings from the corners of the houses, white or black or gray or black-and-white according to whether they mark a relationship of blood, of trade, authority, agency. When the strings become so numerous that you can no longer pass among them, the inhabitants leave: the houses are dismantled; only the strings and their supports remain."

Italo Calvino, *Invisible Cities*

One characteristic of Arab desert society, is its tribal traditions that require non-Arabs to jettison their preconceptions about the positive force that their heritage, culture and ethics have in shaping community by providing strength and social cohesion. The development of the UAE demanded a frantic influx of immigrants and the adoption of new occupations by tribesmen. This, in turn, posed questions about the coexistence of this newly formed society, apparently bursting with different races and thus values and beliefs. Nevertheless, these inhabitants—urban nomads—have intervened in the city to secure their collective memory and to feel at home in a modern society marked by a globalised world. These interventions are restricted by the physical limitations of urban voids and the consensus established in the area by the various parts involved. This can be discussed in terms of dimension: small- to large-scale; and time: temporary to permanent appropriations. Indeed, these interventions are not exempt from conflict caused by the overlapping formalization of community practices among different social groups and institutions both public and private.

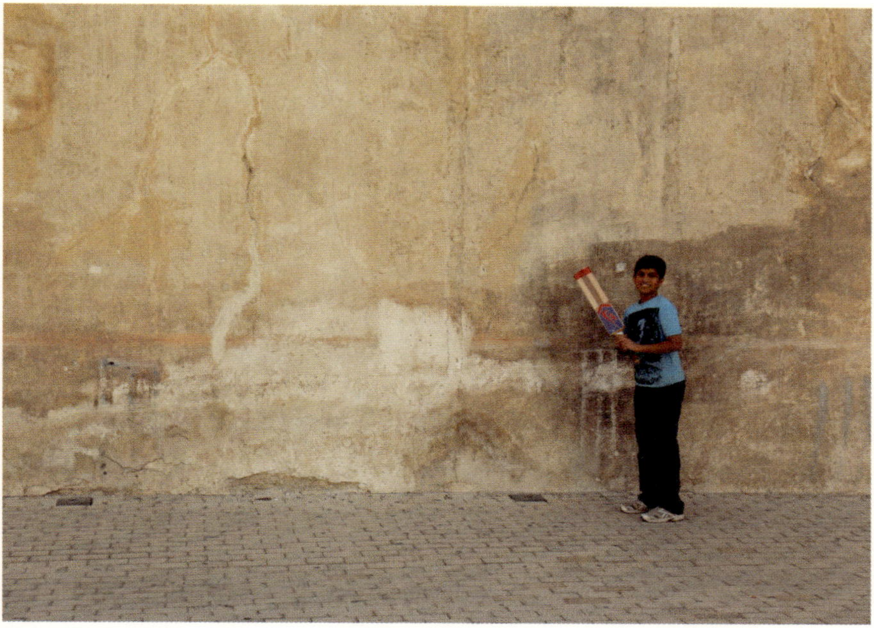

03. TEMPORARY MARKINGS OF THE WICKET ON THE WALL, HERITAGE AREA.
SHARJAH. 2015.

SMALL - TEMPORARY

The first example relies on two key factors, the small scale and the limited temporality of the intervention on private property. This is due to the number of rituals that overlap throughout the day (time) in that limited area (space). The density of activities makes the interventions imperceptible, almost invisible, for passers-by who transit that area. The intervention becomes a silent motif that is meaningful for the people that inhabit that location. Figure 3 (page 51) shows an impermanent intervention, in which inhabitants marked in a wall a wicket so they can play cricket in an open space. Indeed, the number of elements can increase rapidly to further invigorate the rituals of people.

MEDIUM - SEMI-TEMPORARY

The following case deals with a medium-scale and semi-temporal intervention in a property that has been vacant (semi-public). Urban wonderers—they are not necessarily inhabitants of that location—form a community that is responsible of making decisions regarding the ritual. In this case, they borrow a space to intervene with a permanent landmark of their ritual using concrete or car wheels, securing that it blends in with or disappears into the urban landscape. This vacant space borrowed can be taken at any time, and thus their intervention has to be relocated. Their rituals are formal, and thus membership to this group is earned through invitation. Their activities are imperceptible unless people are witnesses of their activity (ritual). Figure 4 (opposite page) shows the permanent landmarks—a cricket pitch or cricket field—built by a community of cricket players in University City Road in the area of Al Shahba. Here, there are groups that have been playing for over 15 years every Saturday on the same location. The beauty of this intervention is the empowerment that members have while changing the space to undertake their ritual.

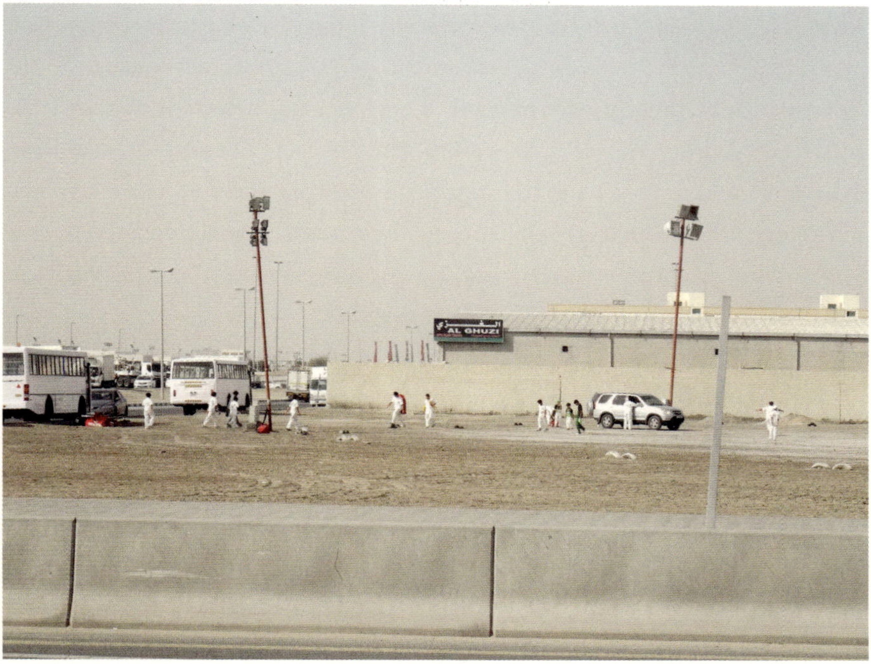

04. PERMANENT MARKINGS OF THE CRICKET PITCH, AL SHAHBA. SHARJAH. 2014.

LARGE - PERMANENT

This case represents interventions that are large in scale and impermanent in a semi-private location. Due to the physical characteristics of the location, it is possible to observe a number of different rituals that occur throughout the day. Therefore, the character of the interventions is impermanent, as informally a group of people claimed the space and transform it far from its true purpose. The space is negotiated and claimed by residents and non residents who do not have the means, capabilities or interests to invest in formal spaces of practice.

Tacit agreements are required between different groups of users to allocate the different activities into that space. Figure 5 (opposite page) shows the back part of a hotel in Al-Qasba that is used for recreational, social activities and city facilities. The space is mostly used as a parking lot, but on Friday morning it becomes momentarily a cricket field. Users manage to bring a repertoire of objects—cones, stones, chalk—to mark their activities and so give visibility to their rituals.

EXTRA-LARGE - PERMANENT

The final case represents interventions that are consciously planned and designed in an extensive urban location for a specific activity that will benefit a large community. As the space is owned by the government, it must be formally managed, and its users held accountable for its regulation. Users have a certain degree of power to establish behaviour codes, but they cannot change or modify the space nor the intervention. The rituals become formal and recognised by the society — including governmental bodies. Figure 6 (page 56) shows an aerial view of Hamriyah Cricket Fields located between the border of Sharjah and Ajman, also known as the Alliance Cricket Fields. This intervention was supported by the Ajman Cricket Council (ACC) in 2006 in order to define 12 pitches

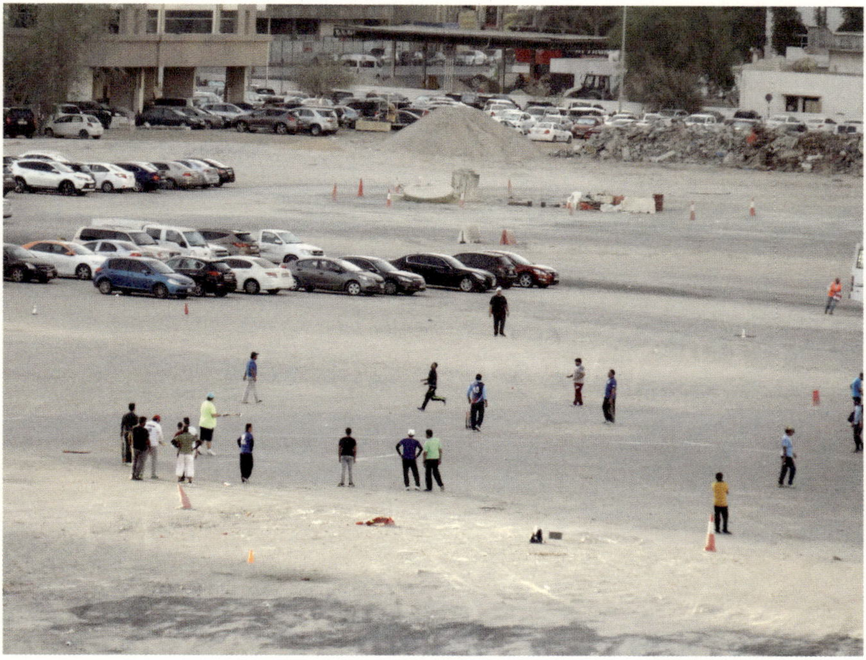

05. TEMPORARY MARKS OF A CRICKET PITCH IN A PARKING LOT, AL-QASBA. SHARJAH. 2017.

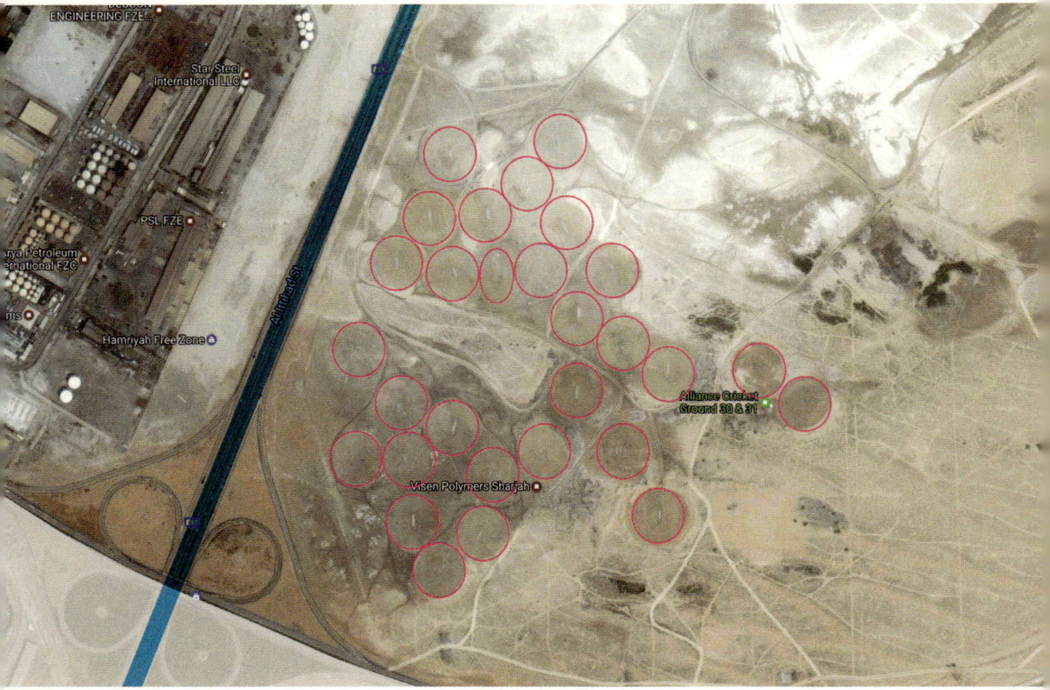

06. AERIAL VIEW OF CRICKET FIELDS, HAMRIYAH CRICKET FIELDS. SHARJAH. 2017.

that have full potential to be used for playing (Figures 7 and 8 on pages 58 and 59)—floodlights for two areas, seating cabins, scoreboards, boundary stoppers, a canteen and a shop (*Gulf News*, 2006.)

FINAL REMARKS

This research begins to reveal how inhabitants use urban voids as liminal spaces to make the city a more functional system. The examples aimed to highlight the intrinsic relation between users and the appropriation of place and engagement of practice. Inhabitants are active participants in building communities, while users, unexpected users and even observers engage in generating a collective memory. Every building, alley, square, or even an empty plot of land is an open space full of potential for the community to make it alive and functional. In this case, the liminal spaces are scenarios of recreational activities—cricket games—carried out by local South East Asian inhabitants. Thus, architects working in the UAE are encouraged to find clever ways to create urban structures that intermingle activities or organize spaces and facilitate their utilization by local residents.

Gulf News (2006). 'Ajman sets up 12 cricket grounds'. [Online] http://gulfnews.com/sport/cricket/ajman-sets-up-12-cricket-grounds-1.255820.

Ledema, R., Long, D., Carroll, K., Stenglin, M., and Braithwaite, J. (2005). 'Corridor work: How liminal space becomes a resource for handling complexities of multidisciplinary health care'. Asia-Pacific Researchers in Organization studies: 11th International Colloquium Melbourne, Australia, 4-7 December 2005.

Sennett, R (2013). The Open City. New York: Theatrum Mundi.

Turner, V (1969). The ritual process: Structure and anti-structure. Chicago: Aldine Publishing.

Zimmerman, P. (2008). 'Liminal Space in Architecture: Threshold and Transition' Master's Thesis, University of Tennessee. [Online] http://trace.tennessee.edu/utk_gradthes/453.

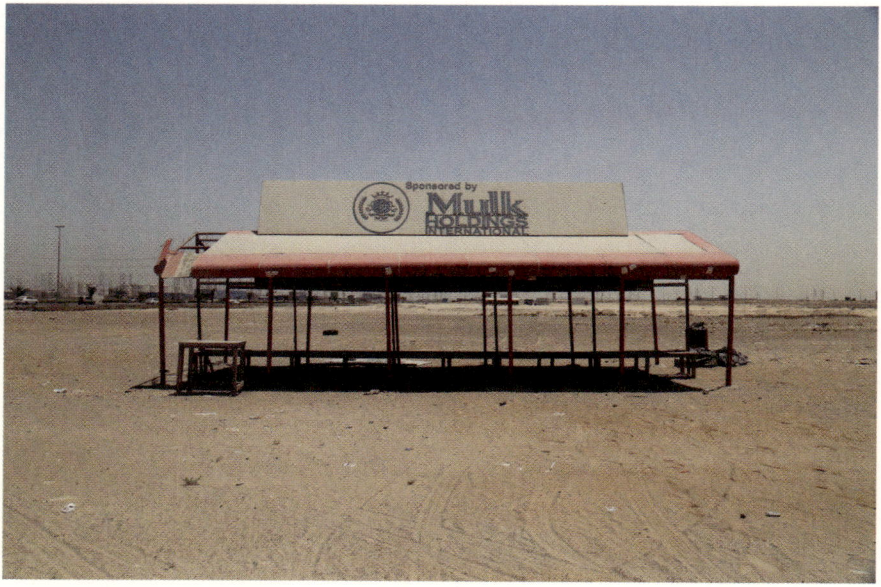

07. SEATING CABINS FOR CRICKET PLAYERS, HAMRIYAH CRICKET FIELDS. SHARJAH. 2017.

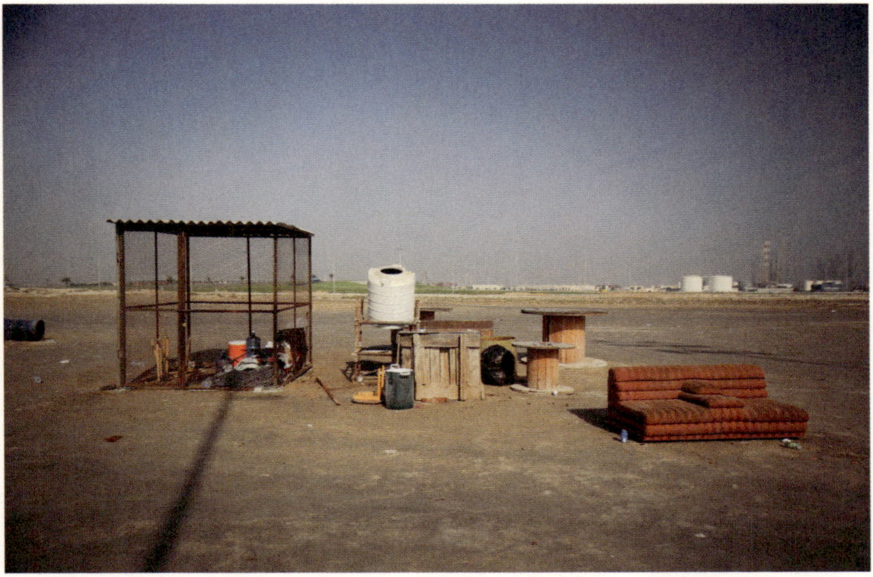

08. HOME FURNISHING USED AS SEATING AREA, HAMRIYAH CRICKET FIELDS. SHARJAH. 2017.

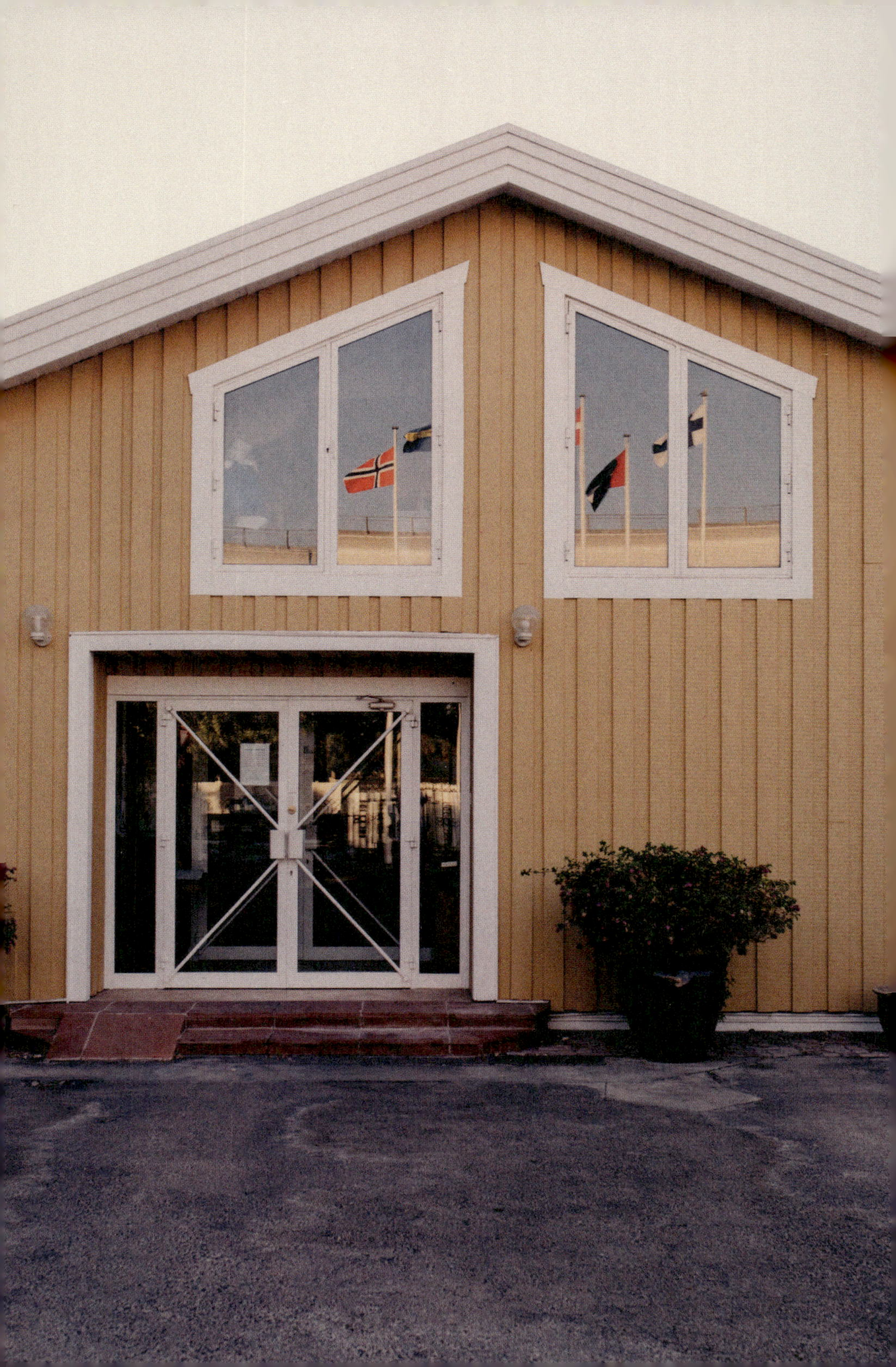

CULTURE CLUB [OUD MEHTHA]

ALEX ATACK

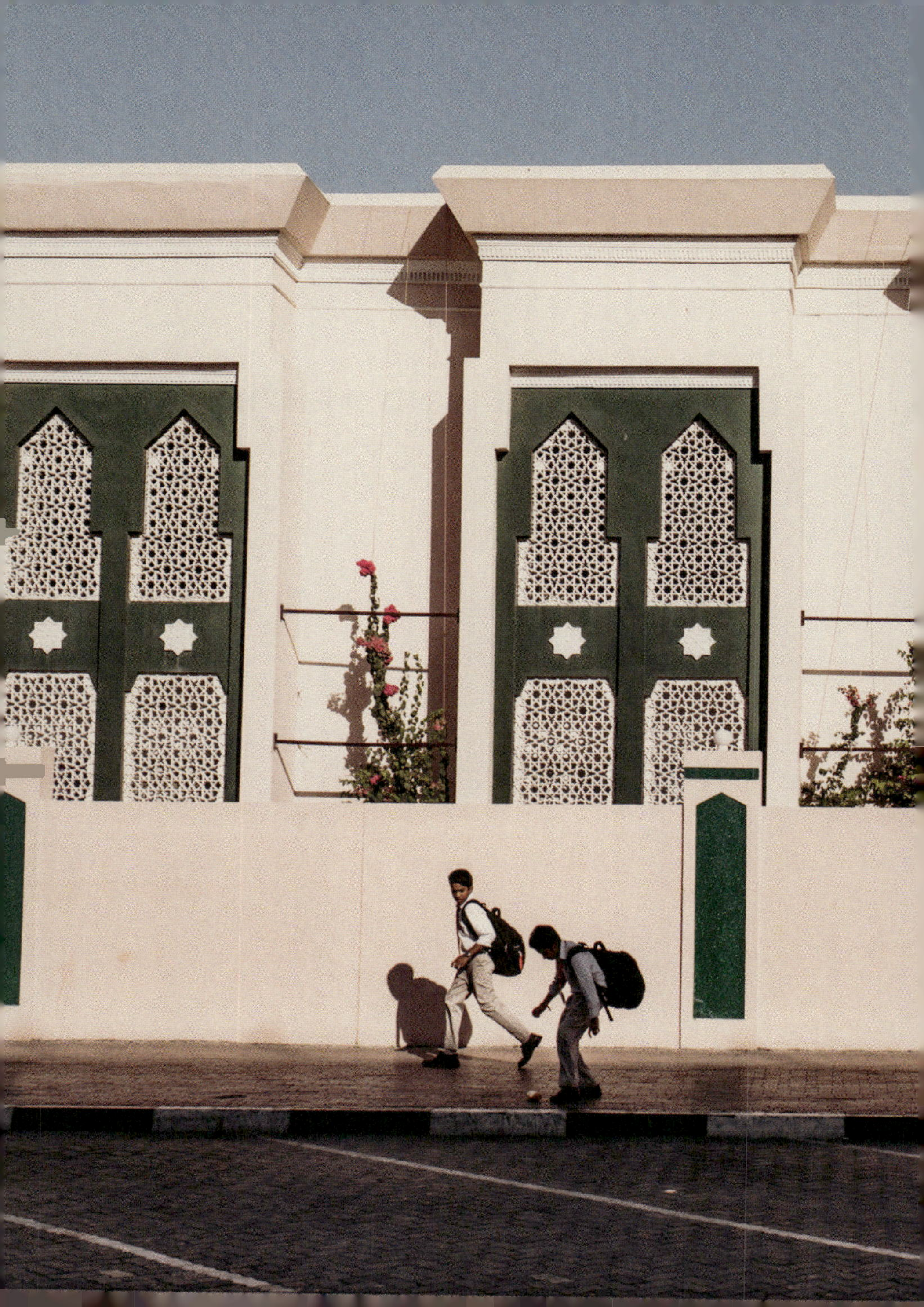

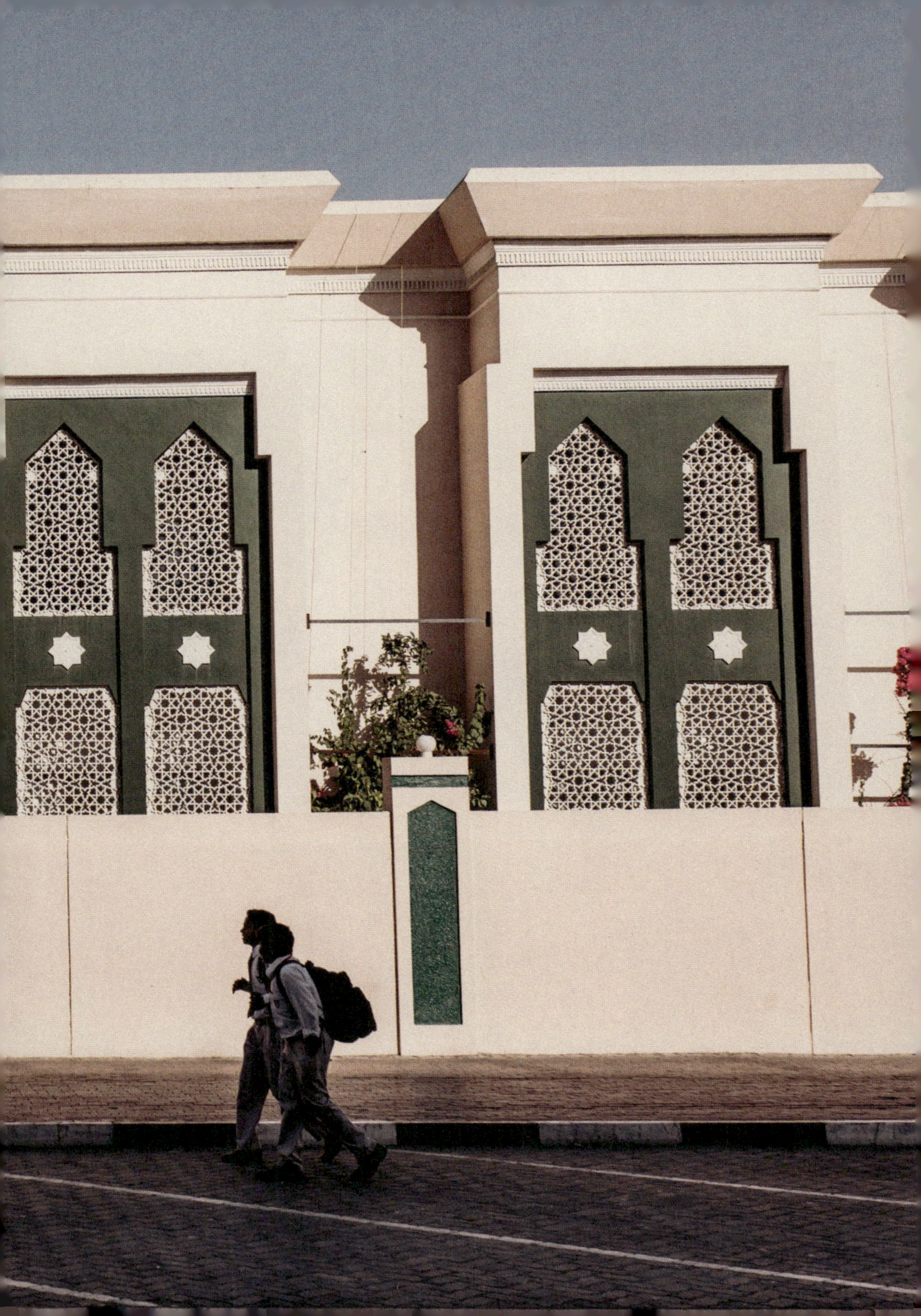

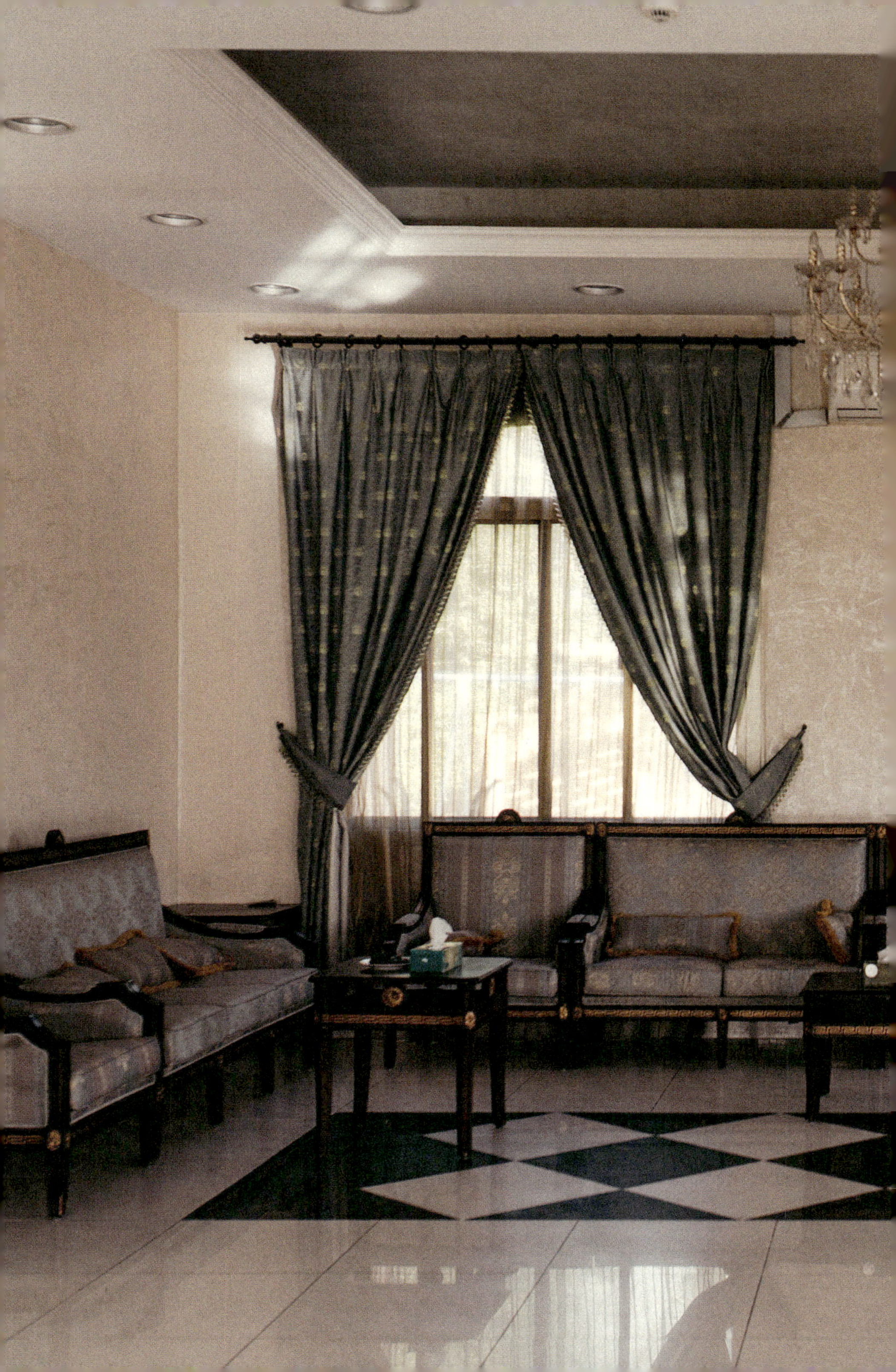

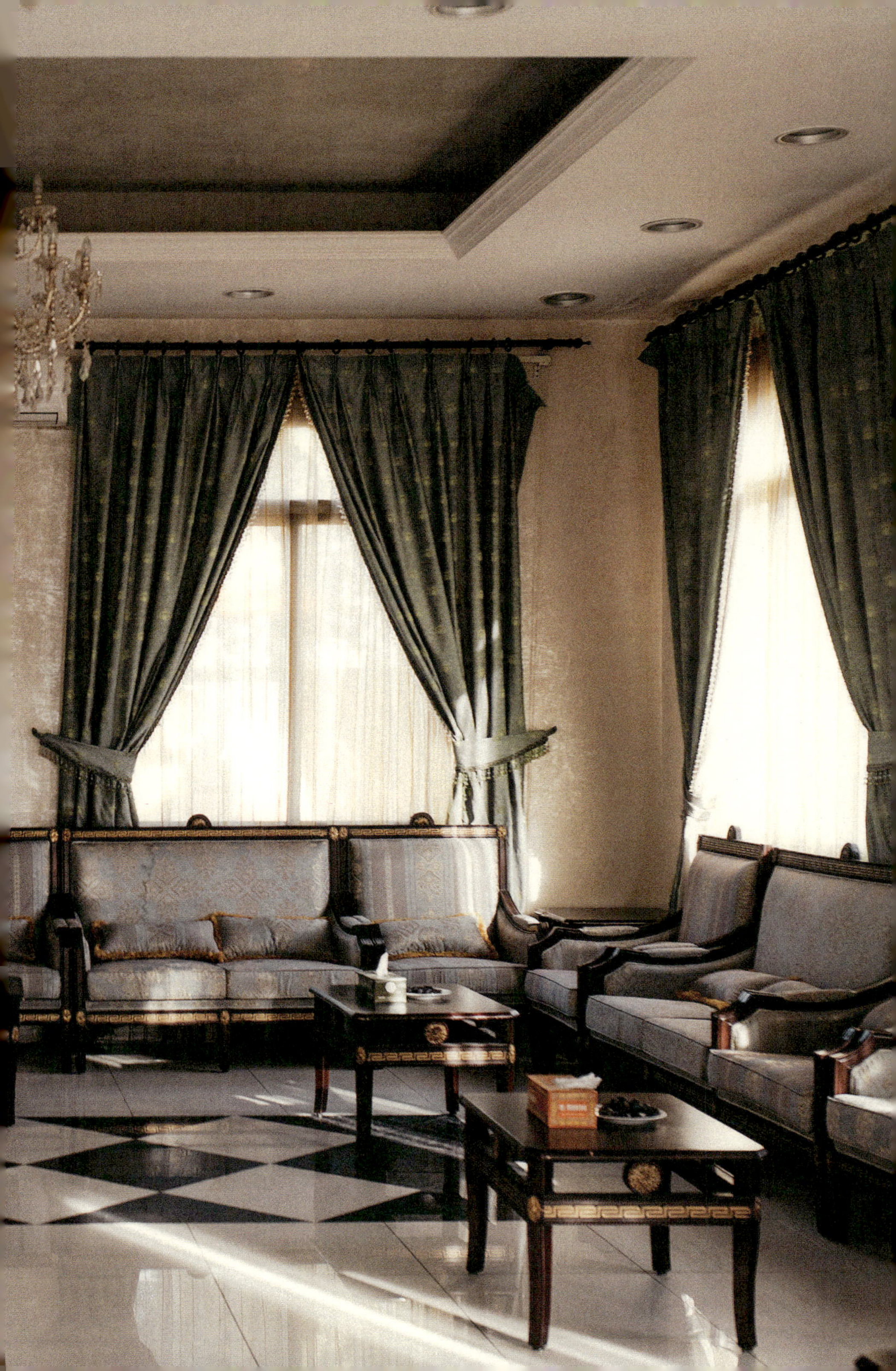

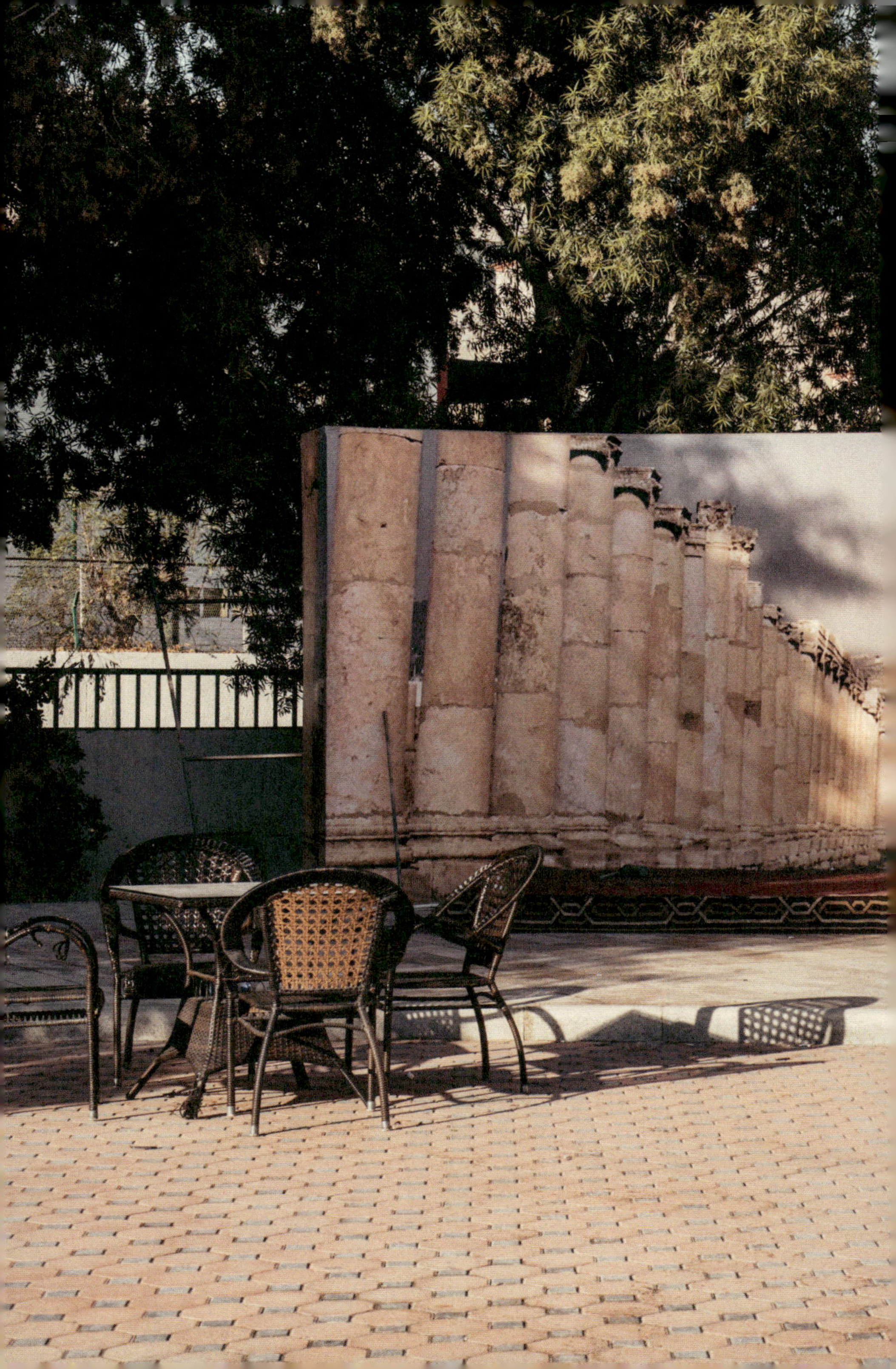

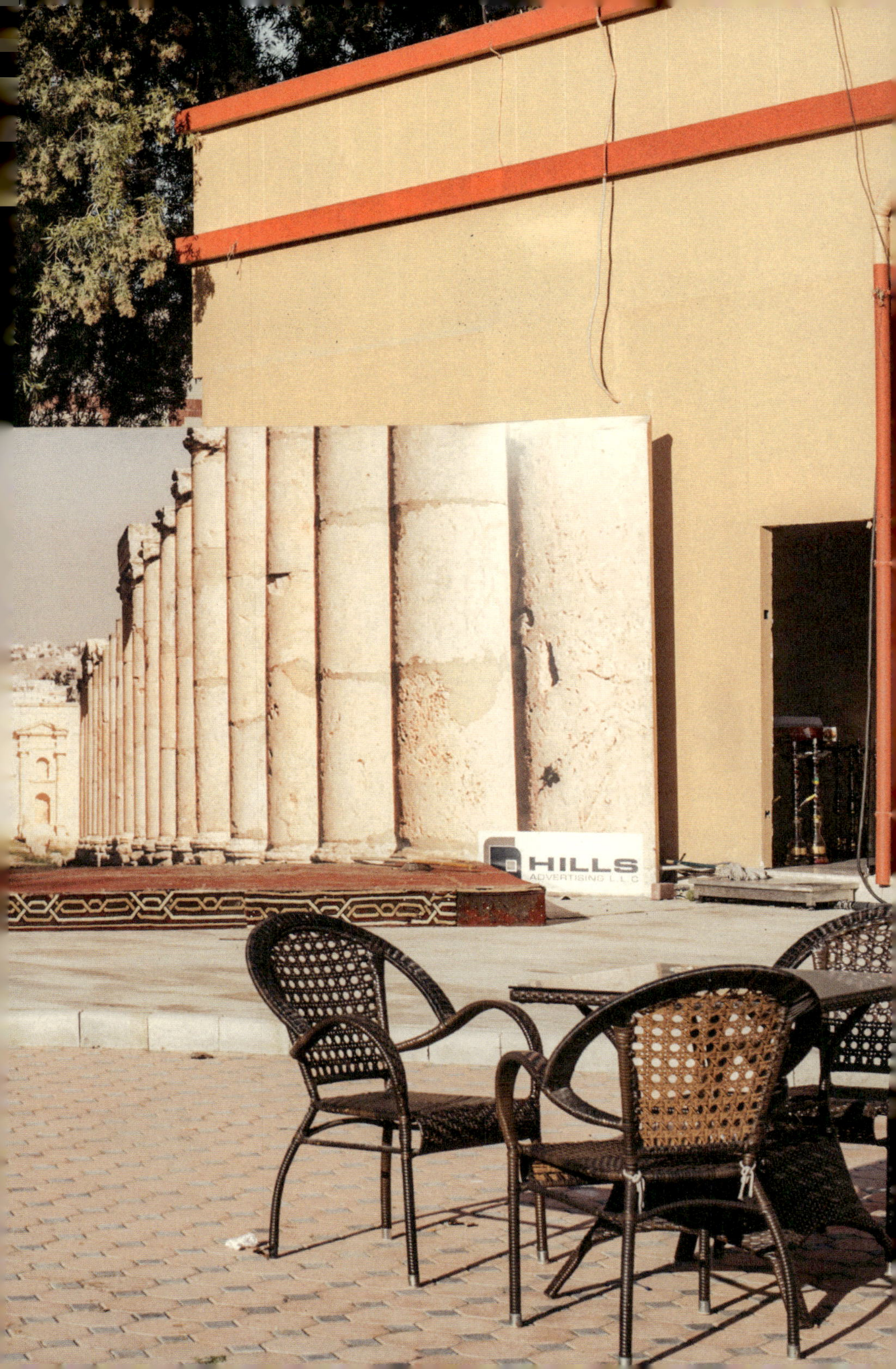
HILLS
ADVERTISING L.L.C

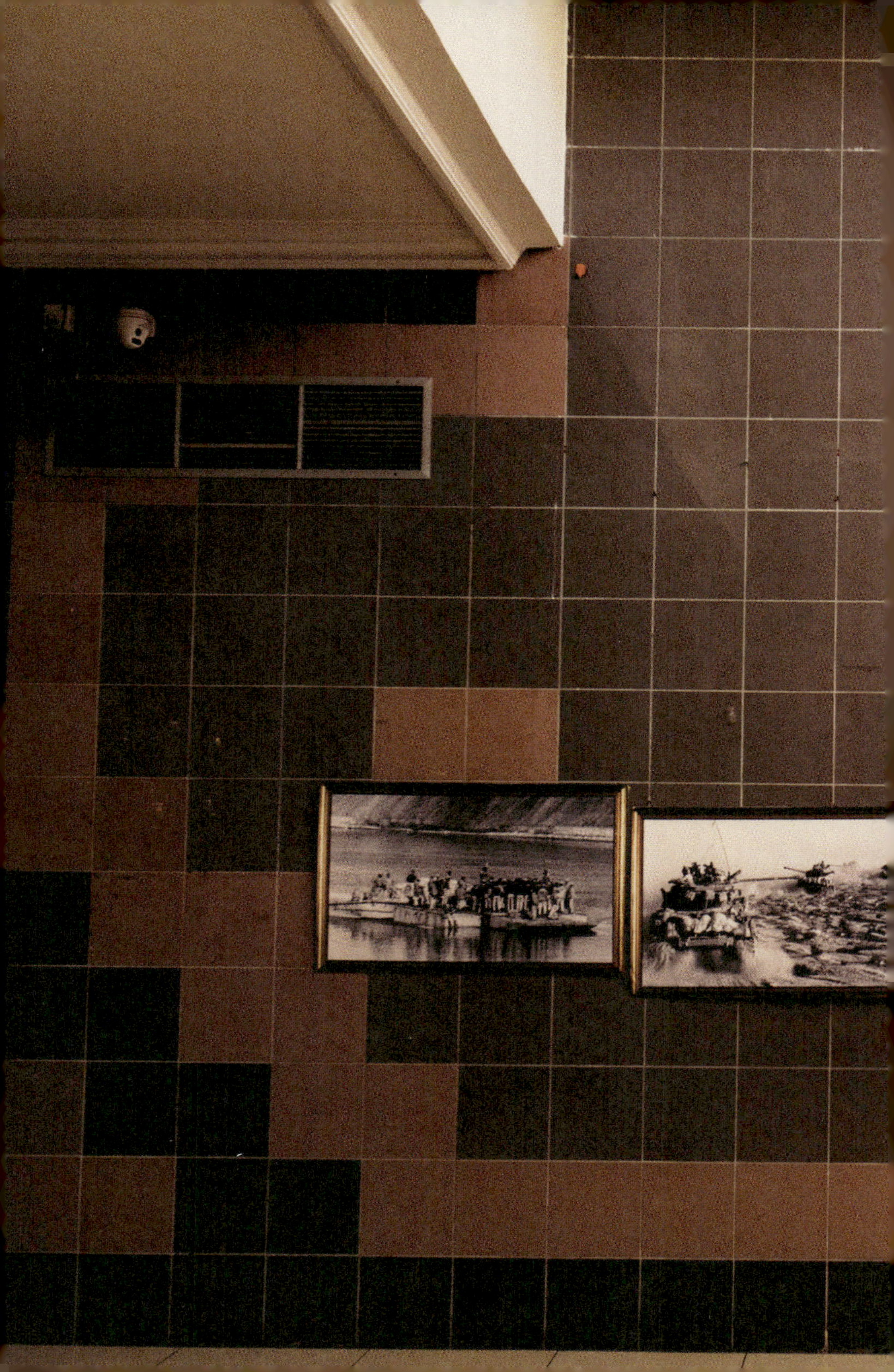

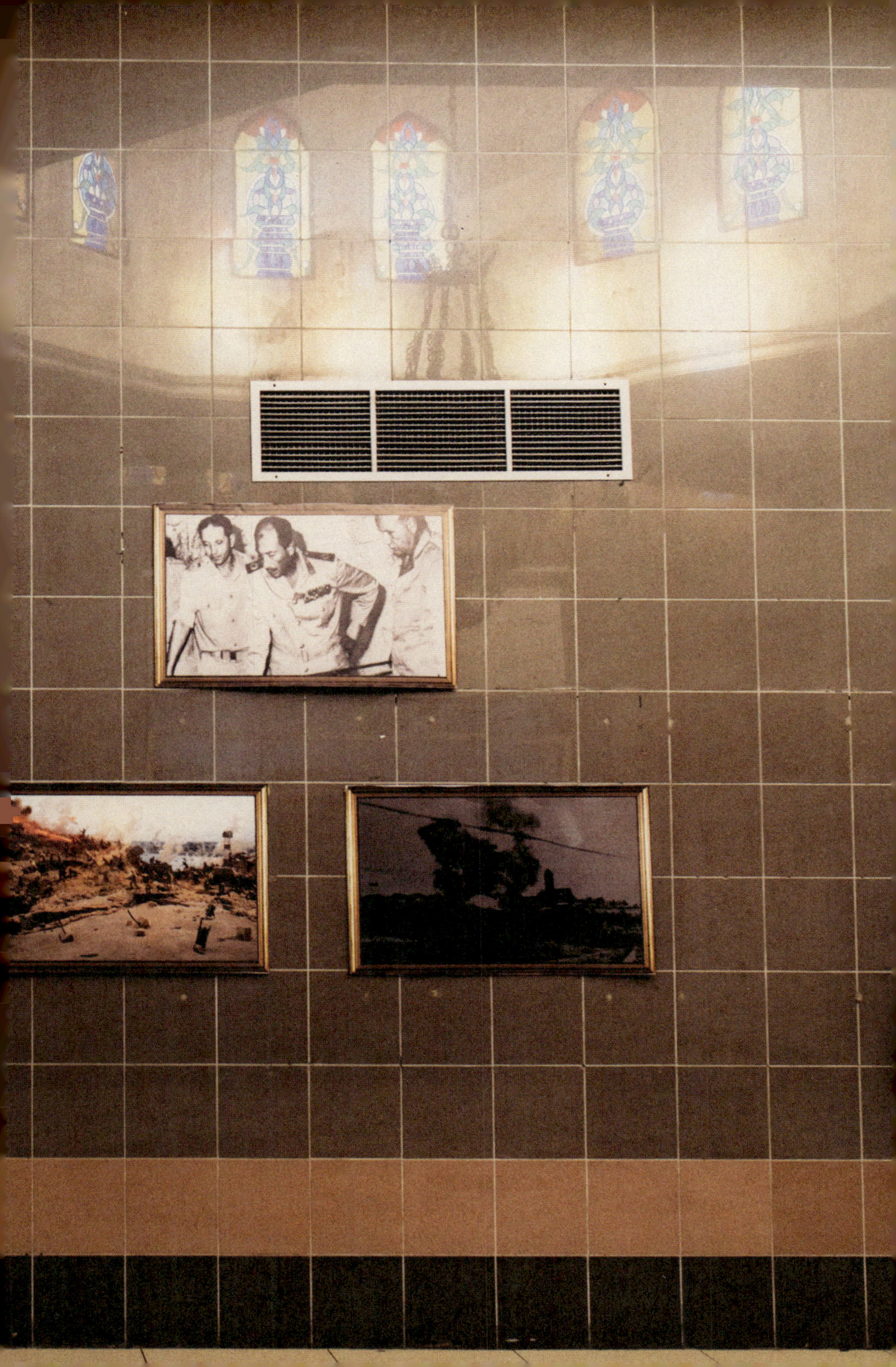

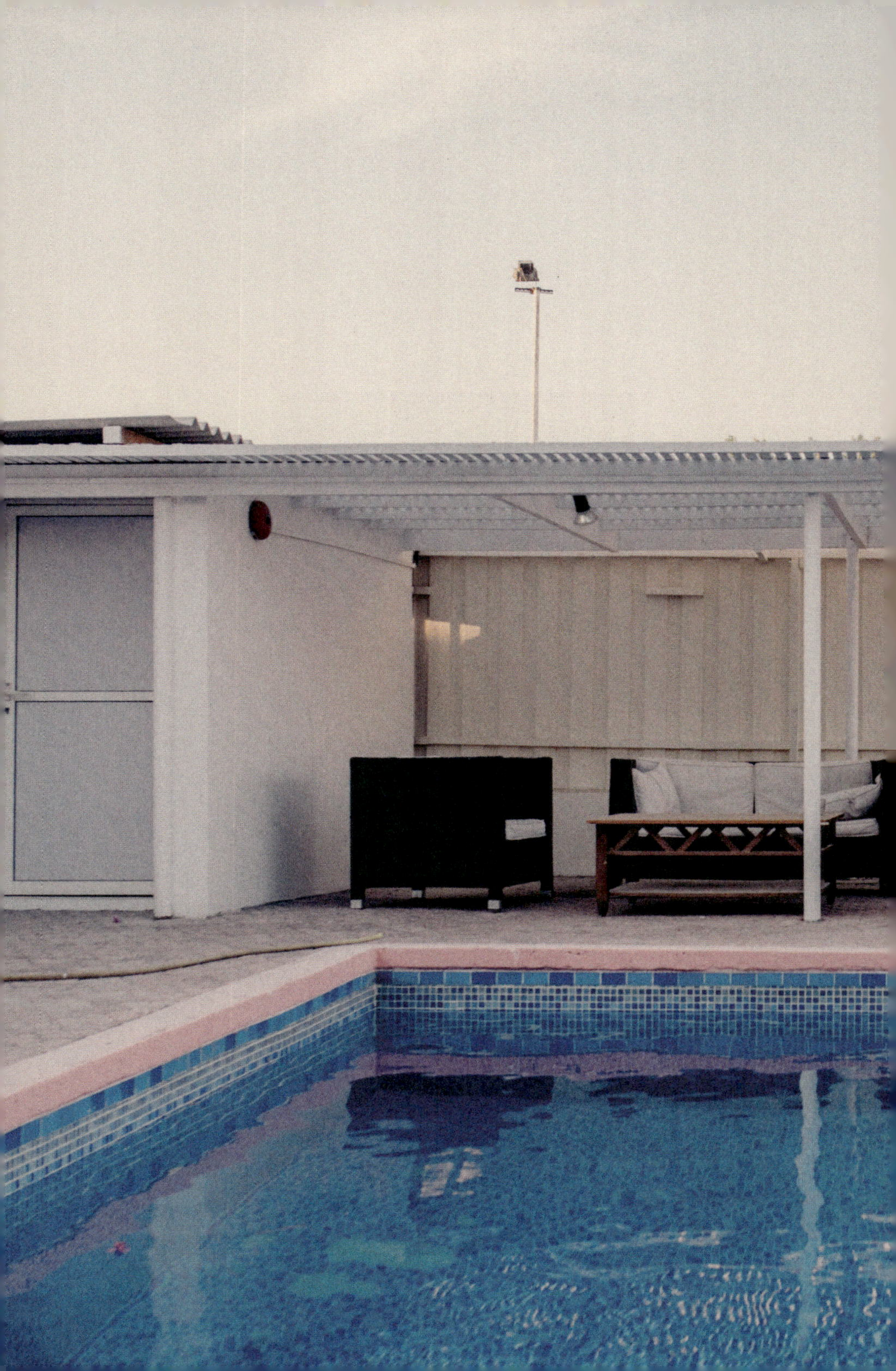

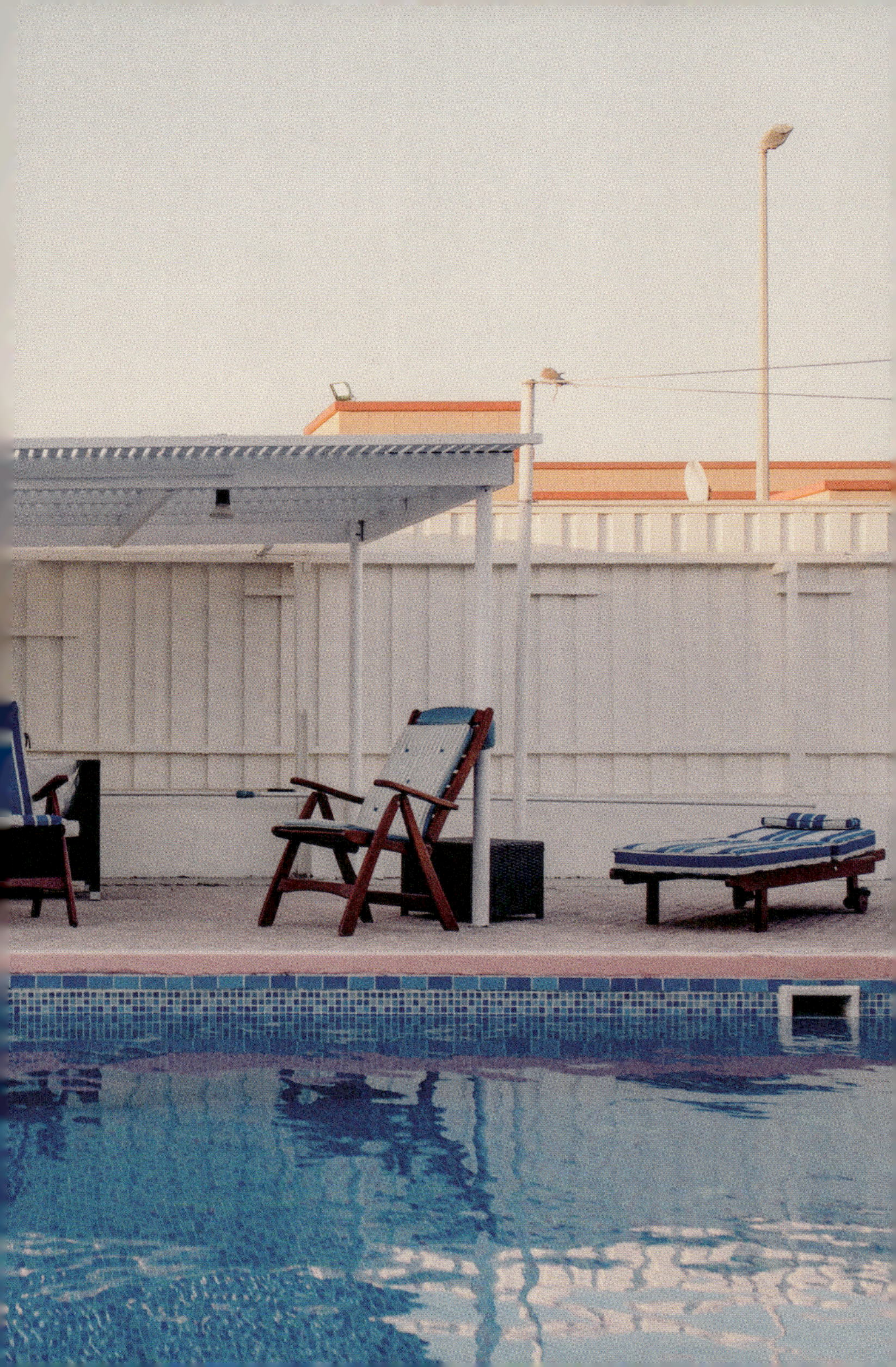

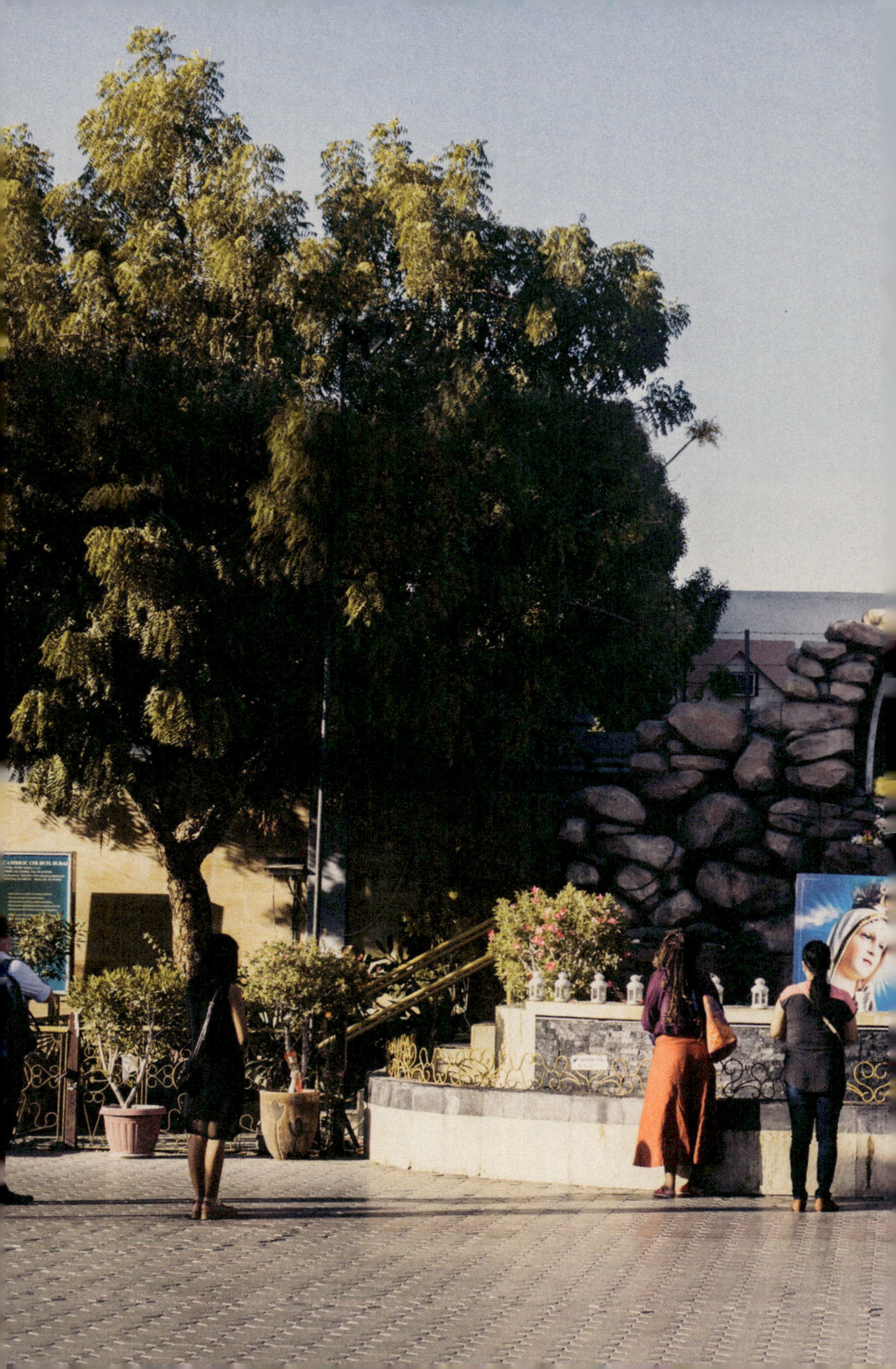

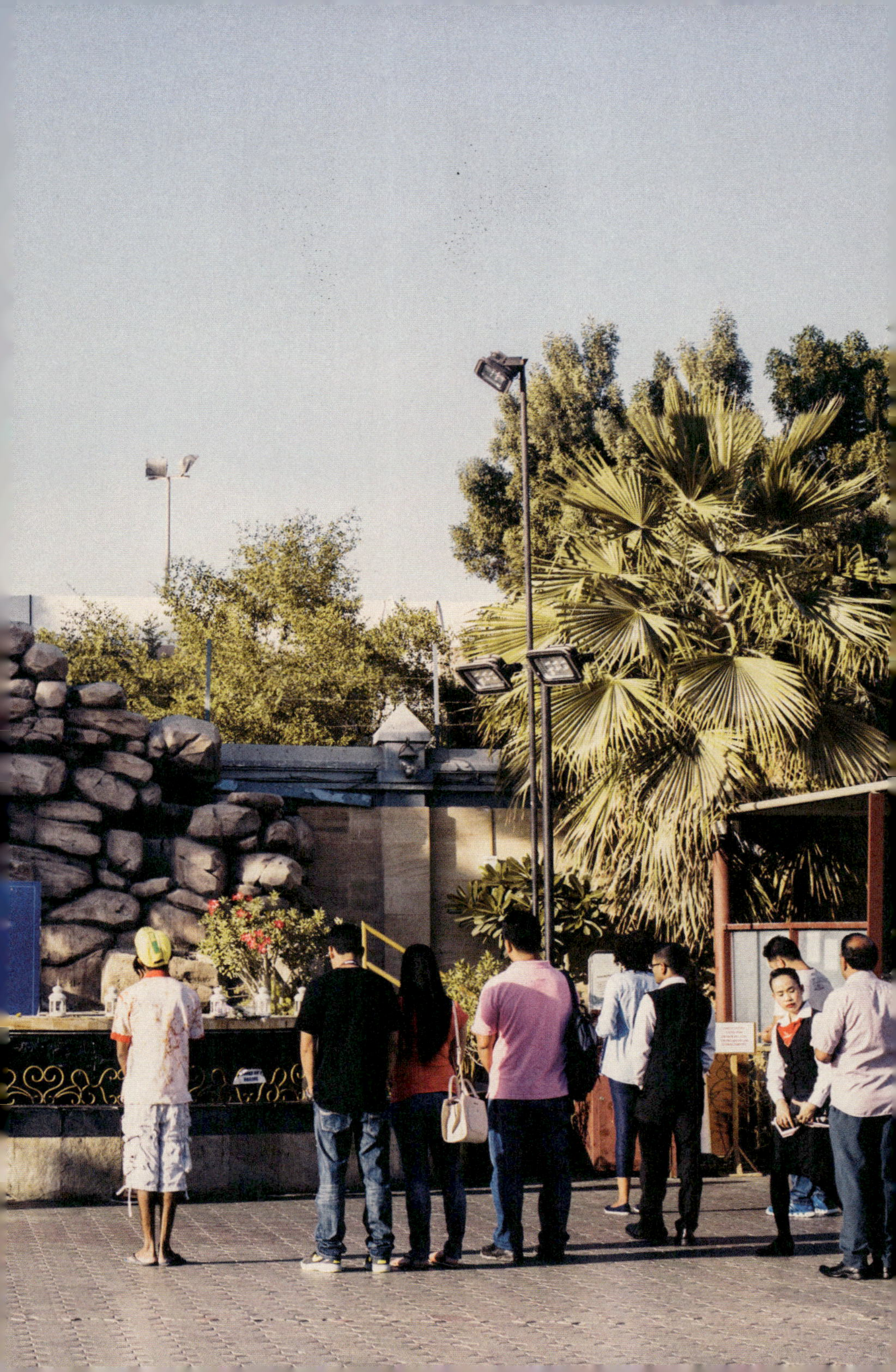

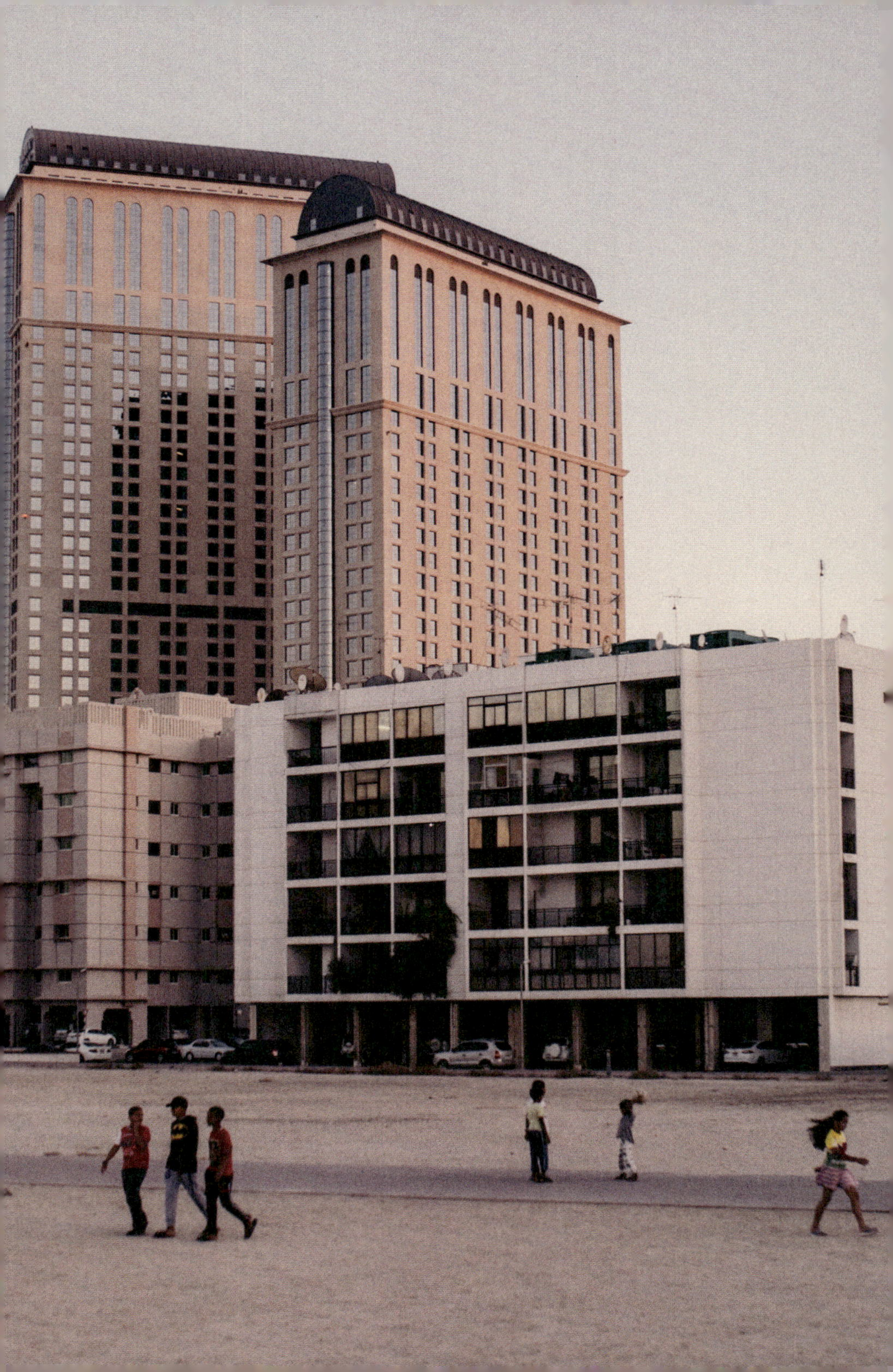

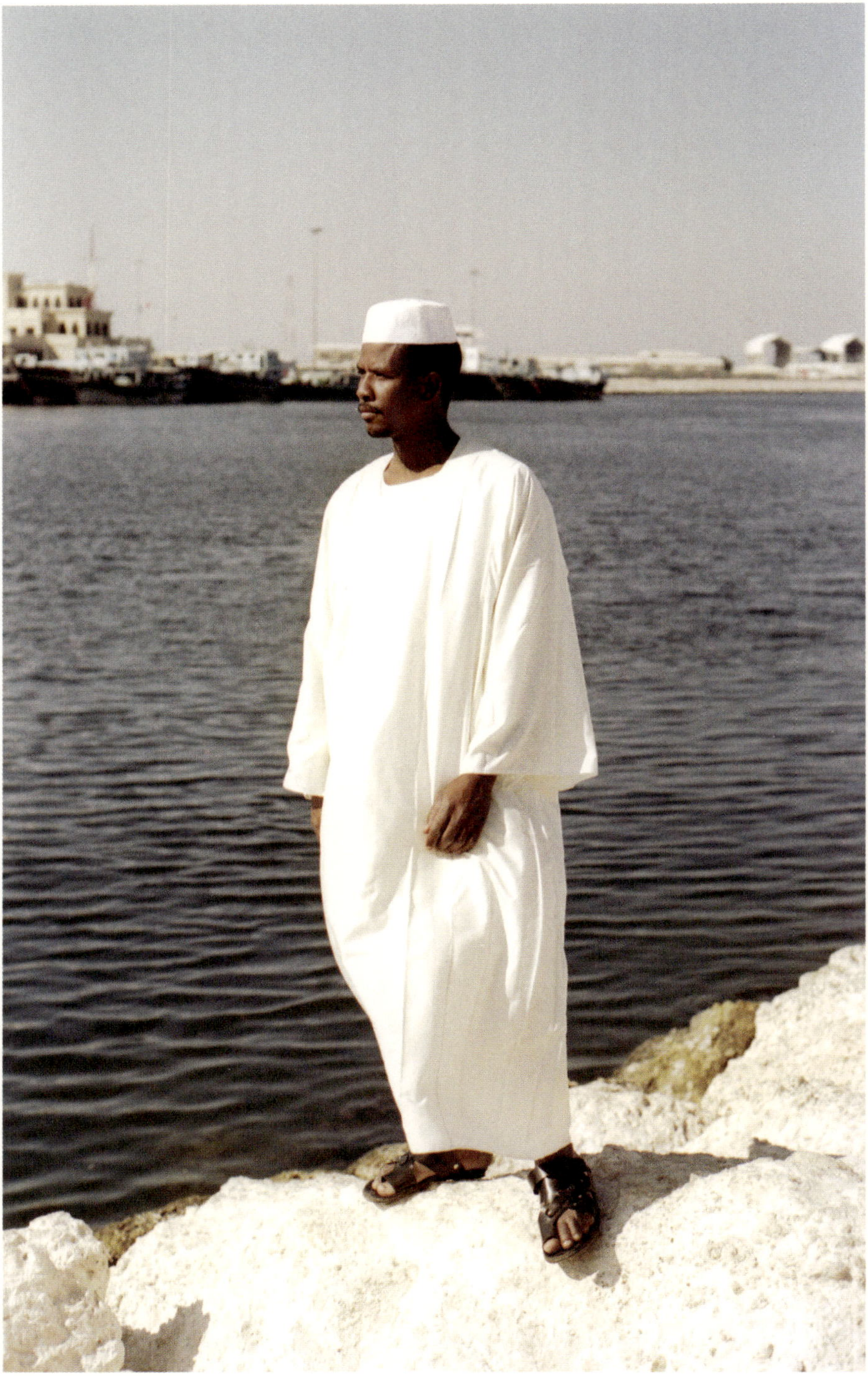

PORTRAITS

KUBA RYNIEWICZ

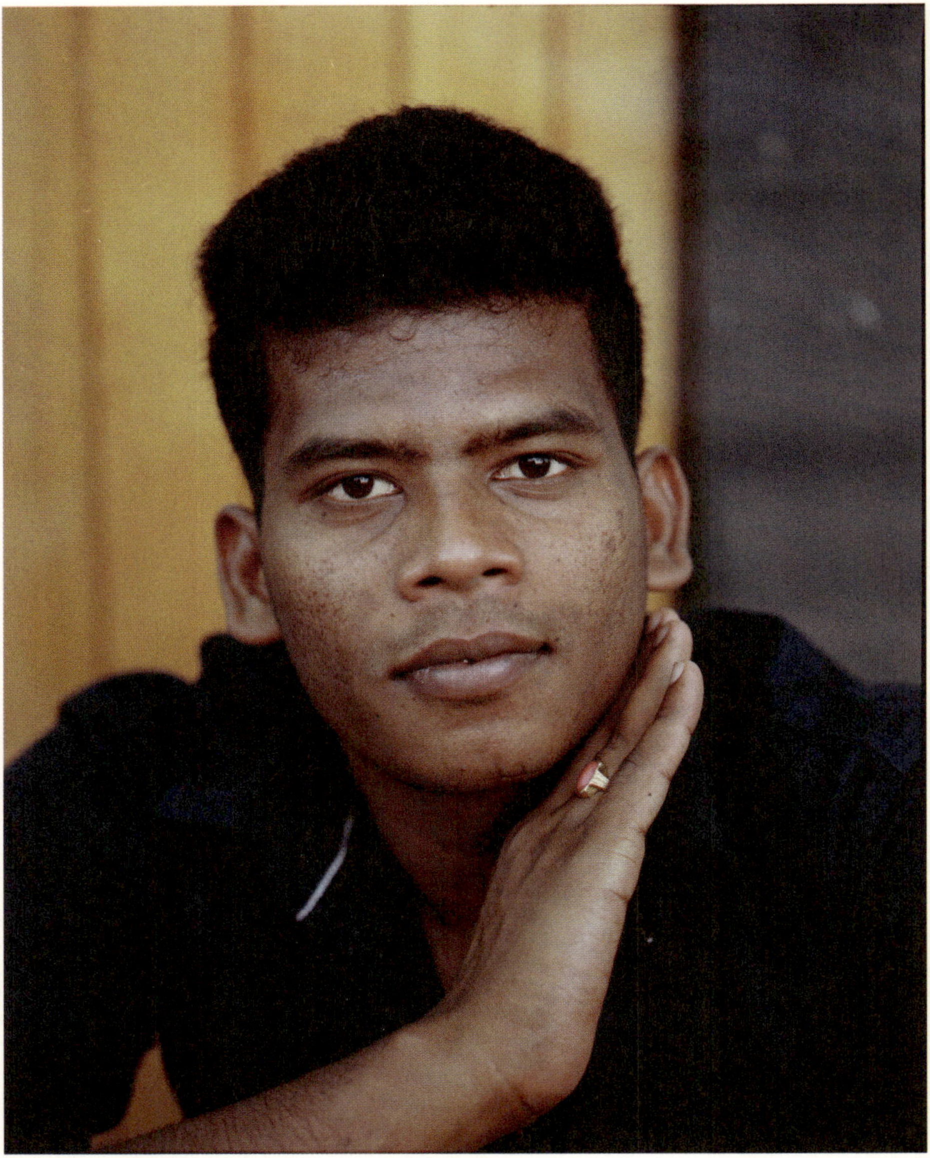

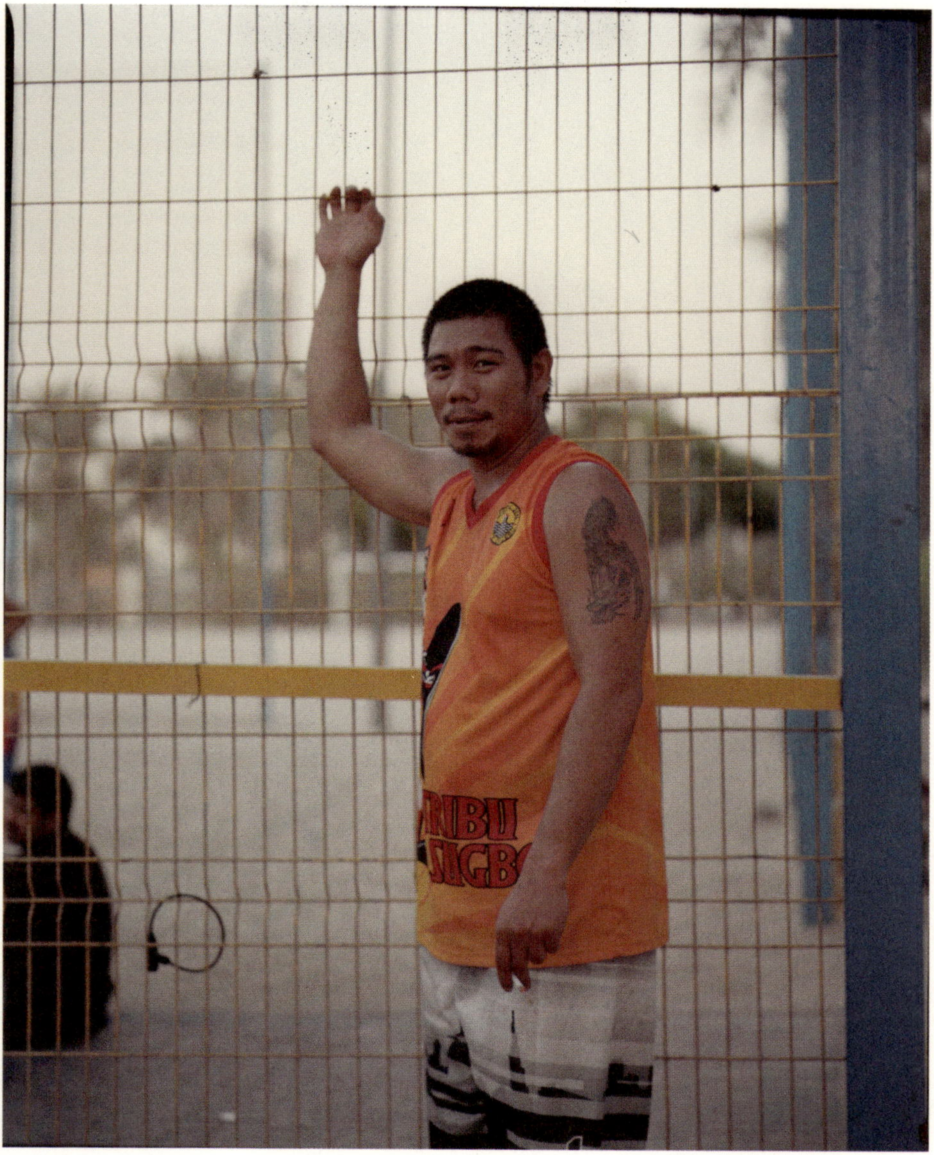
TRIBU
SUGB

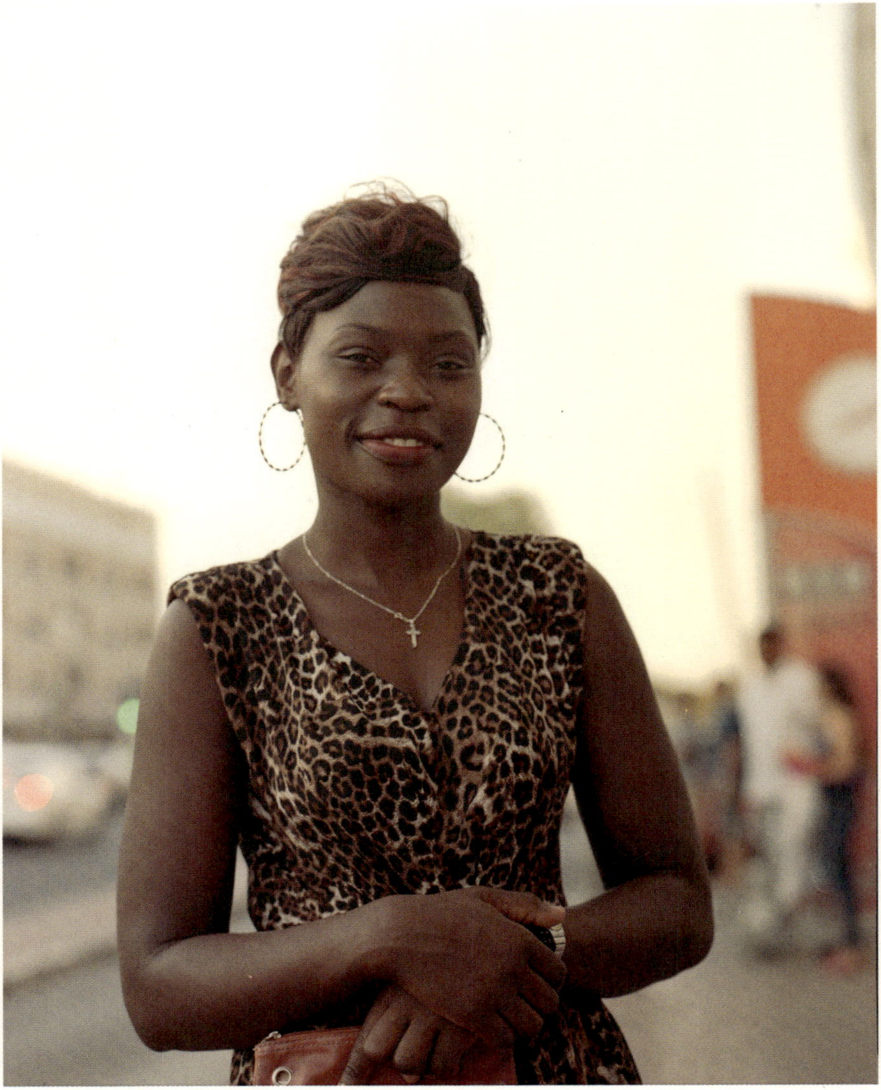

Kuba Ryniewicz

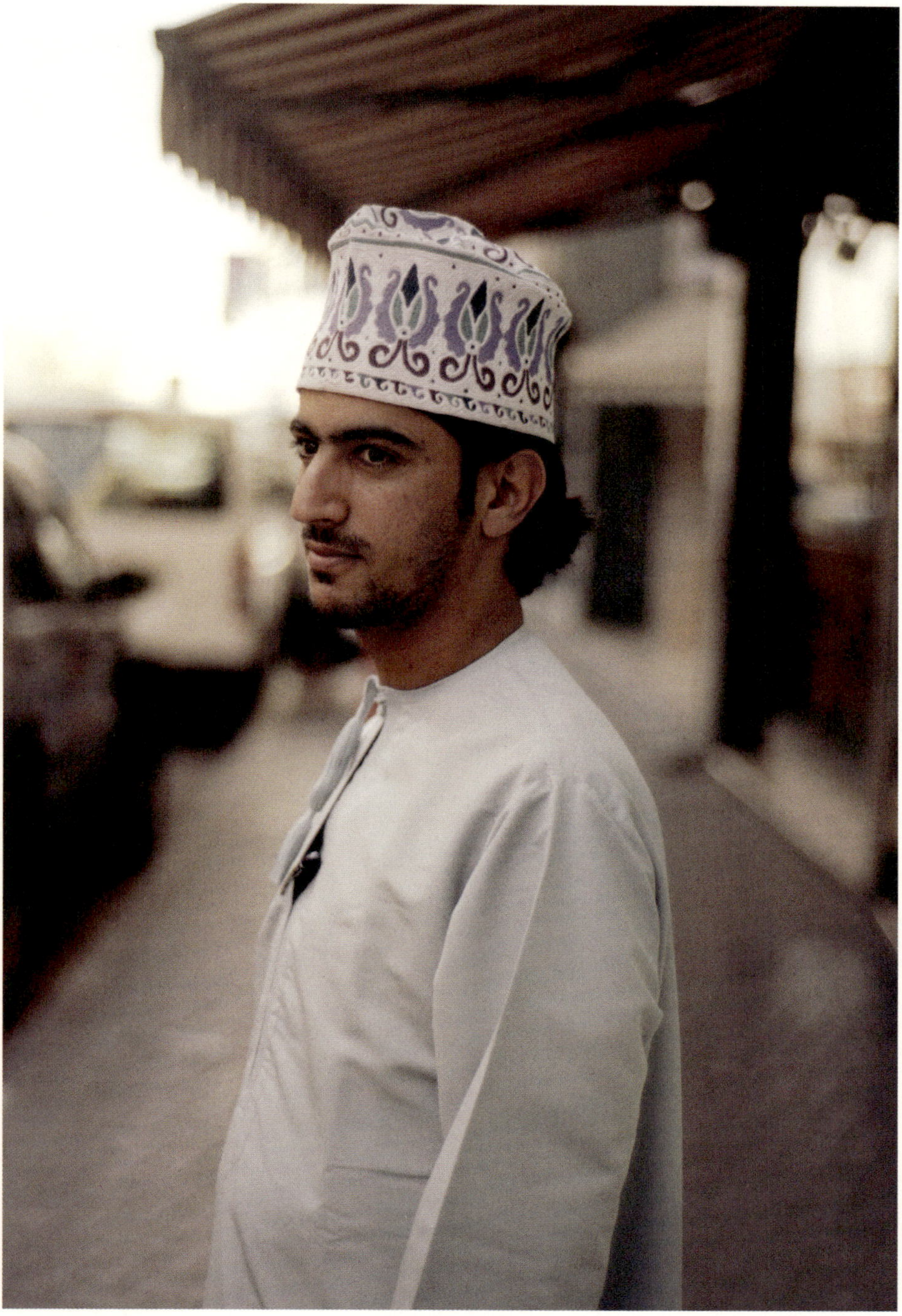

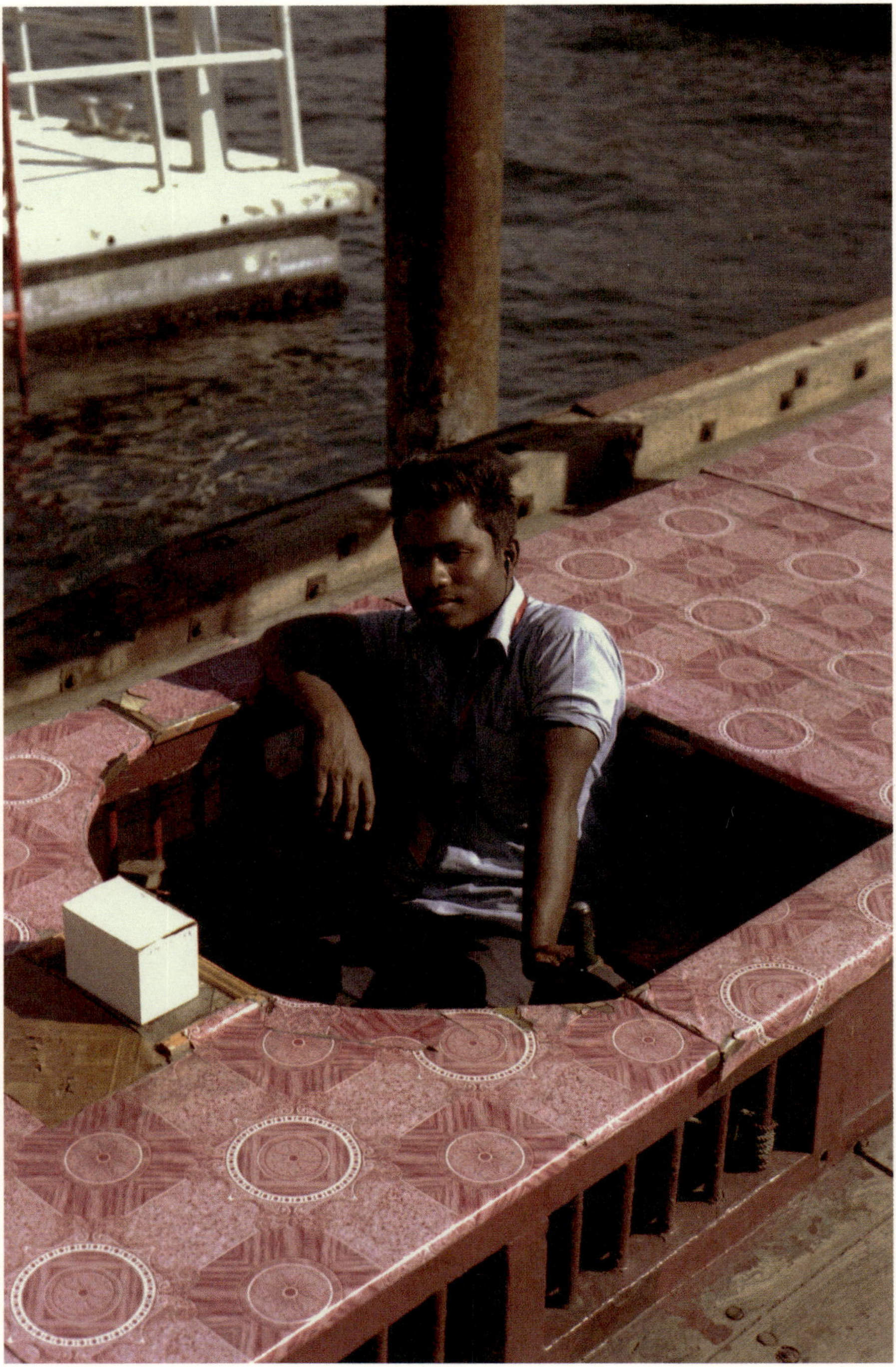

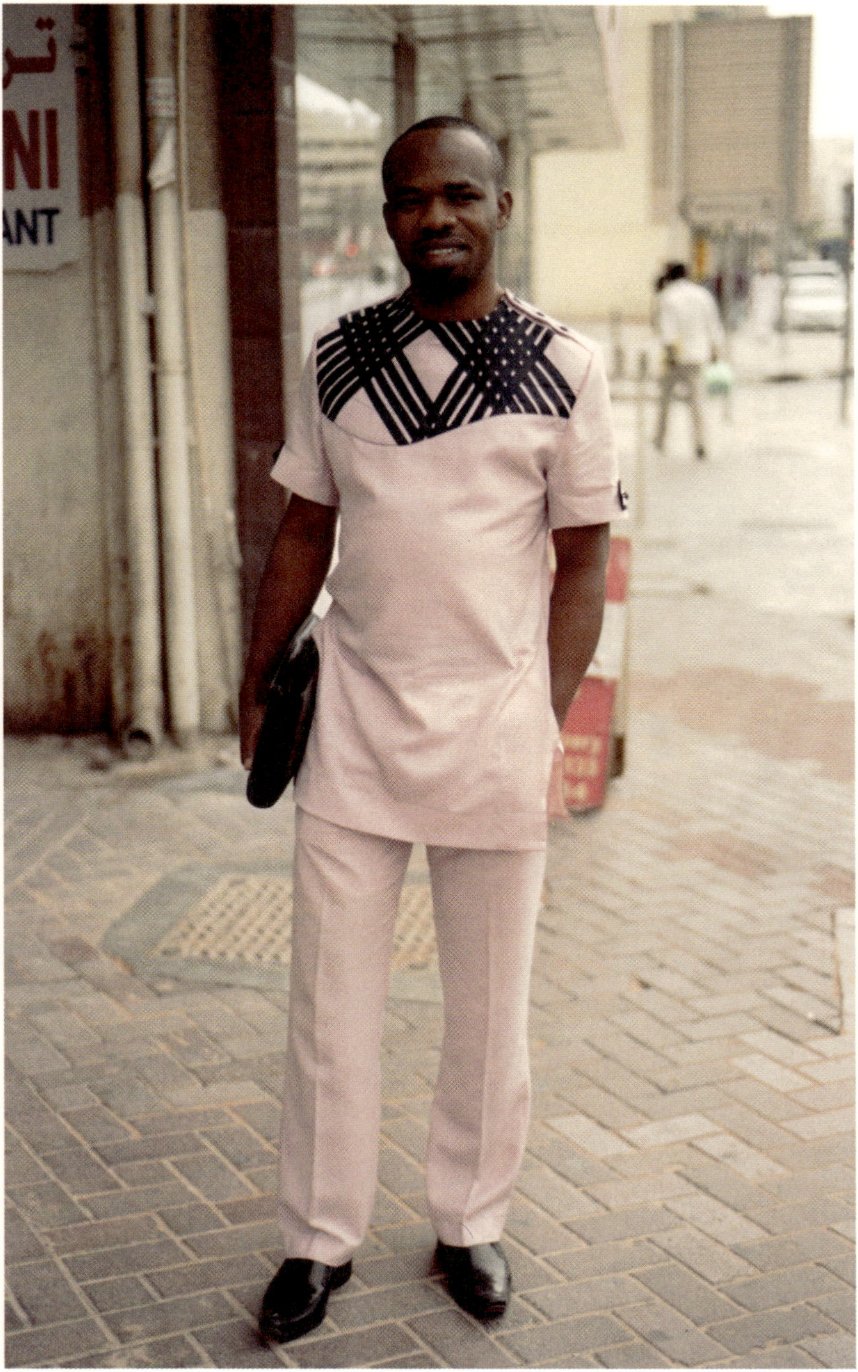

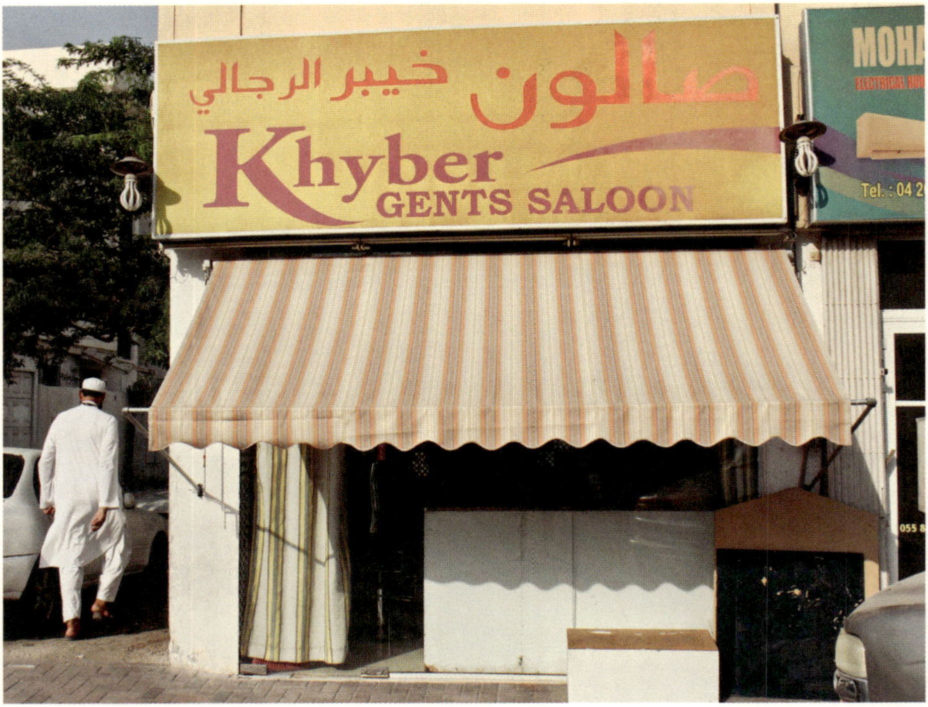
صالون خيبر الرجالي
Khyber
GENTS SALOON

SHAVE AND A HAIRCUT 2 FILS

GAAR ADAMS

I have been called a human porcupine. My wild, coarse beard juts out at precarious angles like quills, threatening friend or foe that dares approach my heavily armored face. The act of hugging borders on farcical —any errant strands of hair latch onto my beard with the sureness of Velcro. Kissing is worse: invariably, my wiry hair will leave a lover raw and irritated (often in both face and mood.) Even just brushing a soft hand across my cheek is like rubbing sandpaper over a smooth piece of wood that doesn't need polishing. So for the sake of those around me, I try my best to keep a clean mug.

But the task of shaving has always been a tortuous ritual for me, a grueling undertaking that inexorably leads to a mess of bloodied tissues and impassioned cursing. The old wisdom of shaving "with the grain" confounds my beard that spirals out like a galaxy from my angular jaw, refusing to grow in any semblance of a uniform direction. And my general shaving resentment is probably exacerbated by the fact that I am Sisyphus with a razor—once, not three hours after I had shaved, a child noted my perpetual five-o'clock shadow and declared me "a pointy lion". (In my estimation, this is only marginally better than being labeled a porcupine.)

When I moved to the United Arab Emirates from the United States in July of 2010, my troublesome beard did not take kindly to the change. Already battling seborrhoeic dermatitis—a mild skin inflammation exacerbated by heat and humidity—the unforgiving midsummer sun left my face redder, itchier, and more inflamed. But I was loath to admit that it was not just my beard struggling with the transition to my new home.

Despite my best attempts, I found the media's standard-issue critiques of the country—the inaccessibility of its cultural spaces, the vapidity of its Guinness World Record superlatives—difficult to ignore during my first few weeks. I was a New Yorker who had just spent the better part of a year studying Arabic in Yemen, and my initial explorations left me with the distinct impression that the UAE lacked both the thriving bustle of Manhattan and the close-knit communality of my neighborhood in Sana'a. I had landed at the start of Ramadan and the height of 45-degree Celsius days—an unfortunate convergence that left me exploring empty streets and feeling like the country's sole defiant outdoor pedestrian in a relentless assault of fancy cars and malls (and sun-bleached billboards advertising fancier cars and newer malls).

Alone with the deserted sidewalks of Dubai late one afternoon a few weeks after my arrival, I found myself craving the vibrancy of a grungy Lower East Side bar. Or the hospitality of a Sana'a *majlis*. But sweaty and irritated after an aimless stroll through the streets of Deira, I mostly just craved a damn good shave. Scratching my face with the fervor of a flea-ridden gibbon, I started hunting for a spot that could rid me of my pesky whiskers. And then a funny thing happened: I noticed that the whole street in front of me was lined with barbershops.

Their fluorescent signs were everywhere. Two of them flashed the word "BARBER" in the same lustrous green on opposing street corners. Up and down the lane I roamed, signboards emblazoned with the word "SALON" igniting the dusky air with deep reds and regal blues. I fixated on one partially obscured by a dusty old awning for "Khyber Gents

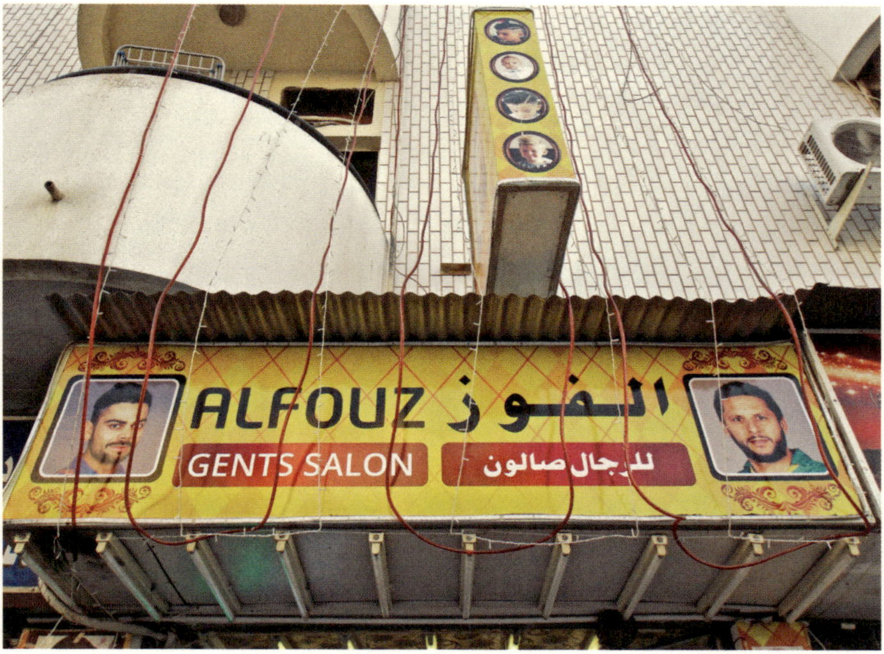
ALFOUZ
الفوز
GENTS SALON
للرجال صالون

Saloon"—probably subconsciously enticed by the connotation of alcohol in American Old West saloons (I would later find out that "saloon" is a common South Asian cognate of "salon"—alas, no illicit booze to be found).

Loitering outside the Al Fouz Gents Salon for a few moments, I was struck by the cheerful commotion inside—men in various stages of shaving laughing with one another and pointing at a Bollywood film on the old television set mounted to the wall. I looked at my map: I had strolled north and east of the Deira waterfront into Hor Al-Anz. But before I could process more, a stout, bearded man in a starched white uniform ushered me in with a persistent wave. A moment later, I was slathered with foamy mint-scented shaving cream, wedged between a Keralite tailor and a Ugandan driver discussing Obama's foreign policy while my Lahori barber shoved two Q-Tips covered in sticky black wax up my nostrils.

'Okay,' I thought, struggling to process the delightfully unexpected scene reflecting in the cracked barber mirror before me. 'Maybe Dubai does have a few surprises worth exploring.'

* * *

The story of Hor Al-Anz is a familiar one: an elegant neighborhood once reserved for the privileged, then neglected to the point of disrepair, but ultimately reinvigorated by an influx of outsiders.

Built in the 1980s as a modern development for Emirati families, Hor Al-Anz didn't serve its intended purpose for long. Just ten years after its completion, local occupants had already began moving out of the neighborhood's squat one-story *sha'abi* houses and into newer developments further afield, like the spacious homes of Mirdif. Hor Al-Anz feels like a block of Dubai that was virtually leapfrogged by a generation during the city's rapid urbanization, built and then cast aside by its intended residents for greener pastures within the same decade.

Today, with the original vision of a quaint Emirati housing development a distant memory, Hor Al-Anz's residences buzz with the energy of a vibrant working class hailing from the corners of South and Southeast Asia. Balconies flutter with the laundry—the drying uniforms of drivers, cooks, and porters catching the wind. Tenants file out of its utilitarian cement housing and into a world of fast-paced commerce—tea stalls serving piping hot *chai*, tandoor bakeries peddling *roti* (flatbread), travel agencies promising the cheapest flights to Kish Island. And lighting up every few meters of sidewalk into the furthest reaches of the neighborhood: the bright signs for the barbershops of Hor Al-Anz.

Fluorescent signs in English and Arabic above the storefronts officially welcome patrons, while iridescent decals for "barber" or "saloon" in Hindi, Urdu, and Malayalam plastered to many of the barbershops' windows speak to a different clientele. But signs in any language aren't really necessary—lingering outside a barbershop's glass storefront regardless of your nationality will result in the same outcome: a hearty wave urging you inside.

To enter into a barbershop in Hor Al-Anz is to enter into a world of improvisation. There is no schedule; no pointing to a clock and asking what time the next appointment might be available. If a barber is free, he'll motion you over—if not, you grab a crisp newspaper from a stack on the table. Finally sitting in the padded barber's chair, you can ask for a particular service from the faded menu taped to the wall. SHAVING 20 AED. HAIRCUT 30 AED. But those offers are just part of the story.

Plenty of the best services are unlisted, with prices negotiated based on length of the treatment. There's eyebrow threading. Steam facials with aloe and avocado moisturizers. Nose waxing. A glorious 30-minute *champissage*[2], where a barber plies your neck, back, and scalp—and sometimes eyelids—with tender strokes. But even if you request just one particular treatment, a barber may have another idea—if you look

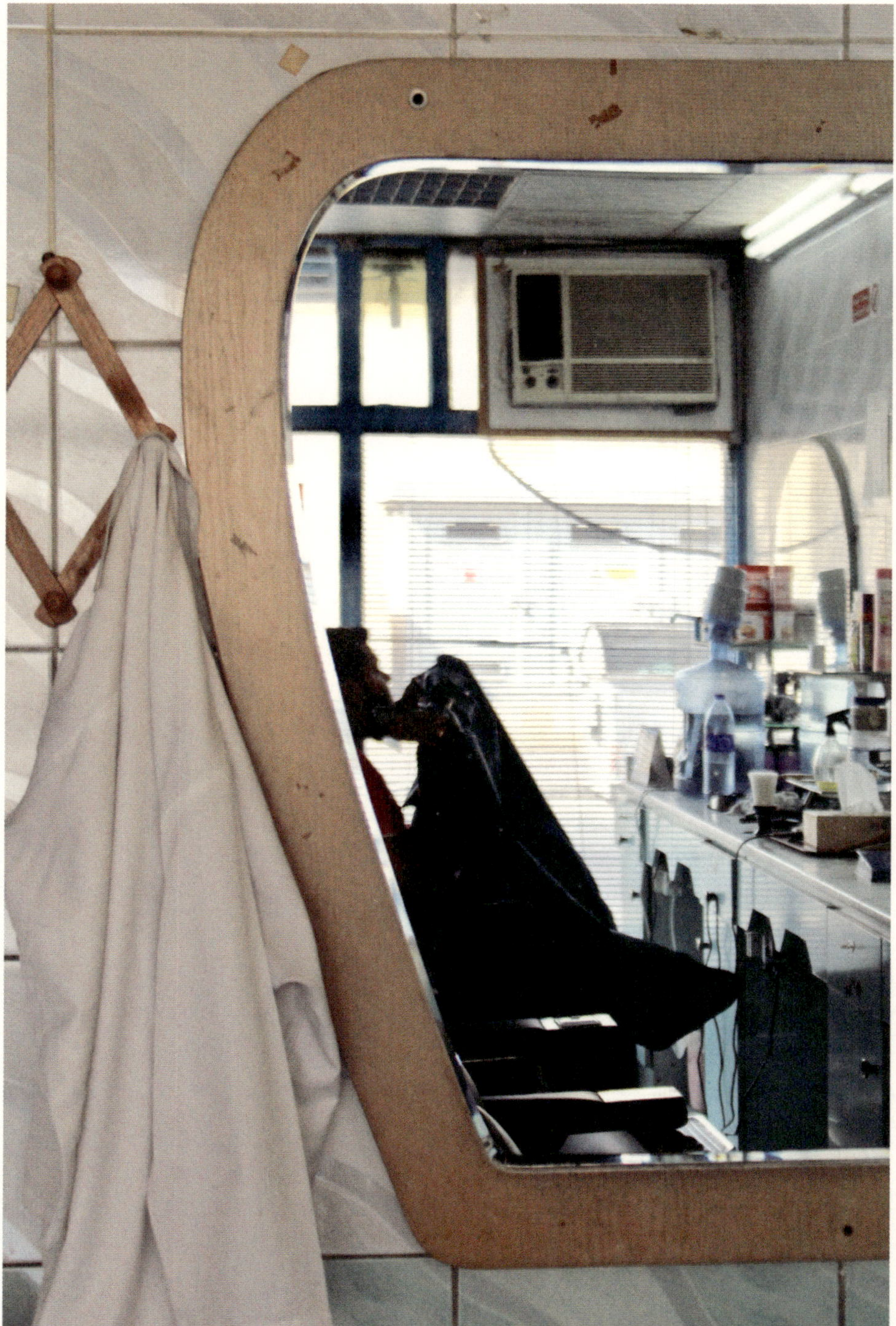

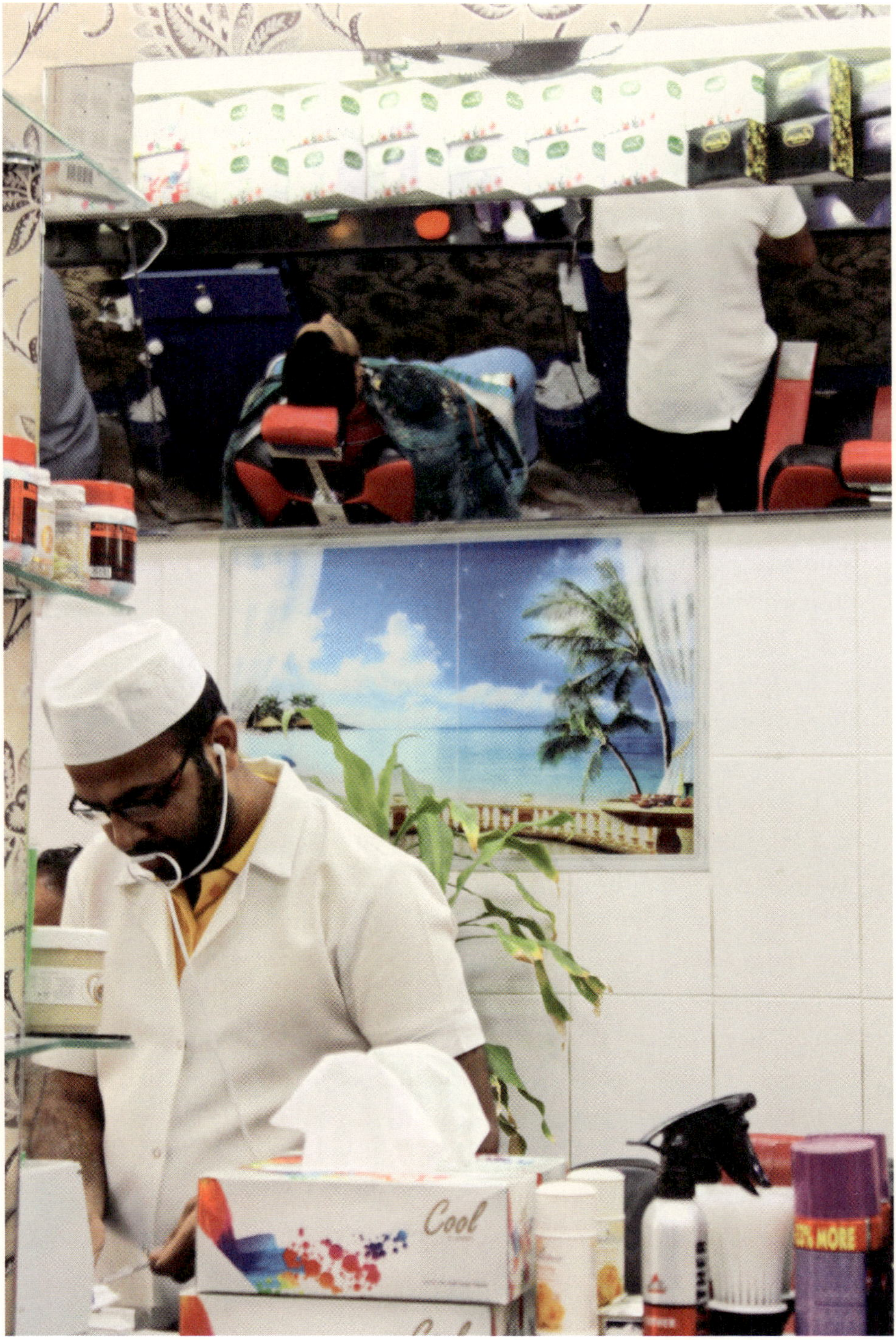
Cool
% MORE

particularly oily one day, you may find your face covered in three layers of exfoliating products. Or vigorously rubbed with alcohol until your pores practically disappear. (Not that my flawless skin has ever needed this, of course.)

Inside the barbershop, time is fluid—you stay as long as the barber thinks you need, and you linger as long as you would like. You can continue reading your newspaper. Or lose yourself in a pivotal scene from the film *Sholay* on MBC. Or finish that chat with a fellow patron. In a city that lacks communal urban spaces, the barbershop is a welcome gathering place without a time limit.

In a country where public spheres are so often cloistered by nationality, the barbershops of Hor Al-Anz subvert that reality. In one salon attached to a Muslim butcher, I have watched numerous men from all different countries point to the same faded photo in the shop's window of Bollywood star Shah Rukh Khan.

"Even today, everyone wants hair like SRK," the Pakistani barber chuckled to me.

At another barbershop behind a small grocery, three Nepali deliverymen regularly frequent a Keralite-operated establishment, undeterred that the language of communication is primarily Malayalam. Shaking hands with the barber that bestows them with matching undercuts in the mirror, they shyly admit their initial inspiration for entering this particular shop: a photo splashed across the storefront of a grinning Cristiano Ronaldo sporting the identical hairstyle.

Sports seem to unite almost everyone in these barbershops. Men ask for haircuts like Lionel Messi and take photos of one another's end results. Patrons help each other pull up photos of sports stars on their phones for beard inspiration. And when a soccer or cricket match broadcasts live, men from India, Pakistan, Bangladesh, and Sri Lanka steam into the shops with the biggest and loudest televisions. During a particularly tense India vs Pakistan cricket match a few years ago, I watched an Indian barber cut the hair of a Pakistani construction foreman while both were standing to watch the television.

"You promise you will not cut me if India will lose," the foreman laughed. Each courteously waited for the other to cheer or curse a particular run, and both ended up surviving the protracted haircut.

If some barbershops attract customers with wide-screen televisions or pictures of celebrated soccer players, others draw in customers with reputations. One of my favorite barbershops in Hor Al-Anz employs a burly former Pehlwani wrestler from outside Karachi renowned for his meticulous head massages that feature luxurious fingertip kneading and expert neck cracks. Inside the unassuming shop where three tightly jammed chairs share one sink, he regales his diverse clientele with stories in simple English of his wrestling career in Pakistan. In both storytelling and basic communication inside barbershops, anticipated language barriers often prove weaker than expected. One evening I watched a Bangladeshi man try in vain to sooth his toddler crying high atop a booster seat in a barber chair. A Filipino man gingerly walked over and tussled the boy's hair, singing *Sa Ugoy ng Duya*, a famous Tagalog lullaby:

Nais kong maulit/
Ang awit ni lnang mahal

"Don't worry," he said, as the boy's wails calmed to a sputter. "This song helps everyone."

While friendly chatter and music permeate most salons in Hor Al-Anz, periods of silence serve to connect as well. A lull between topics can fall over the shop with only the light shuffle of newspapers audible.

Or a conversation will halt to respect a man who dozed off in the corner, basking in the midday sun. It is in these moments of quiet that a barber —be he from Hyderabad or Chittagong—will flick his eyebrows toward the sky: "Lift your chin," his gesture says. Or lightly graze a cheek: "Turn your head to the left," he asks, words unuttered.

This is the nonverbal barbershop vocabulary spoken and comprehended by both barber and customer, regardless of language. Placing your hand on a shoulder mid-shave sends a heartfelt greeting. Holding up two fingers signifies the length of a cut. Smiling and offering a nod across the shop compliments another man's haircut; pointing to yourself asks for the same style. Inside this world, a shared fluency in spoken language isn't compulsory to share moments with the men that surround you.

Having gone for a shave two to three times a week for seven years, I've probably sat in upwards of one hundred barbershops in the UAE—from a windowless storefront jammed next to a refinery in Ruwais to one with sweeping views over the western foothills of Ras Al Khaimah's Hajar Mountains. Most barbershops look and feel strikingly similar, but the ones I most relish and continually return to are that cluster in Hor Al-Anz; they are now the most familiar to me—and that brings a measure of comfort.

I still miss so many things here in the UAE—the *majlis* of my adopted home in Yemen, the bustle of New York, the milestones of my family back in Midwest America. But there is solace in being surrounded by men in the same position—thousands of miles from loved ones and sharing stories of home. And so we all return to a place that brings comfort—from the creature comfort of a fresh shave to the deeper emotional soothing of a communal space.

Each time I'm sitting in that chair, with the last dab of shaving cream tenderly washed away and a splash of lotion applied to my face, the barber peels off my gown and lets me inspect my freshly shorn beard in the mirror.

"*Na'iman*," he says.

It's a closing routine that unfolds at each salon with the same concluding word, an Arabic language blessing offered from barber to patron regardless of either's nation, religion, or language. '*You are fresh. You are clean*,' it imparts.

But it's the kind of word that remains perfectly untranslatable—a sentiment that lingers in the air, best communicated with a kind smile and a friendly slap on the neck. As I push my way back out into the streets of Hor Al-Anz that I now call a part of my home, I hear *na'iman* mostly as an invitation. "Return here when you need, and we will send you back out again, renewed."

Majlis: A 'place of sitting' for social gatherings or legislative assemblies. In a home, a majlis is where the head of the family hosts guests.
Champissage: Indian head massage, where the head, neck and face are massaged. The word originates from the Hindi term 'champi', from which the English word 'shampoo' was derived.

2. REVIEW

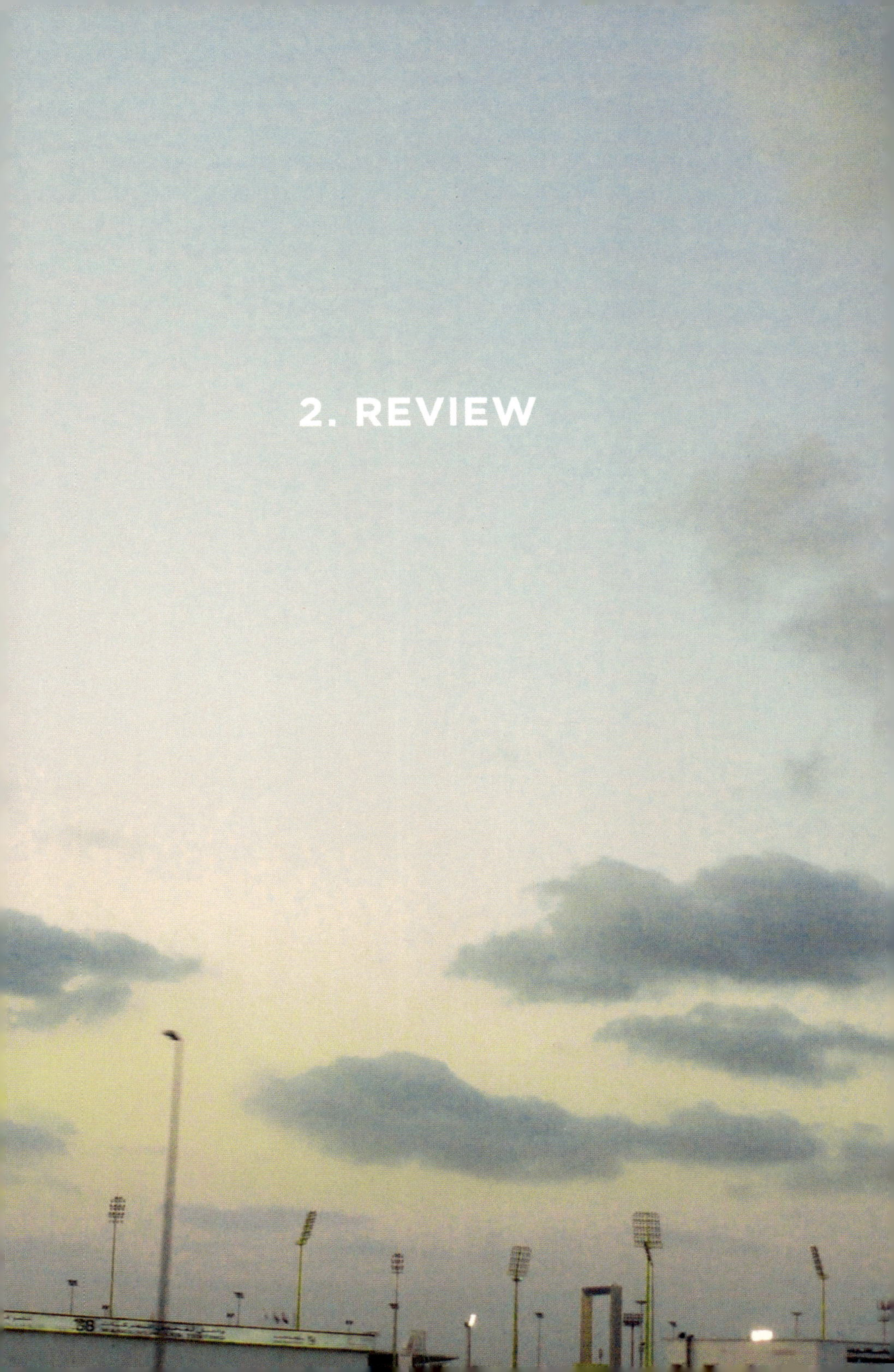

THE ARRIVAL OF LATE MODERNISM

MARYAM MUDHAFFAR

During the first half of the 20th century, life and settlements in Dubai mainly existed around the creek. Known as Al-Khor, the creek divides city life and activity geographically, economically, socially, and even visually into two complementary parts. To the north lies Deira with its bustling mercantile, spice and fabric souqs and to its south is Bur Dubai, home to government buildings and Sheikhs' residences. The late 1950s witnessed a shift from the residential mud brick, coral stone and *barasti* (dried palm frond) houses to Modernist housing districts distanced from the creek. John Harris, a British architect and planner, completed the first town plan of Dubai in 1960 based on aerial surveys and existing settlements; and a later adjusted version in the 1970s. His proposed networks of roads, zoning and infrastructure were extended out to the vast empty deserts of the city, hence guiding the early development of Dubai before and after the discovery of oil in 1966.

These master plans mark a turning point in the architectural language and urban design of Dubai, where traditional practices were altered or were completely abandoned, and the influence of late Modernism began to manifest itself in newly constructed buildings, landmarks, parks, and neighborhoods—most of which were designed by Japanese, British, European and some Arab architects and engineers. The stylistic aesthetics and design principles of Modernism, as an international architectural movement, were introduced to Dubai in the early 1960s. The discovery of oil in 1966 further facilitated the emergence of Modernist structures across the emirate, where they were adapted to local practices and social values. These 'new' buildings, in the context of 'old' Dubai at the time, worked on integrating their Modernist approach to design with vernacular building traditions. For instance, most of these buildings contained courtyards (usually made of sand), abstract ornaments in the form of latticework for screens, windows and shades, elements of passive cooling, techniques of cross-ventilation, light colored paint, repetitive patterns, recessed windows and a respectful play on the dichotomy of public, private and gender-specific spaces. Such architectural manifestations took into consideration a detail-oriented methodology in their built proportions, structural specifications, material selections, evolving typologies and prototypes. They attempted to reconcile local specificities of customs and materials with the colonial innovations of the time—manifestations that had the ambition of belonging to an international movement, but were responding to context.

The prefix "new" customarily implies "successor" to, or "inferior" to, an outdated form. However, in the case of Dubai it implies that 'new' and 'old' coexist synchronically—"an idiom of sibling competition rather than of inheritance." This old/new Dubai spatial matrix is essential to understanding how the architecture of my case studies—being mostly non-iconic buildings—responds to sociocultural, political and economic factors that allowed for the principles of Modernism to be expressed through them. The following case studies show buildings that share Modernist influences but have entirely different functions. They are presented in chronological order.

CASE STUDY 01: DEIRA HOUSE BLOCK, 1961

Architect: Unknown
Date: 1961
Location: Deira
Function: Residential
Status: Still in use

An early example of Modernism in Dubai is best demonstrated in the design of this residential building, which is still in use today. Situated on a corner plot in one of the city's busiest commercial districts —and in the midst of—high-rise residential and commercial blocks nearby, it stands out as an L-shaped three-story whitewashed house that lacks excessive ornamentation.

A plinth bearing wings, just under a vertical window shaft that spans the height of the building, marks its public entry point and commemorates its year of construction: 1961. A ribbon of perforated simple patterns adorns the exterior, its fence, its parapet, and interior walls—creating balanced and repetitive layers of transparency. Greenery visually defines degrees of access; a row of potted plants outside the building periphery introduces the inner front garden of the residential block. The Art Nouveau-inspired staircase and doorway, providing private access to the interior of the building, reveal tendencies for eclectic designs, an outcome probably due to the initial struggle of Modernist architecture to find a language harmonious with the local context and its stylistic inclinations.

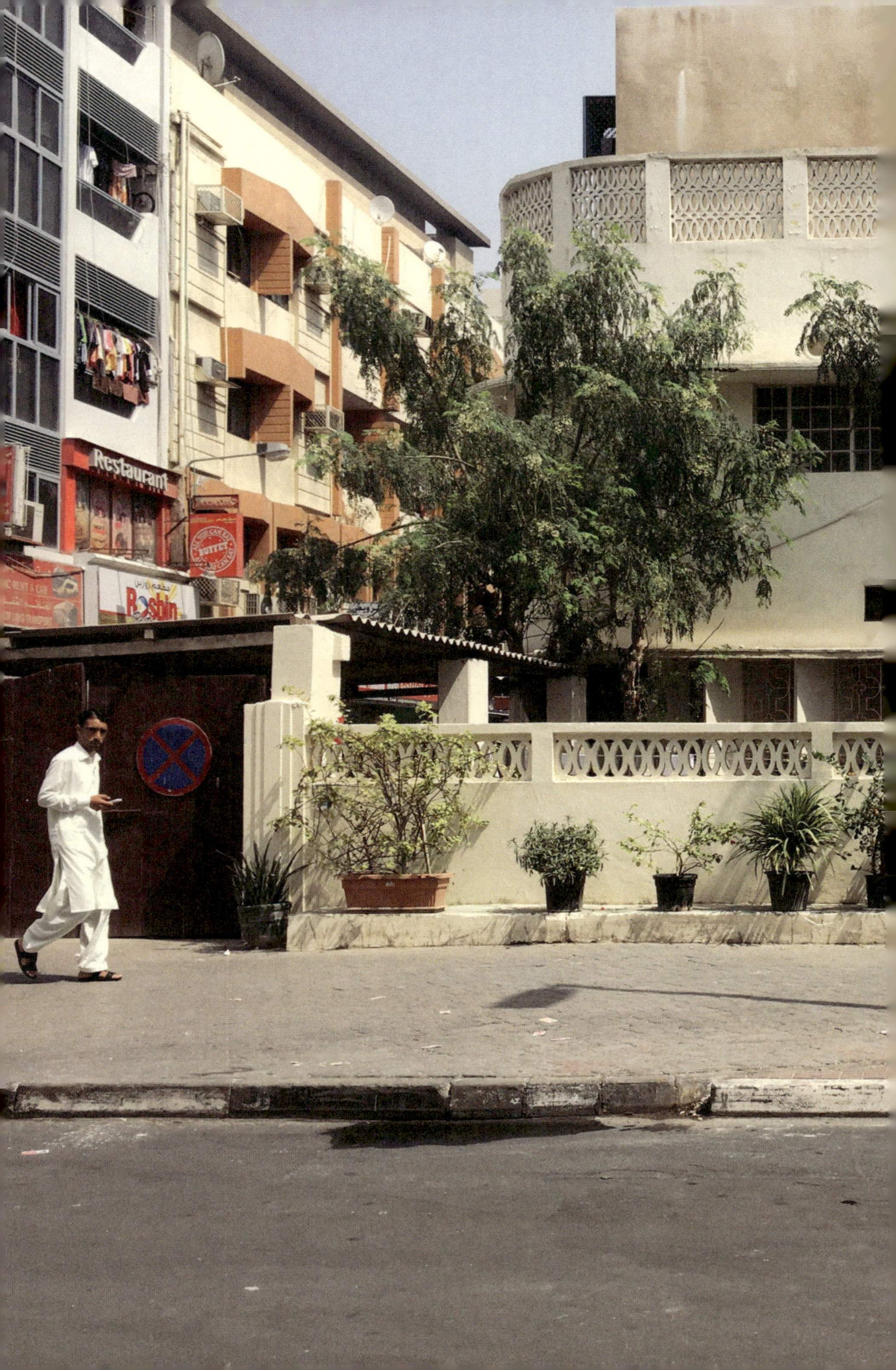
Restaurant

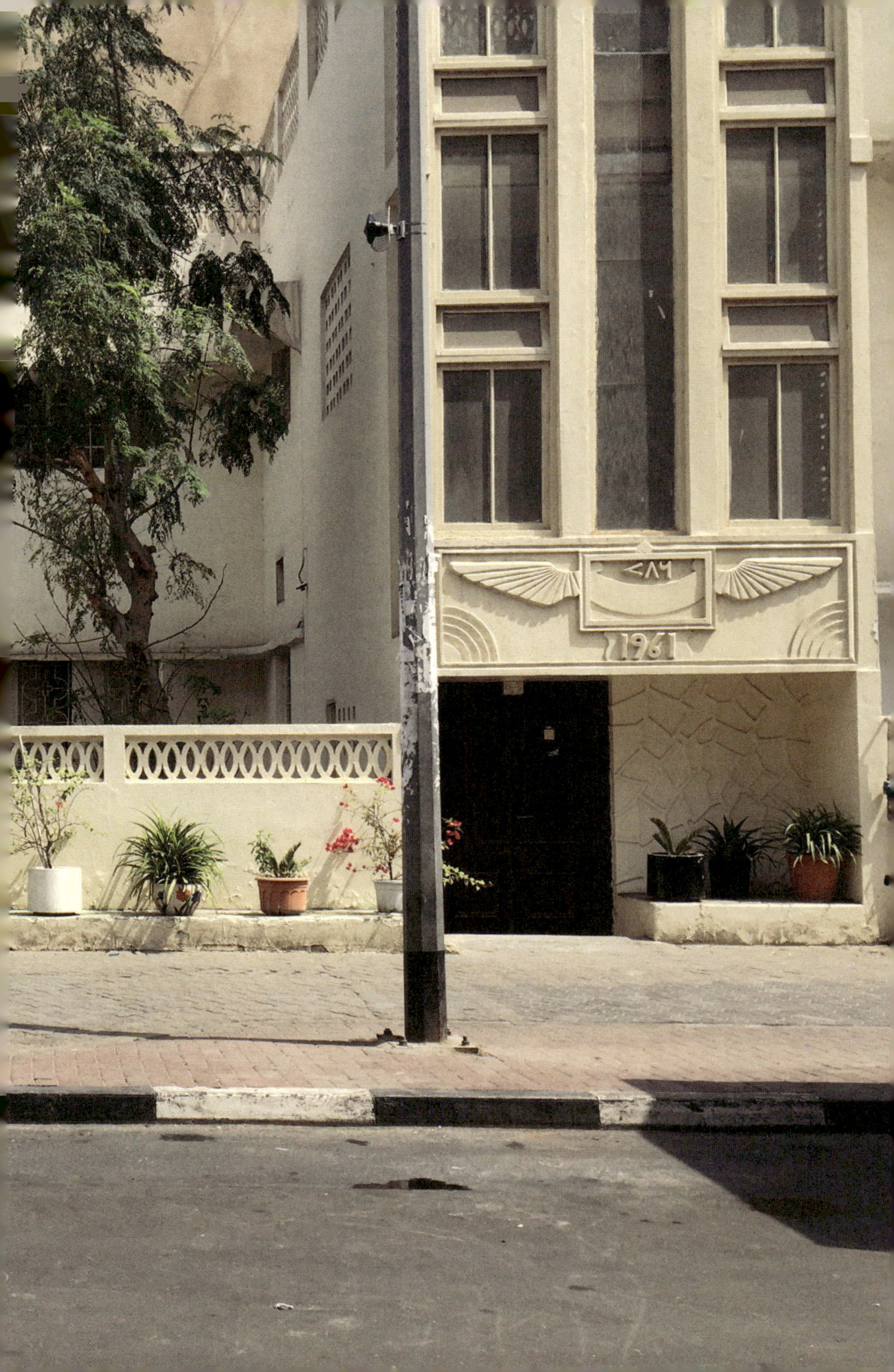
1961

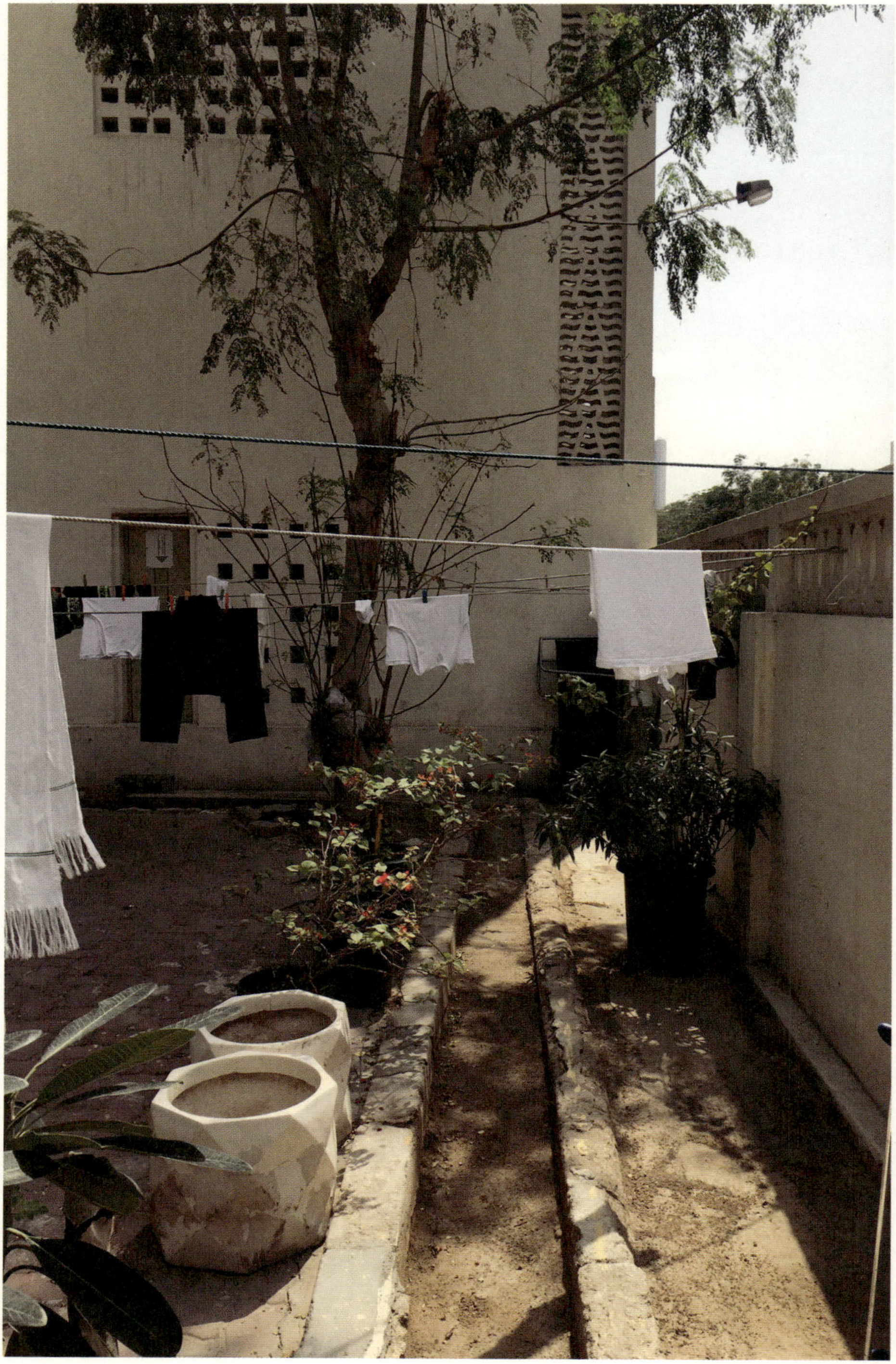

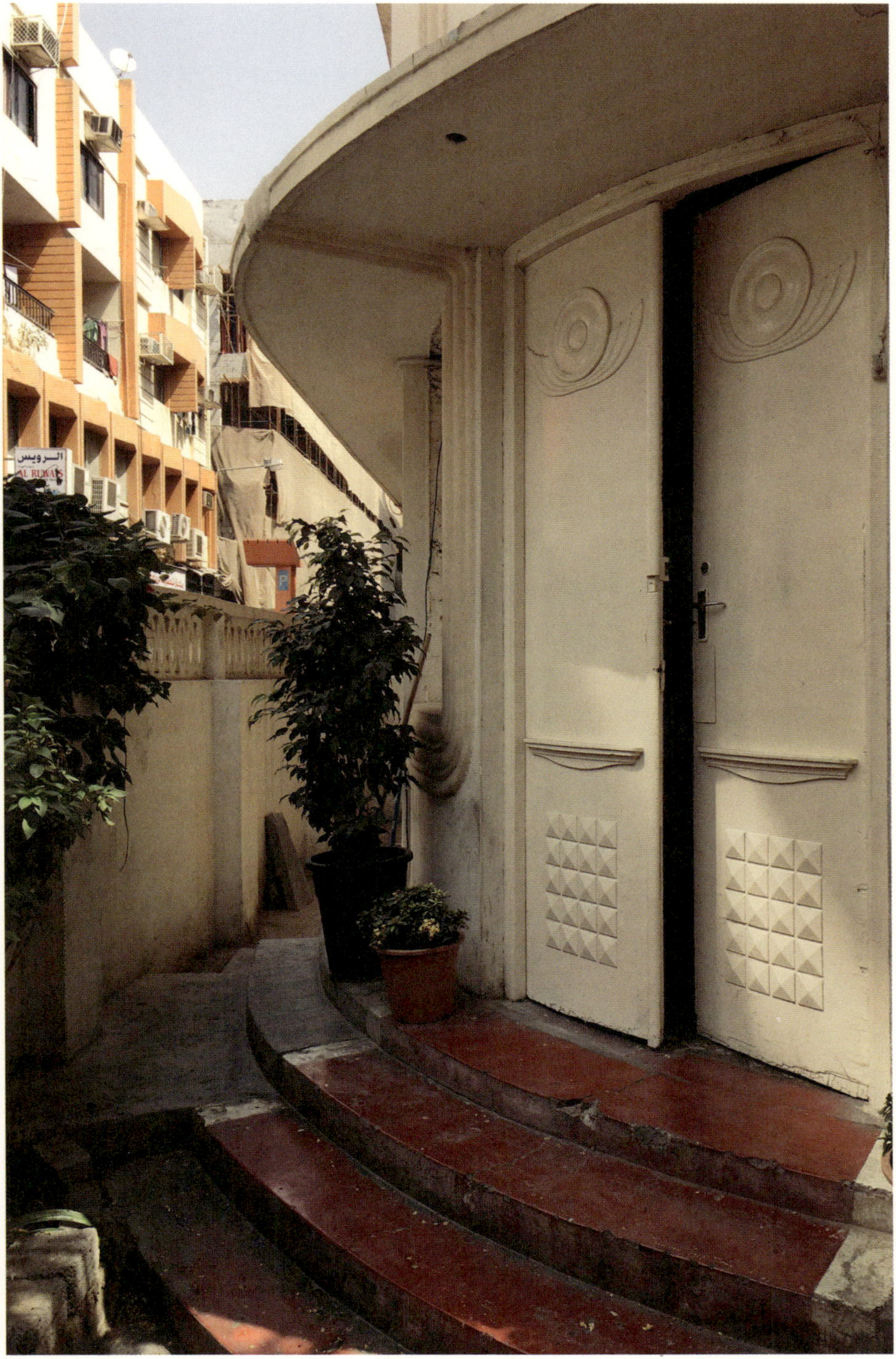
الرويس

CASE STUDY 02: AL AMAL PSYCHIATRIC HOSPITAL, 1983

Architect: John Harris
Date: 1983
Location: Al Wasl
Function: Hospital
Status: Demolished

Al Amal Psychiatric Hospital was designed by John Harris in 1983. Harris designed many of the city's hospitals, but this was the first to be dedicated to mental illness. Its name, Al Amal, is derived from the Arabic word for hope. The design of the hospital embodies a Modernist approach that is nevertheless vernacular in its application. The building is whitewashed, spacious, and contains multiple vast sand-filled courtyards. Surrounding the courtyards are the mental wards, medical facilities and doctors' offices. The exterior of these interiorized built-up spaces contain *brise soleil* window treatments that deflect direct sunlight, allowing for these spaces to become more welcoming and adaptable for the use of the patients and staff living there. A set of abstract patterns is repeated across multiple walls used for screening throughout the facility, thus keeping certain areas private.

These modern design elements are sensitive to the site in which they are employed and to the function they were to serve. They were designed in a manner that portrayed the essence and ambience of traditional houses in Dubai, allowing in-patients to, even if temporarily, feel at home there. With the closure of the hospital, the patients were moved to a new treatment centre in Al Awir that has the same name. The building has been demolished and the land bought for re-development project given the high commercial value of its location between Al Wasl and Jumeirah.

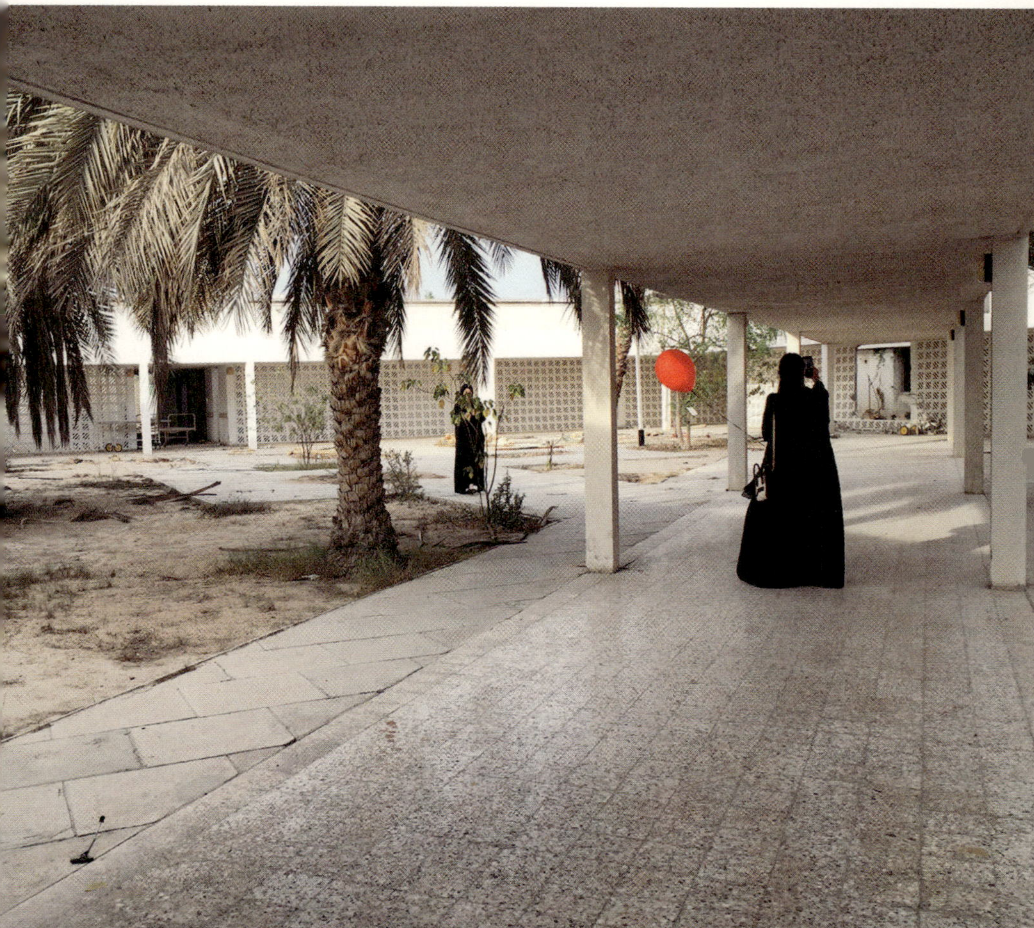

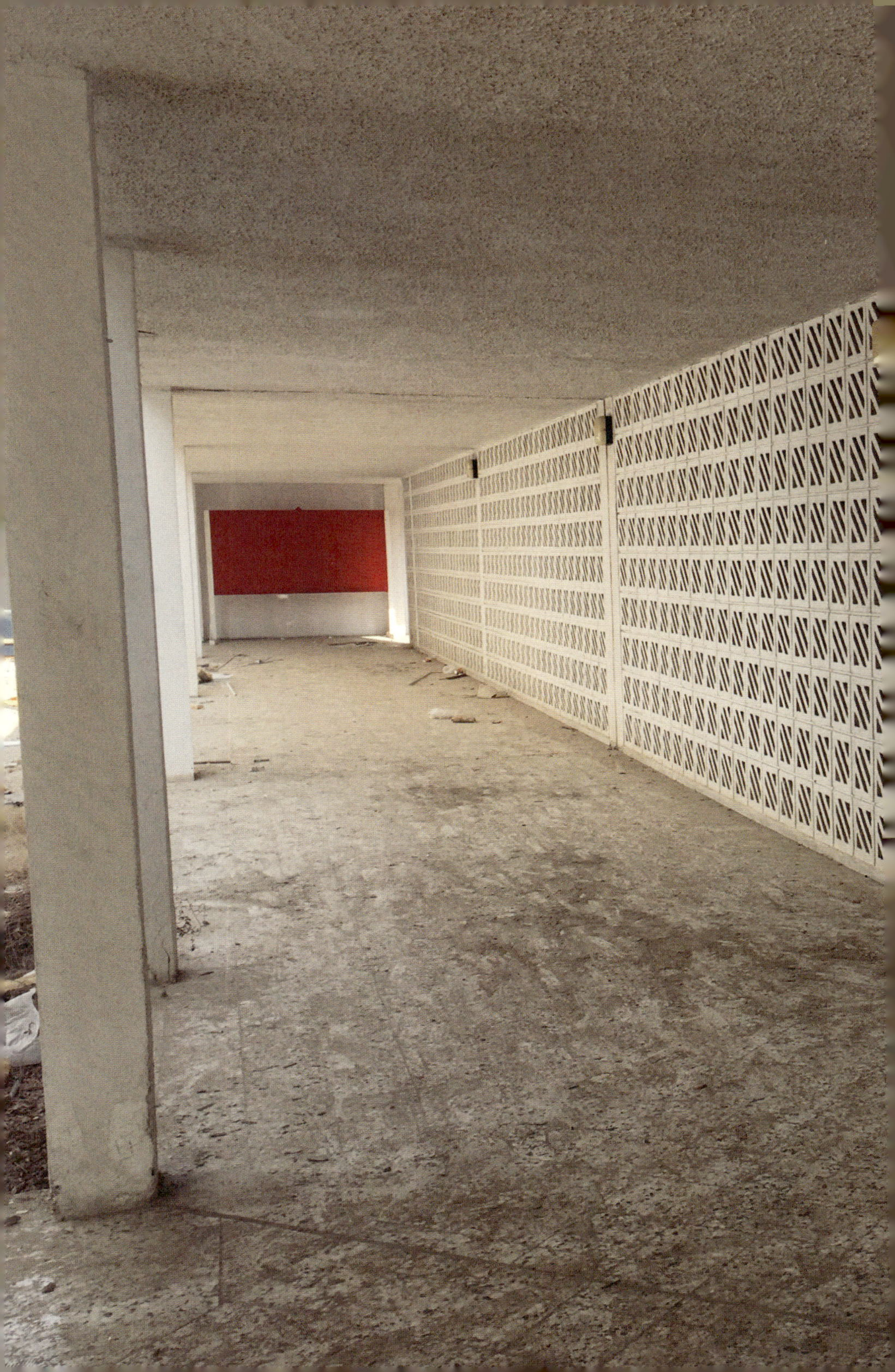

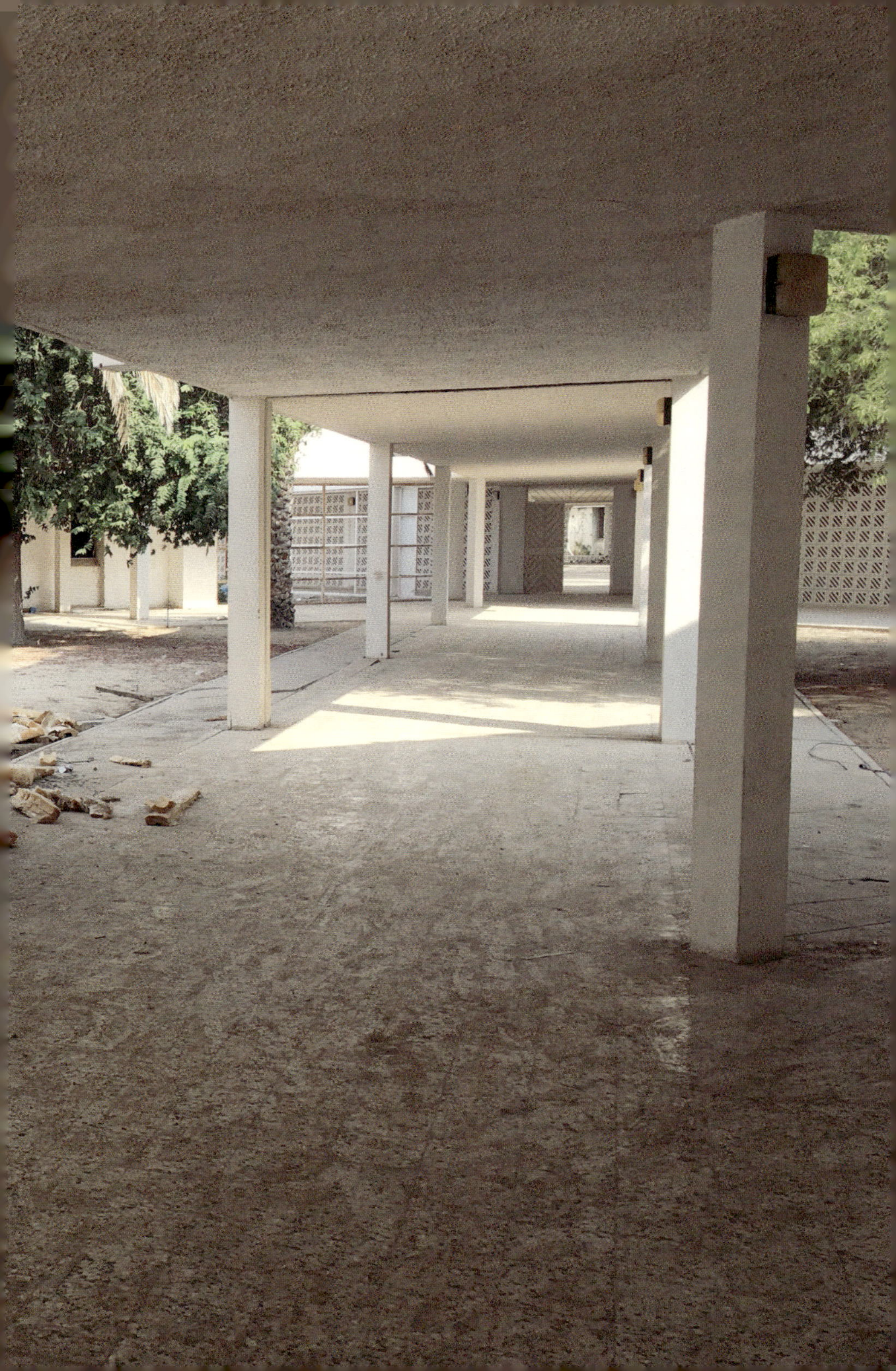

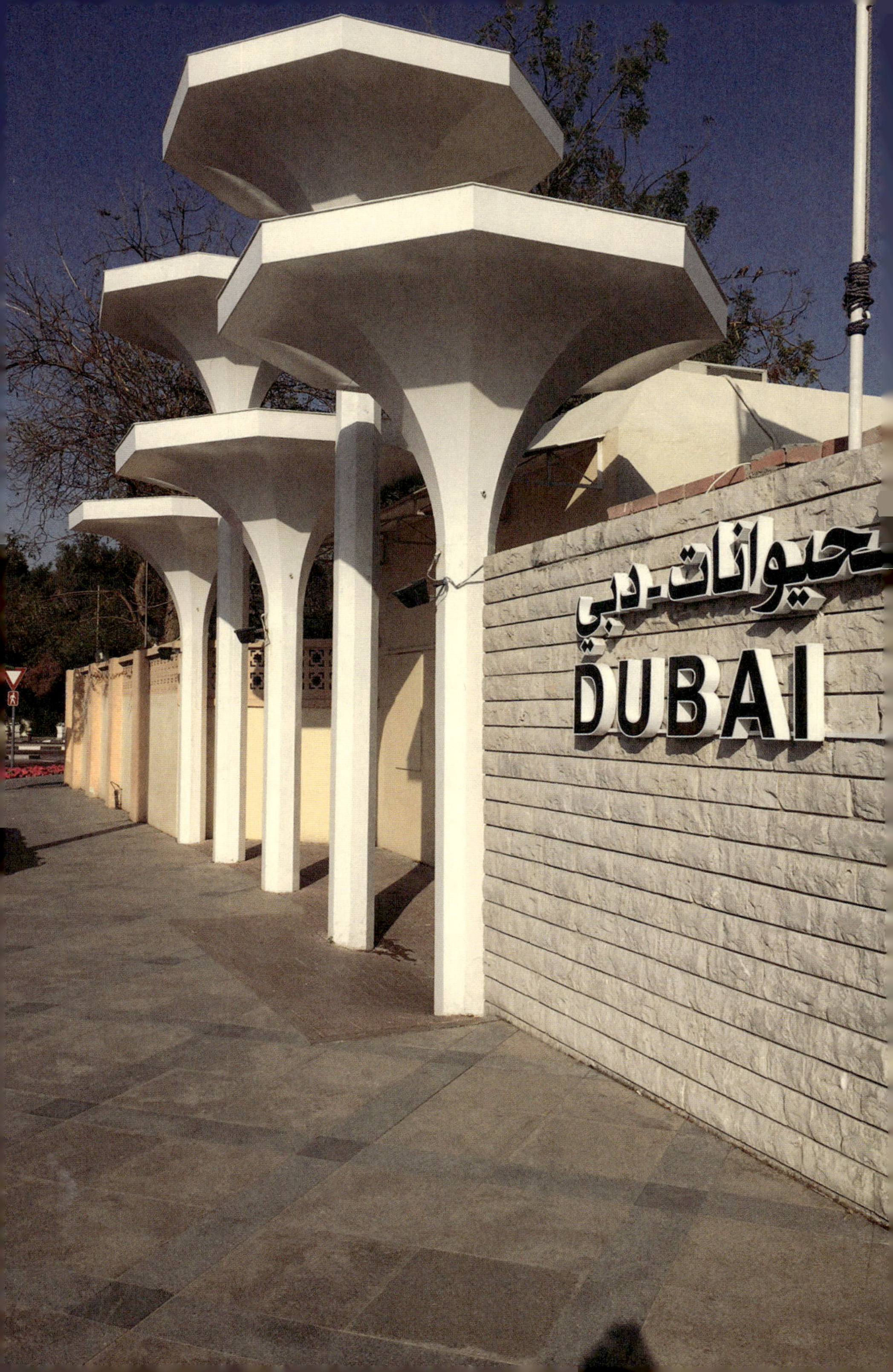
حيوانات دبي
DUBAI

CASE STUDY 03: DUBAI ZOO, 1967

Architect: Otto J. Bulart
Date: 1967
Location: Jumeira 1
Function: Recreational
Status: Closed in 2017

A landmark that once marked what was known in the 1960s as the "end of the town," the Dubai Zoo today sits at the heart of the city in Jumeira1. Austrian architect Otto J. Bulart, who had a passion for wild animals, and a special love for lions, designed the 1.5-kilometer park in 1967. Bulart was allocated this two-hectare site on the far-end of the city by the late ruler of Dubai, Sheikh Rashid. The intention was to develop a zoo as well as house the private collection of animals owned by the architect, which was brought to the attention of Dubai Municipality's Director, Kamal Hamza.

A Modernist approach is evident in the design of the zoo and its facilities. The white-washed architecture features clean cuts, free-flowing open spaces and abstract geometric patterns, inspired by vernacular practices. In addition to the animal facilities, the architect designed a residence for the resident zoologist that encompasses a colonnaded liwan-like veranda space open to an interiorized dynamic garden.

After Dubai Municipality took over the management of the zoo in 1971, a series of constant redesign and renovation works took place, and more residences were added to accommodate the remaining zoo staff as the facility and the wildlife it housed expanded. These additions however are not attributable to Bulart. Another Modernist element is the urban monument marking its entrance, which remains lit at night past operating hours, to highlight the recreational project.

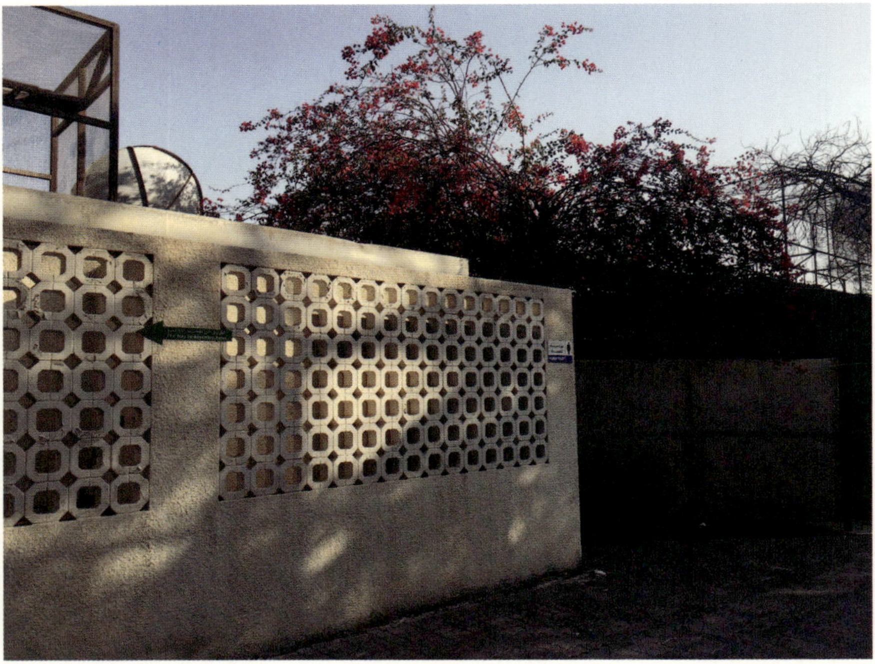

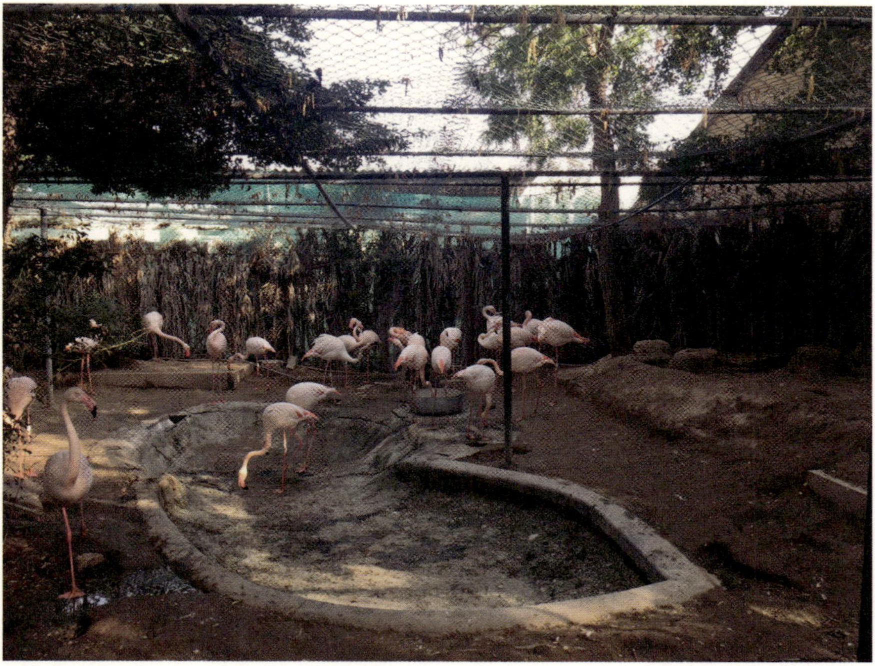

An abstract pattern in a continuous ribbon surrounds the outer wall fencing of the zoo—a pattern that is different in style yet represents a similar aesthetic across both interior and exterior parameters. The animals of the Dubai Zoo will be relocated to the new Safari Park. This sadly leads to the closure and eventual demolition of the zoo. Considering that it is the oldest zoo in the Arabian Peninsula, a suggested re-adaptive use of the building might be a better, and more sensible, option.

* * *

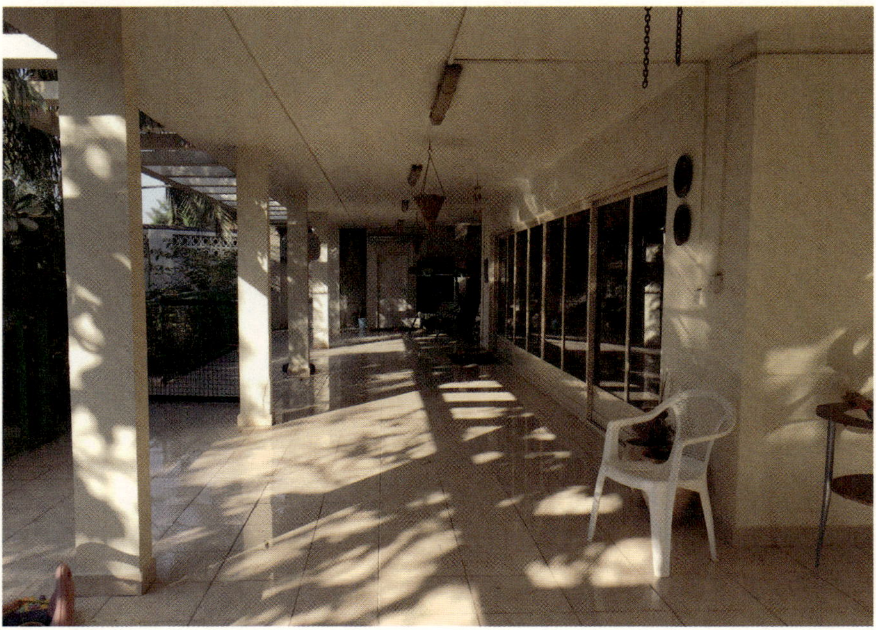

The international standards of Modernism do not completely apply to the context of Modernist structures in Dubai because the fundamental practice of International Style dictates that it be void of contextual responses in its design approach and lack ornamentation. However, in Dubai the Modernist structures responded to the local context and incorporated stylistic—although simplified forms of—elements to adorn the buildings, making these interventions more site-aware, sensitive and specific. This brings us to conclude that although Modernism arrived late in Dubai, it adapted itself to become more regional than international—it was expressing local culture and values through modern design. A style that responded to Dubai's need to become a modern city and respected the transitional period from the traditional to the new in terms of built forms—in fact, it became a hybrid of several styles. As was the case with their traditional and historical predecessors, these Modernist buildings remain conscious in their overall design propositions. Because they strived to be site-sensitive in response to the needs of their end-users, we need to preserve, classify and document the important examples of Modernism in Dubai—our "modern heritage"—since it is not only essential, but also crucial to understanding and contextualizing the architectural development and urban evolution of the emirate as a multicultural metropolis. Dubai's architectural growth did not pause at the 1940s wind-tower houses and palm frond huts, it continues to survive in the memories of these Modernist structures.

I [HEART] DUBAI

TODD REISZ
IMAGES: LAYAN ATTARI

Dubai has a new heart. If Rome is the Eternal City, if Aleppo is the longest enduring city, and if Beirut is the regenerating Phoenix, then Dubai might just get along by having a new heart installed every so many years. Dubai's heart was once split. Between two towns. Dubai and Deira stared at each other across Dubai Creek. The two were eventually stitched together by modern engineering. Tons of concrete and steel hardened the creek's edges into something anyone might believe would last forever. Dubai then had a heart that was in neither town but drifted between the two reinforced shores. Dubai had a heart in its void. Urban planners compulsively drew circles of ring roads around the creek, as if swirls of asphalt and exhaust would keep the heart alive.

Ever since Dubai built an airport with a runway made out of hardened sand, it has been sold as the center of the world, just at the moment it was positioned to lose its own. Conventional wisdom says the heart left the creek sometime in the 1980s, when there was enough commercial attraction in Dubai's newest districts to pull people away from its pulse. But the heart didn't move; it dissipated. Or maybe it just burst, trying too hard to be loved by too many people, too many demographics. Newness, the planners learned the hard way, was marketed as Dubai's heart.

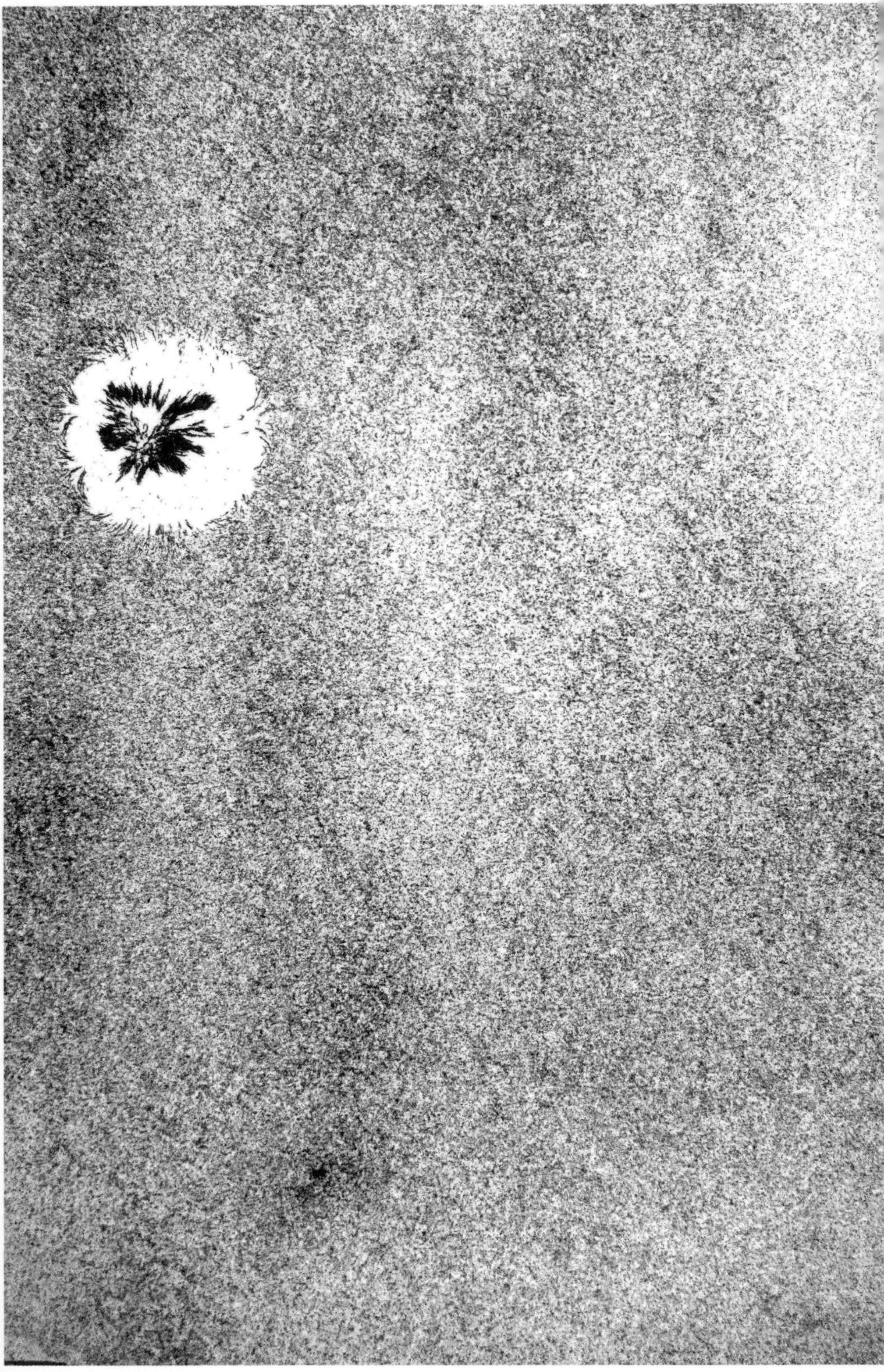

Dubai became a city of cities. Or, if cities are organic, then Dubai was like a starfish, or a sea cucumber, reproducing by fragmentation. By having many hearts, Dubai might have had many ways to be loved. Multiple hearts also meant that one heart didn't have to replace another. Hearts could beat as one. Or not. Hearts can share blood, or reject blood. Hearts were options. Or at least appeared to be options. Some hearts beat better, and longer, than others.

Once Dubai started to get its first fully interiorized living experiences (the World Trade Centre, Al Mulla Plaza, Al Ghurair Centre), its wave pool at Al Nasr Leisureland, a night-lit park in Karama, Dubai's heart was everywhere and nowhere. Always parallel hearts pumping of their own accord on the dashboards of their own proprietary HVAC ecosystems. To be "in the heart of Dubai" meant somehow always to be outside it. It was the city of parallel and contradictory experiences that only through telepathy or heroic empathy could be co-experienced. Desensitization often kicked in. Fear of Missing Out (FOMO) might have trended and ended in Dubai before it ever got hashtagged in this century.

Dubai has taught me something about people, about life. It brings me back to size. What people point to and call "*so artificial!*" gives me pause to feel my own blood coursing through my own veins.

Dubai is certainly about life. Thanks to Dubai's growth philosophy in the previous century, the old heart on the creek was left alone to its own devices, to pump its own ancient systems of circulation. I've always been drawn to the creek and the suggestive parallel worlds it teases me into believing exist, where I recall once seeing IKEA glassware being shipped out to Iran and then another time witnessing a fleet of pink kids' bikes getting boarded on a boat to Pakistan.

Dubai's heart yearns from a long time ago. There's no room for nostalgia though. The city's firmament heckles anyone with a tendency toward nostalgia. I used to heckle them too, until I realized I held onto a Dubai anno 2007. It happens pretty regularly that if I'm talking or writing about Dubai that I get the question, "But...do you like Dubai?" As if Dubai was the talented but unlikable contestant in a pageant. As if my [like] mattered.

On the topic of nostalgia, I'm reminded of "Center of Now," an advertising campaign that ran on LCD screens around the Burj Khalifa and the New Downtown district. It ends with a model, the typical kind in Dubai ads that defies easy racial categorization, singing something operatic from the Burj's lookout balcony. Since the street screens were silent, I don't know what she sings. But then I think of an Oum Khaltoum song that she could sing, one that an Egyptian friend once translated for me while we listened. If Madame Oum Kalthoum is right, then the heart is there all along; it just waits for you to return.

The beautiful nights and the yearning and the great love
From a long time ago the heart is holding for you.

Many watched with a veritable mixture of engagement and doubt when Burj Dubai, as it was known then, started to rise. Its immeasurable accumulation of concrete looked ominous. The tower's construction was relayed in engineering machismo and sheathed in German techno-glass. But concrete and steel had once before made way for a heart. The Burj Khalifa's opening was extravagant fanfare, followed by a quickened and grounded discovery that Dubai had a new heart. The spaces around the engineering feat, misted with the chlorinated water from the world's largest fountain, didn't feel exactly public, but they did feel central and more welcoming than anything before in Dubai. Well, maybe since before the shallow shores of Dubai Creek were hardened into an economizing aquatic machine.

* * *

This new heart I read about today is called Dubai Creek Harbour. It includes a tallest piece of architecture, though not very inhabitable. The needle tower is designed by a famous architect who is new to Dubai. It too will be an emblem of "achievements", "challenges", and "beauty". Santiago Calatrava's "human architecture", we are told, is inspired by the bud of a lily just before it blooms. (Wasn't the Burj Dubai also based on a flower?) It seems then appropriate that the tower is referred to as a "centerpiece".

The proposed new heart now circles us back to Dubai Creek. Dubai's mythology might be meted out to a stomping march forward, but the city has a bag full of comebacks. One soundbite promises that the tower "celebrates the world one more time". This time, the return is to a part of the creek mostly left alone during Dubai's growth spurts. Once, when the creek was still the bull's-eye of the planners' concentric road rings, there was talk about developing this particular part. It was referred to as a "lake", and it was proposed as a marina for Dubai's wealthiest. Here is where Dubai's first man-made island was planned.

Flamingoes now live near this part of the creek. They were once flown in from somewhere along the Great Rift Valley. The wading birds' first days in airport quarantine were frightening, both for them and the ill-prepared airport staff, but even they eventually made a home at Dubai's old heart. Fauna can be imported, too. They are part of a nature reserve that Dubai Creek Harbor promises to protect and even help to make flourish.

When Calatrava came to Dubai, he posed with the model of his design. The tower and its appending tensile wires balance the bud, the heart, at the top. It is like a syringe whose tip is swollen with a sworn-by panacea. Calatrava's pose with his design reminded me of William DeVries, the heart surgeon who once posed on the cover of *Time* magazine with his own model. Like an architect. Except the doctor's model could actually do something. It was the Jarvik-7, the man-made object DeVries inserted

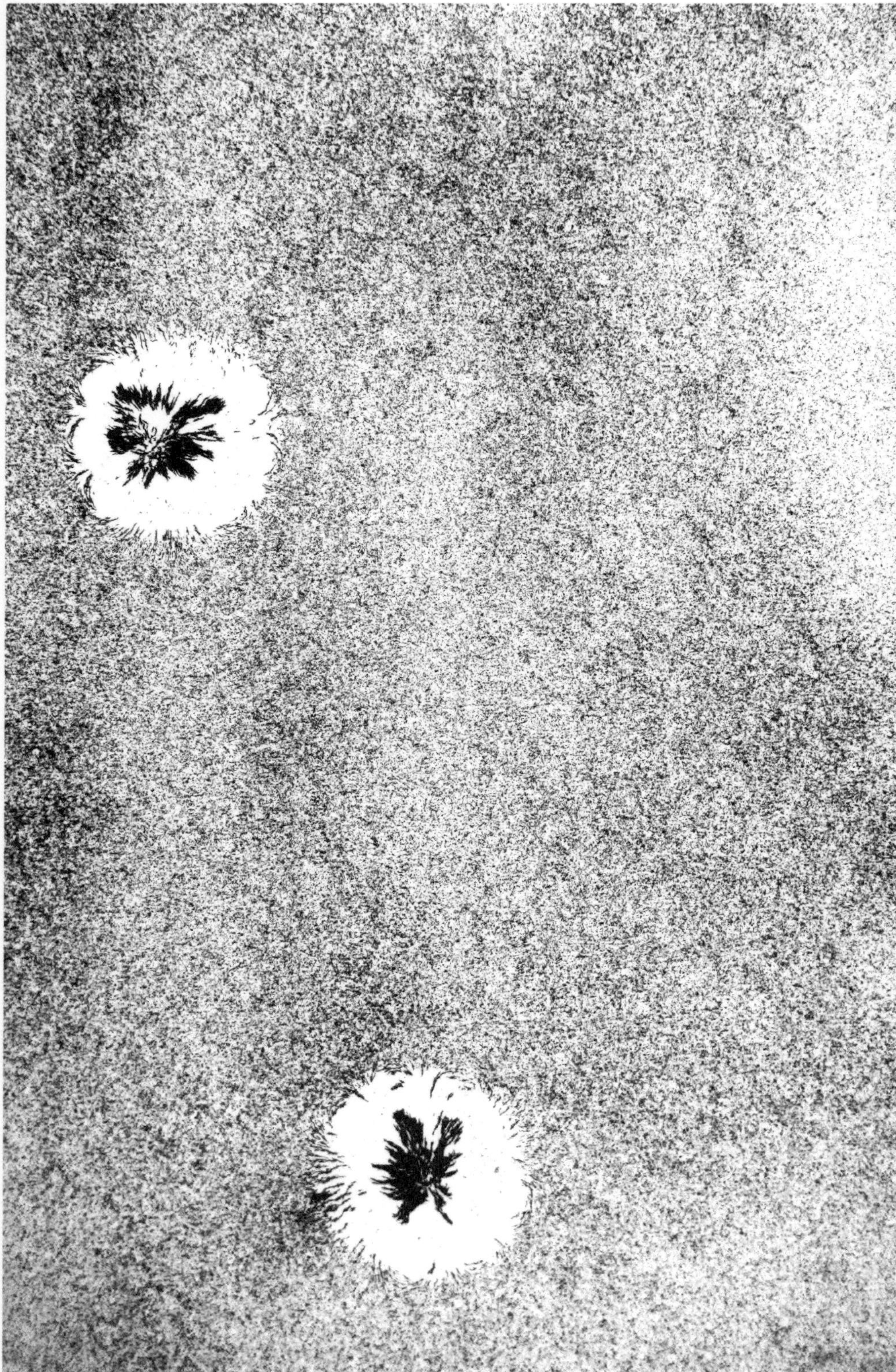

into another man whose own "ravaged" heart "tore like tissue paper" when DeVries removed it.

As I arrived at the sales center for Dubai Creek Harbour, a busload of well-heeled American retirees arrived for a tour. A Scottish member of the development team welcomed them and told them that Dubai Creek Harbour was as big as a Scottish town. Someone told him that his analogy didn't mean anything to an American. The guests asked who would live there. The answer included references to investment opportunities and Dubai's appeal to markets in China and India. What about the environment? The project was actually "giving green" back to the creek, not taking it away. They asked about public transit. They were shown a video of how Calatrava's tower "worked". Only the top part—the swollen tip—was inhabitable. You buy tickets to reach this part. The more you pay, the higher you go. The video demonstrated how the translucent membrane of the bud can open and close. Balconies unfold outward from the interior. An icon of movable parts, not unlike the translucent and bio-mimicking chambers of the Jarvik-7. Plastic and metal promise to pump people and capital. Here, at an undisclosed number of meters above Dubai, another set of artificial chambers, thanks to "precision engineering", will somehow manage high-speed winds so that ticket buyers can take in a peaceful view of Sharjah, of the Burj Khalifa, and, if they dared to look steeply below, of Dubai Creek. A heart's blood finances an altitudinal nosebleed.

"Our project won't look anything like the old Dubai Creek," said the Scot. It was a promise, not a lament. The retirees had no plans to visit the creek, but some spoke among themselves further about environmental risks. "There's nothing here, so what could be the harm?"

As engineers and builders prepare to hoist an artificial heart to a record height, more work continues along the shores of the "old" creek. The horizon-bound dhows, with their boatmen inside, have been mostly shuttled off the creek to a "wharfage development project with integrated

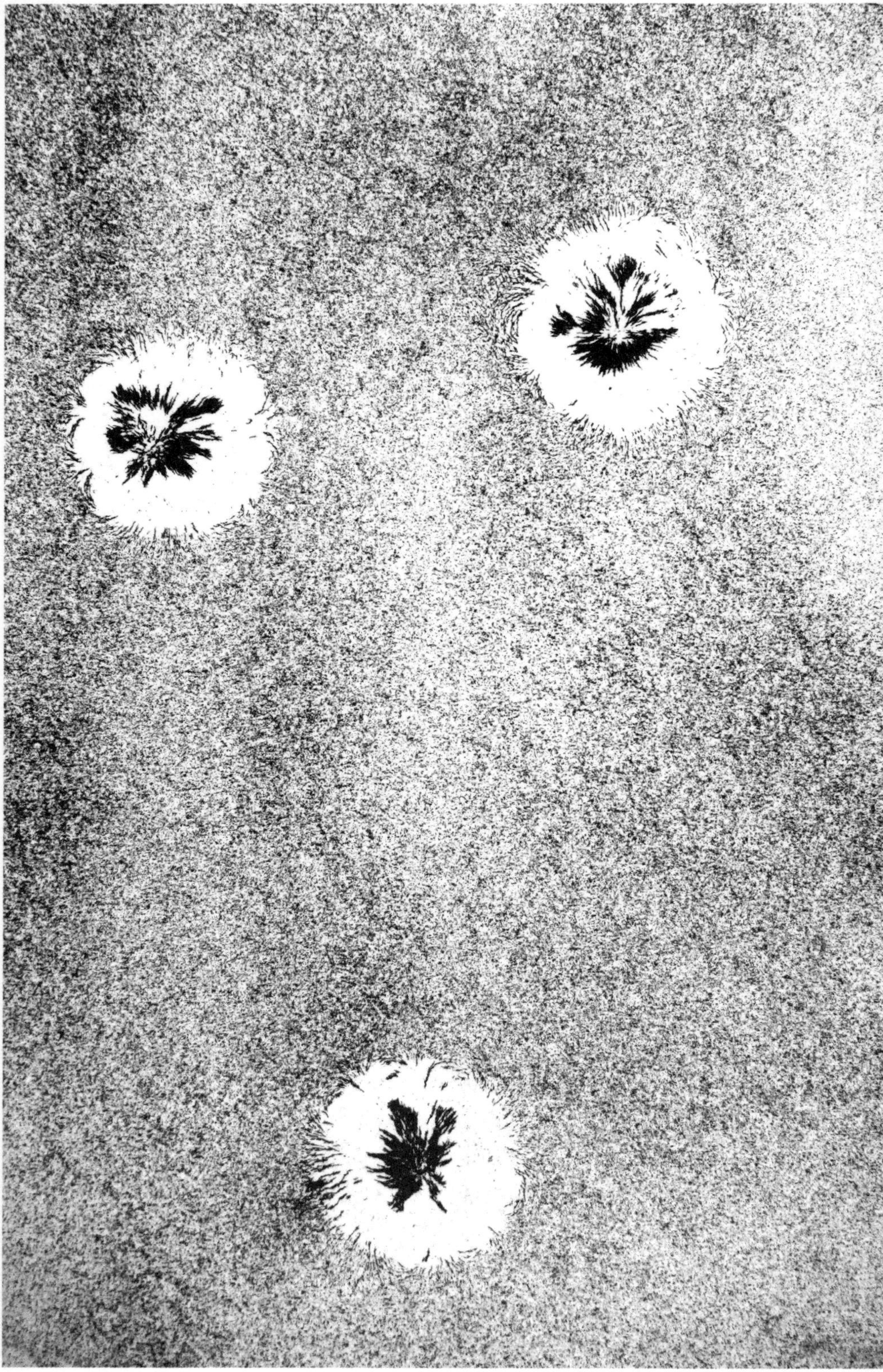

infrastructure". Dhows were once Dubai's most expressive creatures. They proved Dubai's connection to the world. Now they have all but disappeared, accessible only by the stevedores who have to carry access cards to open the guard gates. Back at the creek, the dhows have been replaced by their derivative cousins: floating receptacles for tourists, decked out in colorful LED lights and all-you-can-eat buffets.

Indian investors were essential to financing Dubai's very first building boom in the 1950s. And, if the Scottish tour guide is correct, Asian investors are going to keep his client in business, and maybe Dubai in business too. It can't yet be determined whether today's investors will ever step out onto the boardwalks suspended over the district's rejuvenated marshlands. Besides the financial investors, there were those who invested even more: tradesmen, craftsmen, tea boys and chambermaids who arrived from continents to take a chance on Dubai's broadcasts. The men and women who came to build and fit out Dubai harbored ambitions that were never more virtuous than improving their own lives and those of their family members. It was a trickle that crescendoed into an invigorating pulsation.

Dubai's hearts won't happen in the return to the lagoons at Dubai Creek Harbour. They won't happen in the air-conditioned galleries of a Condé Nast-approved museum. Those are Jarvik-7s. The artificial heart, we've learned, was not a long-term option. It wasn't cost-efficient. The Jarvik-7 was eventually phased out in favor of recycled hearts.

There have been master plans, cultural plans, visions, press releases, closed-door expert assessments, and feasibility studies to rediscover the creek's heart. As if it were ever lost. The creek has kept its heart all this time, even at the moment engineering took its tides and sandbars away, prevented people from dipping their feet into its ripples, and turned a tenuous body of water into a cost-conscious harbor. The creek—at least for now—still has its own rhythms and arrhythmias. It still conducts its essential urban and regional circulations. It's hard to kill this old heart. But it is certainly possible.

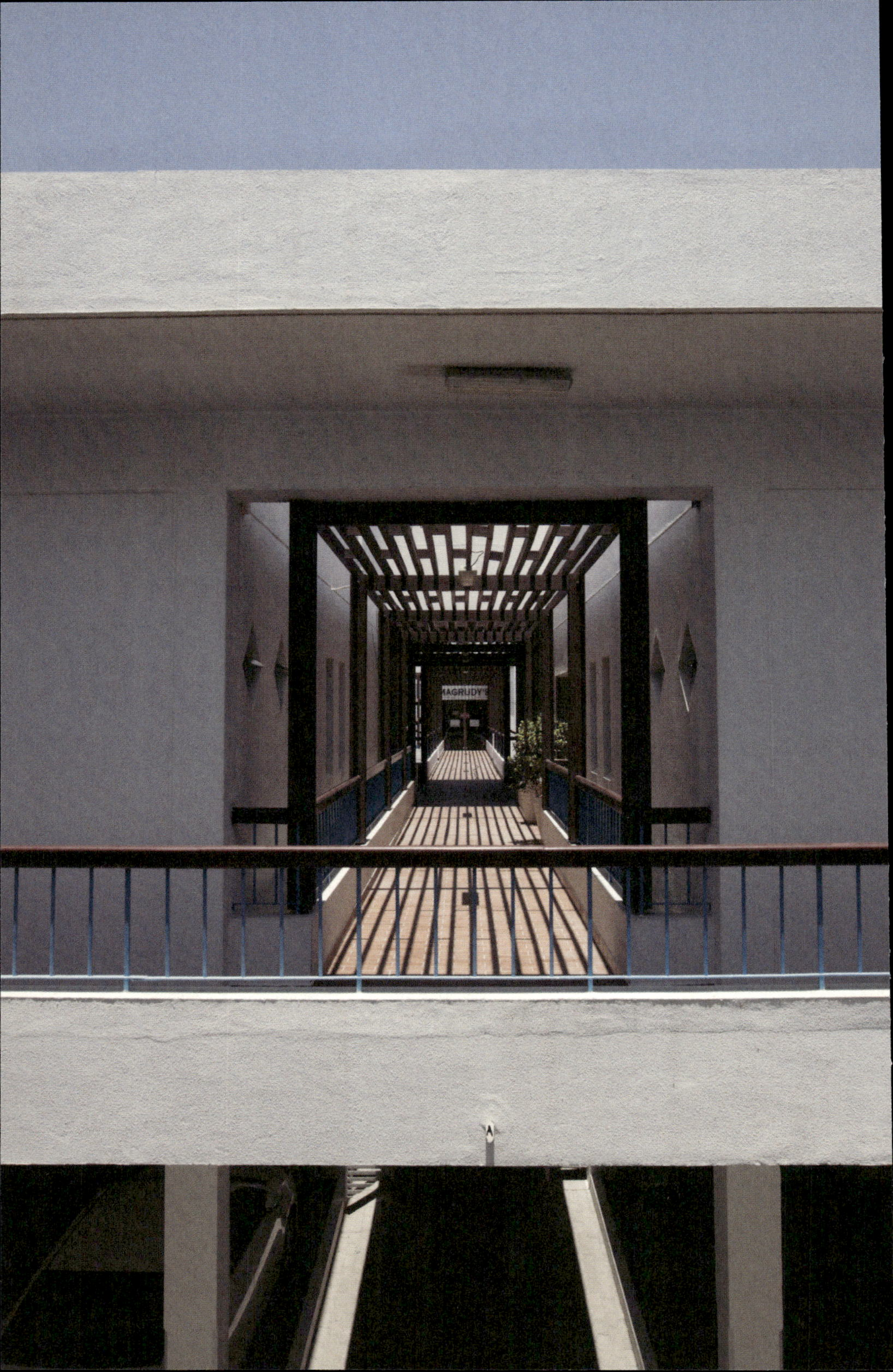
AGRUDY'

MAGRUDY'S MALL: TRANSCENDING THE IMITATION OF IMAGINED PASTS

KEVIN MITCHELL

In a city that lays claim to the world's largest shopping center, Dubai's first, and arguably smallest, mall remains among the most remarkable. Magrudy's Mall, located in Jumeirah, makes a unique contribution to the city through its distinctive architecture that is unconventional in its subtlety. The mall was constructed in two phases, with the first standalone building on the corner of what is now Jumeirah Street and 27 B Street built in the late 1970s. An expansion followed after Magrudy's bookstore moved into the building in 1981 and acquired the adjacent plot. The complex is now comprised of shops and a café that occupy the portion nearest to Jumeirah Street and offices above covered private parking at the rear.

Magrudy's Mall could be described as anti-iconic and antithetical to many of the tendencies exhibited in the majority of more recent buildings in Dubai. Features such as the subdued outward-facing facades and an enclosed courtyard stand in stark contrast to prevailing approaches that privilege individual buildings and treat them as free-standing objects independent of the environment. Architecture in the Gulf often maintains a tenuous connection to the context, whether it be the immediate physical surroundings or the particular sociocultural settings that can vary across the diverse communities residing in the region.

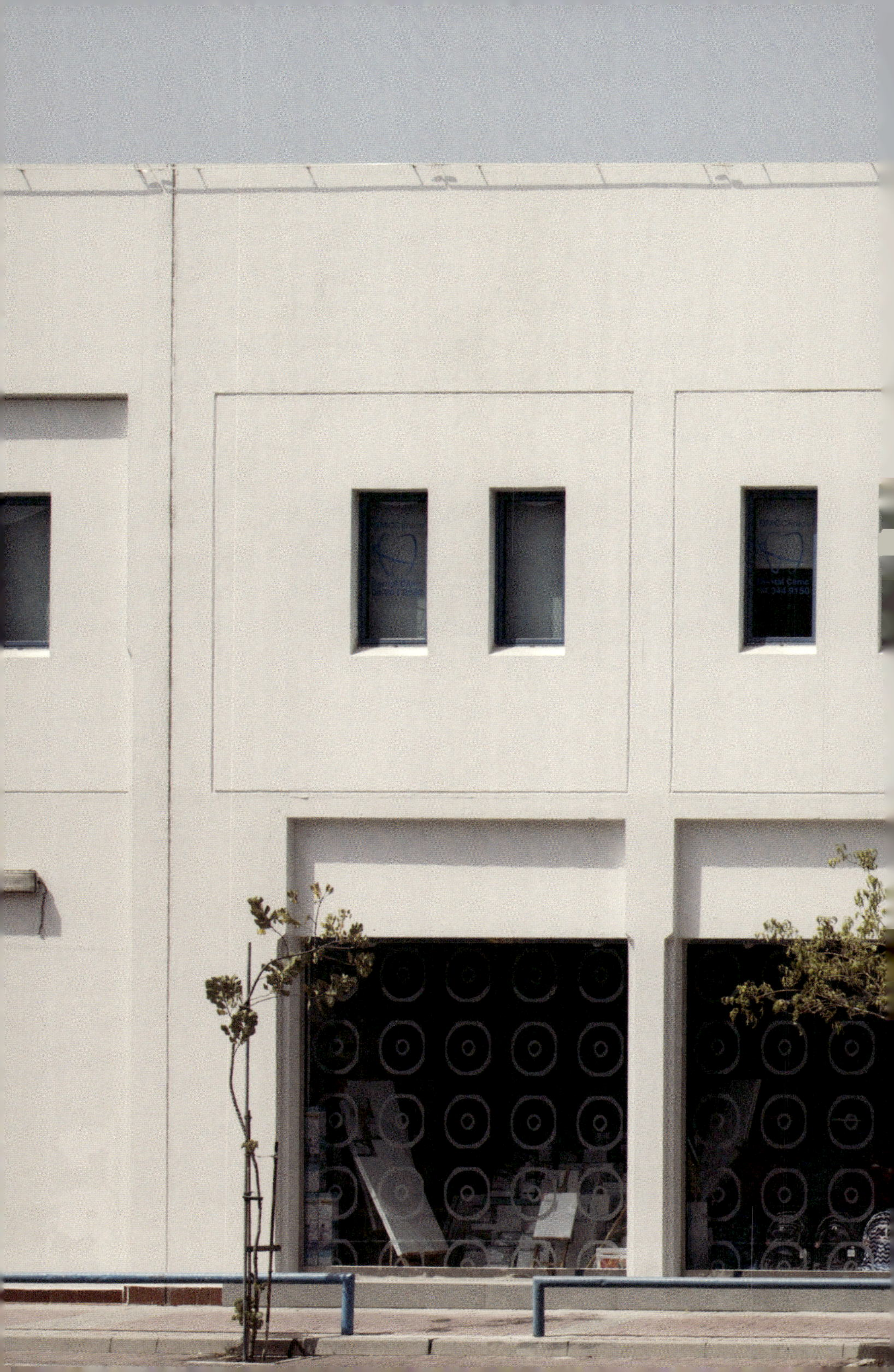

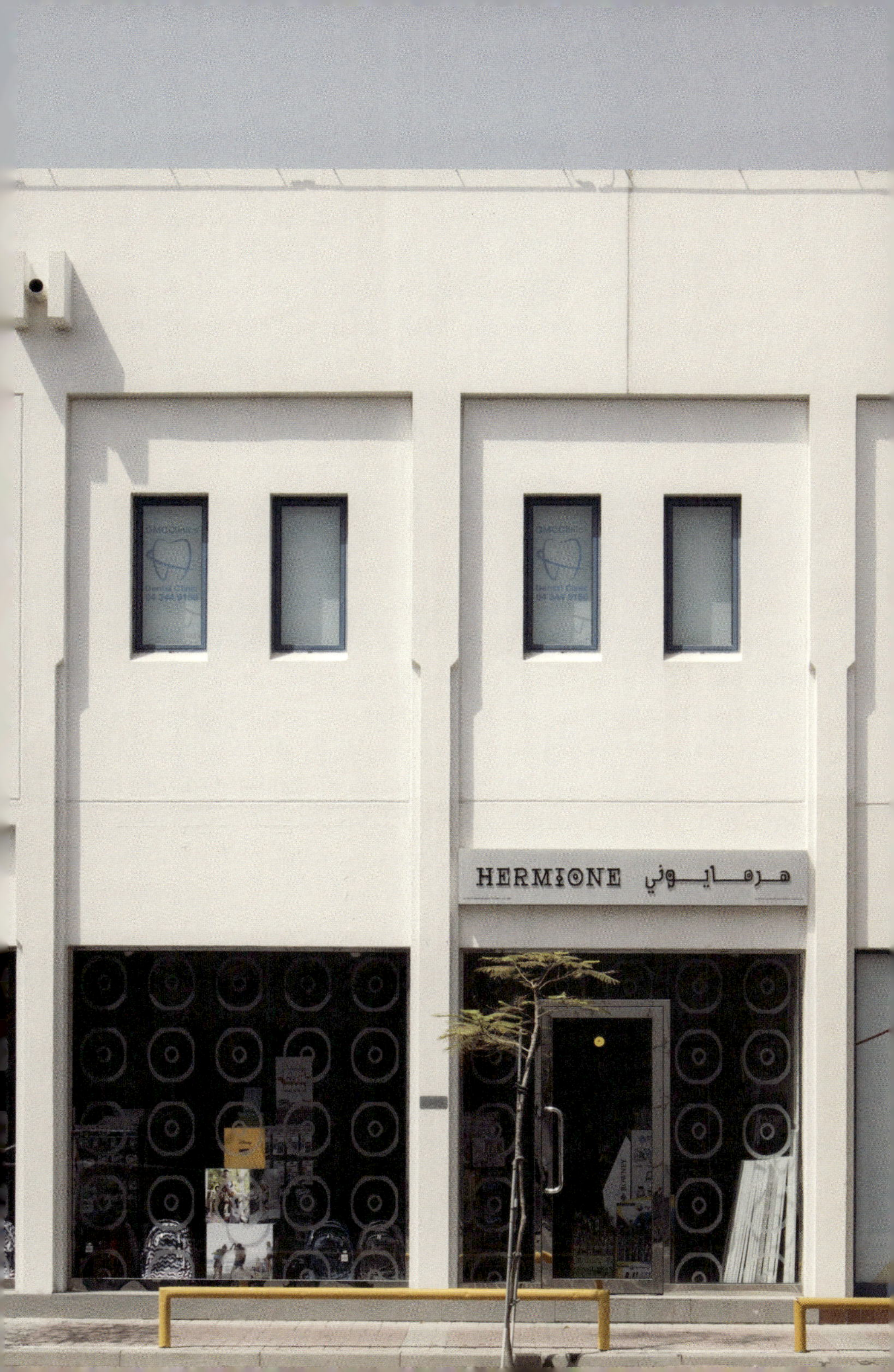
HERMIONE
هرمايوني

This is perhaps because the complexity of the context provokes fundamental questions that defy simplistic answers. For example, should buildings be reproductions of historical precedents or sculptural forms that are described—often superficially—as derivations of sand dunes or desert flowers? Alternatively, should architecture be freed from place-specific concerns and respond only to the individual desires of those who may be commissioning or designing for a building? Rapid urbanization in the Gulf, the ever-changing physical fabric of cities in the region, and the demands associated with the climate have resulted in varied answers to these questions, as evidenced by the range of architectural expressions across the region.

Magrudy's Mall is significant because it represents a carefully considered and clearly articulated response to context-related questions. While the original building replicated features found in reconstructed buildings in the Al Fahidi neighborhood, the subsequent renovation and expansion of the complex invoked references to visual elements from historical structures in a more nuanced manner. The proportion of second-floor openings and the niches in the facades facing the street hearken back to examples from the past, as do details that include three-dimensional arch-like forms carved into columns and surfaces of varying depth that enable an interplay of light and shadow. Rather than present an illusion of a contemporary building appearing to be "traditional", as seen in the neighboring Jumeirah Center, Magrudy's Mall relies on allusion to make visual reference to past works of architecture indigenous to the context.

The complex is also noteworthy for the central exterior space formed by the walls enclosing the surrounding commercial units and the open void at the rear of the site, which allows light into an open second-floor walkway and the parking area below. Characterized by a stepped ziggurat-like form in plan, the humanely scaled courtyard is accommodating, and the bridge covering the walkways and a series of trellises shading the windows facing the courtyard mitigate the impact of the climate.

The fact that the open courtyard at Magrudy's Mall has remained when similar spaces in other buildings have been covered to create additional interior areas is notable. Along with the arrival of air conditioning came the desire to enclose what were previously exterior rooms that were habitable from late fall until early spring. Courtyards, which ensure privacy while providing access to light and air, disappeared from family dwellings and shopping centers, with covered atria quickly supplanted the open-air souk. As courtyards fell out of favor, architecture in the Gulf was impoverished by the absence of the voids within buildings that once served as a locus for private life in dwellings and public interaction in urban settings.

A rather extensive search for respectable coffee and outdoor seating prompted my first visit to Magrudy's Mall in 1999. Then, as now, Gérard Café maintains the ambiance of a local establishment, complete with tables occupied by groups of men from the neighborhood reading newspapers and offering running commentary on the reporting. Given the range of coffee-serving chains providing outdoor seating across Dubai today, one can hardly imagine that there was a time when an extensive search was necessary. But attitudes related to the use of outdoor space have changed significantly, despite protestations that the climate was unsuitable and claims that exterior spaces would never be used. Just as pedestrianization efforts in northern Europe defied expectations and resulted in increasing commercial activity in car-free areas in spite of long winters, developers in Dubai have capitalized on the desire to be freed from confinement to air-conditioned spaces by providing possibilities that range from the provision of patio seating to open-air malls. Although usable outdoor space is now prevalent in commercial complexes, few have matched Magrudy's Mall in terms of the balance and integration of interior and exterior.

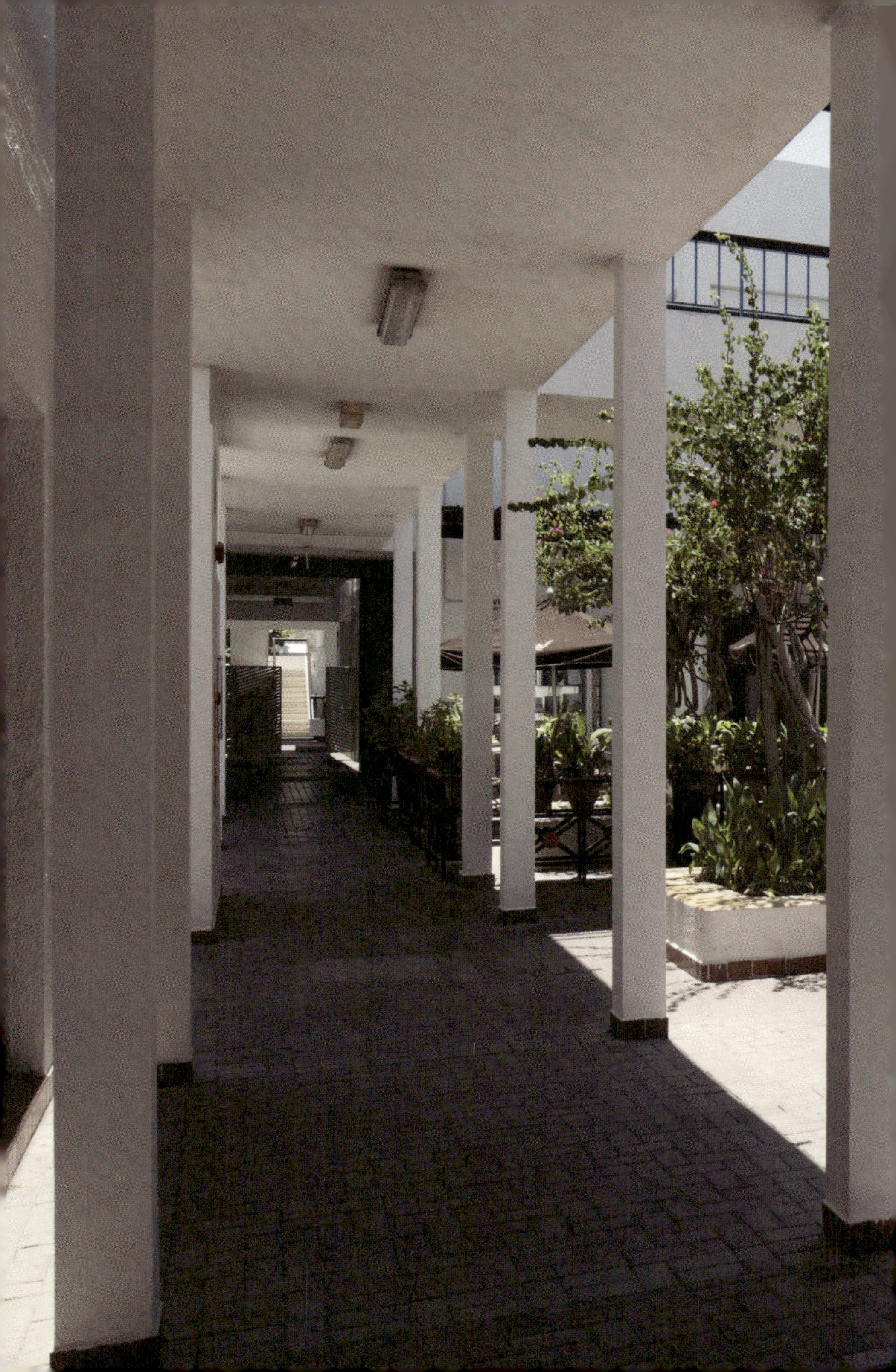

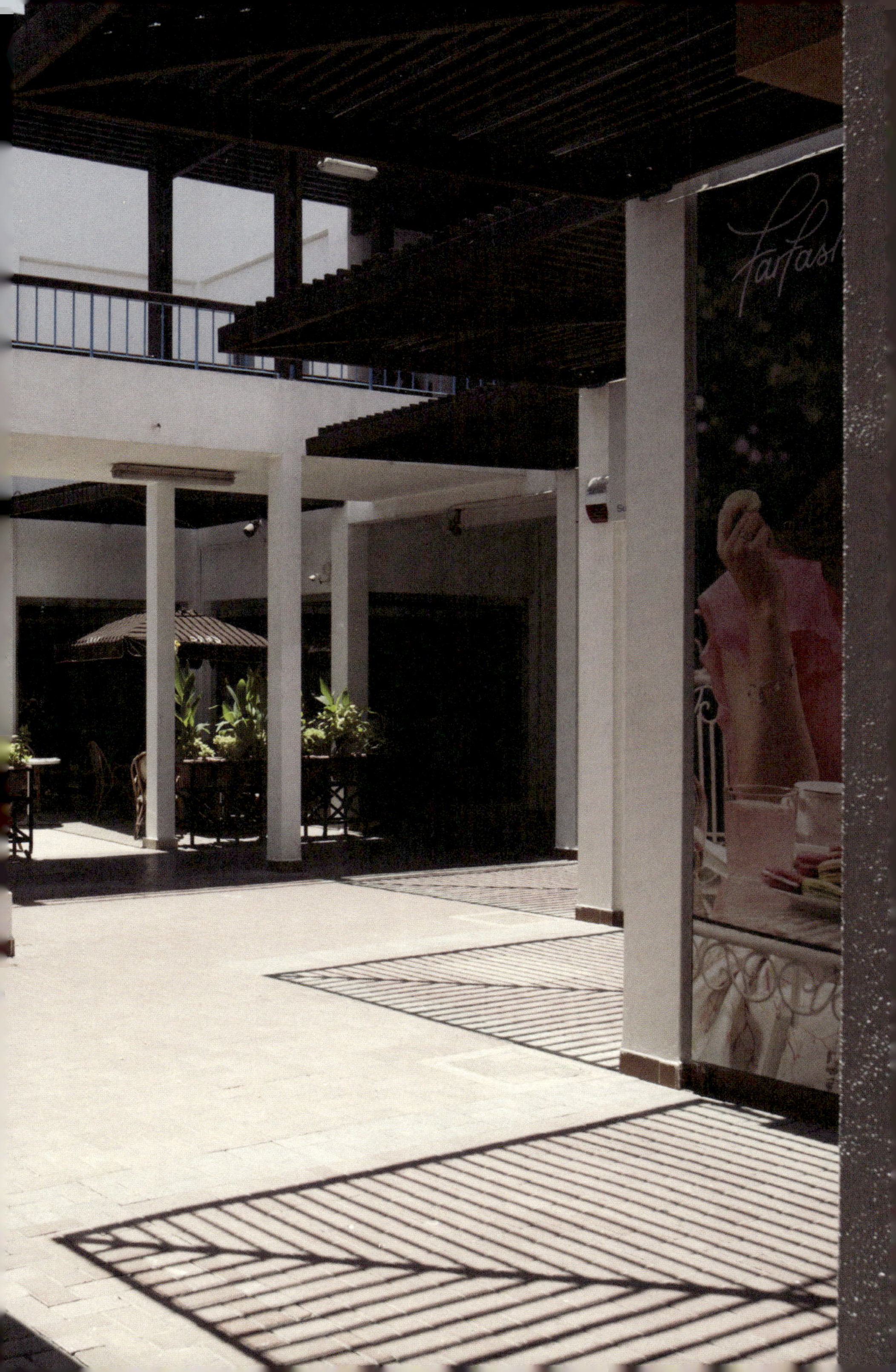

Beyond the specific architectural attributes, there is evidence of thoughtful reflection on the relationship between the mall and the larger urban fabric. The pathways connecting to the courtyard have the potential for connecting to neighboring buildings, and this is the case with the link established to the Jumeirah Center across the *sikka* (alleyway) that maintains a spatial separation between the two shopping centers. If the architects responsible for comparable complexes in Jumeirah would have looked to the sensitive yet significant urban design lessons offered by Magrudy's Mall, the physical structure of the neighborhood would have been very different from what we experience today. The urban model provided by the mall, if replicated, would have created opportunities for winding through the neighborhood in narrow, car-free alleyways and courtyards animated by life between buildings.

Discussions of architecture in Dubai often focus on iconic expressions intended to impress through sheer scale or distinctive appearance. Whereas these structures could be described as 'foreground' buildings that aim to attract attention, Magrudy's Mall is a 'background' building in the most positive sense. Rather than brashly claiming belonging to the context through the application of patterns or non-functional windtowers, the mall displays respect for, and a much greater affinity with the first permanent buildings found in areas like Al Fahidi. Although compositional anomalies such as the way in which the niches meet at interior corners inside the courtyard and the small square openings turned at 45 degrees are peculiar, attributes like the restrained façades and the courtyard reveal a critical position relative to the questions that are central to architecture in the Gulf. By showing how architecture can engage with its context in ways that transcend the imitation of imagined pasts, Magrudy's Mall demonstrates a discerning approach that is all too uncommon.

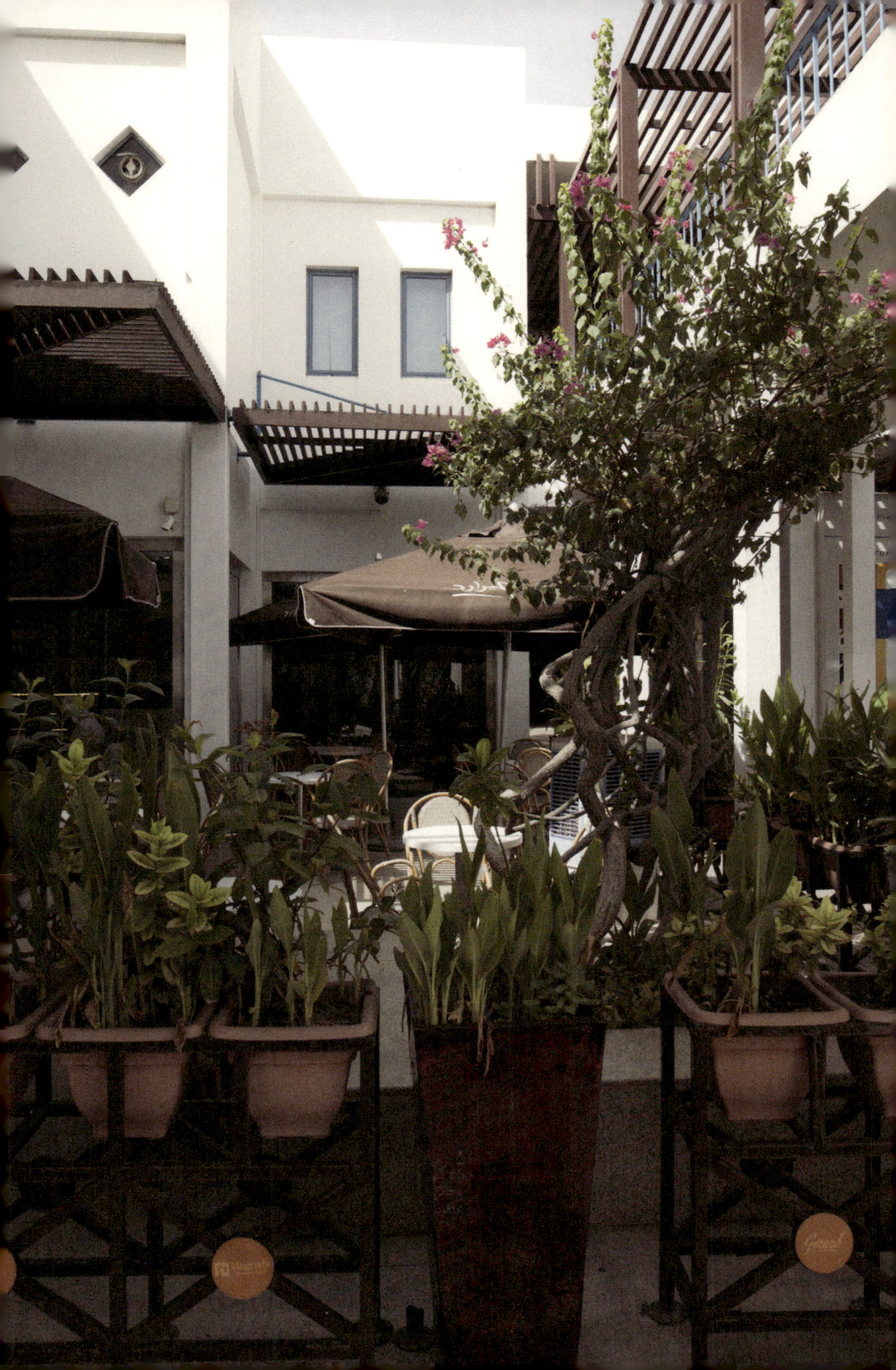

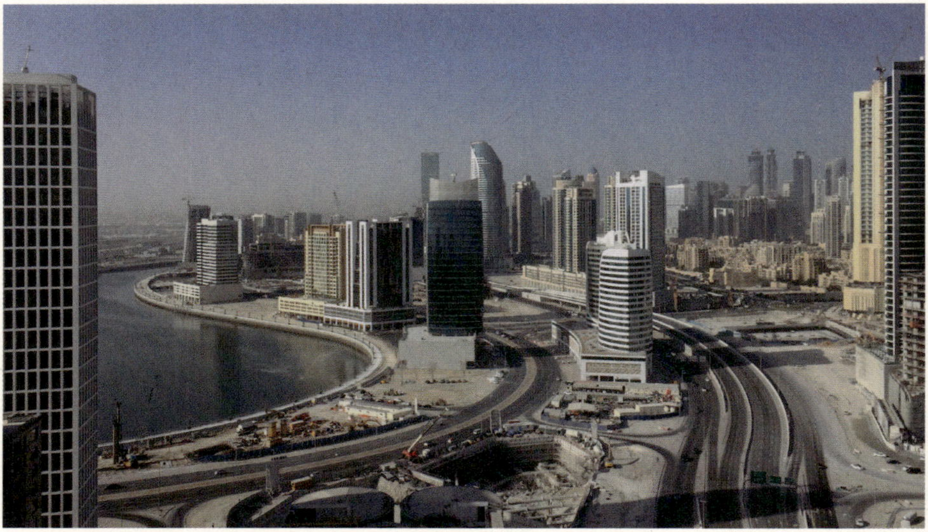

01. A VIEW TOWARDS BUSINESS BAY AND THE DUBAI CANAL.

UNCANNY DUBAI: THE CITY AS AN EXTENSION OF DWELLING

YASSER ELSHESHTAWY

Dubai, in Joseph O'Neill's marvelous novel *The Dog* (2015), echoes the main protagonist's sense of alienation, transience and anomie. The city's rapid rise, its anonymous cityscape and transient population are all colluding to intensify the character's rapid descent into psychological and cognitive despair. In the novel the city is a place that caters to western desires, represented by a placeless and transient architecture. It is an embodiment of a "fragmented, stateless and alienated society" in the words of one reviewer of the book who sees dystopian Dubai as a stand-in for modernity. The city is read as a dystopian space of alienation, in which the main aim is to make its spaces and buildings "indistinguishable from its airport"—as one character in the novel declares.

Such views are not unusual—in fact they are a staple of much of the criticism that is directed at the city. The protagonist's reaction to the view from the windows of his serviced apartment near Dubai International Financial Center (DIFC) is one that many of us would recognize. Sheikh Zayed Road (SZR), that iconic highway leading into the city, where its "six lanes of traffic bowled ceaselessly toward the distant skittles of Sharjah" is the ultimate space where one can experience a sense of disconnectedness (p. 44).

Furthermore, the constant activity of building towers in the desert, waiting to be occupied is another familiar trope pervasive in the narrative. Thus everyone "is looking forward to the day when everything has been built and all that remains is the business of being in the buildings" (p. 79). A view from a hotel in Business Bay towards the Dubai Canal (Figure 1, page 136) shows a cityscape that at the face of it is indeed empty, devoid of life, and where there is hardly any visible street activity. Some have argued that such spaces and sights are what our collective urban future entails (Auge, 2008).

Arguably, the manner in which some of the more visible spaces of the city have been designed and planned may run counter to the very notion of home or *being at home*. There seems to be a desire to project and encourage rootlessness. A constantly moving flow of people coming in and out of the city would be an apt visualization. Yet it is also clear that Dubai is composed of multiple layers that run counter to, and defy, any clear-cut and simplistic narrative of artificiality. Indeed, looking behind the shiny veneer of the visible city, another hidden and invisible city emerges. There, one can find a sense of liveliness and lived-in spaces that would suggest that city inhabitants have found a way—in the midst of the modern metropolis—to create and sustain a home.

To further elaborate on this I would like to explore the notion of the uncanny as it pertains to Dubai. The construct has been used to depict a modern condition that is characteristic of the modern city tracing its roots back to the 19th century. Dubai seems to be an embodiment of this. And, perhaps there is no other space that echoes notions of uncanniness than SZR, the multi-lane highway leading us from new Dubai into old Dubai. A stretch of mega-street that displays many of the city's iconic skyscrapers. Yet it is also a space that conceals, and it is precisely these qualities that makes it a perfect setting for exploring notions of home and belonging (Figure 2, opposite page).

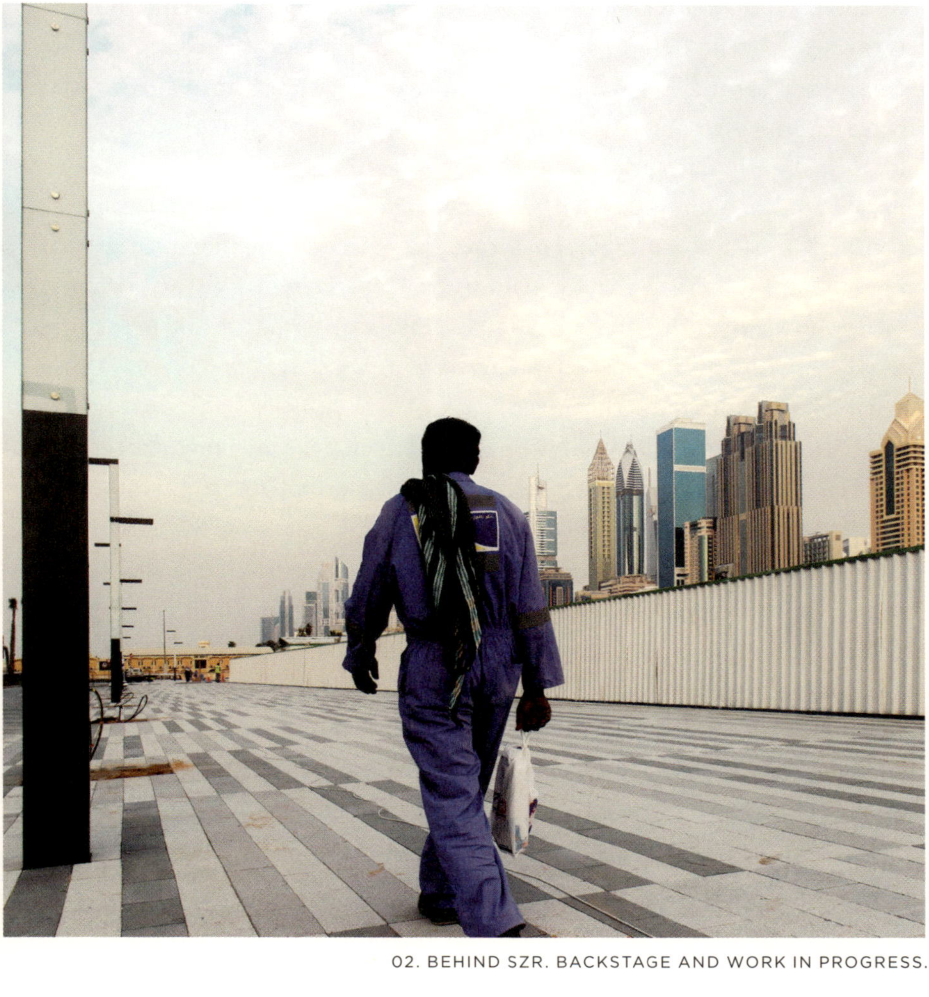

02. BEHIND SZR. BACKSTAGE AND WORK IN PROGRESS.

According to architectural theorist Anthony Vidler, who has written extensively about the architectural uncanny, there is a "contemporary sensibility that sees the uncanny erupt in empty parking lots around abandoned or run-down shopping mall". Moreover, this sensibility "has its roots and draws its commonplaces from a long but essentially modern tradition [...] the heir to a feeling of unease first identified in the late eighteenth century". Such a condition manifests itself through "spatial fear, leading to paralysis of movement, and temporal fear, leading to historical amnesia" (p. 6). The roots of the uncanny are traced back to psychoanalyst Sigmund Freud, master of exploring modern humans' inner psyche. He talks about the "transformation of something that once seemed homely into something decidedly not, from the *heimlich*, that is, into the *unheimlich*", or unhomely. It is not simply a question of not belonging but being "defamiliarized, derealized, as if in a dream" (p. 7). While not a characteristic of the space itself, it is a projection that provokes "a disturbing ambiguity, a slippage between waking and dreaming" (p. 11). The empty spaces created by modern urbanism, the tabula rasa "imagined by modernist utopias" is precisely the kind of setting in which the uncanny proliferates. Georg Simmel, in his classic early 20th century essay on the "Metropolis and Mental Life", writes in great detail about the experiential qualities that confront "modern man", who is transposed from a supposedly communal existence in small towns, to an anonymous presence (Simmel, 1903). Characterizing such feelings as a fundamentally modern condition, it is a theme that pervades much of writings on the city.

AN UNCANNY VIEW FROM THE ROAD

SZR is a multilane highway linking Dubai to the port of Jebel Ali and then further west towards Abu Dhabi (Figure 3, opposite page). Construction of the first section began in the 1970s. The particular stretch that is of interest starts at what used to be known as Defense Roundabout

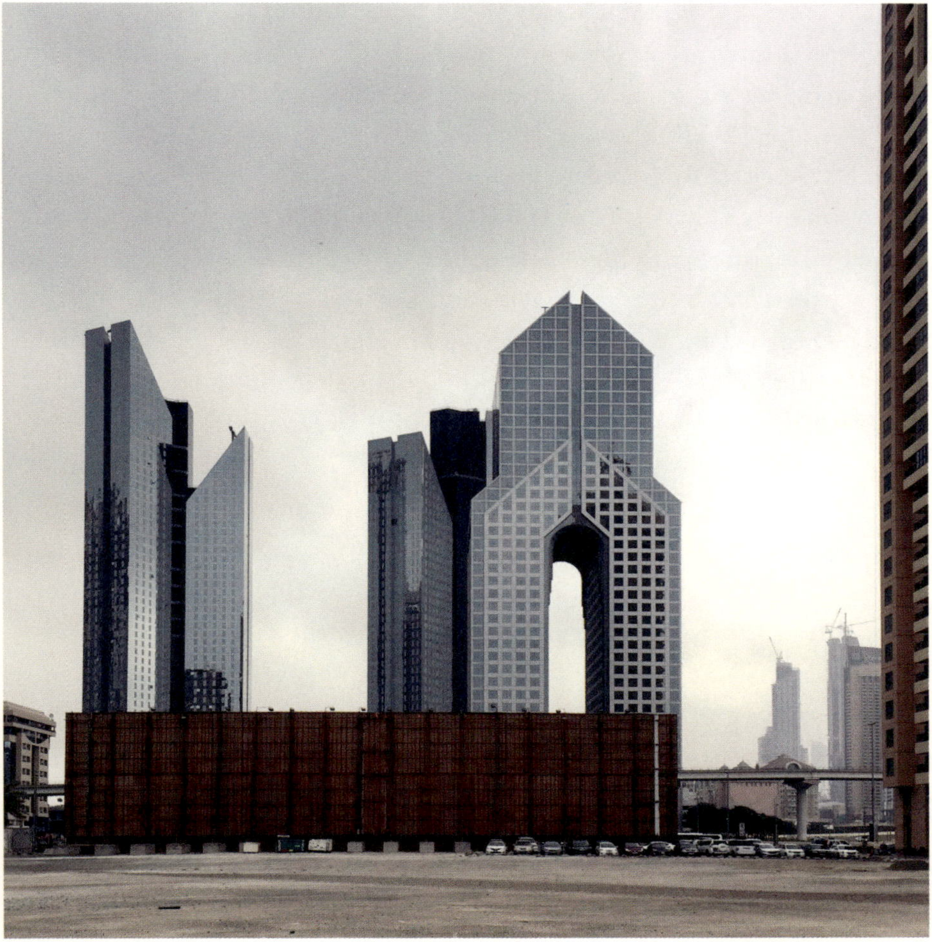

03. A BILLBOARD BEHIND SZR.

(and is now an incomprehensible network of exit/entry ramps) up to the World Trade Center intersection. Aside from its transportation relevance, it contains some of Dubai's most recognizable architectural icons. Arriving from Abu Dhabi, one is immediately confronted with the Burj Khalifa, which looms to the right—only to be faced with a 1970s throwback, the Toyota Building to the left, which stands bravely in the midst of an ever-changing cityscape. It captures a certain modernistic optimism. Further along is the Crowne Plaza Hotel, a 1970s edifice constituting one of the city's first modern hotels. As one moves further along, the twin Emirates Towers appear. Harking back to the 1990s, they epitomize the city's dedication to high-tech architecture. The road concludes with the World Trade center apartments and the iconic World Trade Center itself. Designed by British architect John Harris, it was considered to be the tallest building in the Arab world upon inauguration in 1979. In between these set-pieces, always recognizable to Dubai aficionados, is a series of buildings of varying design quality. Taken together they form an inscrutable wall that appears almost two-dimensional. Moreover, because of the scale of the buildings, it evokes the experience of driving in a canyon. Of course, hiding behind these inscrutable walls are two very different urban experiences. To the left is the ramshackle district of Satwa, housing the city's downtrodden and low-income residents; while to the right, appearing behind the cracks of the skyscraper wall is DIFC, home to the city's financial center and an assortment of high-end galleries, hotels and eateries. Conceived as a free zone, it appears as a kind of "floating environment" catering to the elite and powerful.

Aside from the architectural and urban qualities of this road segment, the particular infrastructural characteristics are also of interest. SZR is a six-lane highway in both directions. In addition, slip roads enable a transition from the main highway to a calmer parallel, two-way, frontage road system. This stretch contains various restaurants, cafés, service shops, and entrances to high-rises. Some semblance of a pedestrian

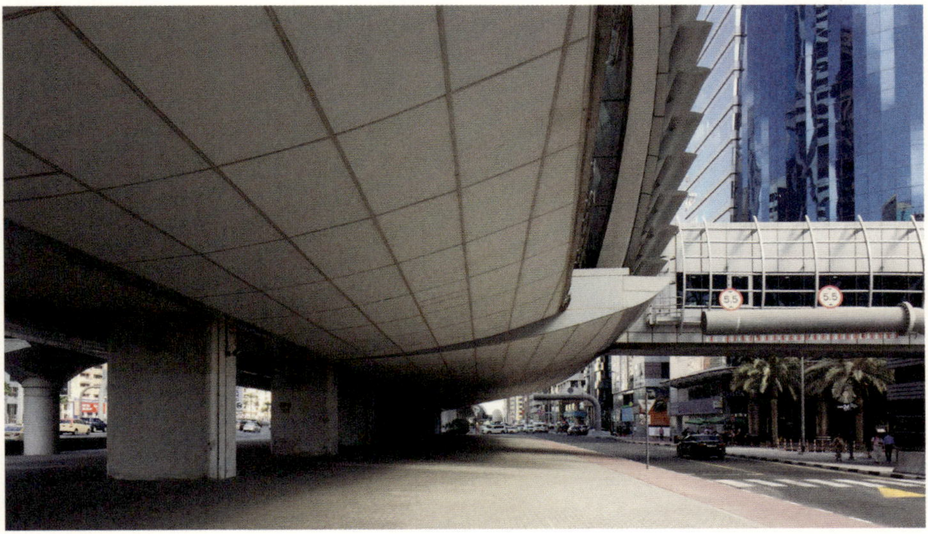

04. UNDER THE VIADUCT. SZR.

walkway exists on which one can observe people hurriedly moving along. This road does not encourage lingering, loitering or simply hanging around to observe. A 19th-century Walter Benjamin-like flâneur would undoubtedly feel out of place here (Benjamin and Tiedemann, 1999). Adding to the experience is the Dubai metro viaduct. A raised, bridge-like structure, it runs to the right side of the road on top of a green median. One major station linked to DIFC interrupts movement. A desolate bicycle rack pays homage to a form of transit-oriented development that may or may not happen there (Figure 4, page 143).

Reflecting on the experiential qualities through the windshield of a car, I am reminded of the work of Kevin Lynch and Donald Appleyard who, in their well-known study "The View from the Road", attempted to capture the experiential qualities of driving in the 1960s Cambridge, USA (Appleyard, Lynch, and Myer, 1964). Indeed, the mere fact that one has to "drive through" from the very outset establishes a certain viewpoint and enables a specific mindset. Confined within the isolated spaces of an air-conditioned car, one is removed from the immediate surroundings. Given the width of the road, any signs of potential life are absent, further adding to the unsettling experience. Most buildings are clad with an impenetrable curtain wall lacking any balconies or possibility for opening windows, making them appear as an *Alphaville* apparition. In some sense, it also reminds us of the iconic scene in Tarkovsky's 1972 movie *Solaris*, equivocating reality and a dream state as the protagonists drive through Tokyo and emerge from a tunnel into the city with its high-rises.

Along SZR, any potential for personalization, and thus a signifier of life, is removed—and is also illegal. The very notion of home, belonging and sense of place is taken away. Thus the space becomes unhomely, or uncanny. The highly utopian appearance of the driverless Dubai metro train as it glides above one's head, with barely visible silhouettes of passengers, intensifies notions of isolation and estrangement. Such feelings of unease are further heightened if one begins to contemplate what hides behind the curtain of this streetscape.

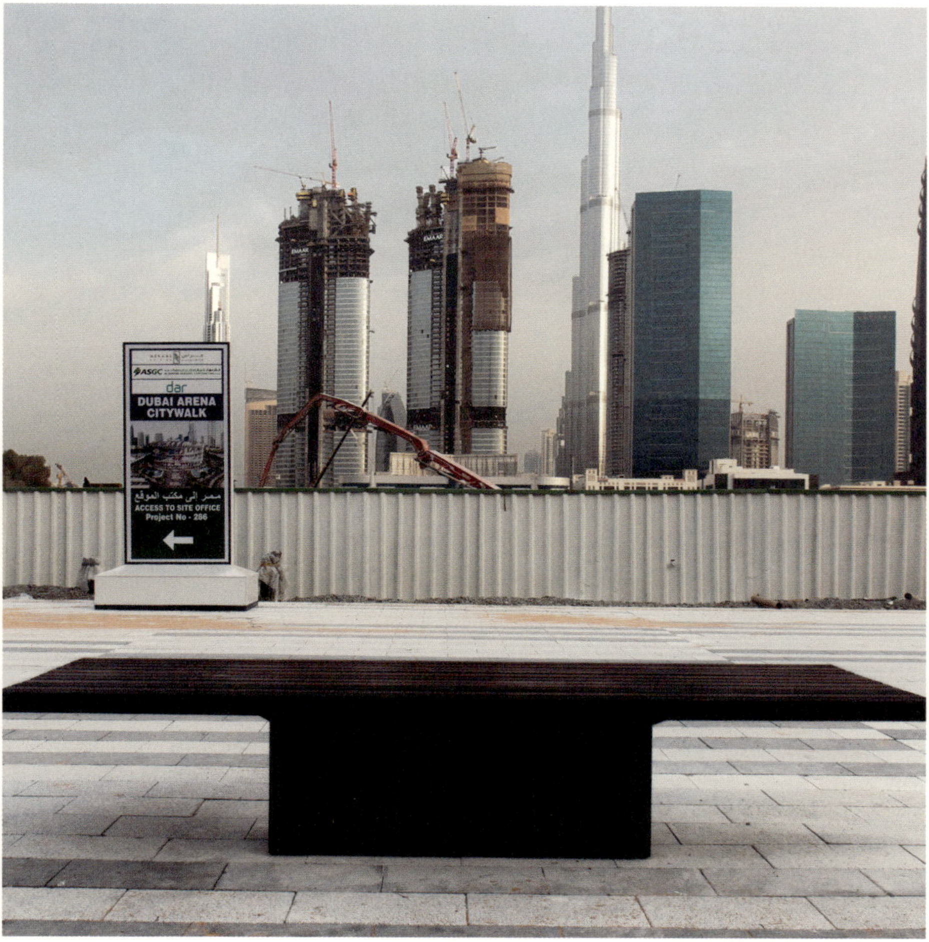

05. WAITING FOR SHA'ABIYAT AL-SHORTA REPLACEMENT.

BEYOND THE ROAD: SUBVERTING THE UNCANNY

As noted, to the right is DIFC, a complex composed of a series of structures, including a Gate building. In many ways it is an extension of the anonymous, transient character of SZR. While its cafés and galleries are teeming with the city's bright and beautiful, it is socially exclusive with most of its activities taking place indoors. Surrounding streets are for car movement, parking, and access to buildings. Pedestrian walkways are perfunctory. Ironically, an interesting outdoor pedestrian network exists, but it is at the upper floor of the complex serving mostly patrons of the facilities—which includes the Middle East headquarters of the famed art auction house Christie's. Of more interest is the space to the right of SZR. The vertical streetscape masks two neighborhoods—Satwa and the now defunct Sha'abiat Al Shorta. In their ramshackle appearance and cobbled-together architecture, both are an embodiment of homeliness—a defiant stance against the neighboring uncanny.

Satwa, which has some of the oldest buildings in Dubai, and over the years, it has evolved into a rich and diverse neighborhood. It was initially home to locals who were given houses by the late Sheikh Rashid in the 1960s in what was then at the outskirts of the city. This explains the repetitive and standardized appearance of its residences. As the city grew, locals moved outwards and a largely South-Asian population moved in (Alawadi, 2014; Elsheshtawy, 2010, 2011) (Figure 5, page 145).

Satwa was slated for demolition to be replaced by a mixed-used development called Jumeirah Gardens, as unveiled at the Dubai Cityscape exhibition in October 2008. The global financial downturn put a halt to those dystopian ambitions and previously displaced residents promptly moved back in. Over the last few years, a fascinating situation has unfolded in the area immediately adjacent to Satwa. The previously mentioned Sha'abiyat Al Shorta is located across the road and is considered an extension of sorts for Satwa. The district is composed of identical courtyard houses from the 1970s and was planned as residence for Emirati employees of the police force. Appearing largely as a curiosity from a bygone era, most of its houses had been abandoned and covered with graffiti and wild vegetation. Yet some were still occupied while I was walking among its dusty lanes in 2014. I met a resident who informed me that they will all soon have to leave. We stood in front of his house, which was completely surrounded by vegetation. He told me that his mother still waters the garden every day even though she knows that she will move soon. When neighbors asked her about why she keeps doing this, she responded that she will continue to do so until the last day of their stay. This elderly local woman refused to accept that this would all soon be gone. The architecture and the urban setting conveys a sense of attachment and belonging that stands in stark contrast to the anonymous and placeless dystopia that exists just across the road (Figure 6, pages 148-149).

Such spaces are the antithesis of the uncanny and are a physical embodiment of dwelling, or rootedness to place. Indeed, the notion of dwelling is critical here, as its loss is used to critique modern life in general. Philosopher Heidegger describes dwelling as the very essence of what is to be human. Hence "the way in which you are and I am, the manner in which we humans are on earth, is [...] dwelling". Furthermore, "to be a human being means to be on earth as a mortal. It means to dwell" (p. 147). Dwelling is also defined as an activity that involves such feelings as to cherish and protect, to preserve and care for. A person's whole being hinges on being able to dwell properly (Elsheshtawy, 2001). Similar notions are also expressed in Gaston Bachelard's meditation on the meaning of home (Bachelard, 2014). In many ways, Sha'abiat al Shorta evokes similar qualities. Through the careful cultivation of a garden, the extensions and additions made by residents, the presence of multiple generations in one dwelling, and perhaps the most important: memories sustained over decades of living. As a footnote to this, the district has been demolished to make way for an extension of City Walk, a high-

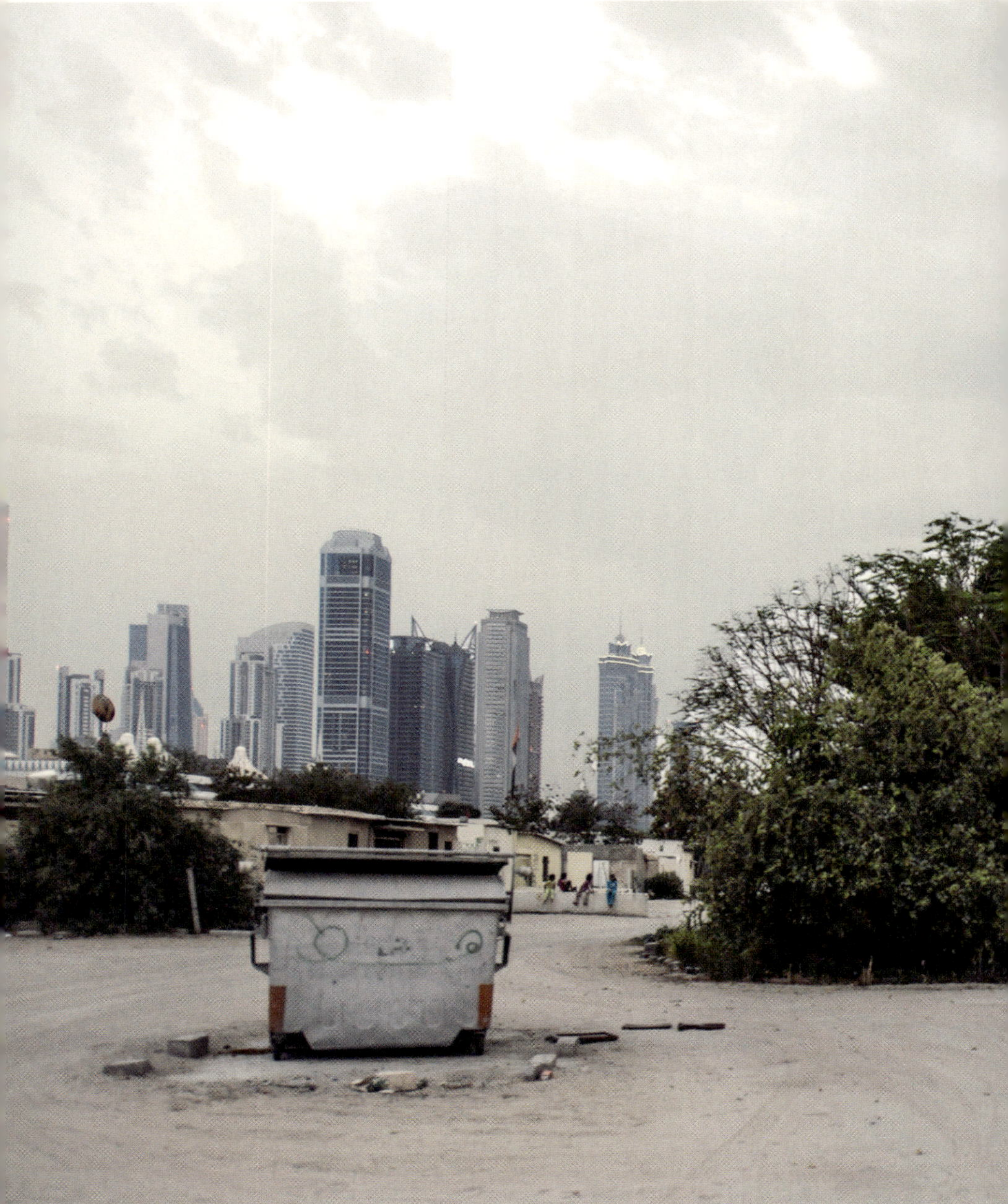

06. A HOUSE ENVELOPED BY VEGETATION. DYSTOPIA IN THE DISTANCE.

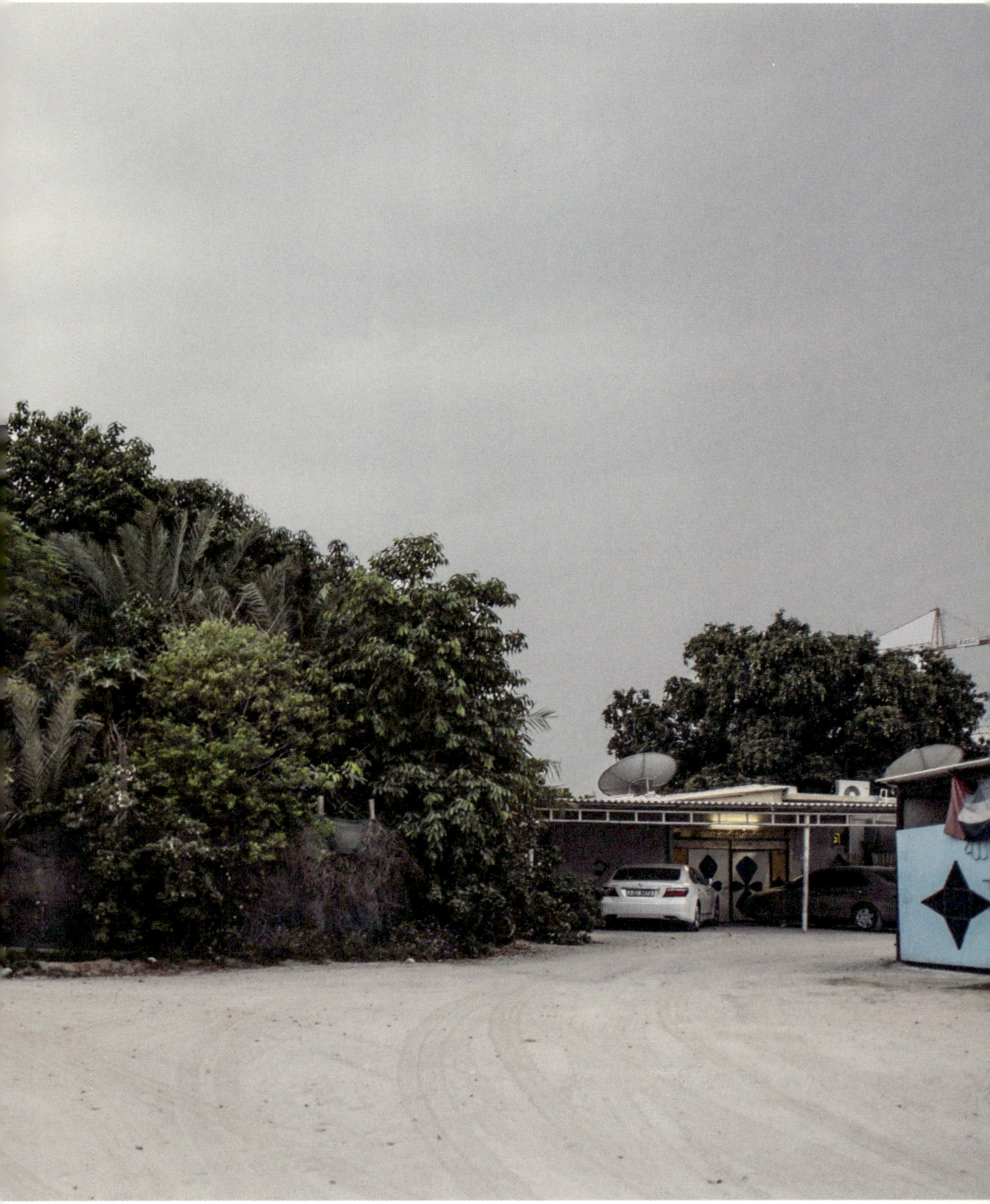

end retail and residential development. The original neighborhood has become a distant memory. Instead, a generic landscape has been put in place, with the requisite universal street signage and furniture. Wide sidewalks and an upscale retail mix cater to a well-to-do clientele that is a far cry from the modest spaces it replaced. In this instance, the uncanny has prevailed.

LEARNING FROM DUBAI: BEYOND THE UNCANNY

> *"... seek and learn to recognize who and what, in the midst of the inferno, are not inferno, then make them endure, give them space."*
>
> Italo Calvino, *Invisible Cities*

The uncanny pervades the city. It is everywhere and its march is unstoppable. This is not necessarily a Dubai-specific problem. Anthropologist Marc Augé argues that such constructs have become a distinct sign of "super-modern cities" leading to the presence of "non-places" which are "spaces which do not integrate the earlier places". It is "a world thus surrendered to solitary individuality, to the fleeting, the temporary and ephemeral" (Auge, 2008). Yet Dubai is not just composed of such spaces. These are the fleeting impressions of the hurried and the biased. Spaces such as the Shorta neighborhood still exist in the city in plentitude and are evidence of a defiance exhibited by city dwellers. Here they subvert notions of transience and anomie.

Juxtaposing these two experiences—the canyon drive through along SZR vs the nurtured spaces of the Sha'abiya—another city emerges. A city that is full of life, in which its citizens dwell in the true sense of the word. And it is these places that must endure against the uncanny drive through an anonymous and place-less architecture.

Alawadi, K. (2014). 'Urban Redevelopment Trauma: The Story of a Dubai Neighbourhood', *Built Environment*, 40(3), pp. 357-375.

Appleyard, D., K. Lynch and J.R. Myer (1964). *The view from the road*. Cambridge. Published for the Joint Center for Urban Studies of the Massachusetts Institute of Technology and Harvard University by the M.I.T. Press.

Auge, M. (2008). *Non-places* (2nd English language ed.). London; New York: Verso.

Bachelard, G. (2014). *The Poetics of Space*. Penguin.

Benjamin, W. and R. Tiedemann (1999). *The Arcades Project*. Cambridge, MA: Belknap Press.

Calvino, I. (1978). *Invisible Cities* (1st Harvest/HBJ ed.). New York: Harcourt Brace Jovanovich.

Elsheshtawy, Y. (2001). 'Searching For Theory: Christopher Alexander's Intellectual Rootss', *Architectural Science Review*, 44(4), pp. 395-403.

Elsheshtawy, Y. (2010). Dubai : *behind an urban spectacle*, London; New York: Routledge.

Elsheshtawy, Y. (2011). The Prophecy of Code 46: Afuera in Dubai or our Urban Future. Traditional Dwellings and Settlement Review, 22(11), 19-32.

O'Neill, J. (2015). *The Dog*, New York: Vintage, Random House.

Simmel, G. (1903). '*The Metropolis and Mental Life*', In J. Lin and C. Mele (eds), *The Urban Sociology Reader* (pp. 23-31). London, New York: Routledge.

Vidler, A. (1992). *The Architectural Uncanny: essays in the modern unhomely.* Cambridge, MA: MIT Press.

AFFICIONADOS OF THE UNHOMELY CENTER AND THE IDIO(TS)SYNCRASY OF THE PERIPHERY

GEORGE KATODRYTIS

From the 'mega' to the 'social', every aspect of the city has seemingly been reported. Yet Dubai has not ceased to inspire constant speculation on its future urbanism. In a hybrid metropolis, which is bigger than the sum of its disconnected parts, every architectural piece takes the role of a prototype in an ongoing urban planning exercise. The city is a conglomeration, morphing from one generic mode of representation to new forms of imagination, but mostly it has adhered to a postmodern formula of predominantly unexciting urbanism. Have individual buildings and their aspiring architects made an impact? Regardless, the city as whole thrives on its own total environment.

The center of the city is familiar but with edited moments of unexpredictable encounters and exchanges. These can only be captured by direct participation and not through any rhetoric discourse. Not dissimilar to tourism, it is an act of being here. Such an approach is neither nostalgic nor idealistic but addresses reality and utilizes the mood and creativity of the participants as the flâneurs, the urban explorers and the connoisseurs of the street.

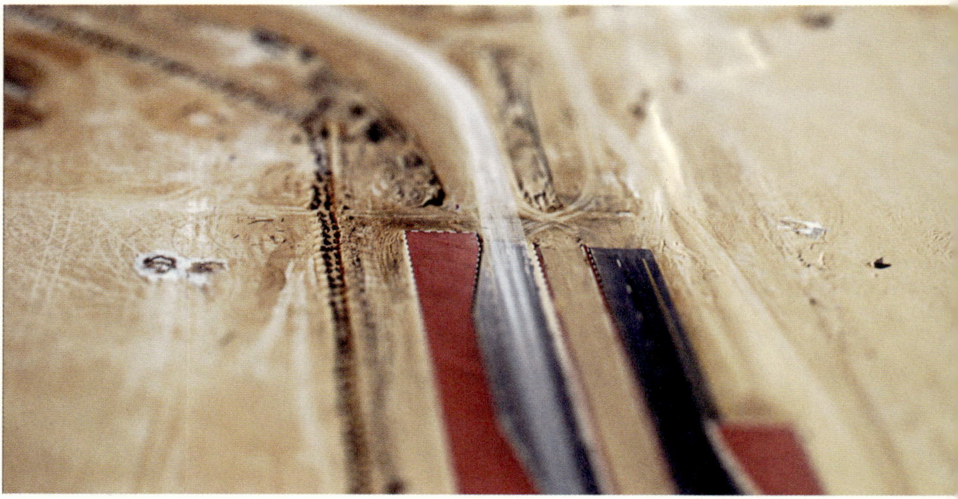

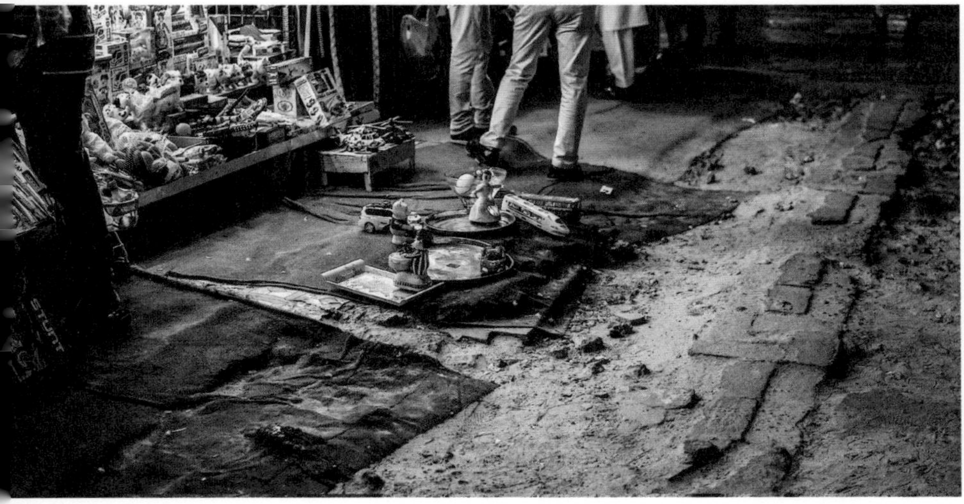

Since the development of hand-held cameras in the early 20th century, these devices have become the tool of the flâneur. The smartphone has now made everybody an instantaneous tourist and an orchestrator, recording and editing the everyday into everything as long as there is a hint of spectacle. This can be applied in unpredictable spaces: the car park, the shop front, in wide vistas, and in front of neon street signs. The space is all the same represented as a city of arrayed repetitions and productions. This can be observed as aerial views but experienced on the street. They are real yet mysterious detailed plastic toy models in total defiance of their reality; the city is an avatar of itself. But the urban is only revealed through a direct participation and a dérive, a voyage and a technique of rapid passage through varied ambiances of the city.

For the tourist and the accidental participant, Dubai might seem peculiar, hyperactive and with no apparent hierarchy, held together by virtue of proximity. The city is delirious; it is about layering everything with anything. It is found everywhere but it has not lost its idiosyncrasy of a hybrid and complex urbanism with an invisible infrastructure of non-hierarchical activities and goods. Everything has become aesthetic. This aestheticization of the world, as Baudrillard suggests, entails a collapse of aesthetic standards at the expense of the fascination with excess. Social space turns into a fetishized abstraction. Yet the fetishized, closed-up urban and street culture imagery is now becoming blurred and melancholic. It is a raw urban experience pointing to a new direction: internal, trivial, human, sensual, and a kind of defiance.

The center of Dubai is frozen in time. Everybody has moved to the outskirts, to technology parks, to free-zone clusters, and to expatriate enclaves. These peripheral districts are a new type of city created by the pure aggregation of a number of apparently unconnected buildings that, by virtue of proximity, form an urban condition. Yet here in the center everything is strangely familiar, with a paradoxical charm of being simultaneously attractive and repulsive, leaving the participant in uncertainty. Much like a scene from the film *Blade Runner*, Dubai's streets are pandemonium. At nightfall, the chaotic operations of bazaars and souks overtake the bland high-street building blocks, reducing them to mere backdrops. During these moments, when urban spaces merge with street culture, the city is truly at its best. Shopping and street chaos are the only space.

Within this landscape, our direct participation is authentic while mirroring the contemporary experience of urban life. In an act of self-stylization, Dubai is a raw experiment in the context of this hybridization. For every fast-forward development of the city, there is a flipside of residual and hidden spaces, by-products, and leftover conditions, which are equally vibrant. The mental map of the city that emerges is both seamless and complex. In this part of the city, patterns of behavior are transformed into urban organizational structures that negotiate, and adapt to, the forever-changing demands and multiple realities of the city. In a domain of abundant real estate speculative developments where the imaginary is sold as the real, there is no longer a place for reality itself.

Paradoxically, the center of Dubai is doing the opposite: the real has become imaginary—filled with blurred images and spontaneous multicultural exchanges. Leaving the manicured lawns and palaces of suburbia and arriving to the center, a new world of images re-emerges. There are no aesthetic values here, only an instinct for survival. While suburbia lives in fetishized images and lifestyles, the center turns into a space of experience that has been codified with signification and hierarchies in a new form of increased sensory perception. It has also been frozen, as though there has been no progress at all.

Since the Surrealists, the city is above all an enchanting dreamscape that fuels the imagination. The very cacophony of the city with its blaring horns and flashing neon lights—the fragmentary, kaleidoscopic impulses of the modern metropolis—provide them with a continual source of stimulation and intoxication. The modern metropolis is entangled

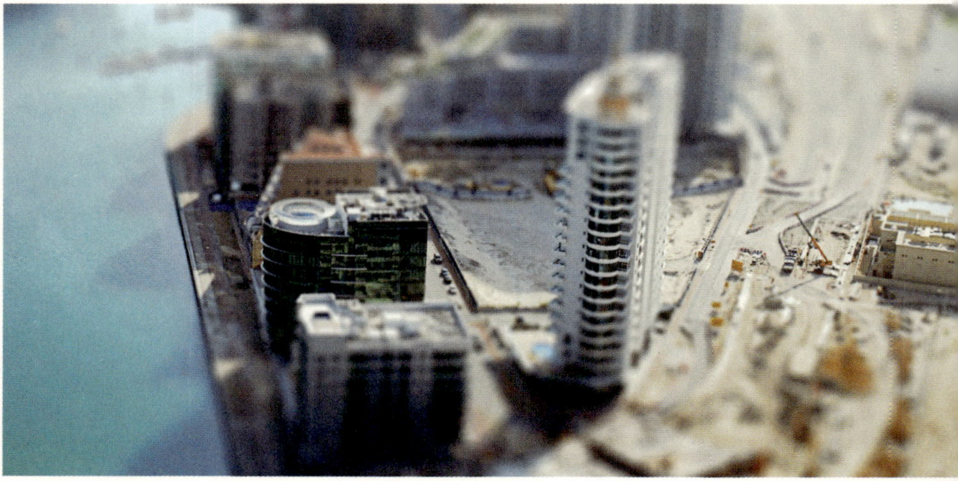

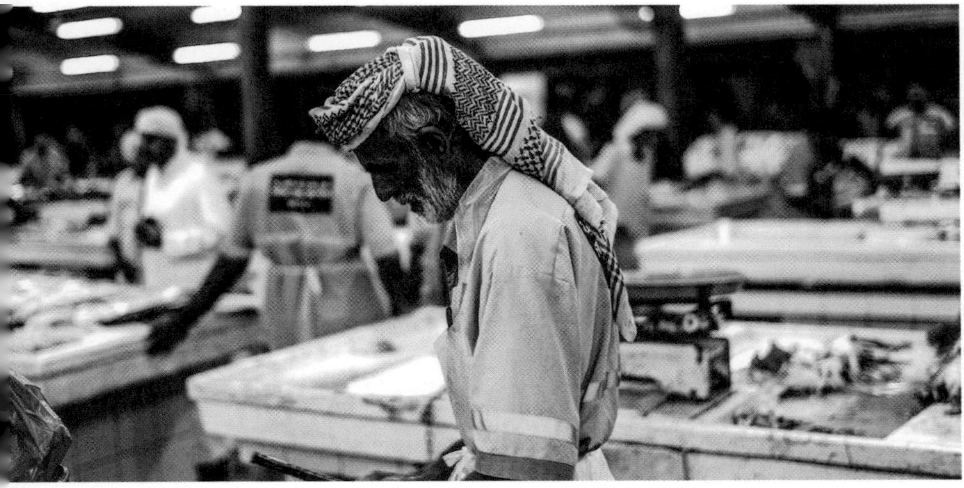

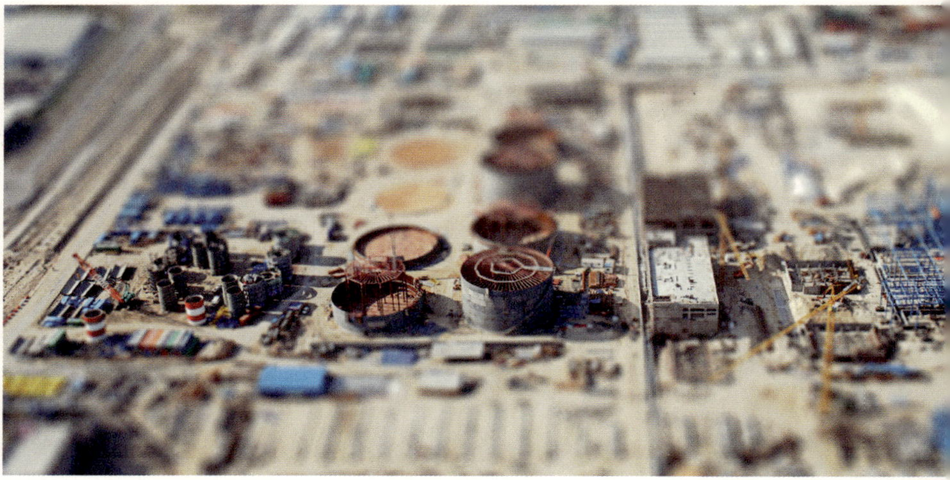

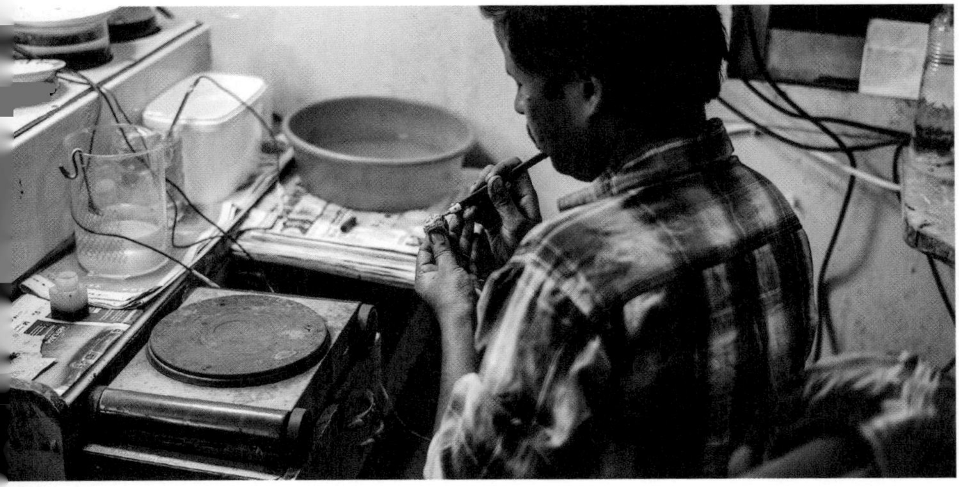

with myth, a form of dreamworld and the site of the phantasmagoric and kaleidoscopic. In such a hybrid metropolis full of complexities and contradictions, the city's polarized condition becomes a sequence of shifting scales from suburbia to the center and from aerial perspectives to dérive into the backstreets.

Would it be too far-fetched if we borrowed from Marx and spoke of 'the idiocy of suburban life', bearing in mind that the original meaning of the word 'idiots' referred to those who did not vote, lived in the outskirts and in suburbia, and ignored the city, that is, took no interest in the affairs of the *polis*?

If the outskirts appear homely, they replicate a passive gaze. They are all the same. Constructed leisure lands and resorts that long to be seen as exotic. Urbanism takes the form of a revised Garden City, or rather a garden with city parts and buildings of the new 'Orient'. New architectural objects are constructed with decorated with fabricated fakes reminiscent of Islamic traditional geometric patterns. This is a new form of 21st-century Orientalism addressing mass tourism. In reality, these spaces are fake, confined between the free-zone office, the beach, and the mall.

Yet the unsettling qualities of the center have become mysterious, dense, and engaging. This is what makes Dubai a true city of production. Every space is used, everybody is busy, and everything is consumed as if in a state of endless transaction. It is a total lifestyle and a system of operations for survival. Nothing is in excess and nothing is wasted. Like a physics engine, all is interactive, performative and material. There is no architectural past to romanticize, only the future to fantasize about, and a present to consume: direct urbanism.

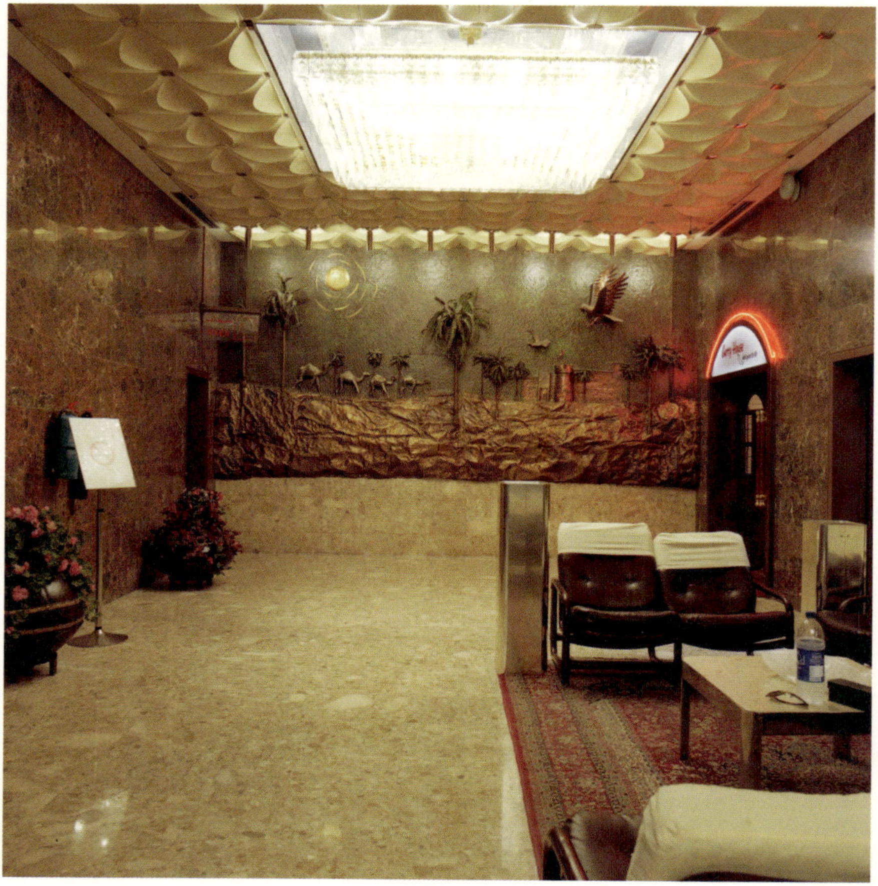

FAMILIAL

LAMYA GARGASH

These photographs, taken in the interiors of budget hotels, trace a period and condition that perhaps we imagine to be already outmoded by the desire to portray a classy, luxurious profile, with seven stars taking over the definitive five. They were part of a series that attempted to explore my relationship with unfamiliar spaces. It is interesting to me, how despite living in one's homeland, one can still feel like a foreigner. There are certain spaces which are not known, perhaps more so for a woman.

These most modest of hotels exist with the obvious aspirations of their owners as symbols of hope and potential. The decadence and vibrancy of their interiors are at odds with how they are categorized and what determines the fate and identity of their rooms.

I occasionally introduced family photographs into the rooms to ask: Once a foreign emotion enters the room, are we able to see them as mere bedrooms? Does the room change its identity? What defines a resting space beyond its basic elements? The rooms seem to transcend a level of intimacy and come to represent the experiences and memories that may soon forever be lost to a hierarchical system where the solo star is a moribund breed.

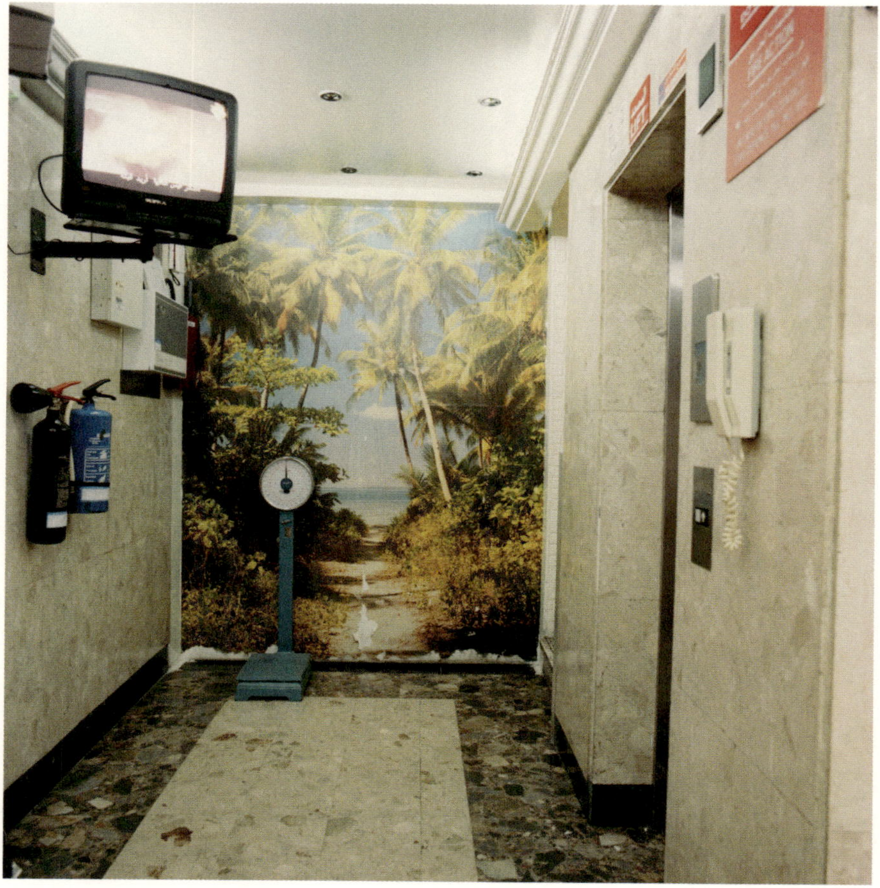

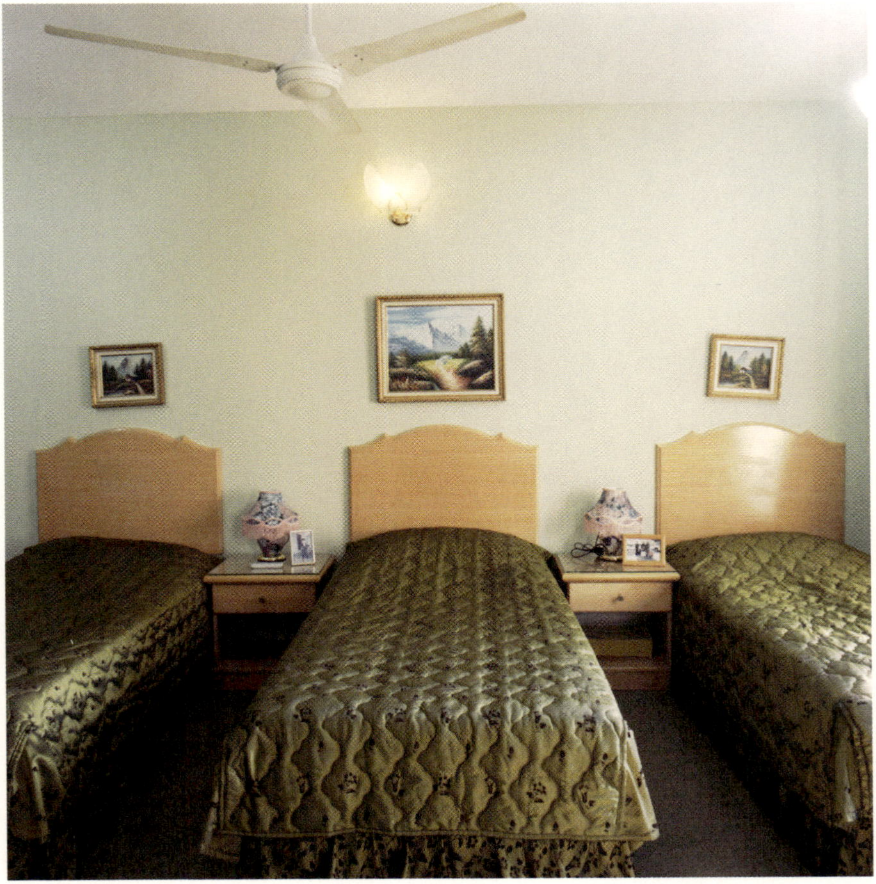

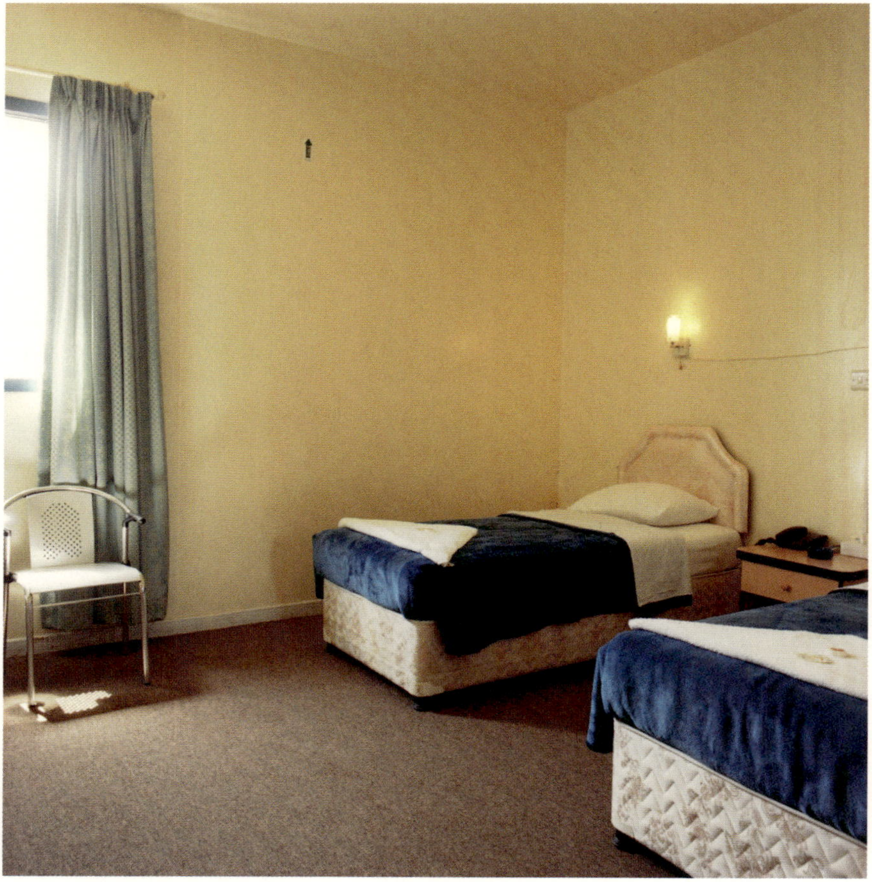

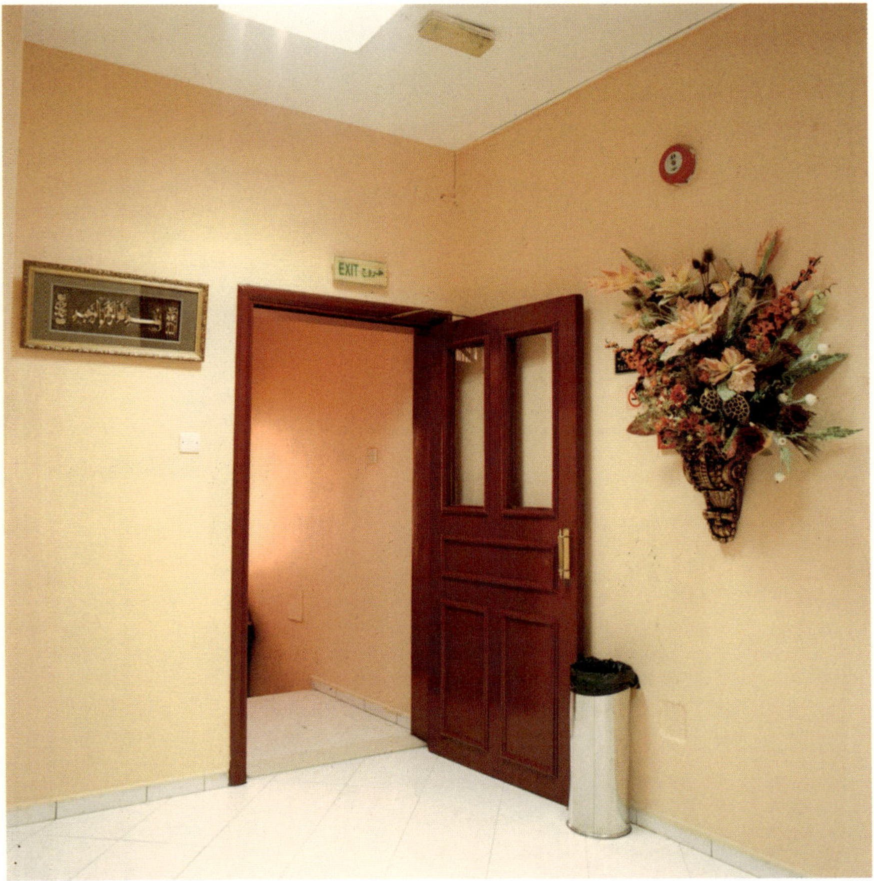
EXIT

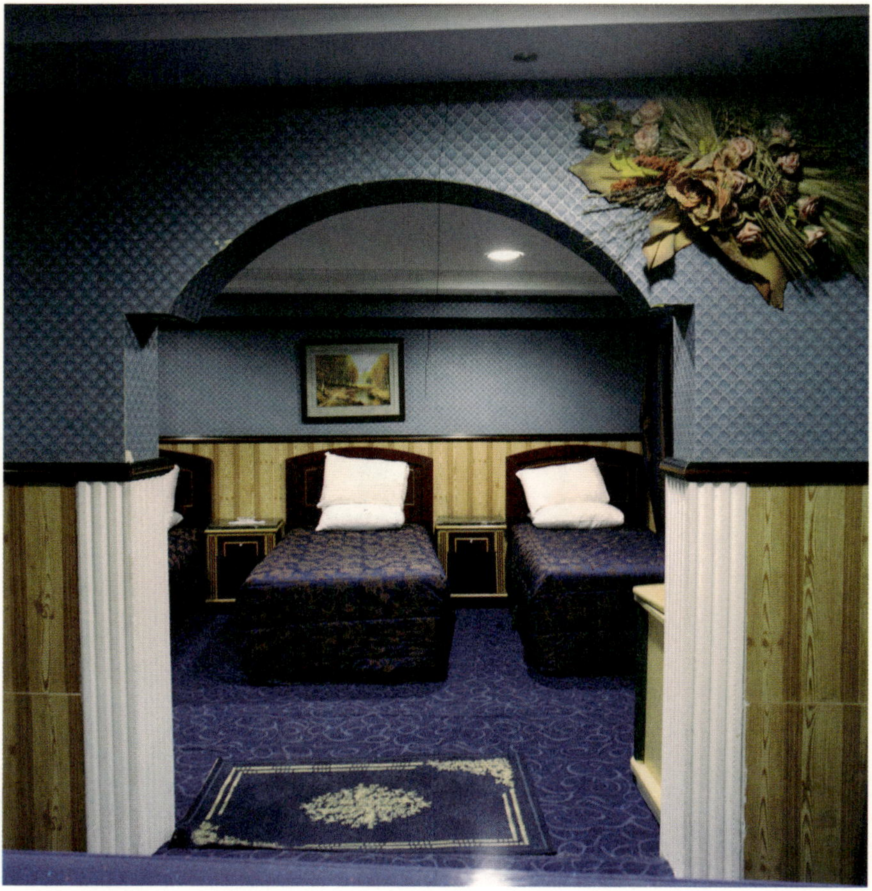

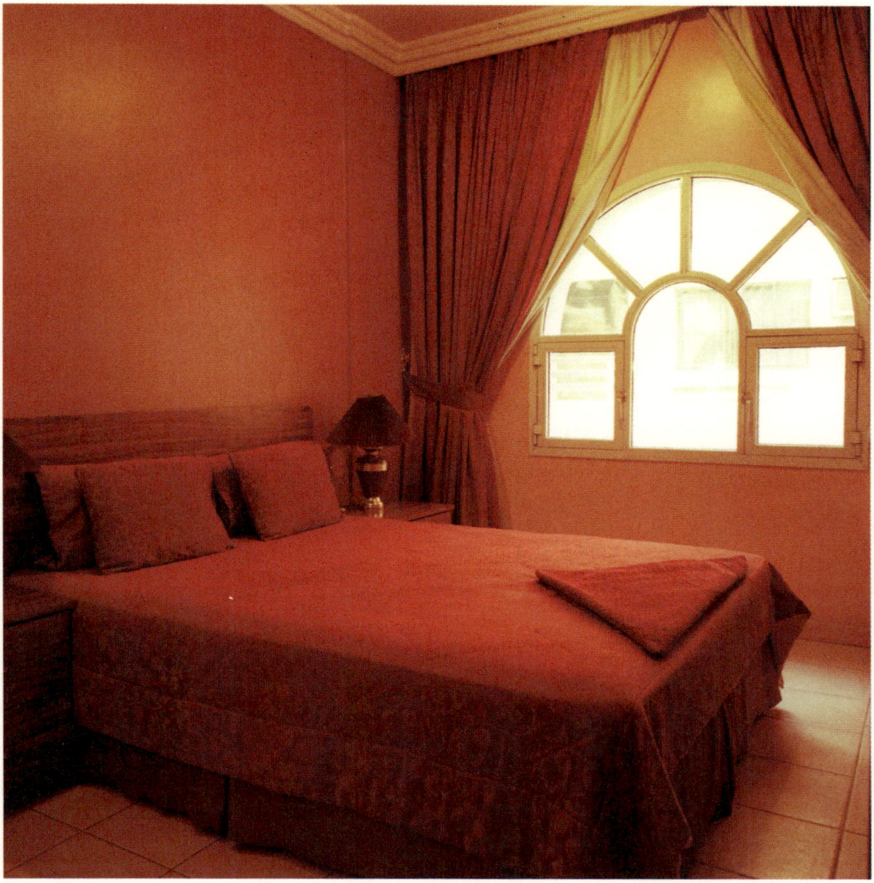

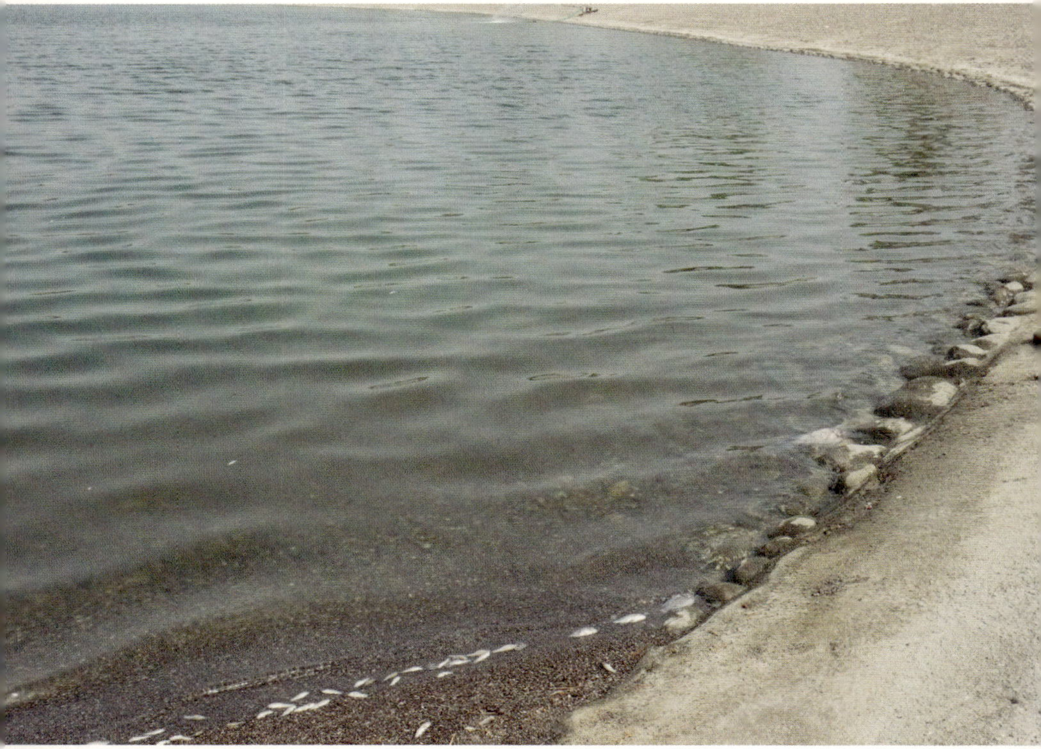

EMIRATES MALL CORNICHE

VIKRAM DIVECHA

As he waved his arm across the water body with a flourish, he christened it 'Emirates Mall Corniche'. This couldn't be the name for an artificial lake that sat between a Mall and a Metro station, I thought. I had asked him, an individual who worked in the vicinity, like many others I encountered, if he knew the name of this lake. Nobody seemed to know for sure. I kept receiving irresolute answers. In this case, our friend couldn't be bothered about someone showing interest in this man-made pit holding still water. It was an eventless body. To dismiss me, he mockingly gave the moniker, which I have borrowed as the title for this text—Emirates Mall Corniche. Despite being intentionally incorrect, his version was generative. The term "corniche" spoke of a pulse that ran along the seafront, where folks are drawn to the sea, sunsets and free breeze. It's the place for chitter chatter, lingering, socializing, stretching, rolling, napping, ambling—all of which, has come to surround this artificial waterbody.

This lake is located in Al Barsha 1, just off the busy Sheikh Zayed Road (E11) highway. It is approximately half a kilometre in length, with a hard-surfaced walking path circling the lake for around a kilometre. A grass patch skirts the path, opening up generously in certain areas. Mature palm trees are mounted at intervals. From Google Earth one notices the lake is contained within a peculiar shape resembling a boomerang, or arguably an amoeba. South of the lake is the colossal

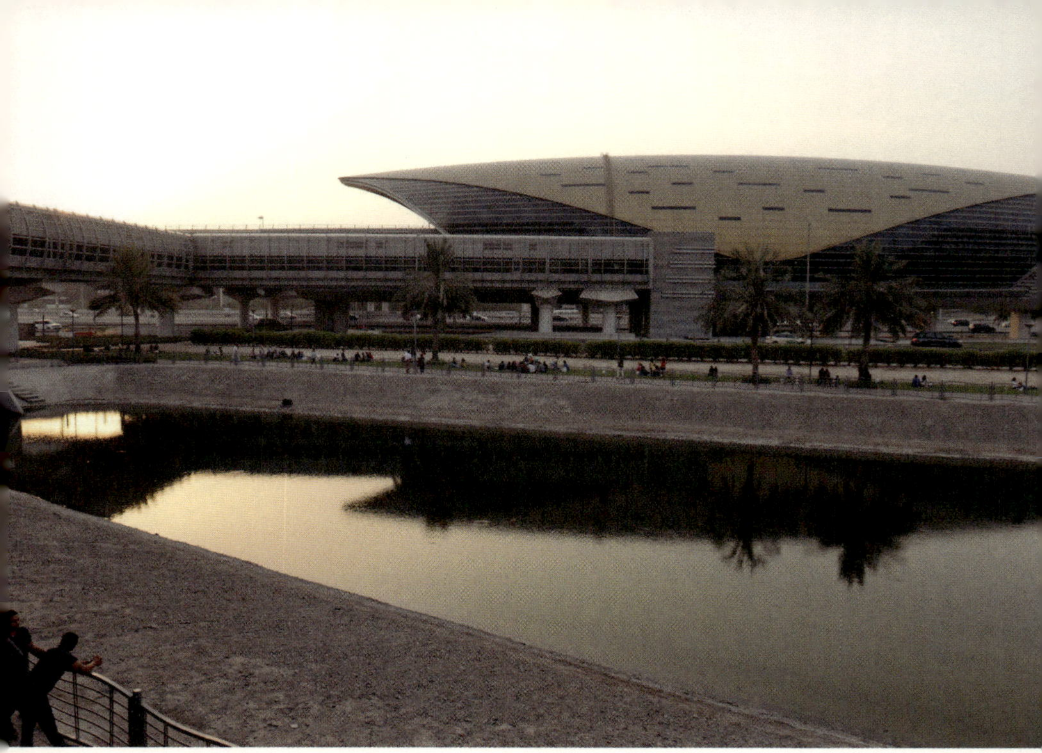

Mall of the Emirates, famous for housing an indoor ski resort and snow park. To top it up, it is flanked on each end with a hotel—the Sheraton Dubai and the Kempinski. Across the Mall, overlooking the lake, is the Mall of the Emirates Metro station, a busy hub that serves the Mall and the growing Al Barsha 1 residential community. A 200-meter enclosed overhead footbridge connects the Metro station directly to the Mall.

A few years ago, during a residency in a mountain village in Lebanon, I found myself in a rather heated debate about public spaces in Dubai. I was trying to convince a Spanish artist that malls are the dominant public spaces in this part of the world. It is where folks get to walk, find relief from the heat, socialize and even meet partners. He didn't seem to be convinced. Today, the irony produced by this unassuming body of water right outside one of UAE's largest malls would make my Spanish friend smile.

A certain strata of city goers have claimed this lake over time. On weekends, even during the summer, they resist the air-conditioned food courts, discount littered hallways and upbeat ambient music that malls in Dubai constantly seduce us with. When I shifted to Al Barsha1 in mid-2010, this lake wasn't as busy. Today it is a regular with the Al Barsha1 community, folks servicing the Mall, weekend visitors, marine species and migratory birds.

After visiting Dubai Municipality, Al Barsha offices and knocking on a few doors I get to meet Garry de la Pomerai—an individual who works with water. His team maintains the lake. Garry points out that Al Barsha has a series of three artificial lakes, all of which are interconnected. The first is a secluded water body in Al Barsha South, and the second is a public lake located within the Al Barsha Pond Park. These two lakes collect treated sewage water from the city for irrigation, which in turn is fed into our lake by the mall. As the last in this series

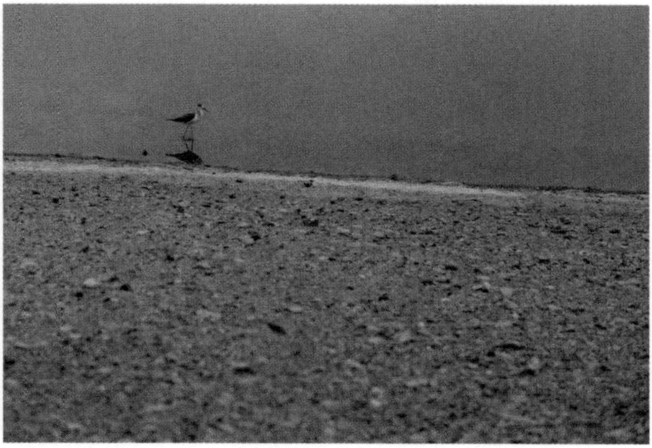

of lakes it has an exit pump from which water flows out to the sea. Storm water and excess water from the mall also collect here. Garry does not work on the other two lakes. To improve the quality of the water, his team regularly magnetize it through a number of pumps placed along the shore. There is marine life in the lake, which I understand was introduced by the municipality early on. Tilapia and minnows populate the lake, the former being invasive in nature. As this reservoir has been turned into a public lake, it demands constant upkeep. A maintenance team cleans the waterline of the lake every day, collecting marine carcasses, waste, and dirt. Garry clarifies that this lake is called "Emirates Mall Lake" on paper, and it would have been around since the mall was built.

* * *

It's 7am on a weekday. Hiron (name changed) is sprawled across on the well-watered green grass along the lake. Dressed in his work wear, he has finished his 8-hour night duty at the Kempinski, where for the last two years he has been polishing marble surfaces. Every day, after work he waits here for his bus to arrive. He enjoys the view of the lake, the open air, and the birds that hop around. I identify Hiron's colleague who is relaxing a few meters away, as he is wearing the same branded uniform. Trucks and large trailers have lined up outside the mall to feed enormous amounts of supplies. The drivers and porters wait by the lake for their turn to offload, while joggers lap and commuters rush towards the Metro station. It gets busier during lunch hours and evenings. One spots many mall employees stepping out to take a lunch or cigarette break through the day. One afternoon, I spot empty safety boots standing on the grass next to a man resting in his overalls. On another, I find a food delivery rider taking a break, while his motorcycle leans on its side stand. Located in the middle of the city, this lake is an easy-to-access oasis.

During the weekend, especially on Jummah (Friday), the lake has a different vibe. Stroll around the lake after 5pm and you will find a gathering every meter, ranging from small groups to a party of more than thirty. Animated conversations fill the air, at times punctuated by shrill laughter. Names are called out loudly, and snacks are passed around generously. As dusk descends the groups keep growing—welcome greetings await for friends who join in. Caps, sunglasses, and hats add to the picnic mood.

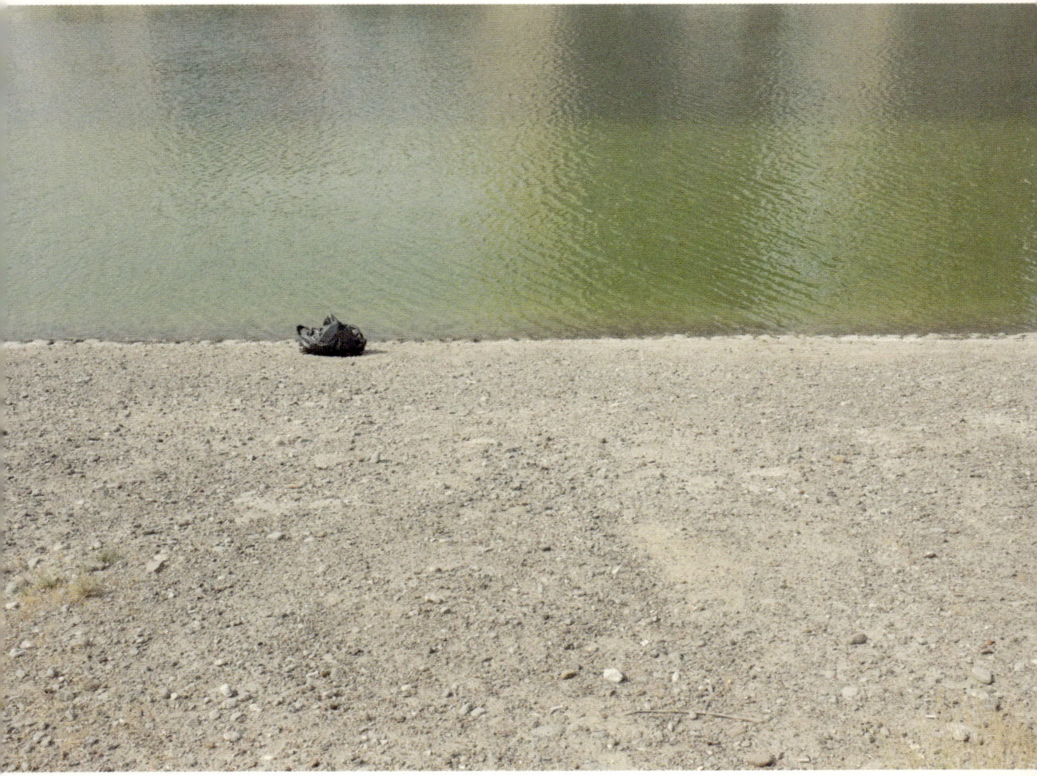

During the sweltering summers, paper plates turn into paper fans, while on a breezy day empty Styrofoam cups roll like tumbleweeds across the grass. Everybody is on the grass. Some are seated cross-legged, some stretch out their legs. Other lie down flat, or rest their bodies against each other. Non-productive hours can be so generative when it comes to variations in poses of relaxation. At some point I consider stopping work on this text piece and picking up pencil and paper to create figure studies of folks unwinding around the lake—but my drawing skills have waned since my art school days. How we can flex, twist and turn, specifically while not working, is something I will return to. I found it difficult to persuade people to be photographed. So, during my early study visits, I would sit close to a group and take notes on their activities, then return the following day and take a picture of the spot.

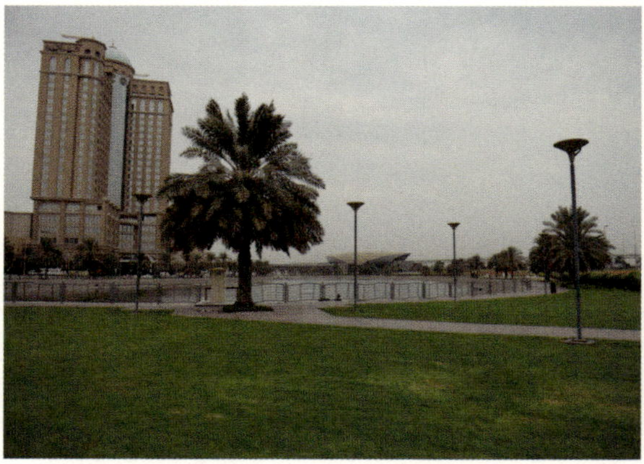

Late evening, Friday, May 2017. A group of 7 adults are seated in a circular fashion on the grass track running along the lake. Being a weekend, they are casually dressed. There are 4 men and 3 women. They are using newspapers as a tablecloth for their takeaway meals. Next to one of them is a laptop on which a vibrant-looking Bollywood film is playing on the bright screen. The group isn't showing any interest in the movie, which has become a mere backdrop to their conversation. The tunes from the film are overlaid by the sound of the cars speeding past on the E11 highway, which runs right behind them. Their footwear is grouped together at the edge, where the grass meets the pavement bricks. It seems like the tradition of leaving one's footwear at the door, before one enters a room.

Not satisfied with the outcome, I resorted to taking images from the vantage point of the Metro footbridge, which was a far more removed exercise. Eventually, I got to know one group and started discussing this piece I was trying to write. They invite me to join them. I am served a large portion of spaghetti. Fizzy drinks and snacks follow. Sitting amongst them I realize this is an active Whatsapp group that surfaces around the lake every weekend. A mix of nationalities, many are single or have families back home. They gather to enjoy a little picnic, finding solace and support amongst each other. Despite knowing the name of the lake now, I come back to my favourite question. One of them labels the lake as singing and dancing park. I learn that many prefer meeting here to other city parks, as playing music is permitted. One neighbouring group regularly brings a portable loudspeaker, from which dance music plays across the lake. It gets the folks to show off their moves, barefoot on the soft grass. After a few weekend visits I notice that there are hardly any children who join these gatherings. But there is a playful mood around. Some nudge each other's bodies, some enjoy long handshakes, while others run around a bit.

As the evening descends, the neon signs reflect sharply on the unruffled water surface. I have never hung around late enough to know how the weekend gatherings conclude or disperse. One unrelated story I picked up occurred in the early hours. A vehicle driven by a likely inebriated driver left one of the nearby hotels and crashed through the railings surrounding the lake, landing in the water. For once the lake wasn't static. Maybe the driver mistook the lake for the dance floor. The vehicle was fished out, but as a reminder a few of the railings are still missing, leaving an opening to the lake. One early morning I walk through the gap, down the angled concrete shore and get close to the waveless corniche. The water is a diluted swamp-green, slightly murky in parts. The negligible breeze produces faint ripples.

Minute bubbles surface and burst silently on the water surface. I look around. It is an immense volume of liquid. At the centre the lake is 2.5 meters deep. I stand there for a while, along with the lake. Week after week, 'Emirates Mall Corniche' has come to witness a lot, drawing so much, and so many.

3. RECREATE

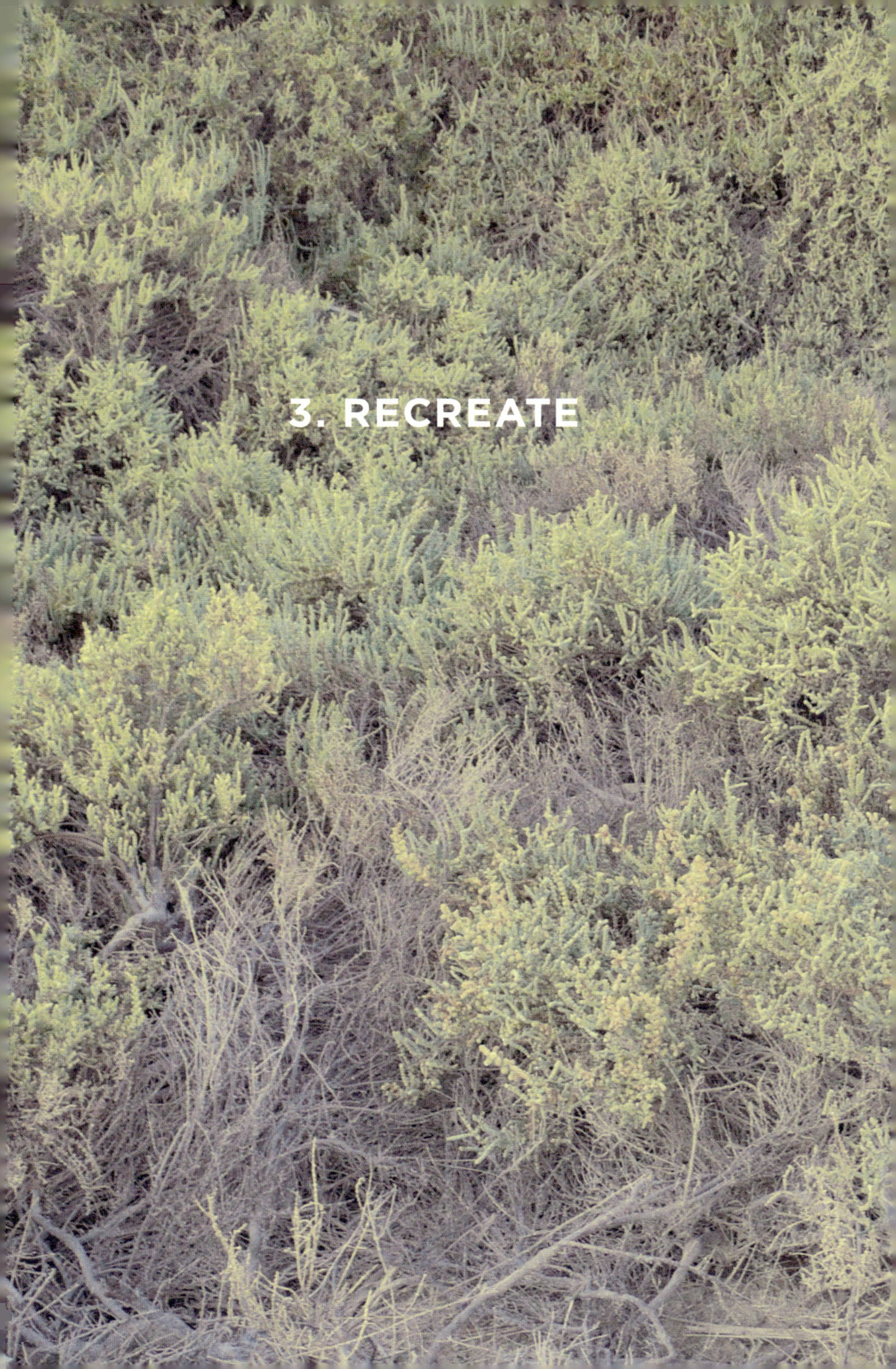

ECOLOGIES OF THE WET GULF

AHMAD MAKIA

I start my day with a singing exercise, usually to Varchavianka. The place I live in is small but has very generous and welcoming windows. I don't actually live there. It is more of a hideout. I am from Dubai; mostly in the ways that I can be. Friends call me by my last name. I am a biogeographer.

What troubles me about Dubai is that with it I am never sure if things can ever be dear to me or if things just become magnified in importance with the passing of time. But no matter, that's a contemplative question I pose for anyone longing for anything. That's not why the city matters to me. It does because I love things here and I love people here.

But please allow me to tell you other things about Dubai. I have an unhealthy and sometimes awkward relationship with our desert; as much as the city does itself. I think we need to abandon it. I mean if you sit and imagine the city, you'll notice how *Urban* Dubai is mainly about deserting the desert. All of us are here to resist it. Here to make sure we do not belong to it; to Nature, whatever that may mean. So I think it is more likely that we will collectively drift, hopefully

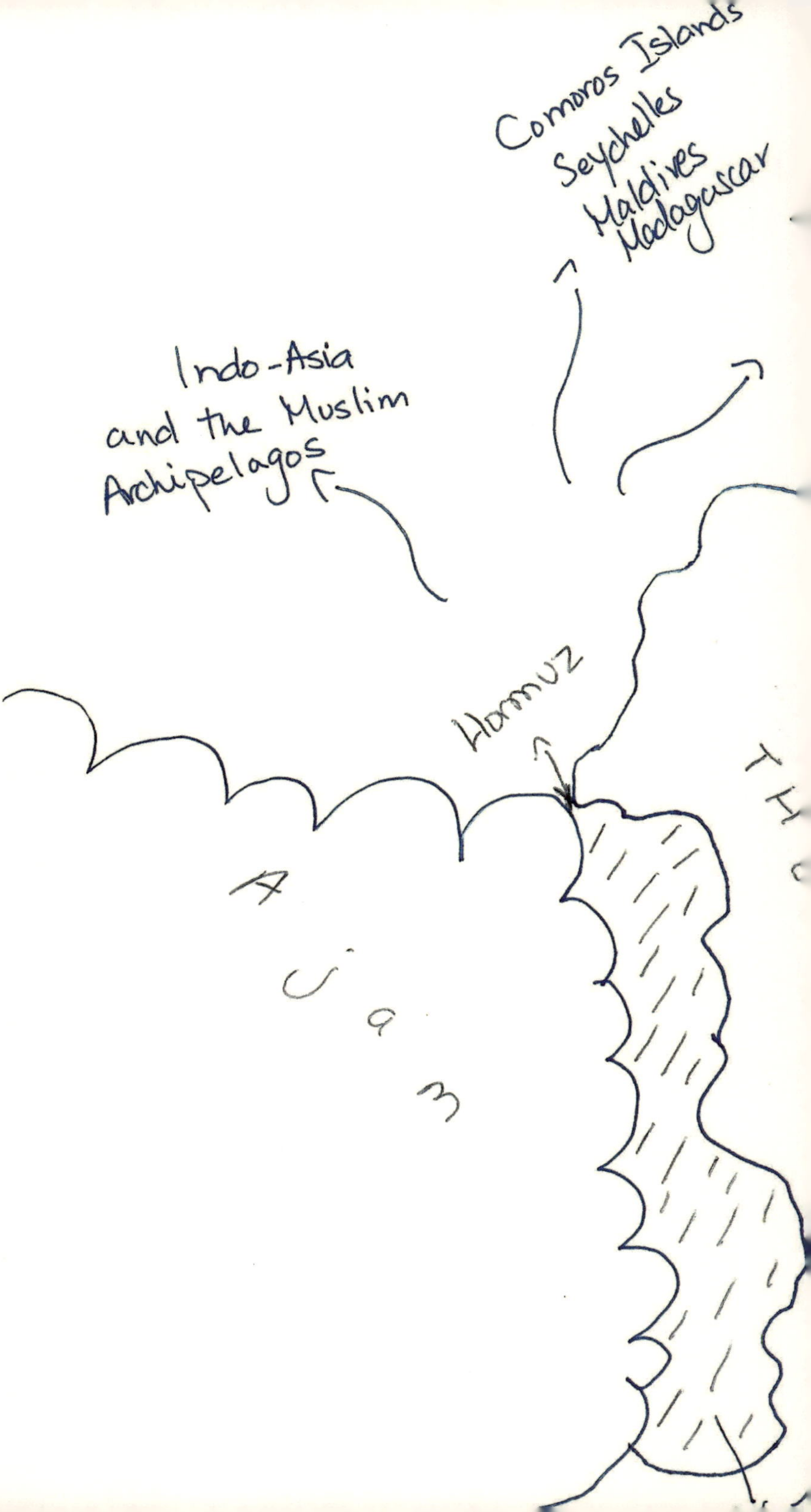
Comoros Islands
Seychelles
Maldives
Madagascar
Indo-Asia
and the Muslim
Archipelagos
Hormuz
Ajam

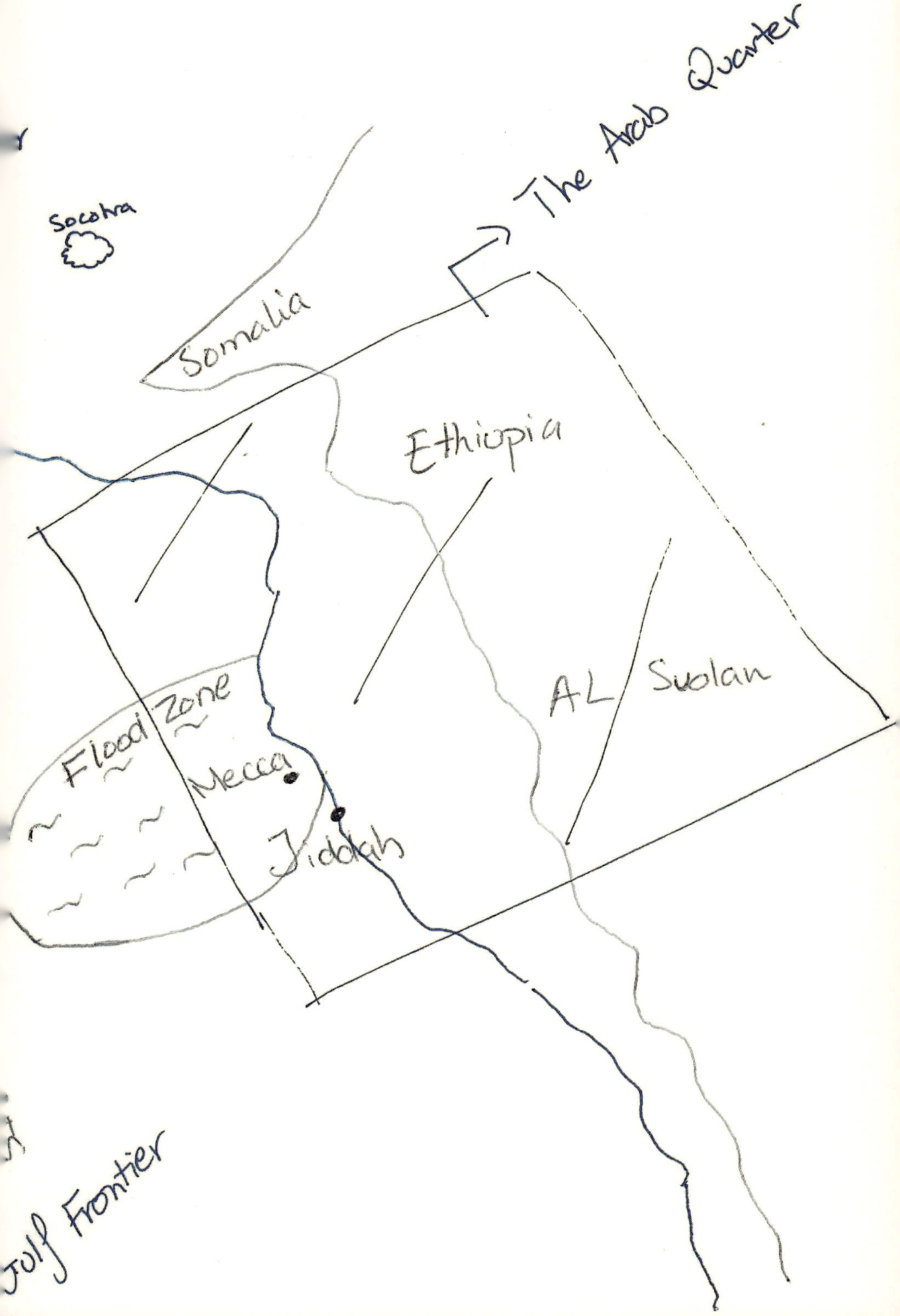
Socotra
The Arab Quarter
Somalia
Ethiopia
AL Sudan
Flood Zone
Mecca
Jiddah
Frontier

towards the coast, away from the desert, rather than just fly away to Mars in 2022. Right? The latter seems a lot more belligerent. So, yes, I think I've found where we are going.

Actually, let me correct myself. I don't think I've found where we are going but I think I've found where we've always stayed. Let me tell you a story I've been investigating: I think the whole history of clandestine desert people is a myth. Rather, I think people in Dubai—and across the Gulf and much all over the world—are actually aquatic species. If you look at the hydrological maps of Dubai—irrigation, sewers, pools, lakes, fountains, islands, creeks—they overshadow, in both density and scale, actual built space in the city. Even more pervasive than the highway or parking or sand!

I wonder if we have lived any other way. During the oil survey exploration era of the 50s, 60s, and 70s, many inland infrastructural developments required a sedentary population for plant operations. Early settled towns were initially staffed with 2 to 3 people (Who? We don't know.) and they today populate the corridor of Emirati desert towns, which act as various processing nodes for the infrastructures which extract, refine, and export national oil. We can call this the federation of *Emirati Urbanism*. Aha! The absence of 'deep', i.e. inland, urbanization in the Emirates means human migration and presence began at the coast then into land, in contrast to what would be the savannah into the bay. So this allegiance to the desert is dumbfounded. It turns out that I don't have anything to do with camels or dunes. Rather, Gulf ecology evolves from phylum, to amphibian, to reptile, to mammal.

Secondly, some research has suggested that the Peninsula sits atop a floodplain, which now might be considered the most ancient submerged civilization. These histories, in addition to all of our public sweating and perspiring, must be preparations, maybe even indications, for some kind of deluge or flood, right? So, no, I don't think we are destined for some dry place, or that we came from one either.

Maybe we are the beginning of the human species; maybe we are even a different kind of species, an amphibian or something. What if we are soggy? I don't think Dubai is only a 'late capitol' experiment: it is a weird hydrological existence too. Similar to Mumbai and Amsterdam. All three of these urban histories indicate that the occupation of the environment is a factor underlying the tendency of living things to expand. In fact, throughout my life I've been sitting around looking through Gulf history and now I've realized everything we have been told about this story is wrong. People are looking for old things, old people, old fossils, but you'll find none of it because you are looking through a literary and imaginary terrain called "the desert". It is an ever-present reality in the city. Everyone is constantly addressed to it through vocation, lifestyle, and perception!

But you can get away. Don't be alarmed. That's why you have my shop. From here, the city appears like an instantaneous emergence from the water. You can be in the city without all that nature; which we think of as mute, deaf, and discreet. Without the desert, it becomes unnecessary to pickle and preserve memories.

Ok, so let's go to my shop. It is about 15 nautical miles north of Port Rashid. Closer to the Bur Dubai side, just before the mouth of the creek. I sell fruit: Different kinds of oranges. Only some are sweet, most are bitter. I also sell slices of loaf cake, vanilla ice cream, Marlboro cigarettes, and Lipton tea. Here, all types of transients and travelers swing by. Most of them are waiting. Actually, no, they're queuing, and as they queue they somehow *lose* themselves, maybe even kill themselves a little. They say, do, and feel the most absurd things. In my shop, I am serving them, yes, but I spend most of my time observing them. I guess it is a little perverse of me. Do you think so? Could I speak to you of what I've noted?

The other day a man and a woman were waiting. Maybe they are married, maybe they are in a partnership, maybe they betray each other, maybe they are siblings. I considered all these things. The woman was speaking, but the man out of deference to her, was not contradicting her.

West Asia | Gulf Frontier
Desalination Plants

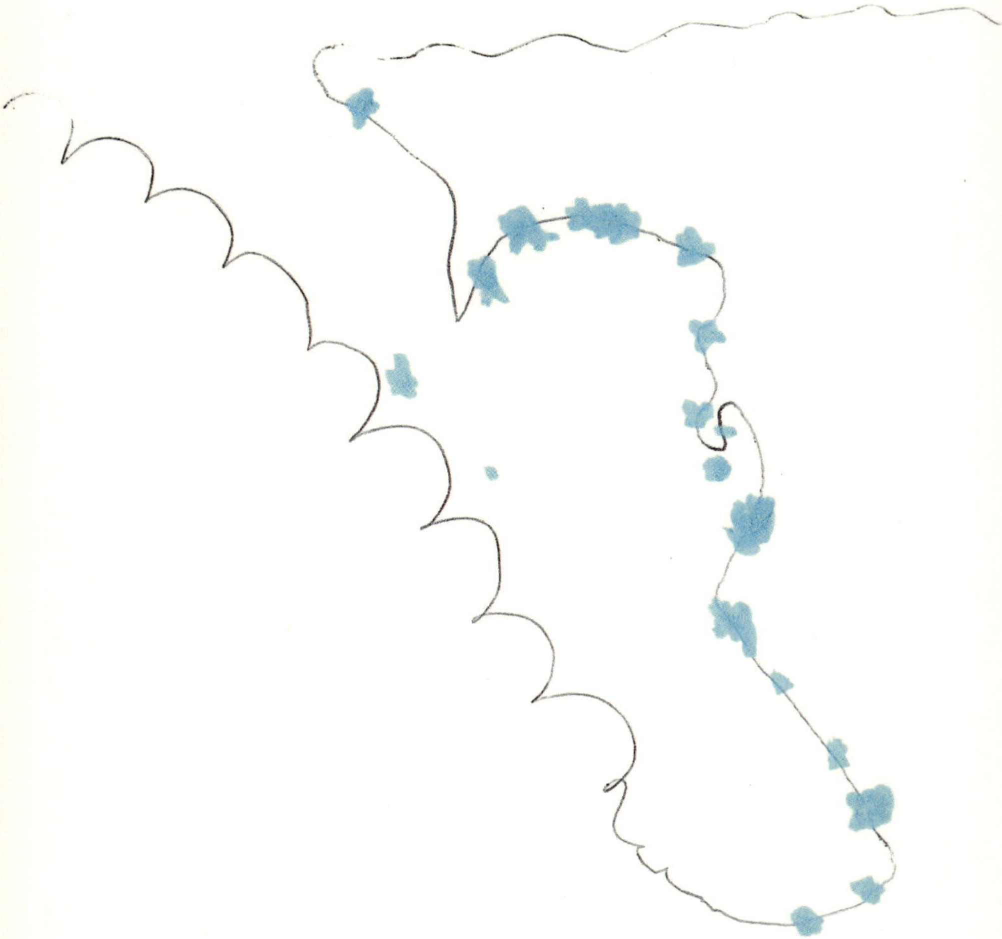

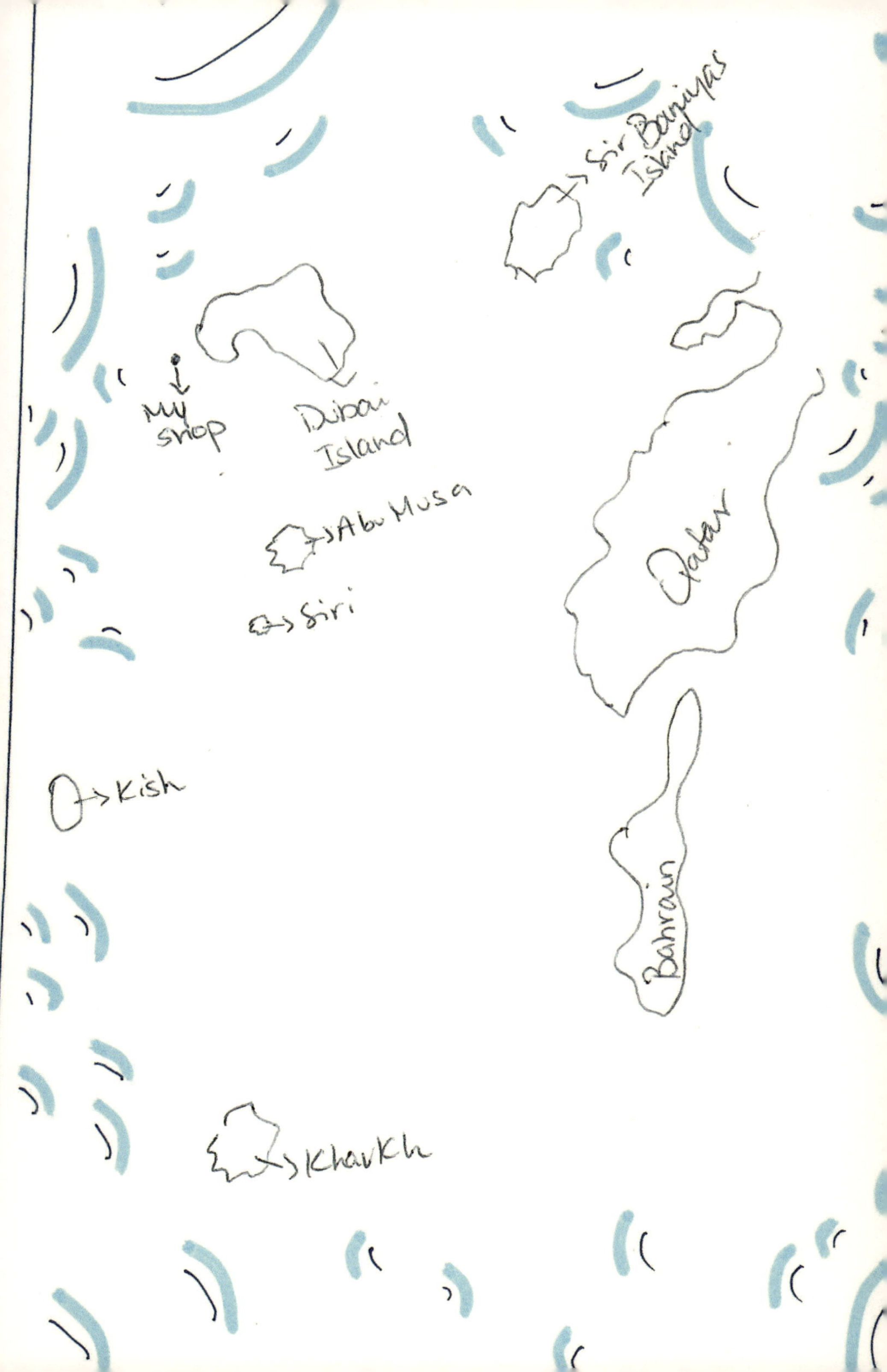
Sir Baniyas Island
My shop
Dubai Island
Abu Musa
Siri
Qatar
Kish
Bahrain
Kharkh

Her expressions were devastating. It was tense. I felt like she was avenging a kind of well-known misery. It bothered—actually, it intrigued—me that I couldn't see the *wwwhhole* of what she was looking at. So I began to imagine her. For her, one must have subtlety and finesse, a little hide-and-seek in wardrobe, speech, and presentation. Something with a good finish, packaged, adept with plot, language, but not necessarily character or situation. One must have broad knowledge—not necessarily good knowledge—of the world and its human affairs.

The man had a style and in it he was fixed. Or transfixed. When he sits and looks at himself, he thinks he is so much more than everything around him. This he makes especially clear to the woman by aggressing her. And she looks at the aggression and dismisses it, excuses it even, but he still won't give in. Who's responsible for this dynamic? You see, you get to exercise such stories at my shop everyday.

Ok, next. The other day a traveler told me he thinks Dubai is gaudy. When I prodded, I was disappointed by his remarks and observations. He, "a creative", believed that most of the things in Dubai shouldn't be there. "I hate you," I quickly reacted. Now, even louder, I went: "I hate you." You have no rigor or responsibility for the ways you've been given, which are more than generous. Maybe your encrusted frames limit you. Who's granted you this title of moral arbiter? You come to places like Dubai and snub the profanity of our limitless and poisoned behavior. Like everything there shouldn't be there; like it shouldn't be ours. Like we are undeserving of it. As if other places were naturally endowed with whatever they are today. Like they are not monstrous continuations of global exploitation, power, culture, knowledge, and information accumulated through the pursuit of many other limitless ambitions.

Anyway, I love my shop, I am sure you can tell. Sometimes, in my shop, I feel like the whole city is playing itself out inside; right now, at this very moment. To be frank with you, you probably shouldn't even go to the city. You probably shouldn't even go to the city because there's probably nothing there. We've polluted it with too many things. Come to my shop...things seem clearer there or with greater meaning. Meanwhile, in the city, all you do is accrue greater meaning for the geography but you never possess the geography itself. And so the city, sometimes, won't make sense to you because it'll feel like a whirlpool of dislocated spirits.

Ahhhh, apologies, I went diffuse, but you know what they say, sometimes you need to go a long way to come back a short distance. So, yes, I have a shop, my marine project via Dubai, and there I study Dubai's seabed. Of course, most of our halophila stipulacea has been entirely displaced and depleted because of all the land-reclaiming projects occurring across the Gulf. Imagine that Bahrain is now trying to reinject the sea with halophila because they have destroyed years worth of their fishing industry. What this illustrates is that the Gulf coast is the terrain experiencing the effects of globalization, via organism displacement and migration, not the cities. Only recently did I discover that there are greater families of reef sharks than initially thought, which means they are over-reproducing. Who's going to give time and thought to learn from their systems? Secondly, I do not have a great knowledge of marine biology, but let me tell you I was able to identify a variety of schistosomes. One of my theories is the Dubai Creek expansion project, or *The Great Leak,* is in fact marine engineering for diluting and recirculating the high concentrations of brine discharged by the Gulf's many desalination plants.

So...what these fluctuations are suggesting is that the future terrain of the Gulf looks like it will need to respond directly to the occurrences of its sea-self, especially since it has nowhere else to go. And so, my shop evolved to also become a centre of awareness about the marine life of Dubai and the Gulf. Along with some peers, we are proposing a marine citizenship co-op where different emissaries are responsible for rehabilitating and transforming existing areas into desirable ecosystems.

Our logic is that since there is no desert and the bay is over-developed, over-populated, and polluted, the Gulf city is dissolving into a "wet" state: Undergoing a process of dilution, an archipelagic shifting. So future Gulf civility must also live with its immediate waters and along this wet frontier. So, for you, dear traveler, the only way to find out where you want to be in this configuration is at my shop; there you'll learn of where you need to be. You might also find out why.

You'll find things because my shop carries a kind of instruction manual from the city, the part brimming with emotion. In this city, we don't have old gods, old things. There is no fleshless, romantic view. No one wants to go back to the desert. It doesn't look like anyone was even there. We play dress-up here but for different motives, not to keep some nostalgic fantasy alive. We are only emerging. I like to imagine that we are emerging as these non-human forms—extraterrestrial, most probably aquatic species. We can sit around and talk about all this at my shop. Actually, you are only welcome to my shop if you want to talk about this. Otherwise, you are more than welcome to the city.

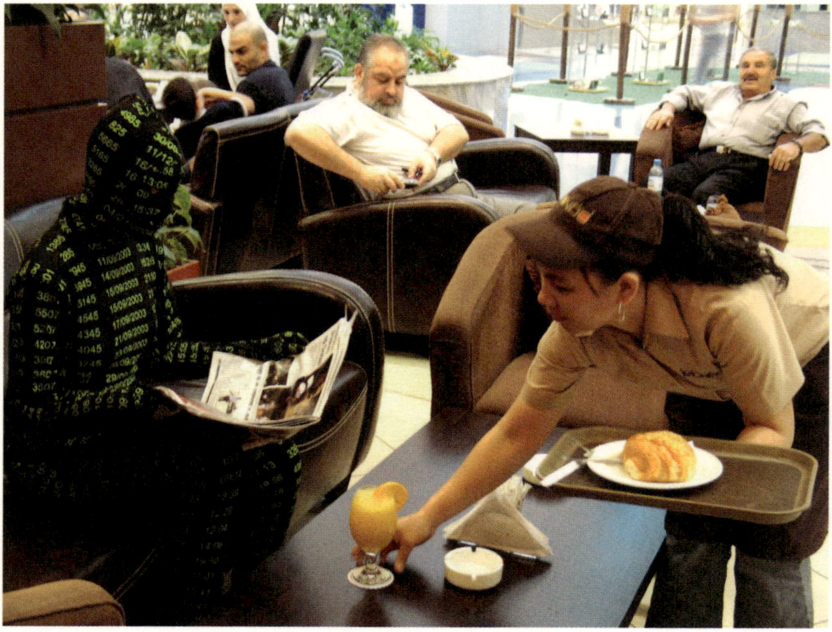

AUTOBIOGRAPHY: A CREATIVE ACT

EBTISAM ABDUL AZIZ

Art has long contributed to the cohesion and coordination between the fundamental directions in civilization and the evolution and history of the city. Modernism was marked by a multitude of possibilities for extracting truth through technical processes, and so art was no longer purely a pursuit of aesthetic expression. Instead, it employed aesthetics in the development of philosophy and modern thinking as a way of understanding oneself and the world. The artistic work now reflects diversity, pluralism, collective participation, open knowledge and creativity that combines culture and vision of the society. We see this in the rebellion of the contemporary artist and through it develop an understanding of their relationship with place and the role of art in initiating discussions about its relationship with political, social, economical and human aspects.

Each city arguably has its own art that has distinctive features, its own way of expressing knowledge, ethics, fears, development, and acceleration. This could explain, or at the very least express the strong relationship that I and perhaps other artists sense between artistic practice and place. My practice is only evident when read through the traces of my everyday life and was inevitably influenced by cities I grew up in. The forms and in the materials, from photographs, videos, installations, numerics and geometry, have been adopted for different purposes. Some attempt to document the acceleration in urban and social development, others offer a way to present miniature schemes for large environmental projects.

The Emirate of Sharjah, particularly during the time when I joined the Emirates Fine Arts Society (EFAS) had an immense impact on my artistic education and refined my conceptual interests. The EFAS played a fundamental role in the establishment and advancement of fine arts in the Emirates and formed a culture in its own right. It facilitated generations of new artistic directions, and ensured the growth and incubation of artists and cultural thinkers. It shaped a unique identity for the emirate of Sharjah, centered on heritage, arts and culture in the region.

In "Autobiography 2007", I documented landmarks in Sharjah as facts, events, opinions, and behavior as they pertain to my relationships with the place and the people that inhabit it. It was an attempt to combine documentary and theatrical aspects of the place and took on the form of a play that reflects human aspects of the society in which we live. I showed the individual as insignificant in the middle of a consumerist society with objectives of profitability and material gain.

Motion in the video together with photographs provided a scene of intentional movement, the same one we perform on a daily basis, though I presented it in a contradictory way to the reality of class stratification. The performance was intended as a critique of the reality of the consumer world. It depicted the changes in human behavior, how we have been reduced to mere numbers, the artist's body simply a familiar icon or a well-known brand to be printed on t-shirts or billboards. Like all other performances the artist's body in the focal point where the physical and the social component meet.

The performance took place largely in the markets that define the Art and Heritage district along the creek, attracting new and regular visitors and consumers. I witnessed a collective curiosity: children

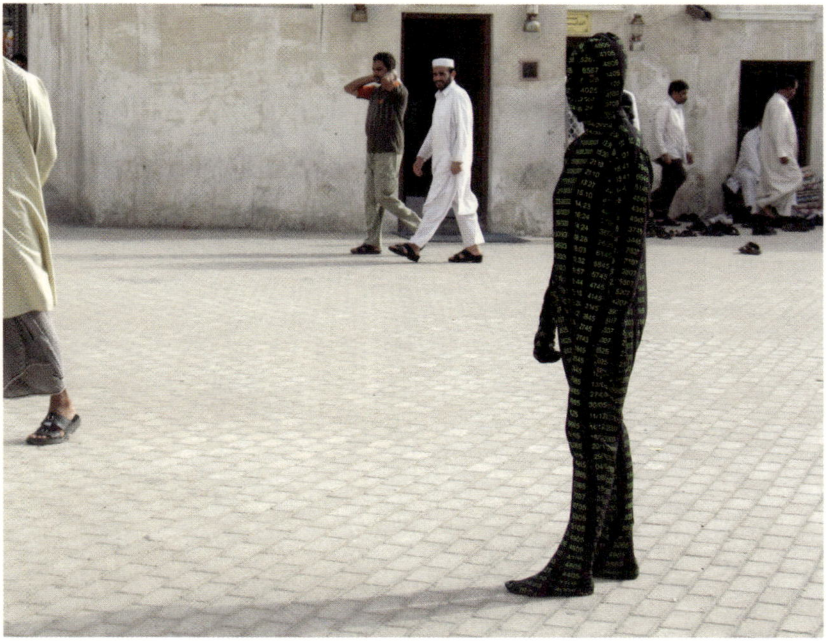

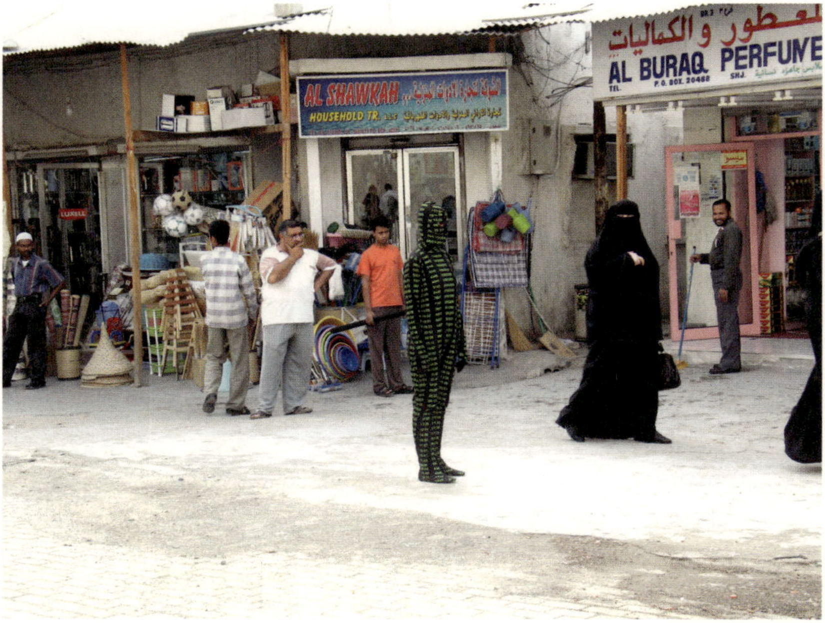
AL SHAWKAH
HOUSEHOLD TR.
AL BURAQ PERFUME

insisted on talking to me, others wore puzzled smiles on their faces. Some called me Spider Woman. As I continued the performance in a restaurant in a mall, I overheard debates over interpretation, invoking dialog on the importance of the human subject and what it means to be a member of society. When I wore the uniform, carrying my own autobiography in the streets of Sharjah, it became a symbol of abstract things in the context of the current era: fast, successive, accumulating events stored in our memory.

Certain characteristics of particular historic pockets in the Emirates have provided an energy and stimulation vital to artistic response. When I was an artist-in-residence, I spent three months working from a studio in the historic Al Fahidi district in Dubai. It felt like time travel. I found myself quickly immersed in research using old maps as a reference to trace the place, constantly searching for both material and intangible histories. I did not care about tourists' preoccupation with taking pictures. I was busy searching for scents and smells from the past, circling the relics of the old wall and and the stories to which it could testify.

The Emirates, its urban history and the diversity of city dwellers provide an environment in which artists can flourish, and be fully aware of the present. These cities call for documentation as well as a new vocabulary. How are these places contemplated about? What affects do they have? What changes are possible or likely? These questions can be tackled by the artist within the context of their practice. The process is regularly serialized in events, showing new subjects first, then new content, and finally the new forms of objects that appear. Most of them are things we see on a daily basis, but can be read in the context of both its charged present and an equally energized past which lies within reach.

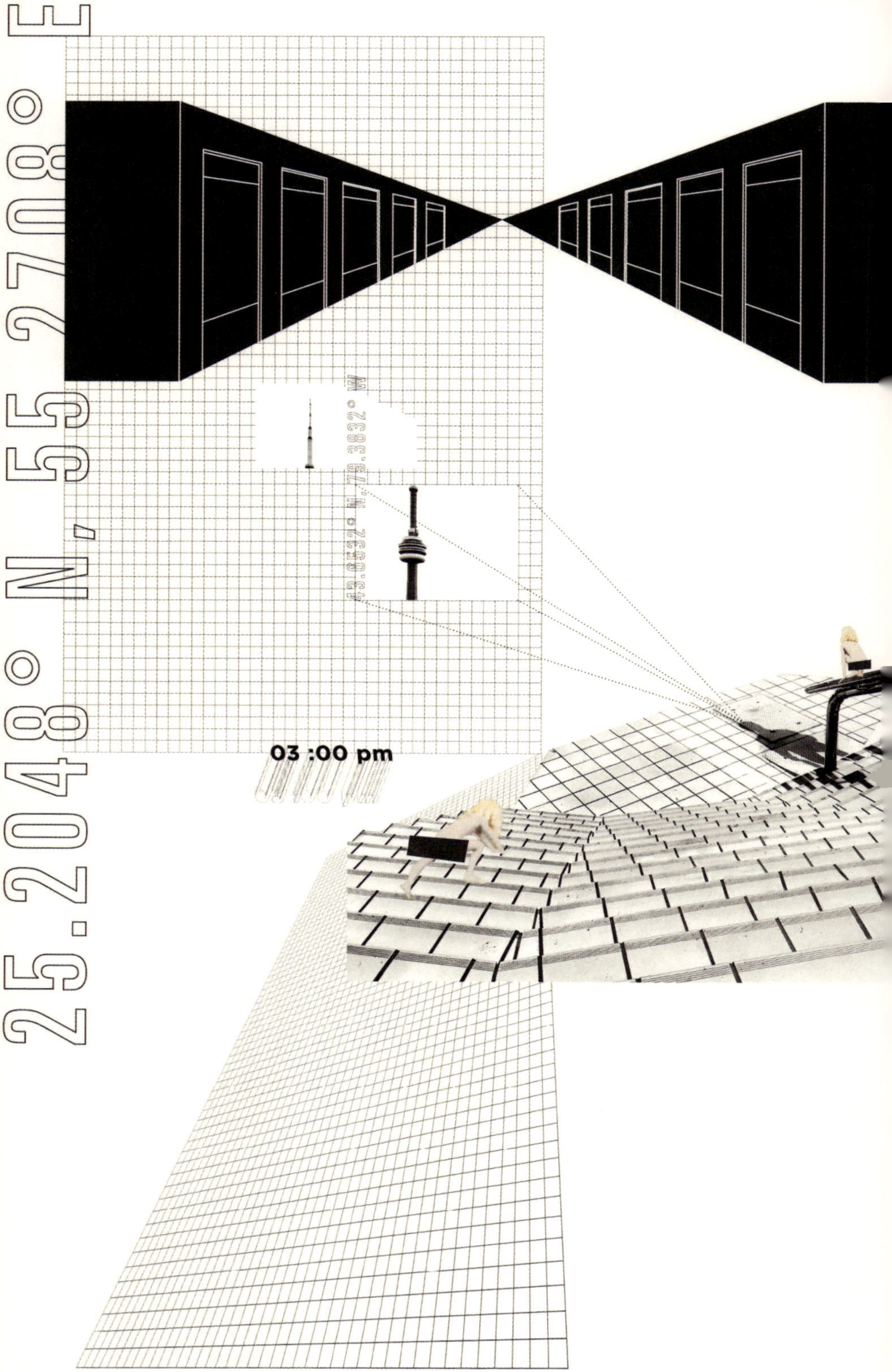
25.2048° N, 55.2708° E
43.6532° N, 79.3832° W
03 :00 pm

OVER THE HILLS AND FAR AWAY

JOOBIN BEKHRAD
ILLUSTRATION: MAHYA SOLTANI

Ringlets of smoke, splotches of gold. It was around three in the afternoon, that most lethargic of hours, when shadows flit by on gummy sidewalks and nausea rears its ugly head. Eyeing myself in a cracked mirror in the gold souk, I tried to ignore the rumbling in my belly and the godawful outfit I'd chosen. Who wears white on white? I tried to get Mum's attention, looking at her askance every now and then, but to no avail. I just wanted to go back to the flat, play the Led Zeppelin record I'd bought the other day (why had they covered up those nymphs with magic marker?), and stare outside at the wide blue expanse through Aref's binoculars, thinking about her all the while. What would I say to her? I hadn't figured that out yet. Just as I was penning the words in my head, I heard Mamak's heels clacking behind me. *Ey Khoda*, I thought, wishing Mum would hurry up. I didn't feel like talking to anyone, least of all that dolt Mamak. I feigned a smile as she lit yet another Virginia Slim between her painted lips, sucking in the sight of its burning tip with pleasure. "Handsome boy," she said. I blushed as bright as those embers then, not knowing what to say in response, only thinking about her. *Handsome, huh? Maybe there's hope for me yet!*

I didn't want to go back home, but I did. I didn't want to leave that city by the sea and the sounds of Amr Diab, but I had to: I'd found a purpose. I had to go back and tell her everything. I didn't care what she'd say in response, if anything at all; things simply couldn't go on the way they had been. She, whose face always appeared to me against hues of deepest red, was my only hope in the soul-destroying suburbs of Toronto. If it hadn't been for her, I might have stayed there, in Dubai, which was slowly growing on me, Berjer Kenj and all; but I couldn't go back looking the way I did; no, that was no way for a lover-boy to present himself. I needed some new clothes, and decided I wanted to look just like Jimmy Page at Knebworth in 1980, before he'd seemingly showered in his blue button-down shirt and white trousers. Don't ask me why.

The next day, I told a noxious-smelling Mamak that I'd be back in a second. I left her to enjoy her cigarettes and tepid Americano while I went to see what I could find in a nearby boutique. It was then and there that everything came crashing down upon my bony little self. Trying on all those posh-looking shirts and trousers beneath the sickening draft of an air conditioner in a changing room, I felt an overwhelming heaviness, an anxiety I couldn't explain, like the ones still brought on every day by the hour of three. In a couple of days, I would say goodbye to Daddy again, and travel to the other end of the world to waste away in my teenage nightmare. What was waiting for me back in snow-covered Toronto? More cautionary tales by sicko teachers, more mind-numbing essays, more talk about how I should have the whole, wide world worked out in my head, and... *her*. Would she want me as I wanted her? What if I scared her silly, as I'd often done to other girls? "For God's sake, don't go up to girls and say you love them," my grandmother always told me when I was a little boy. What other choice did I have, though? Fastening the buckle on the last hole of my belt, and noticing how soft my fingers had become since I'd left my shiny black Stratocaster behind, I resolved to tell her—no matter what.

Later that evening, as Pagey played the blues, I began scrawling down the words I'd say to her—somewhere, somehow—on an old notepad. I thought I'd nailed it, and afterwards went to dinner at the Marina, as heady as I was nervous. Some of Aref's relatives from London were there, and one guy was banging on to me and some other kids my age about how he was going to score big as a banker. The very thought was making the odious little creature grin like a madman, and I soon stopped pretending to pay attention and let my gaze wander off to the waves before me, mottled with light. Lost in a daze, my Persian heart close to bursting with excitement and apprehension, I felt my father's fingers squeeze my nose. "*Joon-e baba*," he said with affection. How could I leave Daddy and the stars on the waves? Would that she and I could have been there that evening, she not against burning crimson, but the night sky, and I the giddiest lad in all the world; but baby lived far away, and the sticks were beckoning once again. I didn't know what would happen—only that I would soon return to the sparkling city by the sea where I'd realised, for the first time, that I was [truly] in love.

LETTERS FROM THE PORT

LEN CHAPMAN

30th April 1971

Dear Mother in Law,

We arrived safely in Dubai and are starting to settle in. Our flight from New Zealand was long and tiring. The children are good.

It was strange flying into Bahrain—despite having lived there for four years, it seemed remarkably different upon return. Gray Mackenzie (my new employer) greeted us. We had some rest then boarded a Gulf Aviation flight to Dubai via Dammam and Doha. We disembarked in Dubai. Only passengers to do so! The remaining passengers continued to Oman. Formalities were easy—two uniformed people behind an old wooden desk on the tarmac nodded us through. My new boss met us and drove us (in his Australian Holden!) to our new home. J was very quiet. First words she uttered were "What have we done?" I must admit I had my doubts too. Lots of sand, few modern buildings, very little road traffic.

Our new home is a brand new three-bedroom apartment in Al Owais Building on Al Fahidi Street. Nice view of Dubai Creek but noisy in the evenings. Nearby local cafés are packed with men watching Indian movies on TVs. At the road junction outside our apartment block they've installed Dubai's first official traffic lights. Drivers sound their horns if they think traffic lights take too long to change. Lights turn off at night and are back at 6am—so we don't need an alarm clock.

There's a small grocery store around the corner—KM Brothers—has room for two customers at a time no more. They sell mostly frozen meat, pickled eggs or powdered milk and other tinned foods. Surprisingly the powdered milk comes from New Zealand. A bread van parks each evening on an open sandy plot nearby. The bread is fresh and warm but sells out quickly. We do have an excellent fruit and vegetable market nearby. And there's the not so appealing meat and fish markets.

Workwise it's exciting to see Port Rashid being built from scratch and it's a unique opportunity to play a part in getting it up and running. I am optimistic about this move. Having said that, I've not had much to do since I got here. In the meantime I am looking after a high-speed offshore launch for our parent

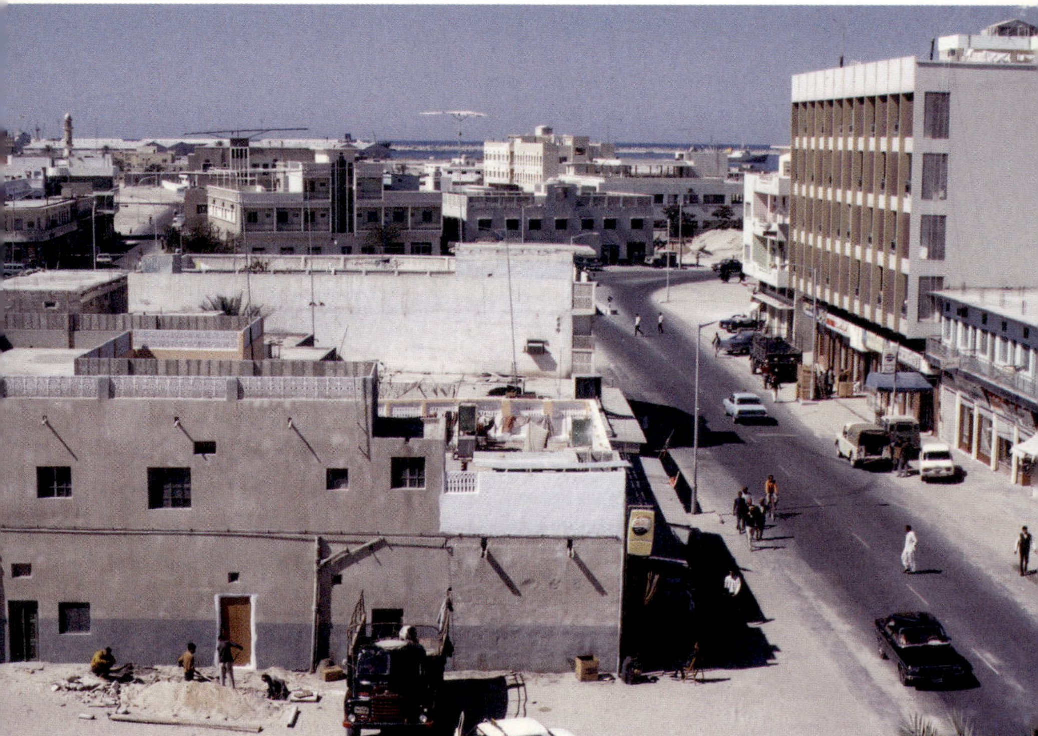

company. Its engines were worn out and required rebuilding. I gave the job to a recommended workshop on the basis that they had a modern engine test bed, only to find out later that the workshop owner was a gold smuggler. The modern test bed was put in place to check his dhow's engines before gold smuggling runs to India.

I'll post another aerogramme soon.
Len

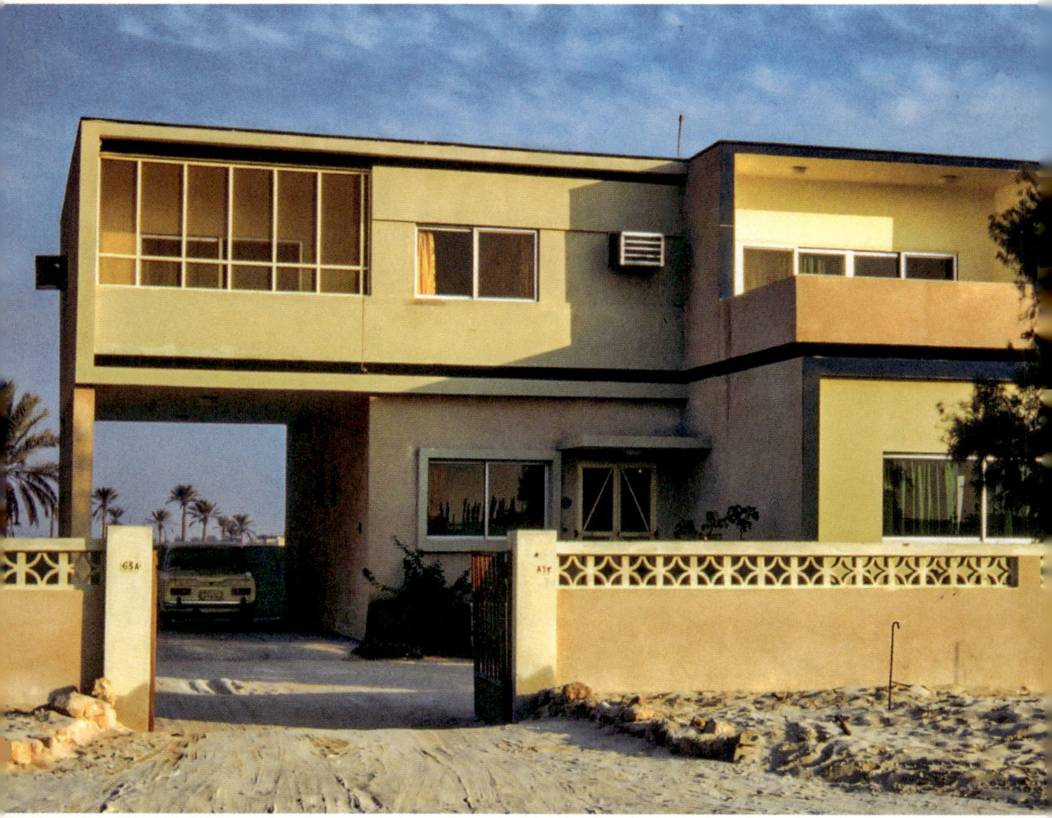

19th November 1985

Dear Son,

Last weekend we were woken up in early hours by a loud explosion. The Gulf War had come to our door! A ship was attacked with rocket propelled grenades off the Jumeirah Coast. There is an upside to this conflict—Dubai Drydocks is now busy repairing damaged ships.

Sunnier updates. I'm now on the Golf Committee at Dubai Country Club. We are working to organise a visit of UK's top golfers to play Pro Am matches at DCC's Sand Golf Course. They're sponsored by British Caledonian Airline and they'll be put up as guests in club members' homes for the week they're here. I'm still playing squash, and well, it has changed a lot since I first played at that sole open-air court at Port Rashid. There are courts popping up all over the city and we've had top players such as Geoff Hunt and Jonah Barrington regularly playing in Dubai.

There's quite a bit constantly changing in the city. The mains sewage installation has finally finished across Dubai. No more Cesspits. Sewage Works produces "black stuff" which is a fantastic fertiliser. Even I can make things grow with it. Everyone is using it here in their gardens and beyond so Dubai is really starting to go green. Water supply is getting worse though. I installed a pump to try and get more water from the mains. Everyone is doing the same thing so no real improvement. Power supply on the other hand has improved. No more blackouts! The new gas turbine power station at Jebel Ali is making a huge difference and the old diesel generator power station in Deira is to be shut down.

We will be moving to a new house soon. Our current house is starting to crumble. Apparently, it was built using unwashed beach sand so is now suffering the same issues as the Clock Tower. Clock Tower was renovated but suffice to say our house will not be. The new complex has its own clubhouse, swimming pool and sports facilities plus a café. So, no complaints.

I'll write again soon.

Dad

10th September 1995

Dear Son,

How's the new job? Enjoying London? You will be amused at what I'm about to tell you.

As you know, until government merged Port Rashid and Jebel Ali Port, I'd held the same job for twenty years before becoming Technical Director of the new Ports Organisation. Well, last Monday I was told Ali is to take over my position (you remember Ali—he was one of the trainees we took on in 1984. He's been my deputy for the past few years). I was to take over Corporate Planning. Two days later I was told to take over Information Services as well. 3 jobs in 3 days—beat that.

Do you remember my telling you about the private floor in Jebel Ali Port's Marine Control Tower? I took a visitor to see it. Harbormaster pulled a face. He said we may or may not get access but we could try. We did try. When we knocked on the door it opened—just slightly—and we saw half a face. After a brief explanation, we were let in. The old sofa where Sheikh Rashid would sit and gaze out over Jebel Ali port and his Free Zone was gone. Instead there were three camp beds and three American sailors equipped with binoculars, telescopes and radios. The USS Nimitz was in Jebel Ali Port and the sailors were watching out for any possible seaborne threats.

Our new house is great. Just as we moved in, the landlord spread chicken manure over the garden (he has a farm in Dhaid). He claims we could put a stick on the ground and it will grow. What he didn't warn us about were flies—hordes of them. It's amazing to see we now have bananas and paw paw growing in our garden. No more sand and tamarisk trees!

Well, that's all for now. Take care,
Dad

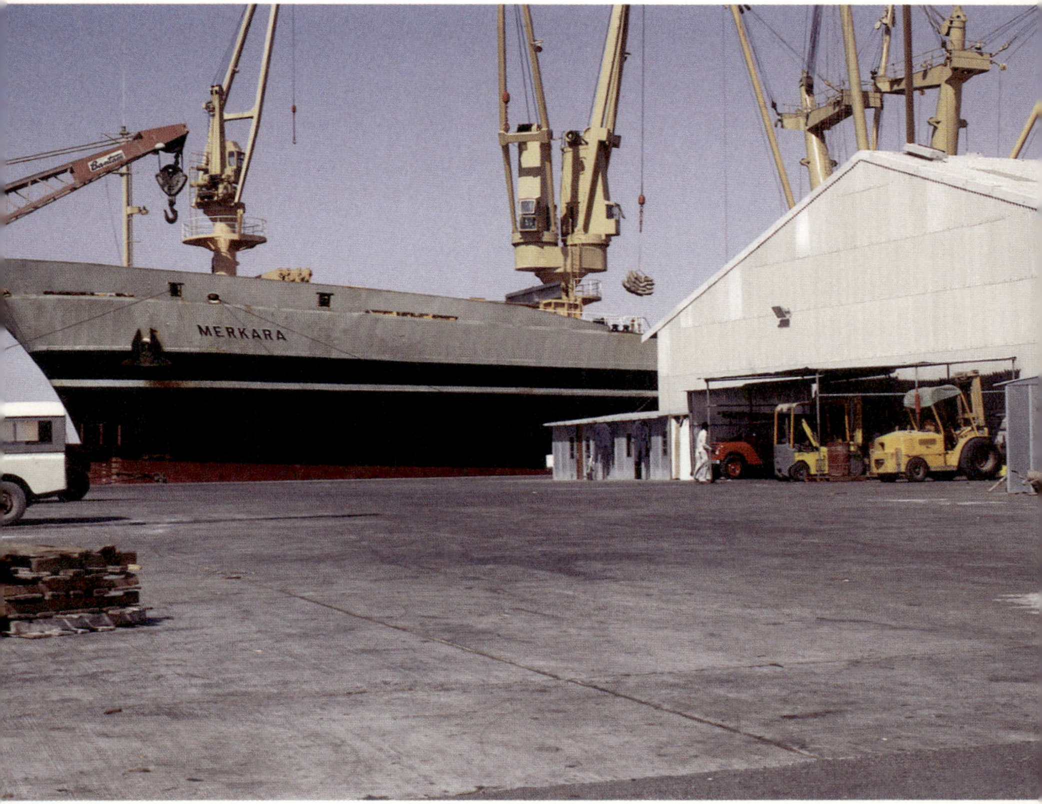
MERKARA
Bantam

2nd June 2003

Dear Son,

How's the new job? Settled in to life in Brisbane? Some surprising news from my end. I am retiring. My resignation is submitted so now I wait for things to happen.

I actually expected to retire three years ago before being moved to Dubai Customs. A marine engineer solving problems for a Customs Department. I remember that day the Director General had called a meeting of his managers in their conference room to introduce me. The room resembled the United Nations—a huge room with an enormous U-shaped "podium" behind which sat fifty managers, each with their own microphone. DG and myself sat at the top of the "U" and each of us gave a short speech, both received in silence. I then left and went to my new office, which is also huge—ballroom size in fact.

Port Rashid is to close soon. Its container traffic is being moved to Jebel Ali Port. Cities no longer want ports on their doorstep and heavy trucks with containers on their streets; the container terminals are moving out of town and city ports are closing. The closing of Port Rashid will be the end of an era and an appropriate moment for me to leave Dubai, don't you think?

We fly to Brisbane next Thursday on Emirates. Thirty-two years ago, we arrived at Dubai's first airport terminal. It had just one gate. I'm told our Emirates flight will depart from Gate 297!

See you soon in Brisbane!
Dad

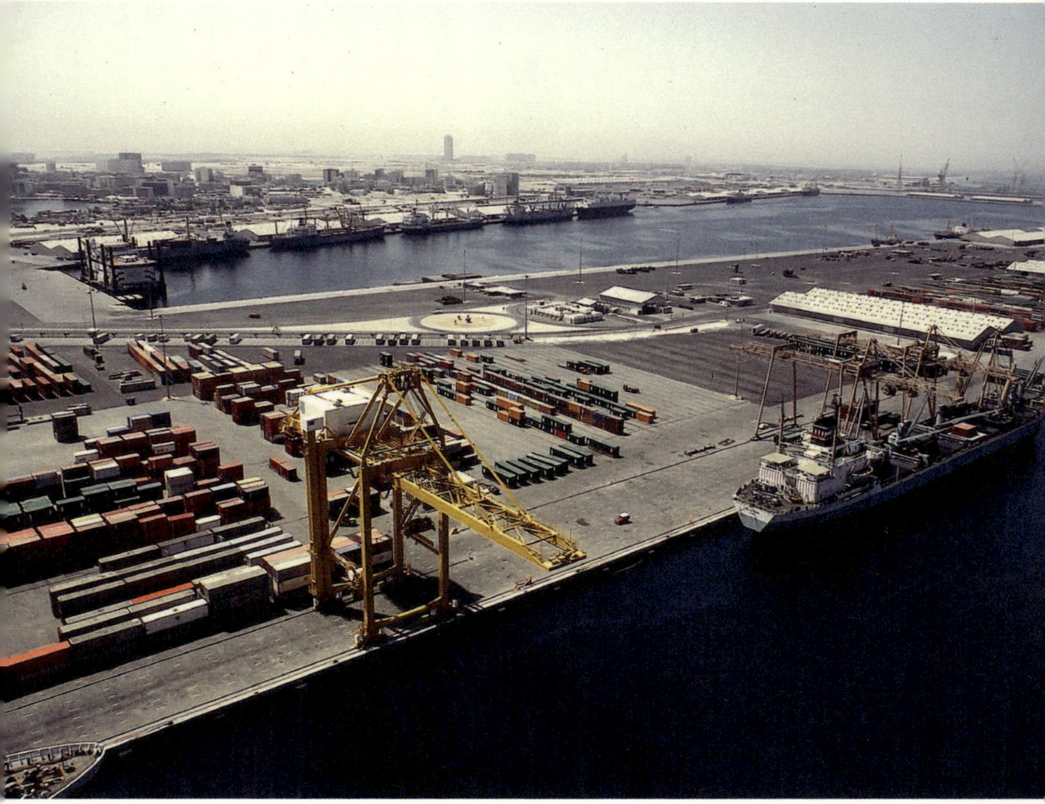

In memory of Corrina . . .

DAUGHTER OF THE CAPTAIN

CRISTIANA DE MARCHI
PHOTOGRAPHS: MOHAMMED KAZEM

I.

Will you remember me
When you will leave this country
That is no home to us
Or I will be forced to
Before you and replaced?

My daughter was not one
When I left her behind
and flew for the first time
"Poor life we had
    Husband already a past
reality not presence".
A countryside without poetry
The true essence of poverty

I had no choice but to go
And confide her to my mother
"It's youth's duty
to support their families"
that voice repeatedly echoes
and obsesses me
the burden of cyclical time
inflicted at birth time

When I first saw you
I couldn't stop myself from rejoicing
"A baby boy to take care of
a second chance to hold my baby
into my arms"

Mothers here are always busy
They don't have time for family care
They come and go
And always come back with something new
Or a disappointment

Twice I went back *home*
Twice in 10 years
And on occasions:
My daughter's first communion
Her 10th birthday.
Unable to fill the void
and create a space
For later contemplation
And future remembrance

Am I still a mother?
What did I sacrifice our memories for?
Not to build any other ones
As never I was pictured
holding the baby then a child
a blanked presence

I build imaginary worlds
For myself and my daughter
This is my reality now
As she grows up quickly
And I am still far
Soon she will be gone
My same destiny
I couldn't avoid

Two memories of her mother
a light luggage to carry

II.

Once again I stare at myself in this mirror
Excessively made up for the occasion

Weekends ultimately land in similar rooms
Low sofas and lights
Mirrors and reflective floors
Loud music and the promise
of distraction

I've changed a lot
Dismissed my old clothes
Wore those of a role

Becoming a cliché
Is easier than expected
A twist in attitude
The acceptance of a new one
a forgetful forgiveness
on loan

Like in an album or a gallery
The hand leafs through faces
And plucks the petals off

Is there any woman
who wouldn't feel powerful
by knowing powerful men?
The time of a moment
And later in remembrance
Even though, in doing so,
One would have to remember that this man
Has devastated the landscape of your innocence?

There are images
I cannot share with my family
When I get back home
and visit them
Taking cheap duty free presents
Between short stays on a visa entry

Even with the other girls
Better to avoid words
And the chitchatting
That ridicules men
We had to please
Without respect
Mutually

What for, to remember?

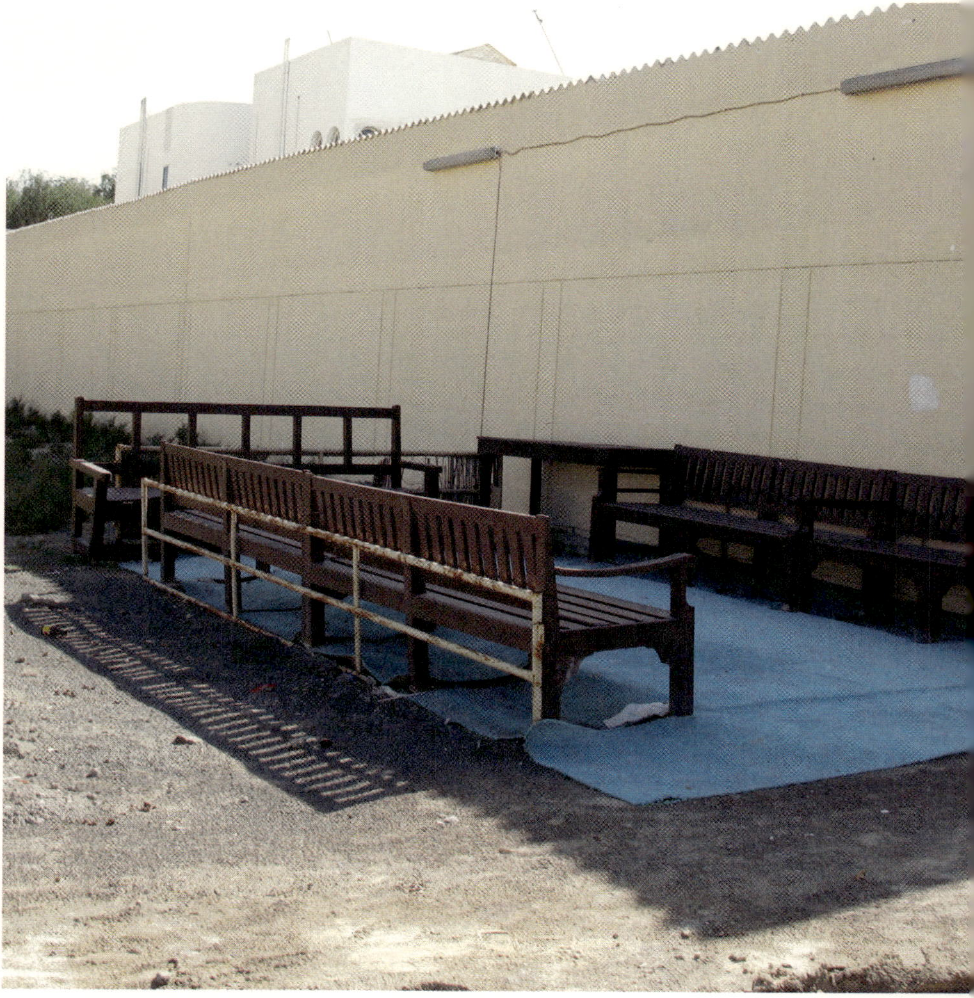

III.

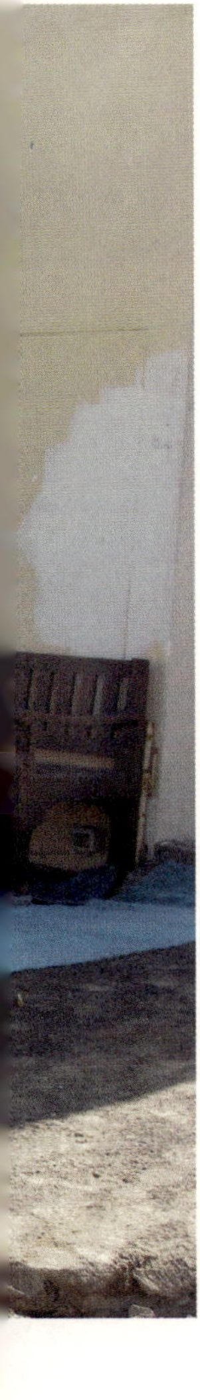

Those were the days when we used to laugh
While reading the news
Statistics like Tales
from the western world
So overestimated yet disregarding
Timeless pleasures filling hours

Light occupied the room
Our hands slowly moving
- Different directions
Yet the same
In our shared obsession with our respective
Obsessions –
Not a word pronounced
Only sobbing sometimes
Or the soft introduction
Of a syllable

What can one share with their mother?
She had one man only
And never told him
"I want you now"

Centuries of women
Transferring the impossibility
Of cleaning the dirtiness of their deflowering
Over their homes
Cleaning and washing
What a waste! All this for a rhetoric figure

Which memories of hot nights
The tropical line, a belt to open–
And lazy days lost in following
the line of a thought
or just dissolving the hangover effect
made up of mixing drinks and guilt feeling
Could we share?

The language of the body
Is not my native one
Rather one that I learned later.
To free the limbs
And decline them
To other inclinations

This is the language we share
The one you use
To ask me more

Dry is the maternal idiom
Humid and clayey the daughterly

(April 2017)

IV.

Flat roof of a popular neighborhood
Memory of other roofs – terraces –
Childhood wasted surfaces
Adopted spaces of the adultness

Roofs embody the privilege of transitions
They are made symbols of the shift
impressed to one's life
The migratory movement
That can take elsewhere

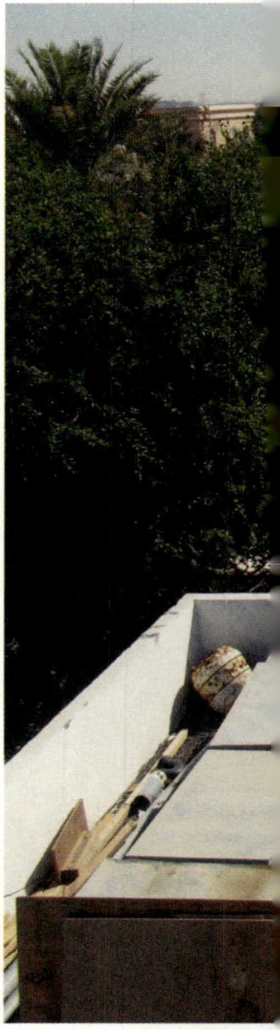

Petrified silhouette
Attracts my attention
Slightly clouded
in the impossible attempt
Of a recognition
Of an identification

Dazzled the vision almost absorbed
By the severity of the complexion
the intensity of its pigmentation
Dampens edges, dissects roles.

Not a demon to tower
The house-roof
But a man of other latitudes
Still exotic to me, as it seems.

To my regretful admission.

(April 2008)

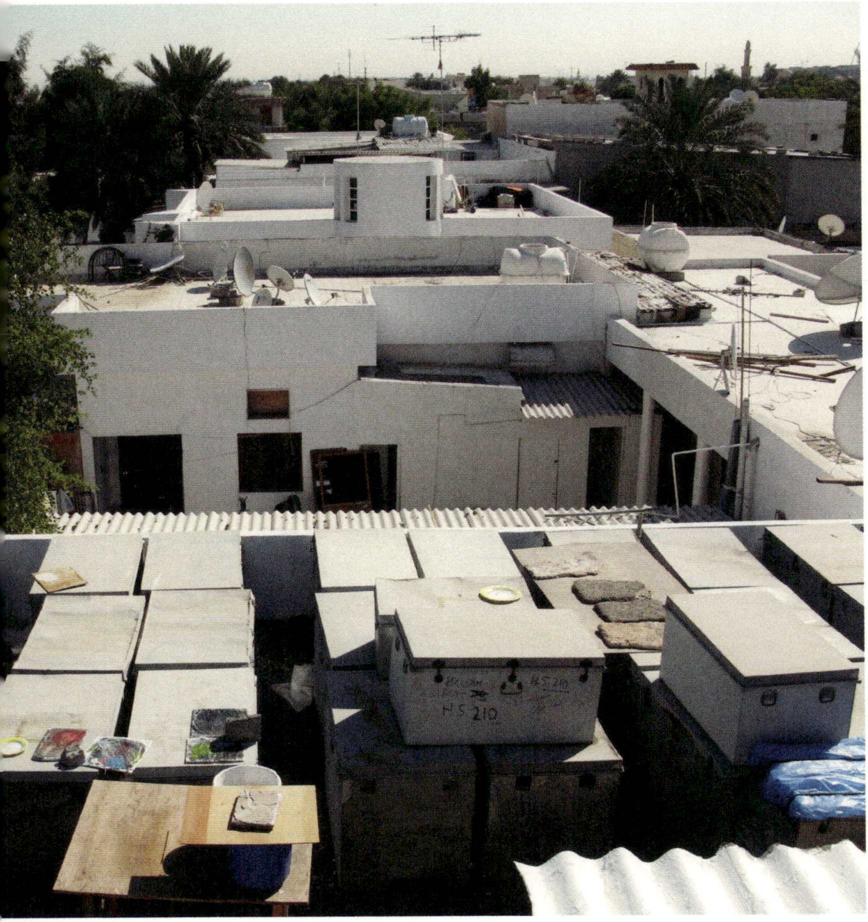

4 POEMS

NJ STALLARD
PHOTOGRAPHS: FARAH AL QASIMI

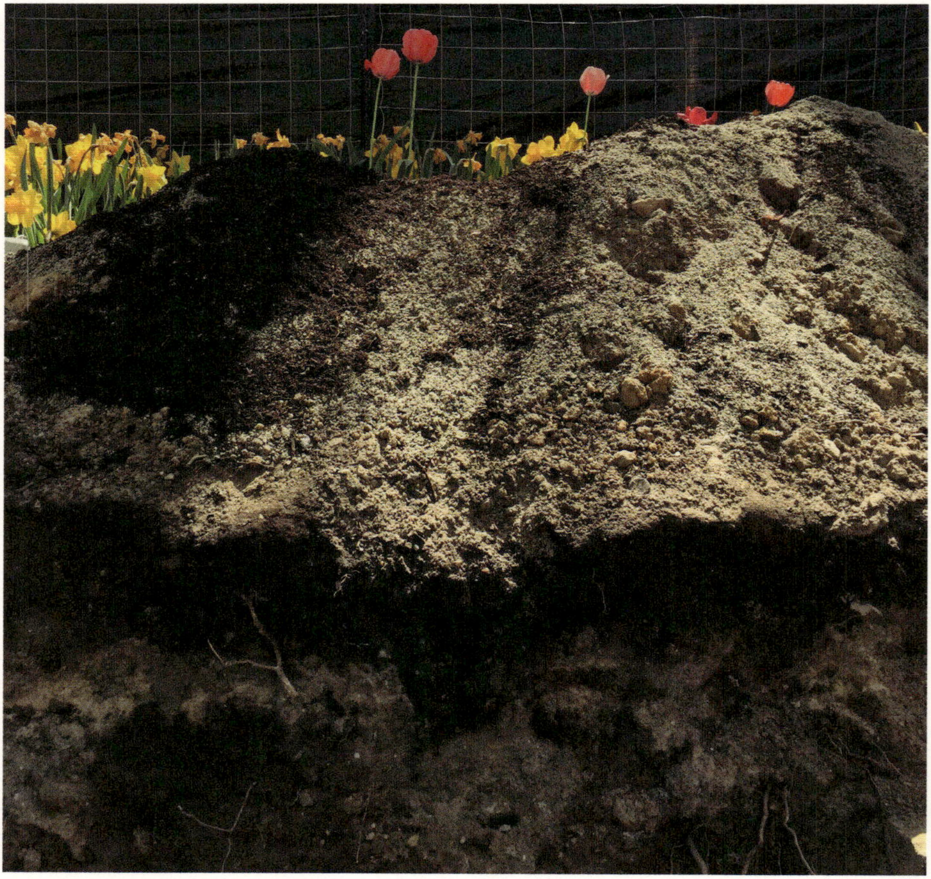

The Hiatus

As the moon rose over the houses,
as calm and cool as glass,
the two women declared a hiatus.

They packed up their belongings
and drove into the desert.
Why build a utopia, the first woman said,
if it won't be appreciated?
We have everything we need here,
the second woman replied,
let this sand be the proxy gold
of our alternative currency.

They ate cans of beans
and slept in horsehair tents
strung up between the palm trees.
When the first woman died,
the second buried her in the sand,
as calm and cool as a coin.

She drove to the airport,
glass still on her fingertips,
and never told a soul.

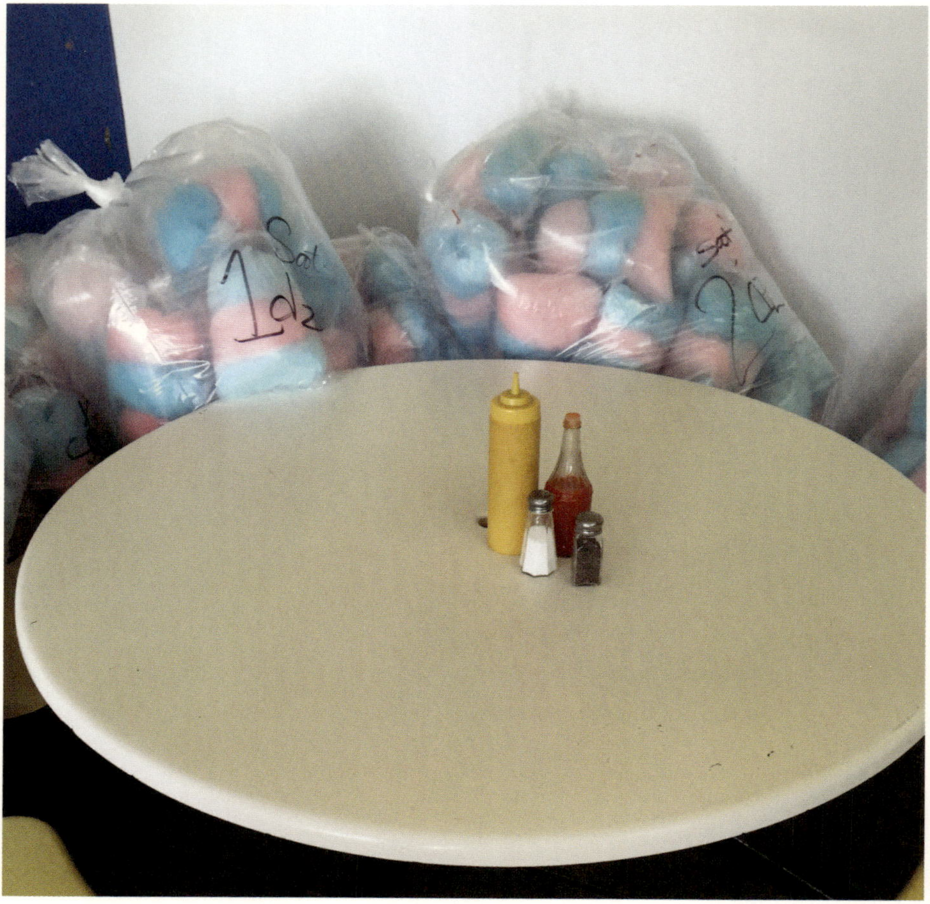

Saudi Aramco Magazine, 1967

In the day of leopard-print bikinis,
hip talk and high-priced abstract art,
distinctions between the primitive
and modern in dress, language and art
have become notably
fuzzy.

In the realm of architecture,
they have occasionally become meaningless,
as the enigma of the
beehive houses
of northern Syria
demonstrates.

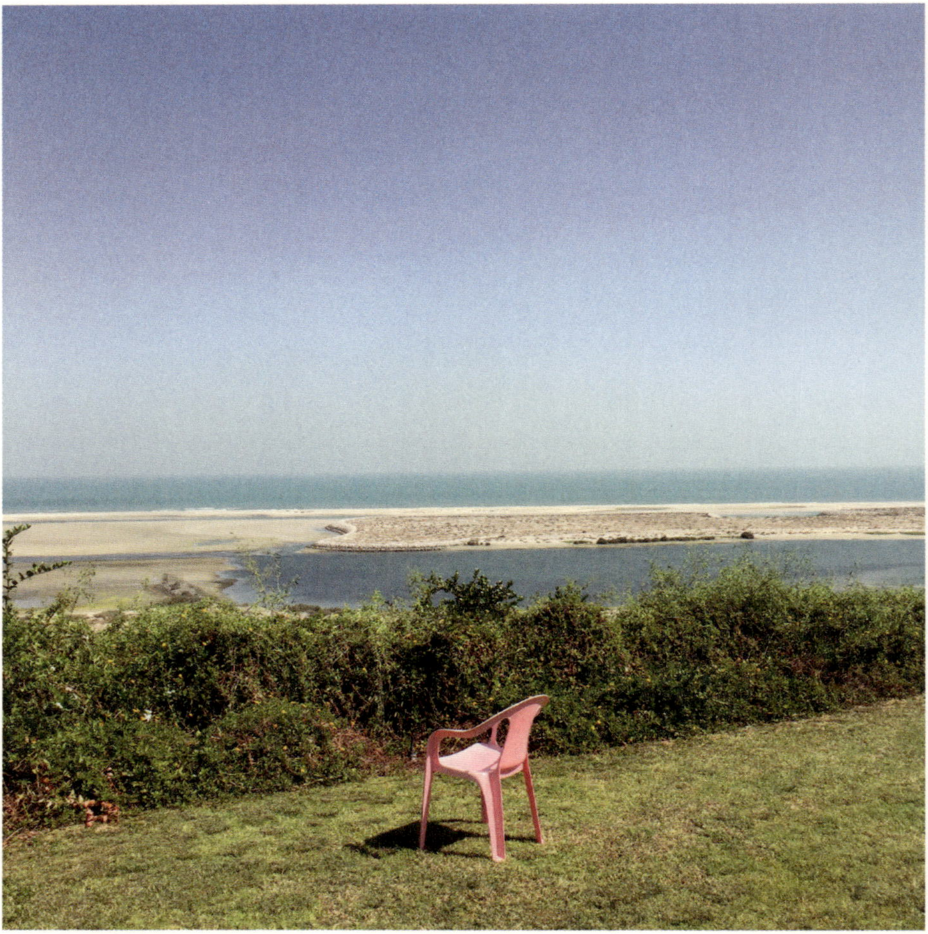

Gloria

Imagine the pipes.
Imagine the disaster
of a 40 floor building crumbling
to dust.

Standing on the balcony
you hesitate to throw your cigarette
over
the edge.

The sky an unbroken blue
the reflection of a thousand swimming pools
on a thousand rooftops.

I laid out my years for you on an embroidered tablecloth,
like my best jewels. Some worn,
some broken.

Imagine the rust.
Imagine the girders, beams and rivets,
showers, sinks and mirrors,

Imagine this whole wonderful building
falling.

The Map

Did I ever tell you
how the fighter
tattooed a map of the Sahara
onto his grandmother's back?

Hot black scabs
from the clay tempered blade
and unclothed ochre
clung to her cotton vest.

Who would bother a grandmother?
the fighter must have thought.
Our secrets will be safe.
When the enemy came
to raid, or if they did, they would lie her
on her back, the map
pressed against the ground,

like two palms poised in prayer,
like one thing returning to another,
like the day we caught that fish
and threw it back into the water.

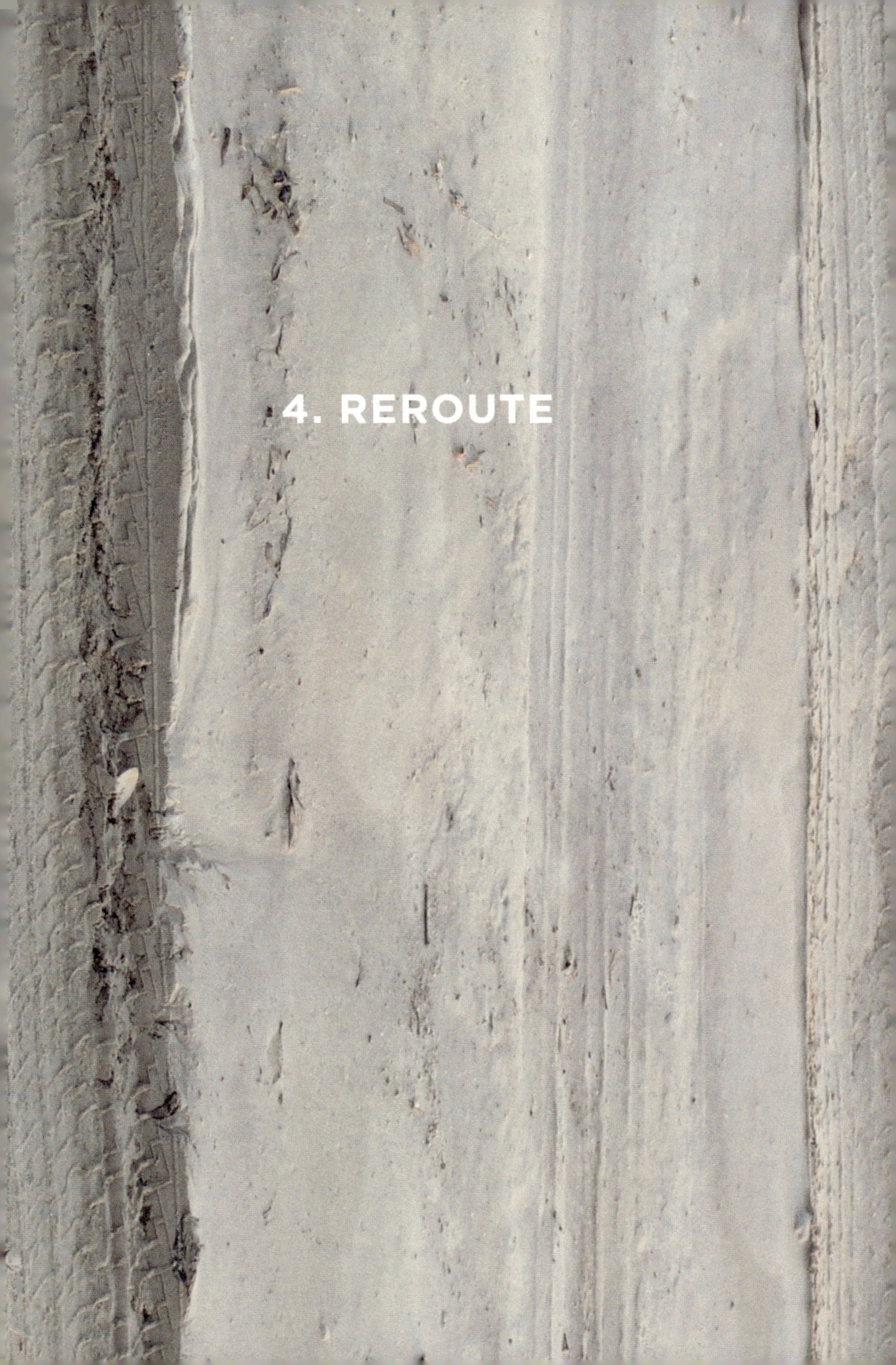

4. REROUTE

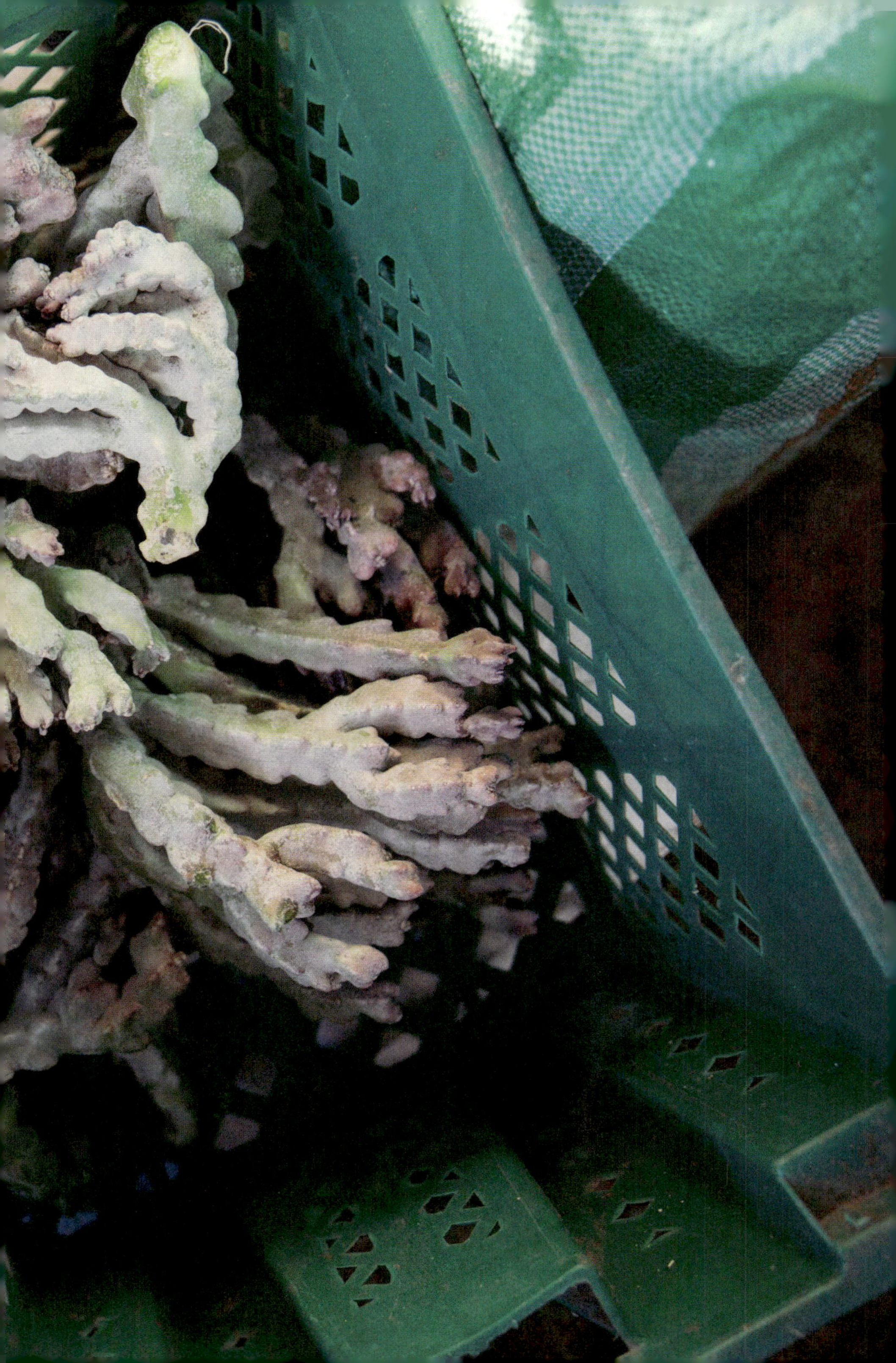

FRIDAY MARKET [MASAFI]

SOUAD HERVÉ

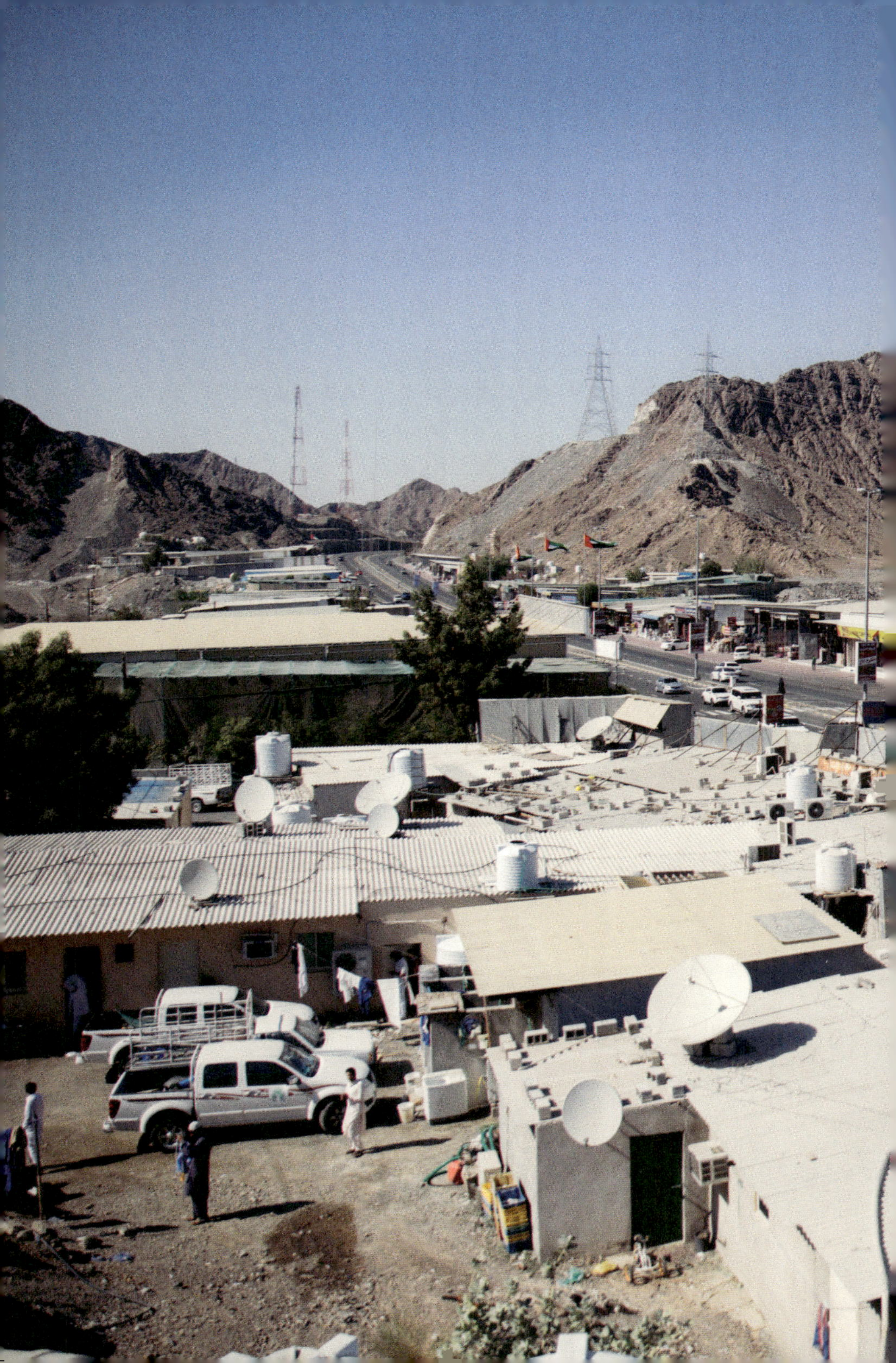

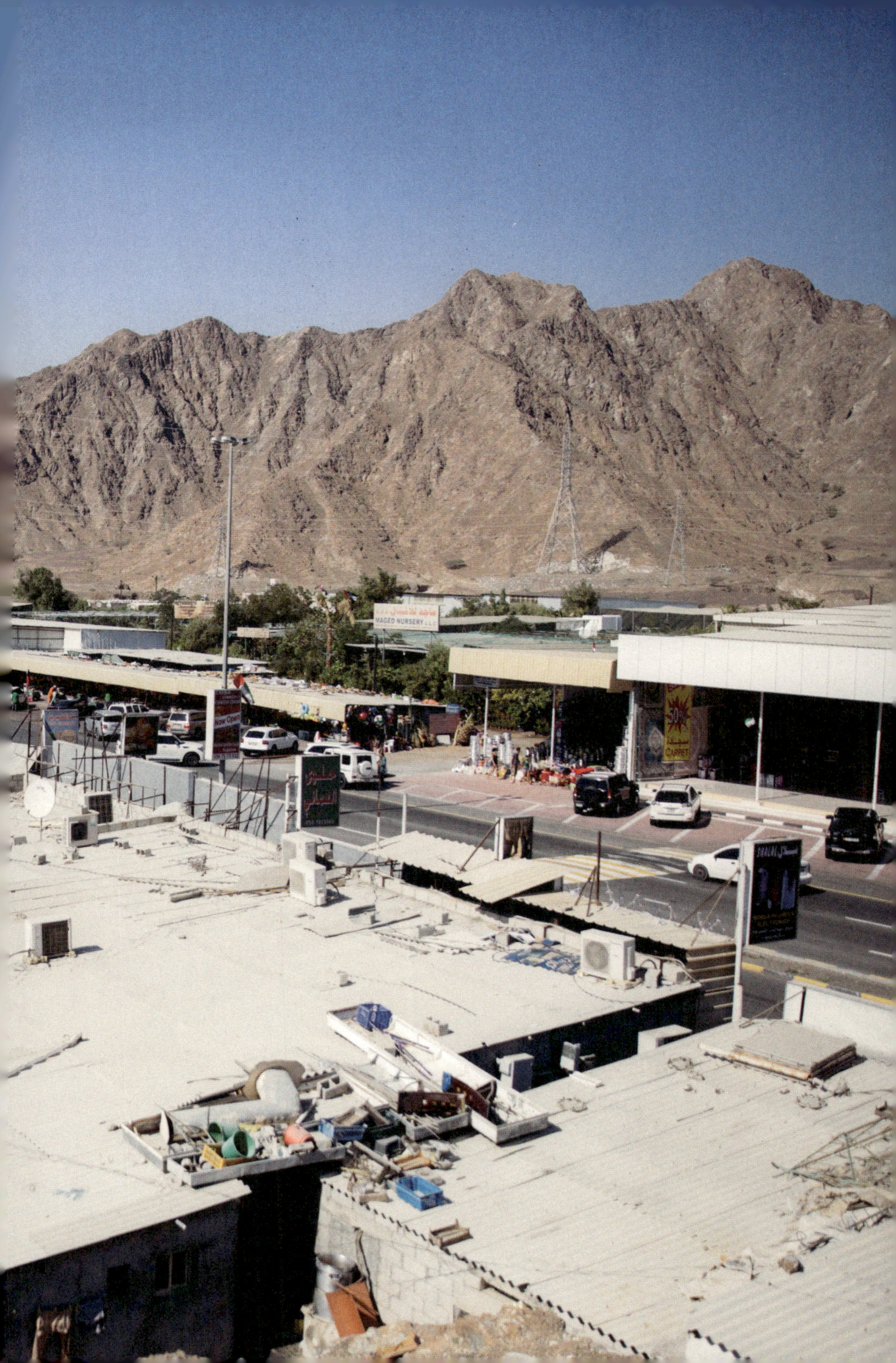
MAGED NURSERY
Now Open

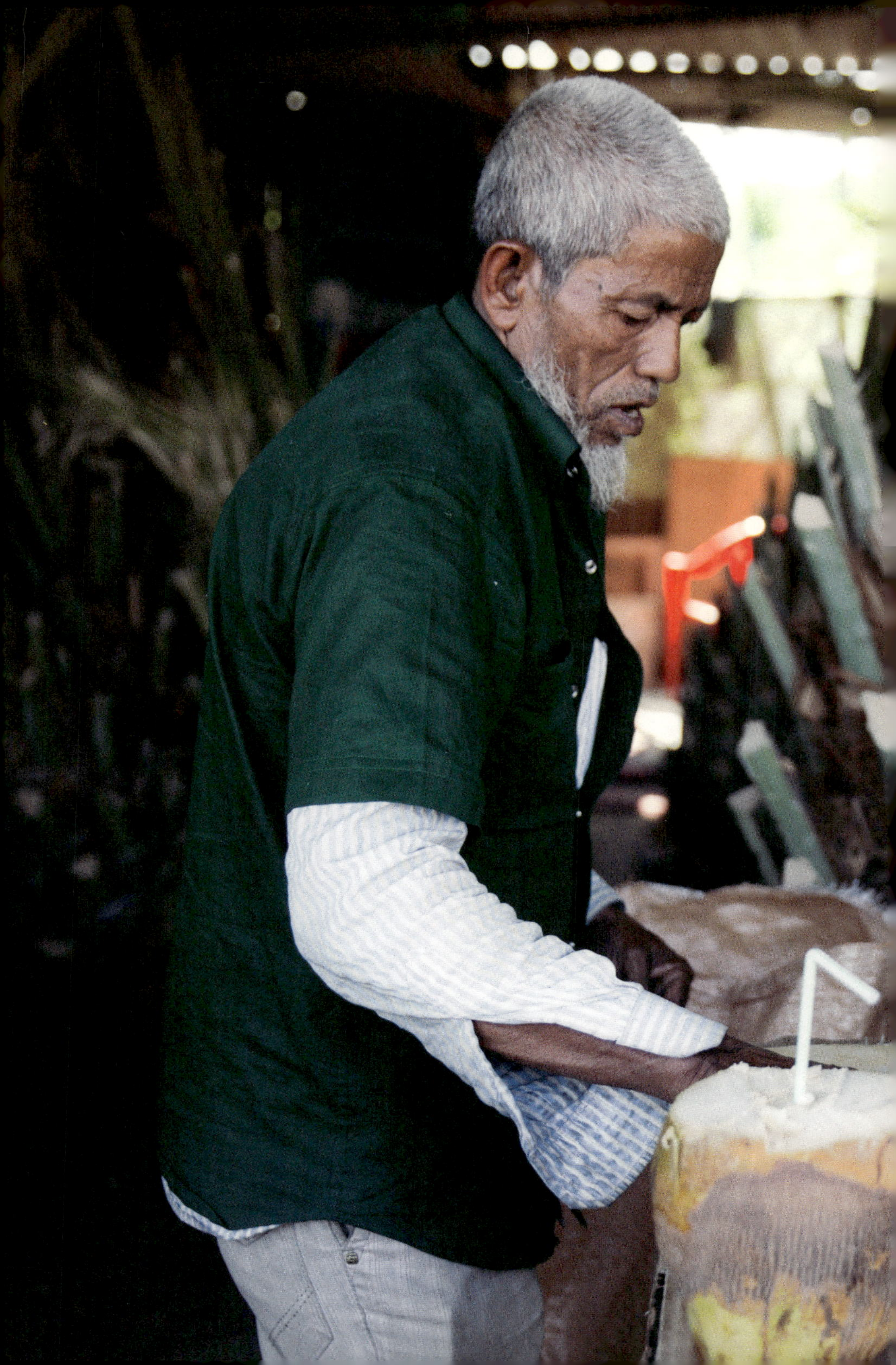

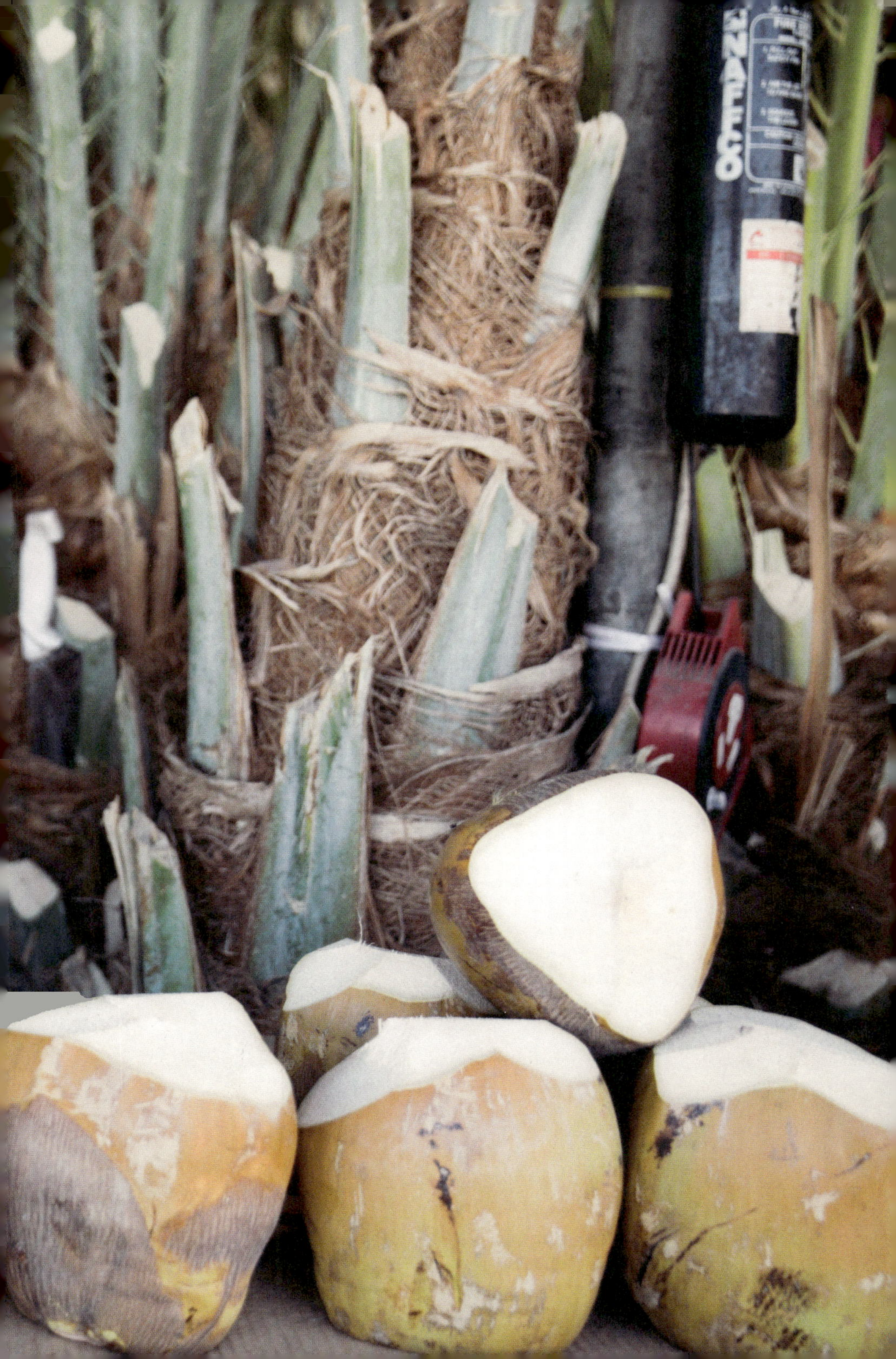

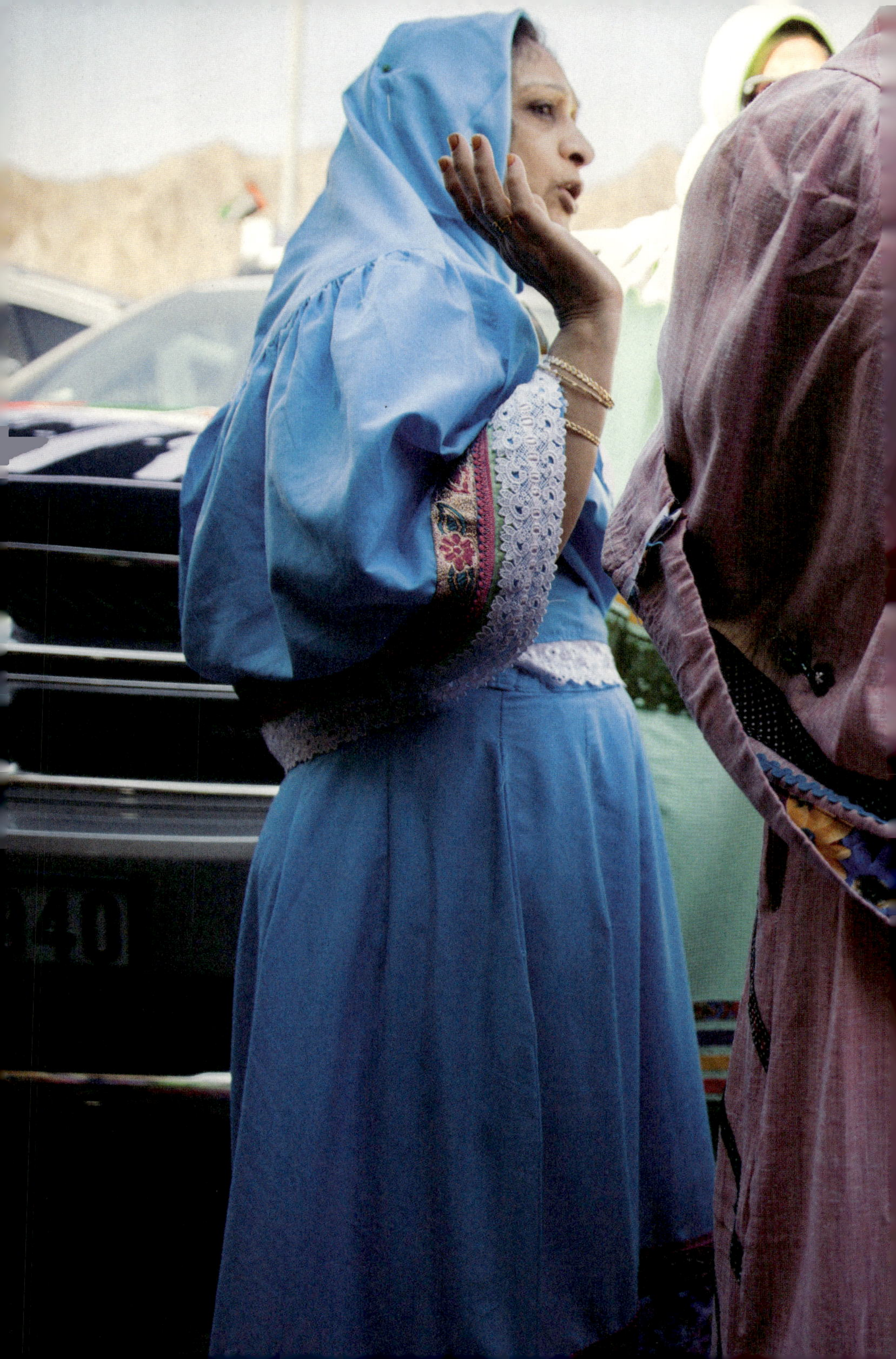

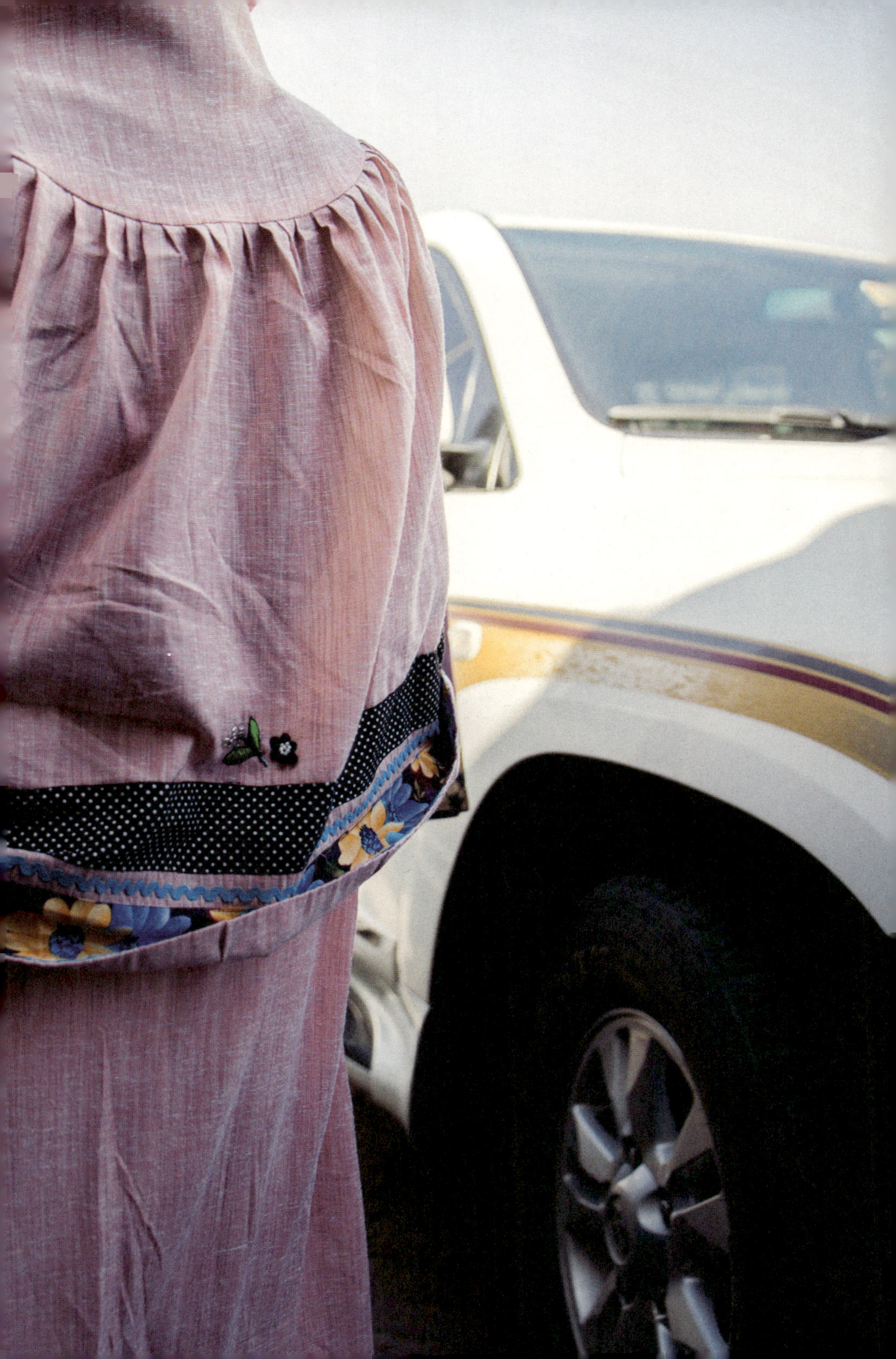

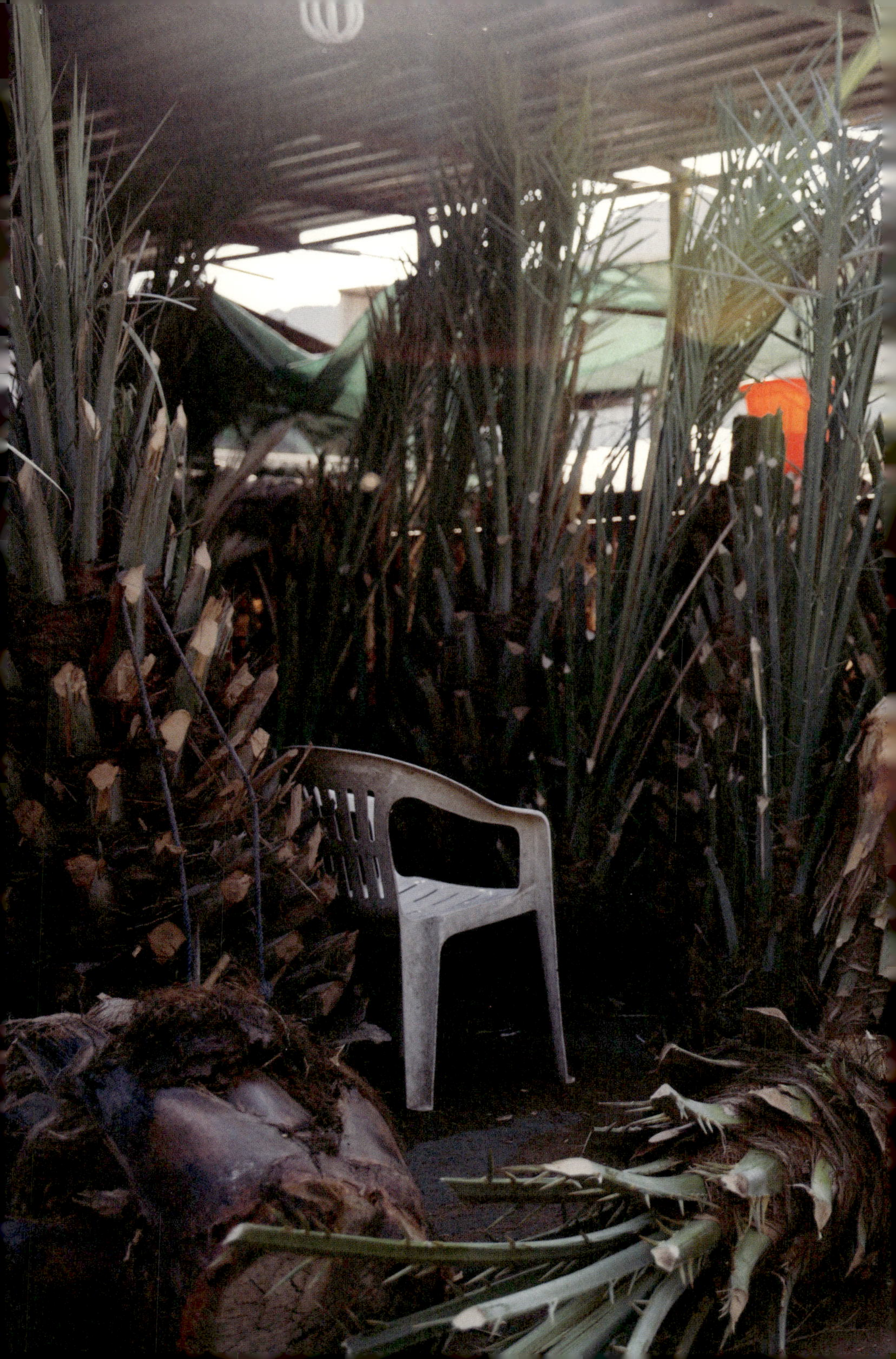

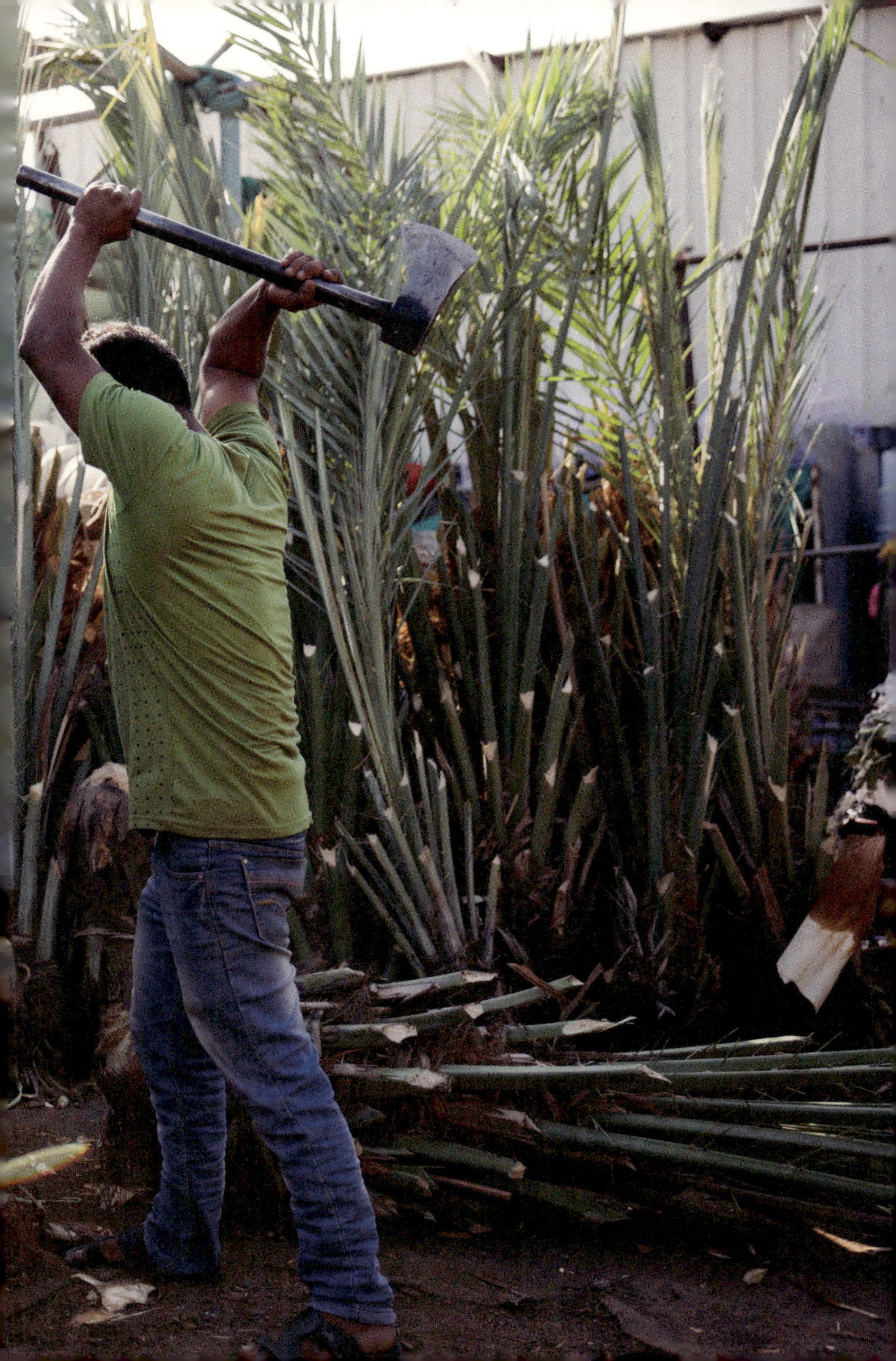

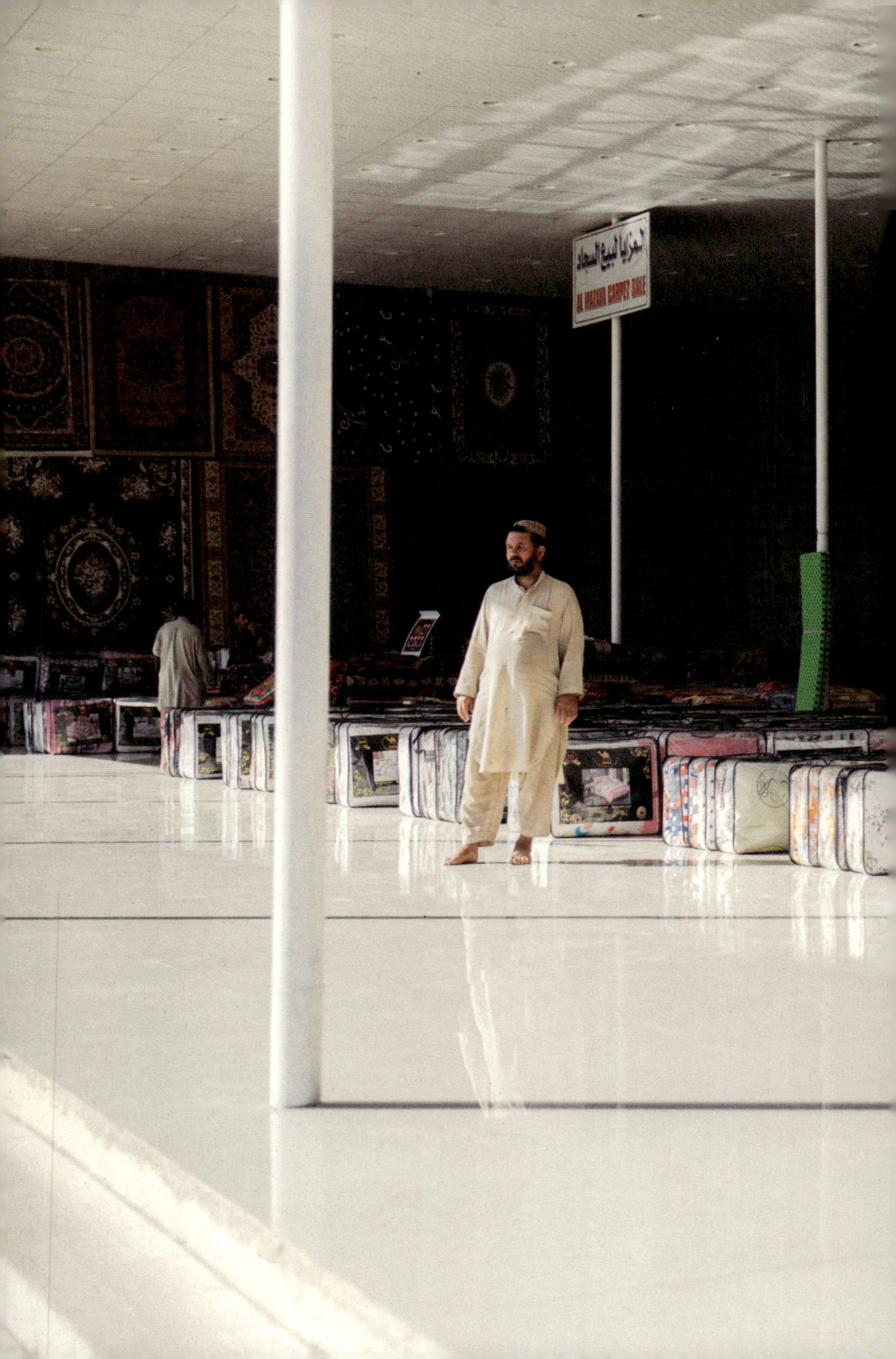
المزايا لبيع السجاد
AL MAZAYA CARPET SALE

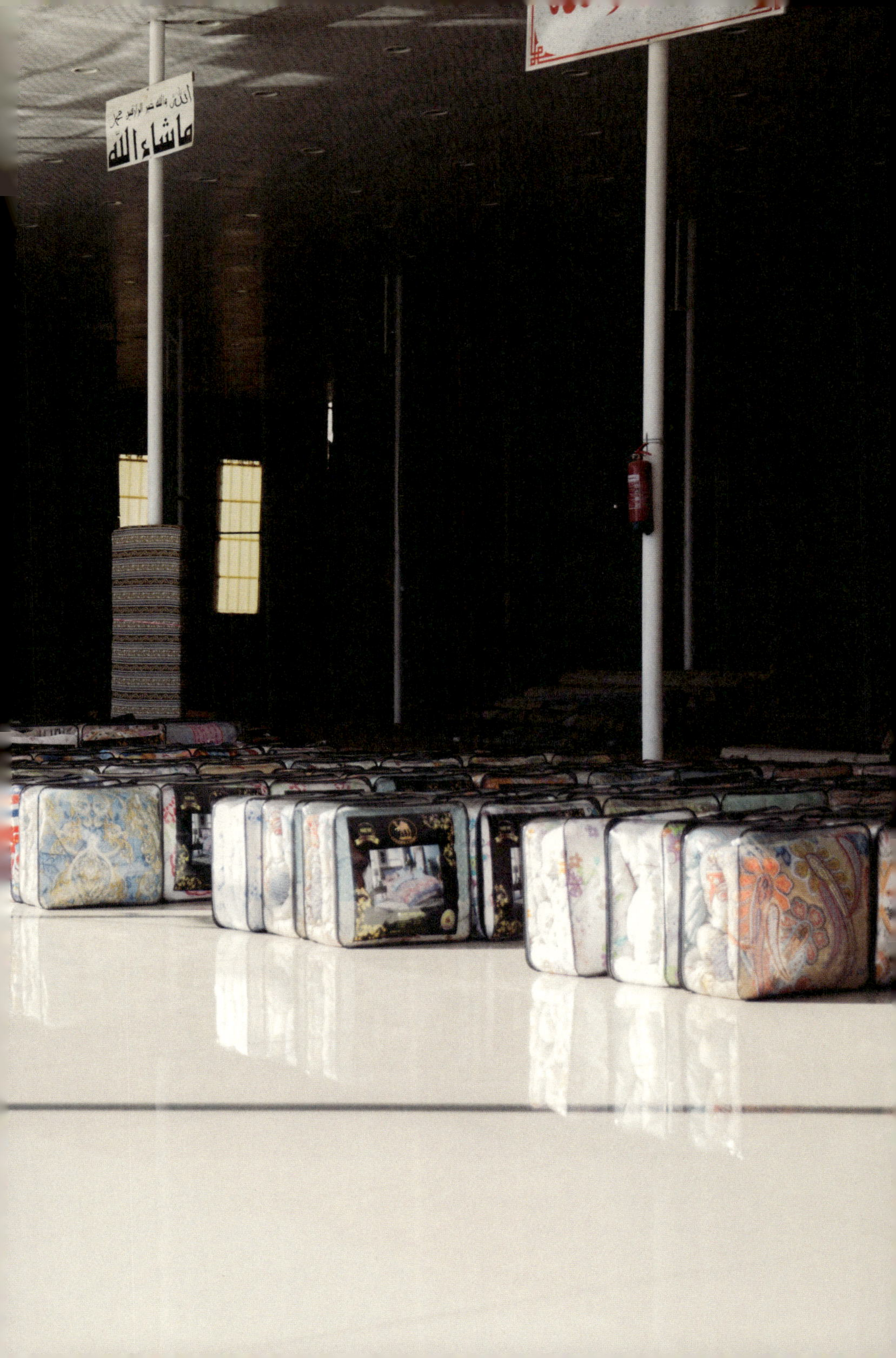
ماشاء الله

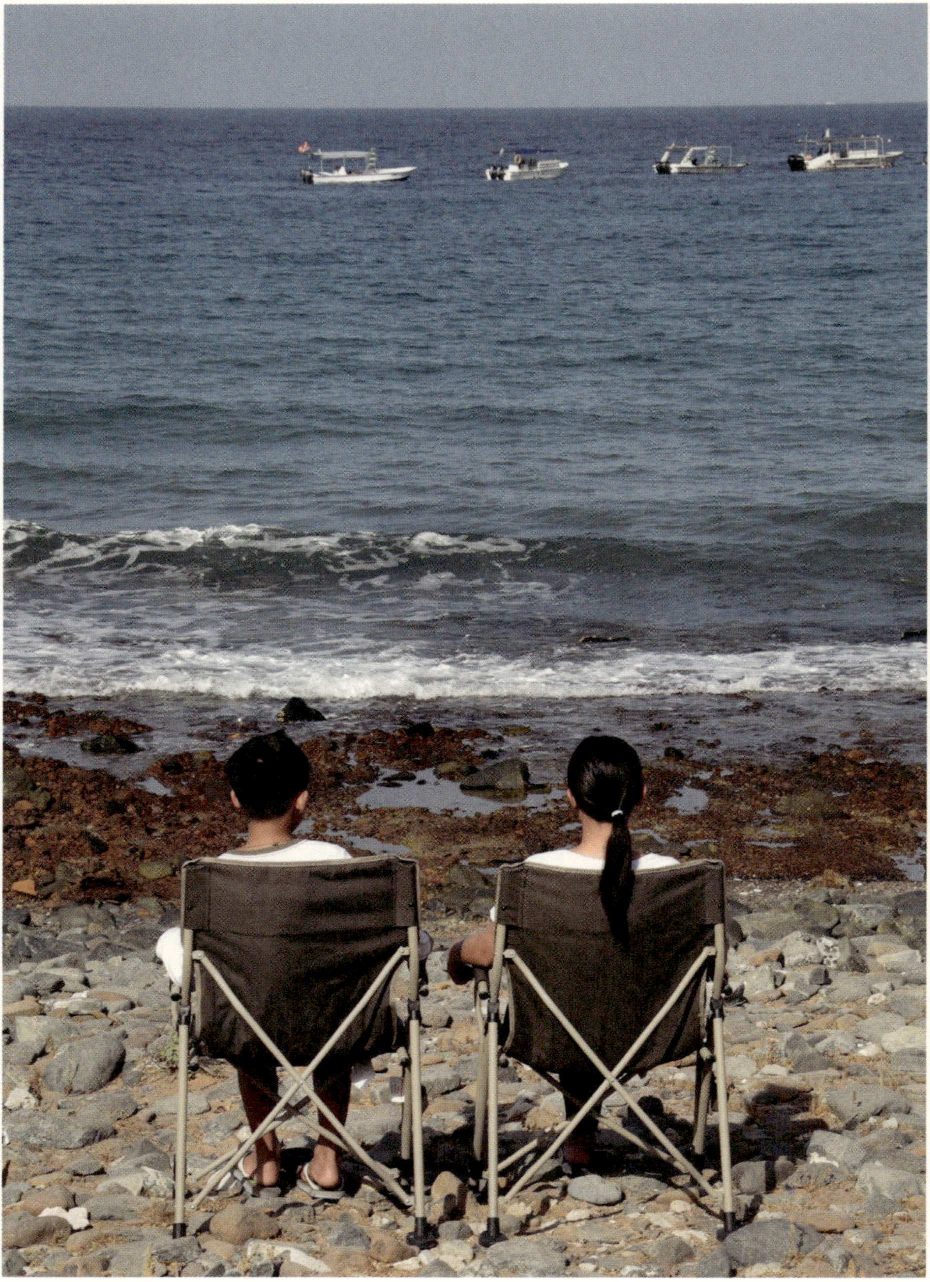

TRANQUILITY: THE CALM SEA BREEZE AND THE STEADY WAVES AT THE ROCKY SHORE OF AL AQAH BEACH IN FUJAIRAH.

THE ADVENTURES OF BEVERLY

BEVERLY CASTRO

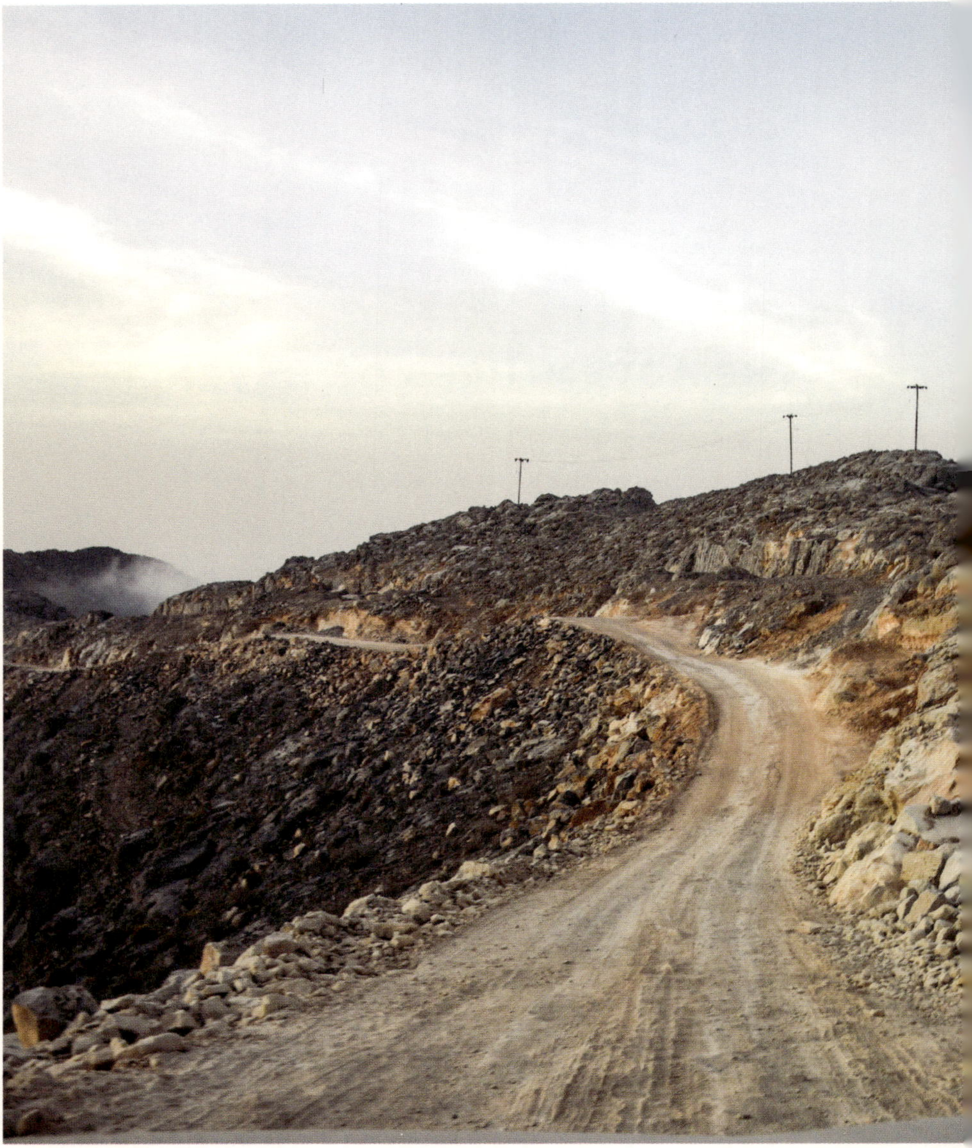

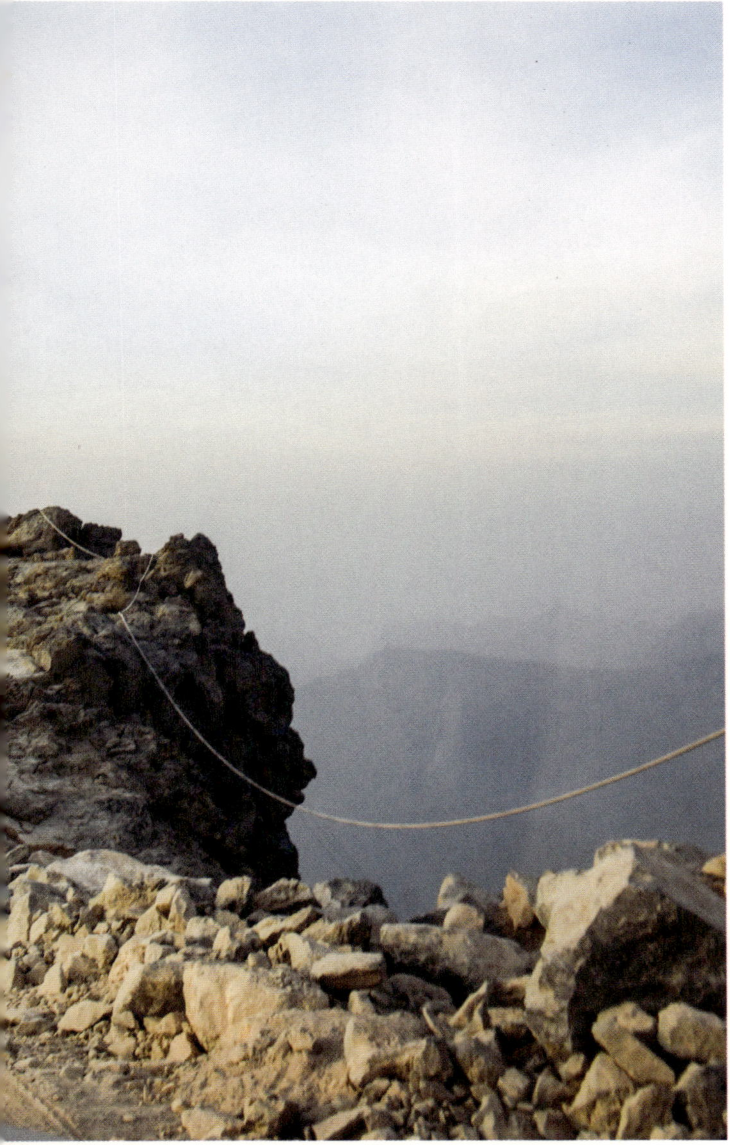

ELEVATED AT 1,911 METERS, JEBEL JAIS IN RAS AL KHAIMAH IS THE HIGHEST POINT IN THE UAE. THIS IS A ROCKY MOUNTAIN RANGE WITH WINDING ROADS.

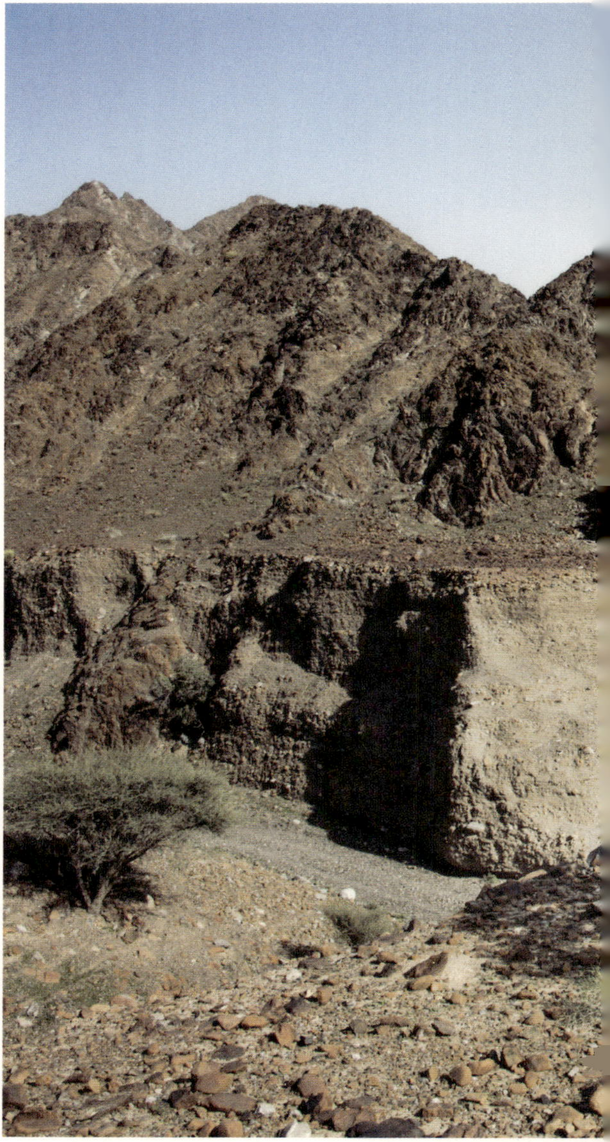

THESE DARK-RED ROCKY MOUNTAINS LIE BEYOND THE HIGHWAYS OF FUJAIRAH. SOME ARE PEAKED, WHILE OTHER PARTS OF THE RANGE HAVE FORMED HIGH FLAT TABLES. THIS PHOTO WAS TAKEN ON A SUMMER AFTERNOON IN MADHA, WHERE WE ENJOYED OUR LUNCH UNDER THE SHADE OF A THORNY TREE.

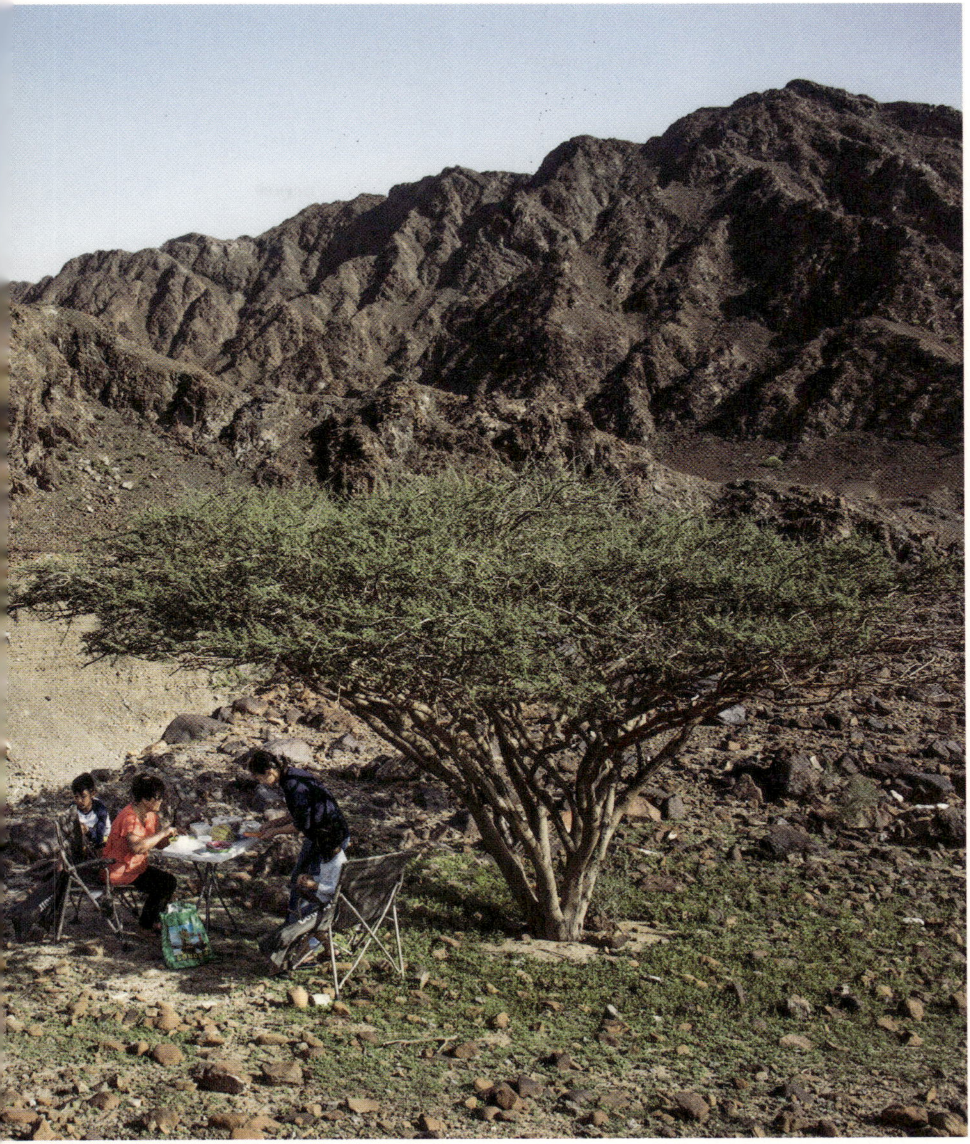

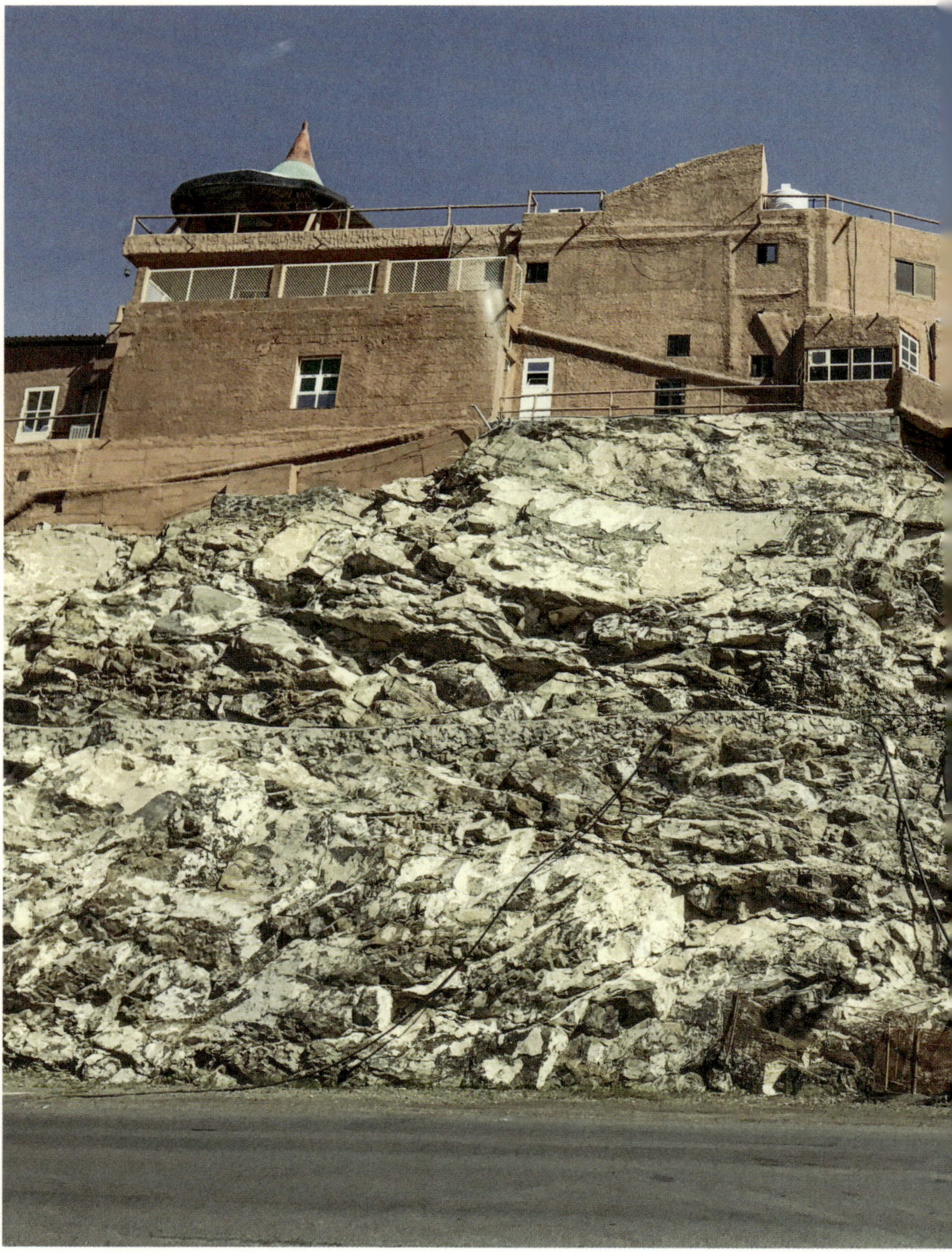

A HOUSE IN THE MASAFI COMMUNITY, RAS AL KHAIMAH.

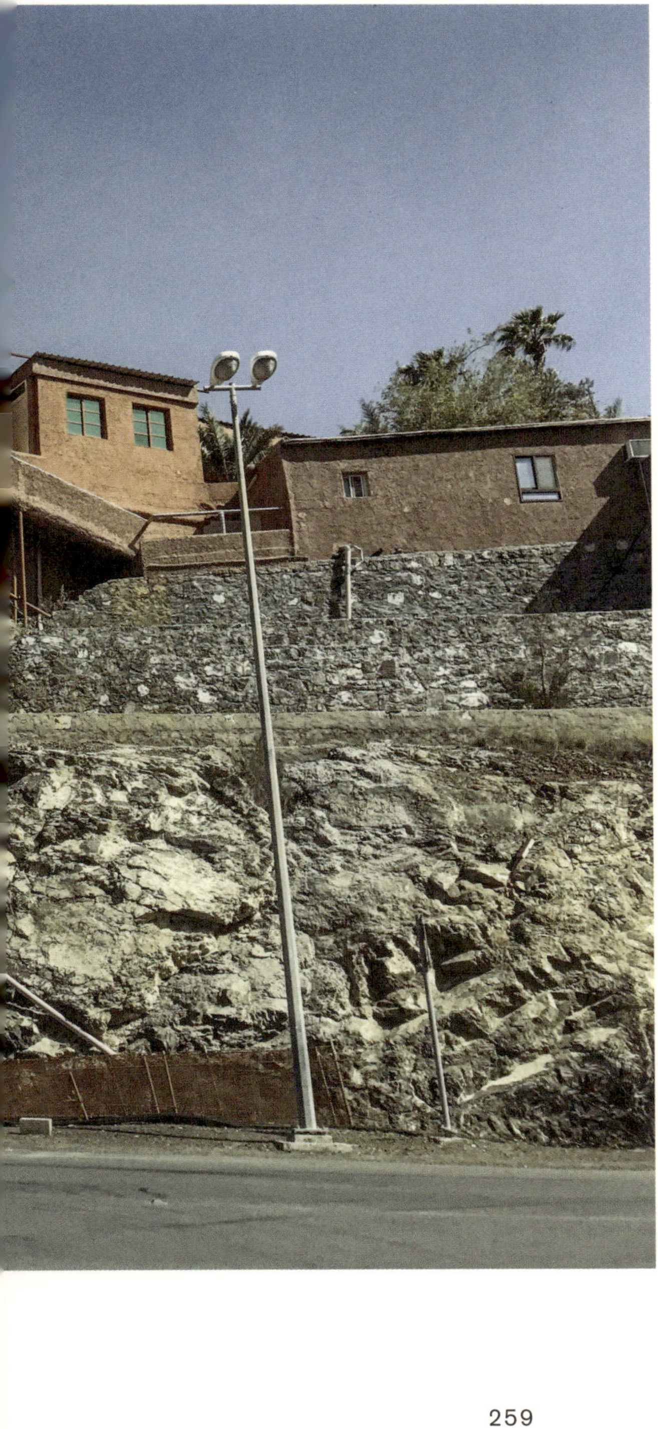

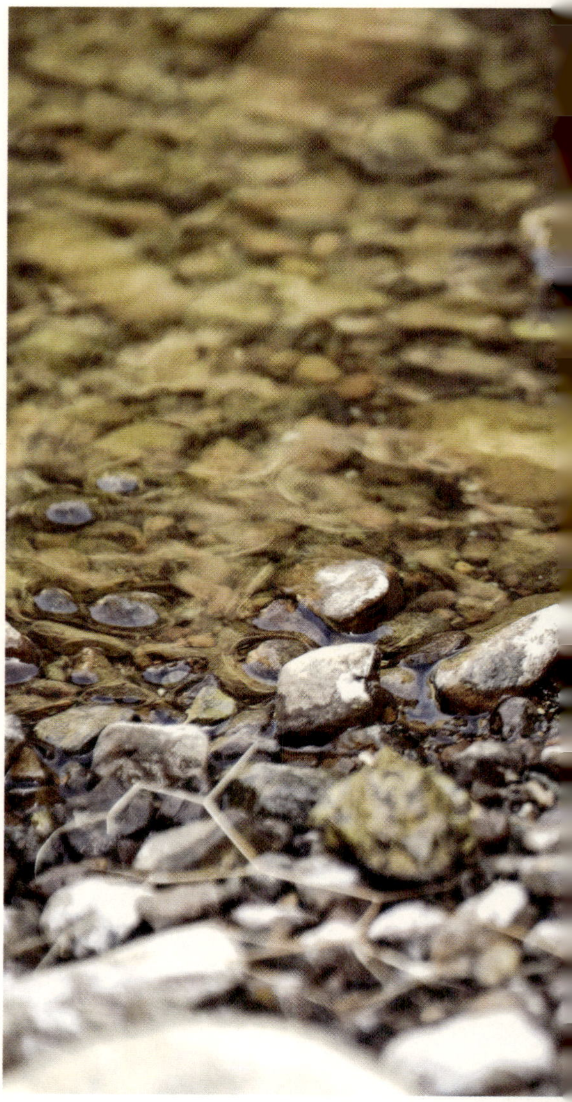

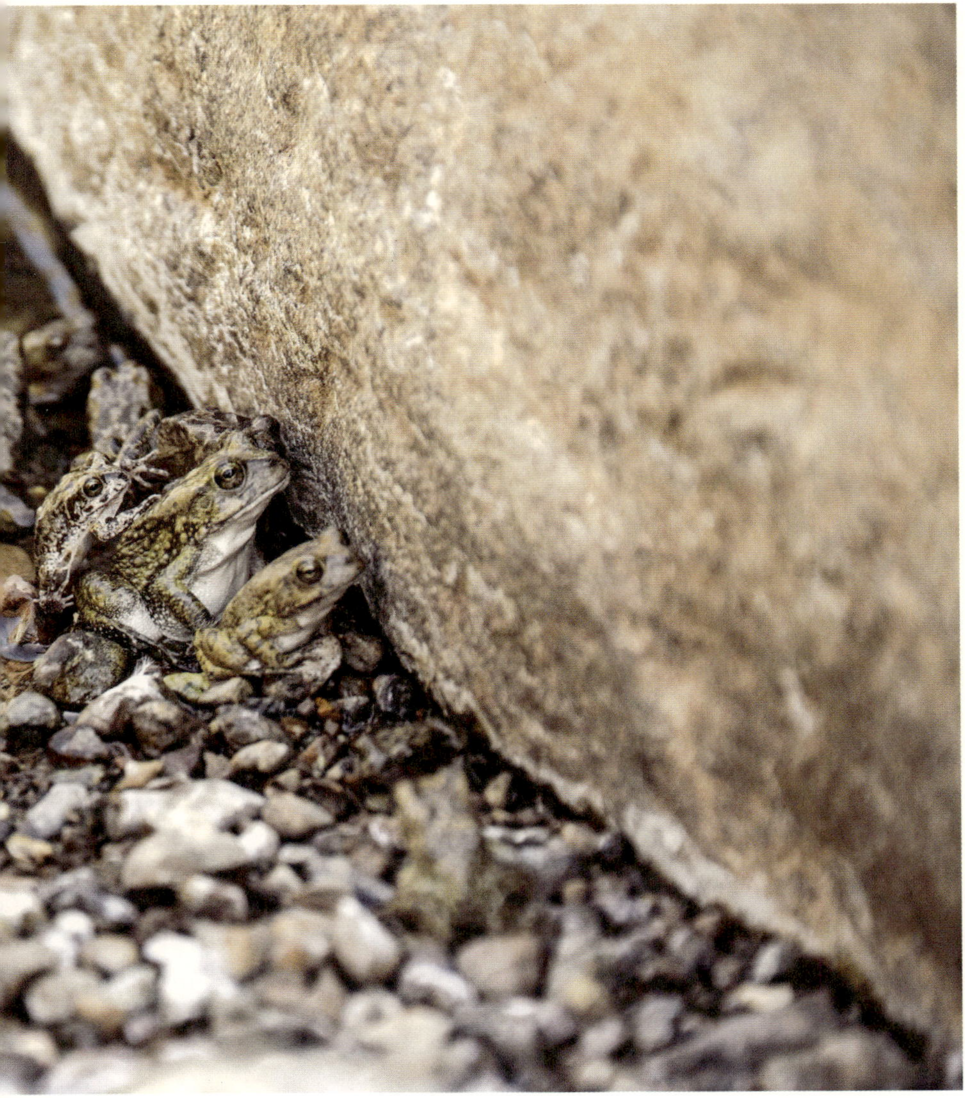

THERE IS A DIVERSITY OF FAUNA IN THE ROCKY MOUNTAINS OF SHOWKA, RAS AL KHAIMAH.

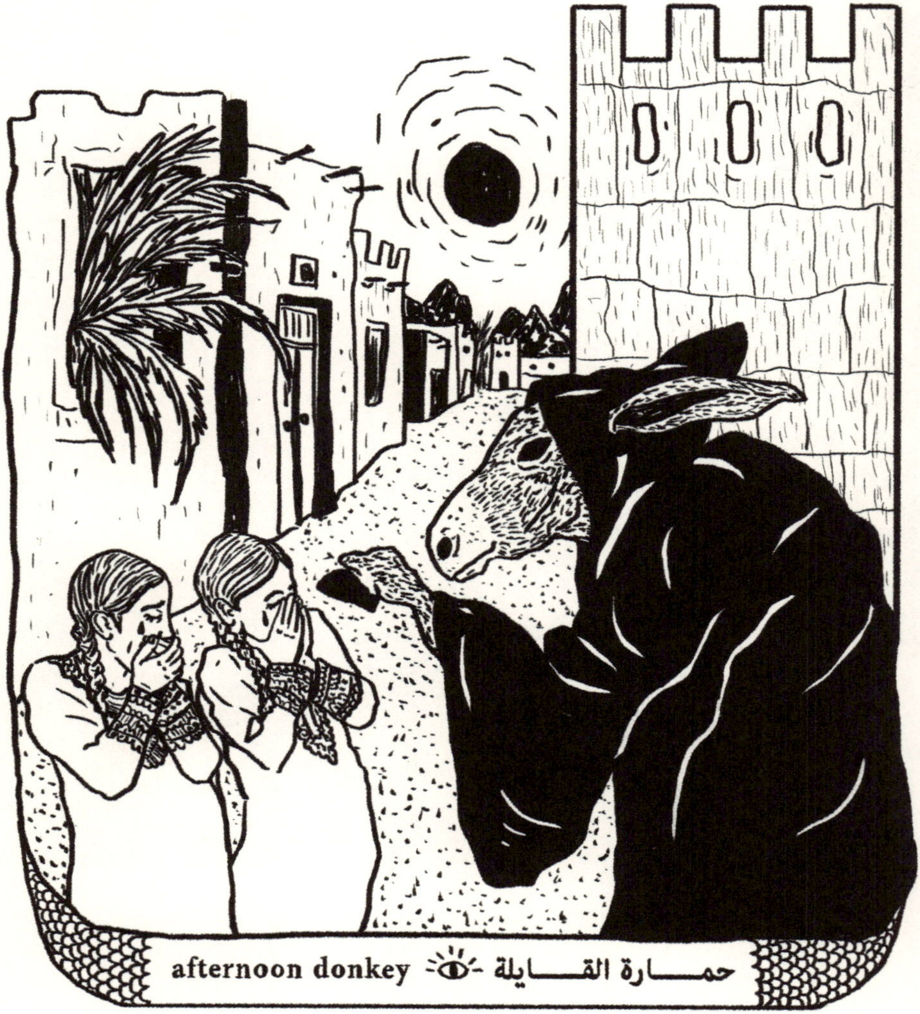
afternoon donkey
حمـــارة القـــايلة

TALES FROM OLD RAS AL KHAIMAH

ANNA ZACHARIAS
ILLUSTRATIONS: TULIP HAZBAR

There are three times of day in Ras Al Khaimah (RAK). There is the morning, the evening and the night, but there is no afternoon because the city is in hiding from the heat and the noontime donkey, a fabled spirit who wanders the old town and gobbles up little children at this hour, when they fry in the sun.

So start your walk when the day begins to cool after late afternoon prayers, at a coffee shop near the fish market in the old town. Here, you'll be in the company of the last pearl divers and captains who sailed the Indian Ocean currents. This is how they spend their retirement: friends, tea and dominos.

They may keep to themselves but when they talk, what stories they tell. There's Abu Daria and other nautical *djinn*, there are sad memories about relatives "swallowed by the sea" but the favorite stories are about a magician who lived here not so long ago or who maybe did not live here at all.

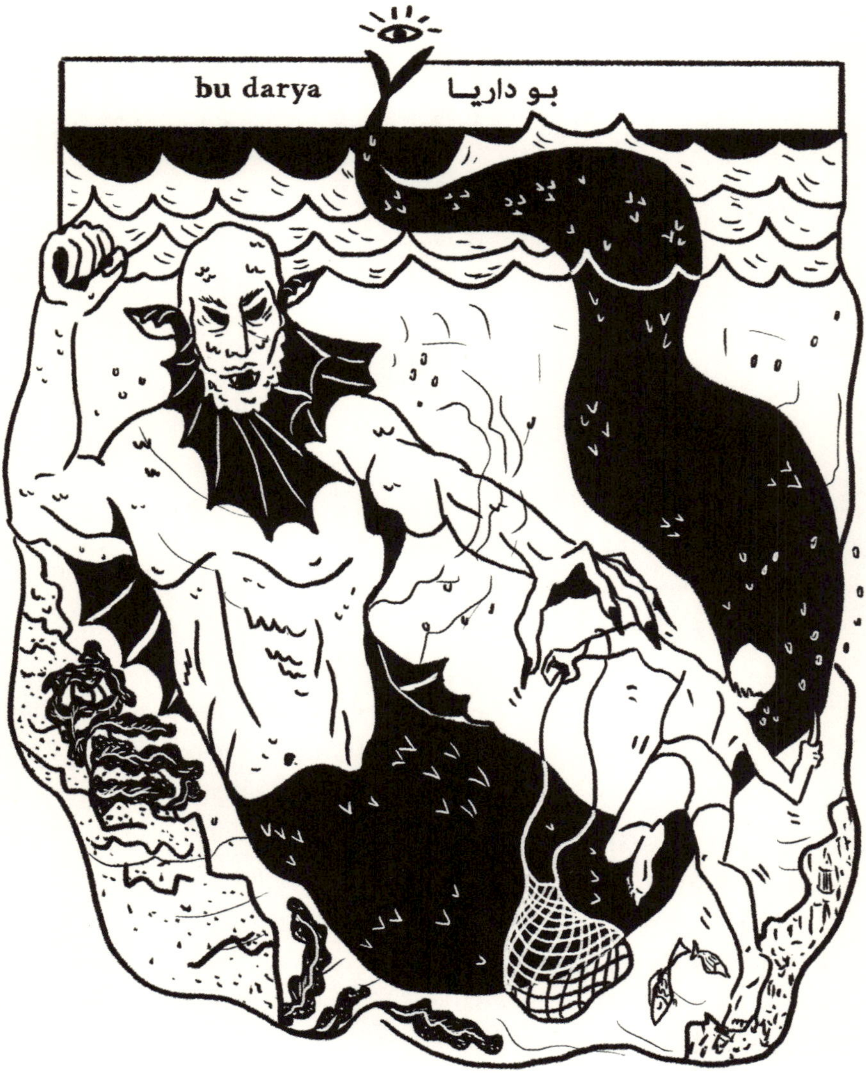
bu darya
بو داريا

It is said this magician could only use his magic for good. I am told that one day, while he was driving along the old coast road to Dubai, he was stopped by a policeman.

"Your plates need changing," the policeman told the magician. "The front ones say Sharjah and the back plates are from RAK."

"Are you sure, officer?" he said.

To the officer's great wonder and astonishment, when he looked back at the plates, they had changed. Dubai plates in the front, Umm al-Quwain in the back. At this, the policeman shook his head in disbelief and let him go.

Another story from the Ras Al Khaimah coffee shops:

The magician's mother was cross. He had run into friends on the street and invited them home for lunch. "I have nothing to feed them but coffee and a few dates," she told her son, mortified.

"Are you sure?" he said. "Go look in your pots."

To the mother's great wonder and astonishment, when she lifted the lids, they were filled with steaming *harees*, *machboos*, rice and *khameer* bread for her guests. At this, the mother shook her head in disbelief and served her guests a feast.

When your tea is finished, wander behind the fish market through the covered alleyways, past the hardware stores and grocers, towards the Iranian souq on Sheikh Mohammed Bin Salem Road. Here, Mohammed Al Awazi sits outside 'HouseHold Applians' Shop at the center of the Irani market every afternoon. Mohammed's family came when people travelled back and forth across the Gulf regularly and communities were bound by the water instead of divided by it. Mohammed likes to recall the souq's glory days, when traders thrived.

"There were no thieves," he once told me. "I mean, they existed, there were bedu thieves but they were outside, not in the city and we went to Dubai by boat. People had rifles but they didn't need them."

A passerby shook his head, laughing at the idea of a market without thieves.

"You can't have a mosque without a lavatory, am I right?" he said.
"That's different," said Mohammed.
"This place is sleeping now," said the passerby.

The souq has been empty since the arrival of the city's first modern shopping mall at the turn of the millennium. Empty, too, is Mohammed's shop. Bare shelves hold a few honey-filled Vimto bottles and clay frankincense burners.

Down the street are a few Baluchi silversmiths, who craft the short-blade *yerz* axe used by mountain tribesmen. Once used as protection, the axe is now an accessory for dancing at weddings.

Behind the swordsmiths are the old houses of Ras Al Khaimah, the neighbourhood from which the emirate takes its name. Its coral stone and cement houses are now labour accommodation where workers often live eight to a room. It's poor and cramped but workers prefer life here to isolated labour camps outside the city. Among these alleys and mosques, there is community and commerce.

My friend's father was raised here in the 1940s and 1950s. A prominent sailing captain, he was on board when his father's ship sank off the coast of Seeb, Oman, in 1958. When his father went to an office to report the sunken ship, he ran into a neighbor from Ras Al Khaimah, another merchant, who took him to the Muttrah hospital for treatment and saw to it that they made it back to Ras Al Khaimah safely. Such were the bonds of this maritime neighborhood in those days, that one could count on neighbors to come through in a foreign city across the ocean, hundreds of kilometers from home.

At one edge of this neighborhood is the Al Qasimi palace on Al Hisn Road, a fort built in the early 1800s that is now the museum of Ras Al Khaimah. Beyond the fort and towards the sea is the Kuwaiti Street souq, a market on a one-way street, its entrance marked by a prayer on a signboard. The street takes its name from the Kuwaiti Hospital, a reminder of a time of pan-Arabism when the Emirates had little wealth and received support for education and healthcare from neighboring states. Nowadays, the street is synonymous with *abaya* shops and sequined dresses. Frankincense burners dot shop doorsteps.

Take a shortcut down an alley to the seaside at Al Qasimi Corniche and you will reach Malik Al Karak, a cafeteria that serves RAK's most popular cardamom tea, best enjoyed at sunset on the old Corniche.

After sunset, wander back to Kuwaiti Street, past gold shops where traders carry suitcases of gold jewellery from the bigger centers of Dubai and Sharjah. Just up from here, you'll reach a junction.

Turn left and head to the Irani herbalists who moved in fifteen years ago. At Al Hosam Herbs, Abdolhamid Mohammed will offer you herbs for indigestion, frankincense for protection against *djinn* and honey for strength, a favorite request of old men. I can remember one day when a man complained bitterly that the honey he'd bought was not strong

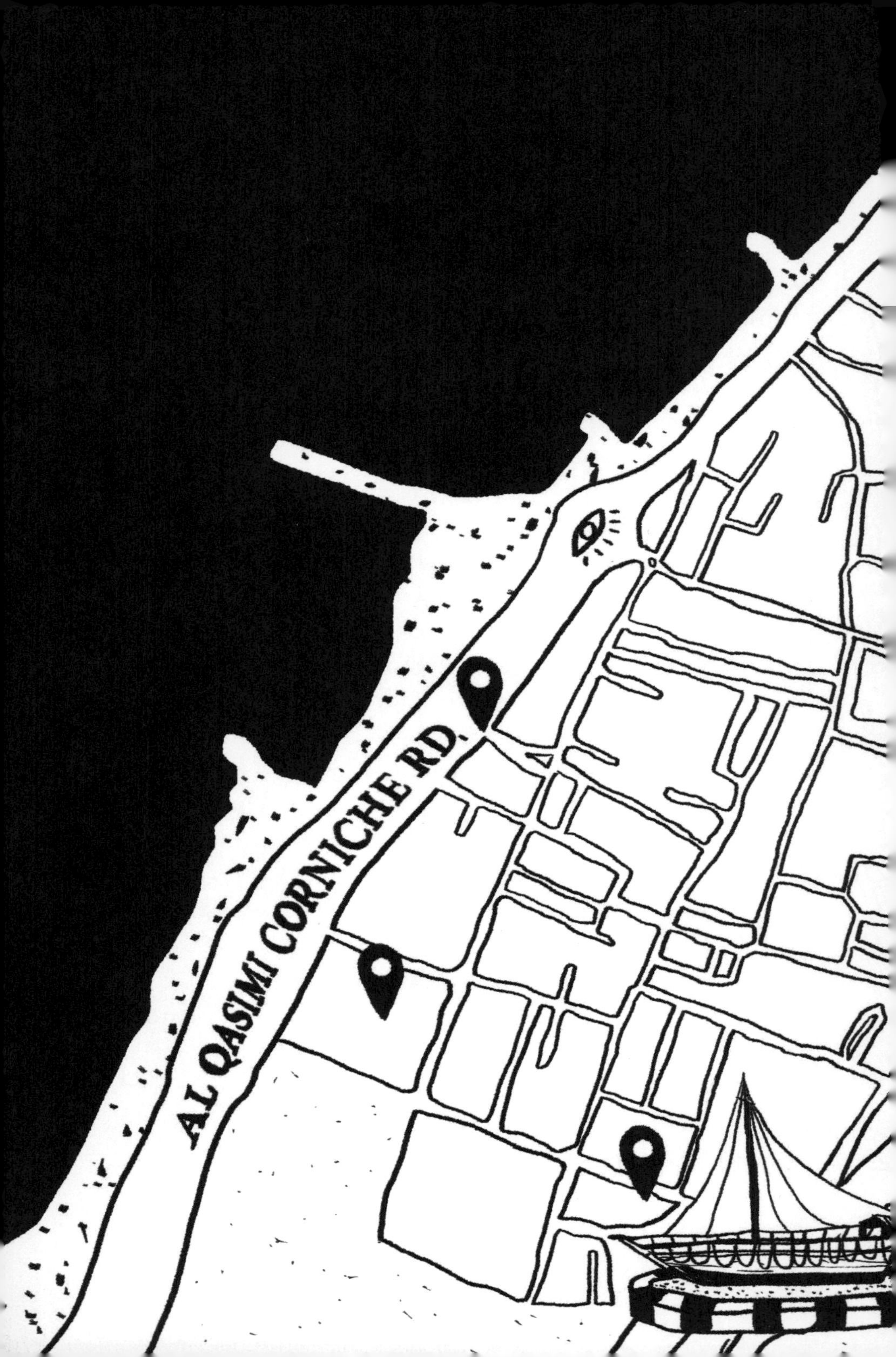
AL QASIMI CORNICHE RD

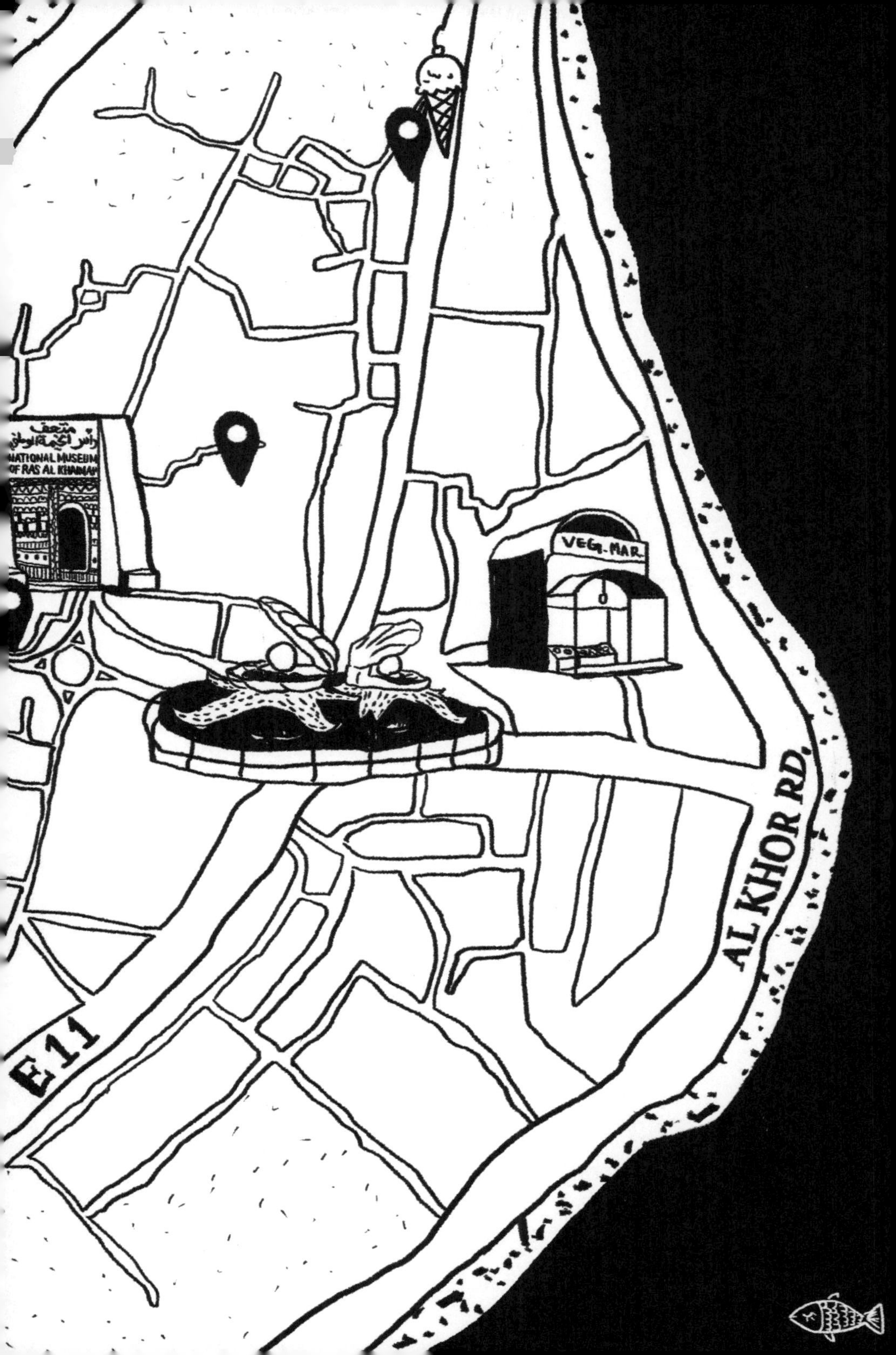
متحف
رأس الخيمة الوطني
NATIONAL MUSEUM
OF RAS AL KHAIMAH
VEG. MAR.
AL KHOR RD.
E 11

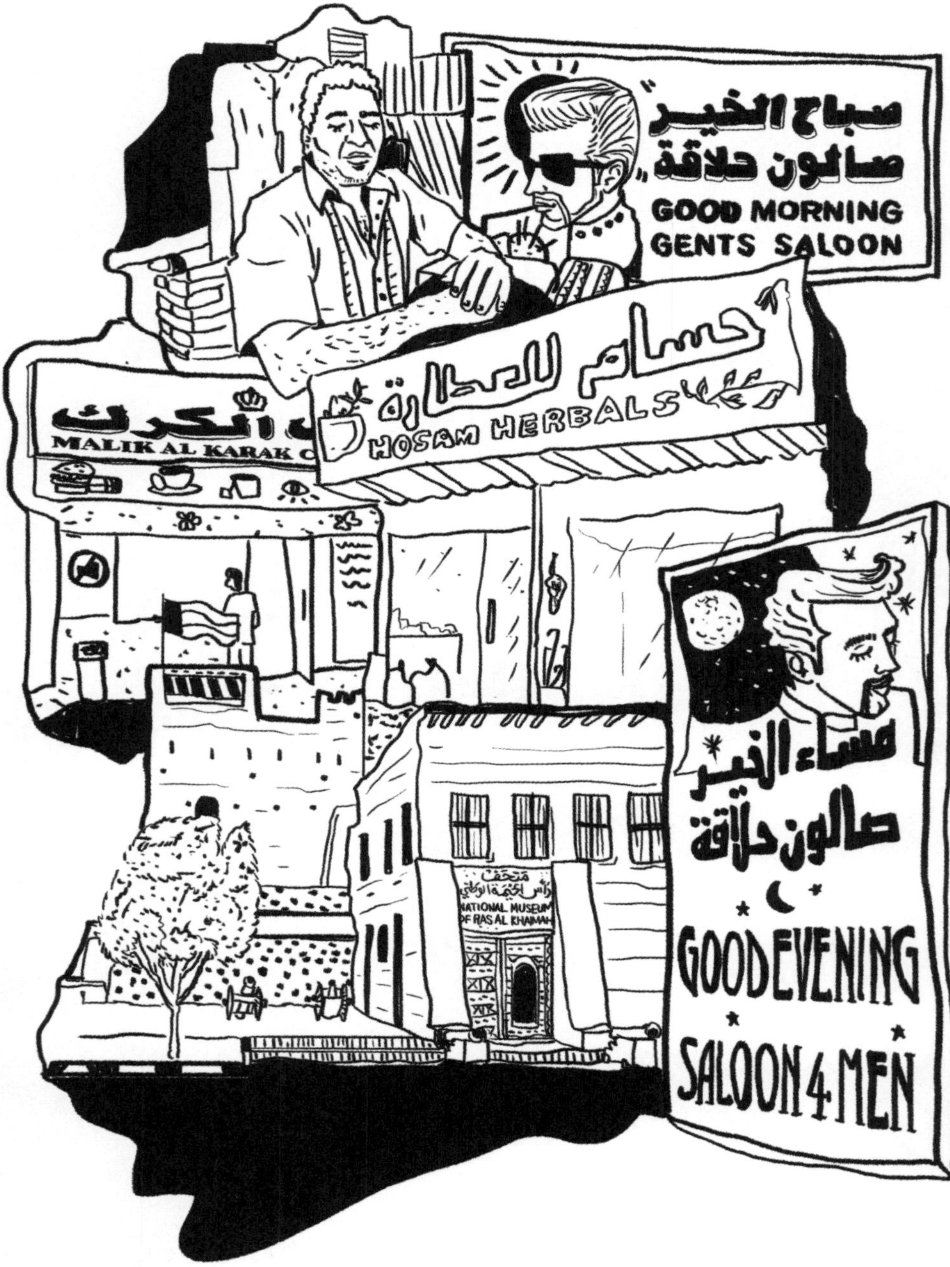
صباح الخير
صالون حلاقة
GOOD MORNING
GENTS SALOON
حسام للعطارة
HOSAM HERBALS
MALIK AL KARAK
متحف
رأس الخيمة الوطني
NATIONAL MUSEUM
OF RAS AL KHAIMAH
مساء الخير
صالون حلاقة
GOOD EVENING
SALOON 4 MEN

enough. Abdolhamid sighed when he left. "You know what this man wanted? He wanted to be Superman. He wanted to be young. But he is an old man." Contentment, Abdolhamid will tell you, is key to good health and low blood pressure.

Across the street, men can get a *kandora* tailored by Sultan Mohideen Liyakath, who journeyed across the Indian Ocean three times before he was allowed to stay in the Emirates. The first time, he came on a ship full of onions from Goa and was turned back at Fujairah because of insufficient paperwork. ("Oh, too much smell," said his son Mohideen.) The second time, Mohamed's ship was turned around because of military tensions between Pakistan and India. The third time, persistence paid off. Sultan landed in Dubai in 1973 with ten US dollars in his pocket.

If you're going to wear a *kandora* then you'll need a trimmed beard to match. Head back to Sidroh Street at the junction to find the barber, Shahid Mehmood, a third-generation Gulf migrant who runs the Good Morning Gents Saloon and the Good Evening Salon for Men next door.

Shahid Mehmood will not simply give you a shave and trim your beard hair by hair with a few fine clips of the scissors. He'll also tell you what has kept his family here for so long.

"The first time I saw Ras Al Khaimah, I said, 'I have come to the jungle.' I was crying too much. It got better. First of all, there were people from my village, the same village as me. We shared everything, every problem. We were like one household together, you know?" After an evening here, you will feel like part of the family too.

Djinn: In Islamic mythology and theology it refers to a class of spirits capable of taking human and animal forms

Harees: A staple dish in the UAE, especially during Ramadan, it is made from mashed wheat with either lamb or chicken.

Machboos: A traditional rice dish in the Gulf.

Saloona: A bedouin meat or fish stew dish.

Khameer: A round flatbread of bedouin origin that can be stuffed with either sweet or savory fillings.

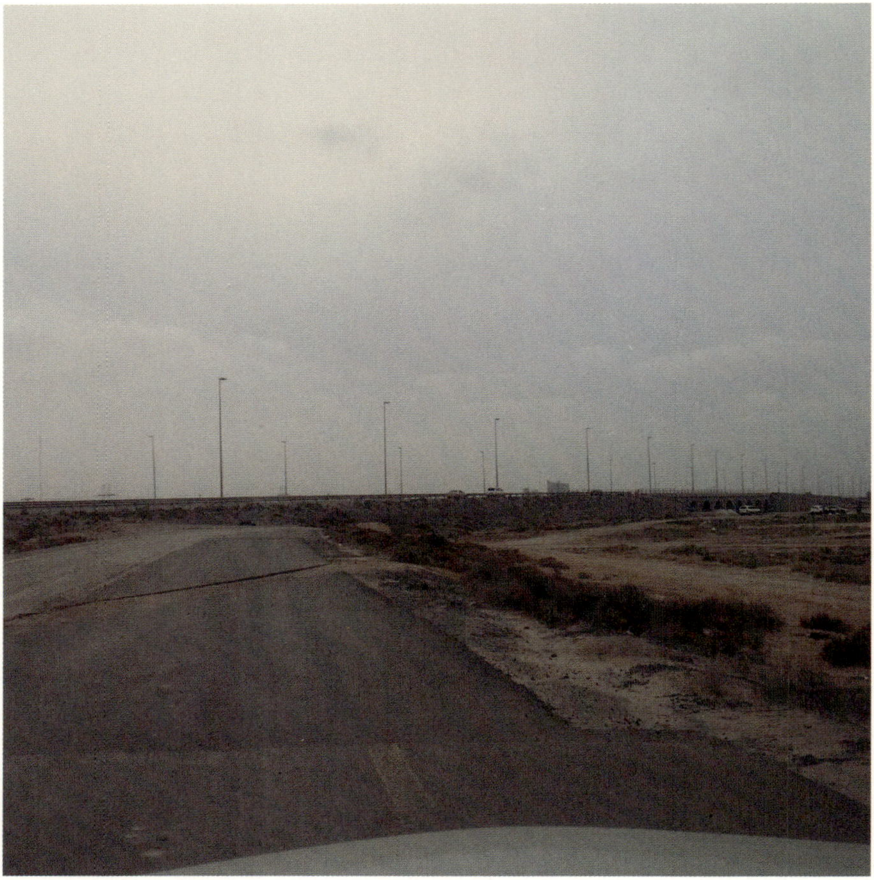

NORTHBOUND

MATTHEW MACLEAN

Talk to expats and Emiratis who lived in Dubai before the city's amazing growth over the last two decades, or scroll through the "Dubai—The good old days!" Facebook group, and you might be overwhelmed by nostalgia for a place you probably never saw. Nostalgia for a small, tight-knit place where people knew their neighbors, when the rent and the restaurants were affordable, and people of different nationalities mixed and mingled because the place just wasn't big enough for everyone to be segregated. Back then, there were no traffic jams and one could get from Deira to the World Trade Center in just a few minutes, or so it is said.

I never lived through those days—I first came to Dubai in 2004—but as a historian of the UAE I can't help but try to imagine them. The closest I've come to living them was my year in Ras al-Khaimah, a 110-kilometer drive to the north. Ras al-Khaimah still embodies today many of the qualities that people miss about "old" Dubai. People know their neighbors, you can be recognized a "regular" at a shop or a restaurant, and there really are no traffic jams. It's easy to find history, too; buildings from the 50s, 70s, 90s, and yesterday jostle against each other, and the city feels more lived-in and less name-branded than its more famous neighbor. One can't escape the natural world either; Ras al-Khaimah lies on an ever-narrowing plain between the Gulf and the mountains, and every day you'll probably see both.

Rightly or wrongly, Ras al-Khaimah and the other "Northern Emirates" are something of a mystery to many Dubai residents; as in other regions, the periphery has a much better idea of the center than vice versa. Even the name is telling—we speak of the "Northern Emirates" and the "East Coast," but do we ever hear Dubai and Abu Dhabi described as the "Southern Emirates"? Do Fujairah residents talk of going over the mountains to the "West Coast" to escape the hordes of tourists looking for a weekend getaway? No, it is simply assumed that Dubai is the center, and other regions have names that describe their relation to Dubai. But I've always believed that no center exists in isolation, and that the burden is on the people in the center to escape and explore.

But how does one get from Dubai to Ras al-Khaimah? For most of the 5,000 years humans have lived in this region, the answer would have been by camel, foot, or boat. Only in the 1950s did automobiles arrive in the region, and they were scarce. There were no paved roads, and one drove along the beach at low tide or followed the tracks of earlier cars on a more inland route. Today, the explorer has three options. Most drivers take E311 (Mohammed bin Zayed Road), fighting their way through impossible traffic at the Dubai-Sharjah boundary, six lanes in either direction. The E611 (Emirates Road) is for the most part free of traffic jams, but takes you way out in the desert, avoiding the booming Dubai-Sharjah-Ajman megalopolis completely. Soon it too will be swallowed by advancing developments. Both options have little to offer other than speed; your standard ADNOC Oasis stops, a fast-food chain or two, and not much else.

The third option takes the longest by time, but the E11 is part of the UAE's poetic geography and history. It was the first paved road linking different emirates (Dubai, Sharjah, Ajman, Umm al-Quwain, and Ras al-Khaimah; roads to Abu Dhabi and Fujairah would come later). At its start in Deira, the road is nothing like it was in "the good old days". Known here as Al-Ittihad Road, its traffic is appalling at all hours. Once a small, two-lane highway, it is now six lanes on either side; there are flyovers and underpasses, service roads and Salik. But it wasn't always like this; as recently as 1965, the area between Sharjah and Dubai was empty desert and a long stretch of untamed shoreline. Yet that desert was the site of intense diplomatic intrigue that led to the construction of the E11.

In the 1960s, there was no UAE federation, just seven independent Sheikhdoms under British protection collectively known as the Trucial States, the Trucial Sheikhdoms, the Trucial Coast, or Trucial Oman. Whatever its name, the Gulf's new-found oil had made the area strategically important. As oil funds had yet to flow to the people of the Trucial Coast, they went north to wealthy Kuwait to find work as electricians, carpenters, taxi drivers, and much else. They brought back new sympathies for anti-colonialism and pan-Arab nationalism. Egyptian and Palestinian schoolteachers brought these ideas to the youth in Dubai, Sharjah, and Ras al-Khaimah, and Gamal Abdel Nasser's speeches on *Sawt al-Arab* radio thrilled listeners in supposedly remote places at this edge of the Arab world, turning them against the British.

By 1964, the Arab League had tried to take advantage of this situation, proposing to fund a road connecting different Sheikhdoms in the name of Arab brotherhood. British diplomats were worried—they too had to promise a road, even though there were less than one hundred automobiles in Ras al-Khaimah at the time. At stake were multimillion-dollar contracts and the proverbial "winning hearts and minds". Ambassadors were chased onto airplanes, British diplomats woke ruling Sheikhs out of their beds in the dead of night, secret oaths were sworn. In June 1965, the British kept the Arab League out by force, but then Saudi Arabia's King Faisal outfoxed them too—he had more money at hand, and could

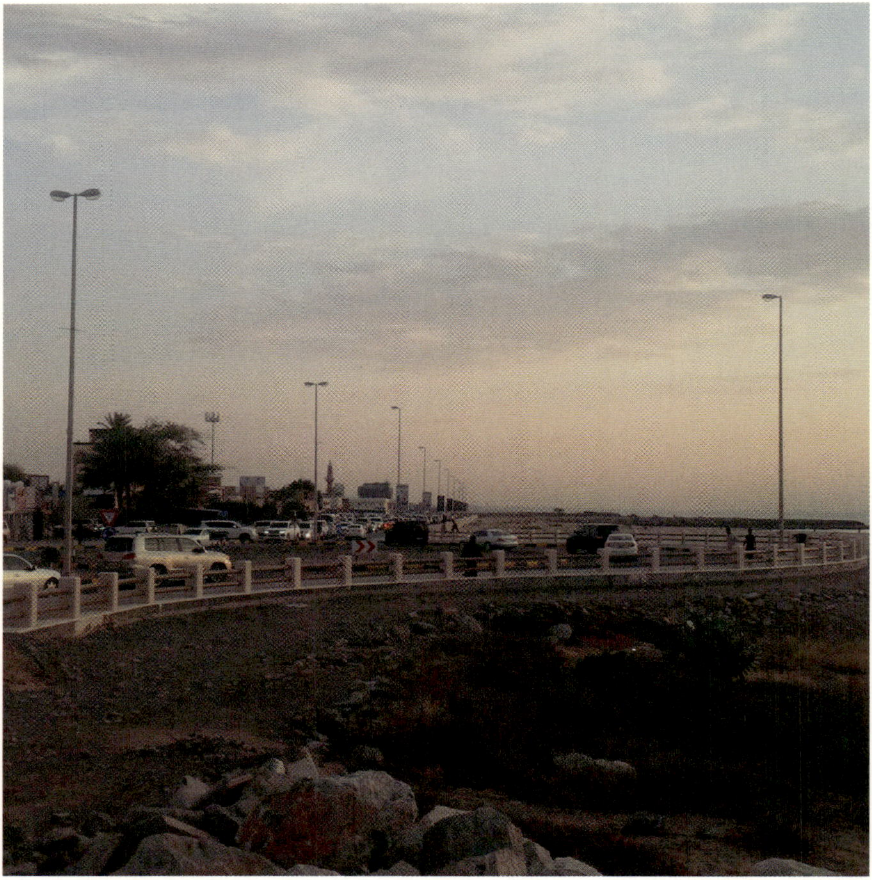

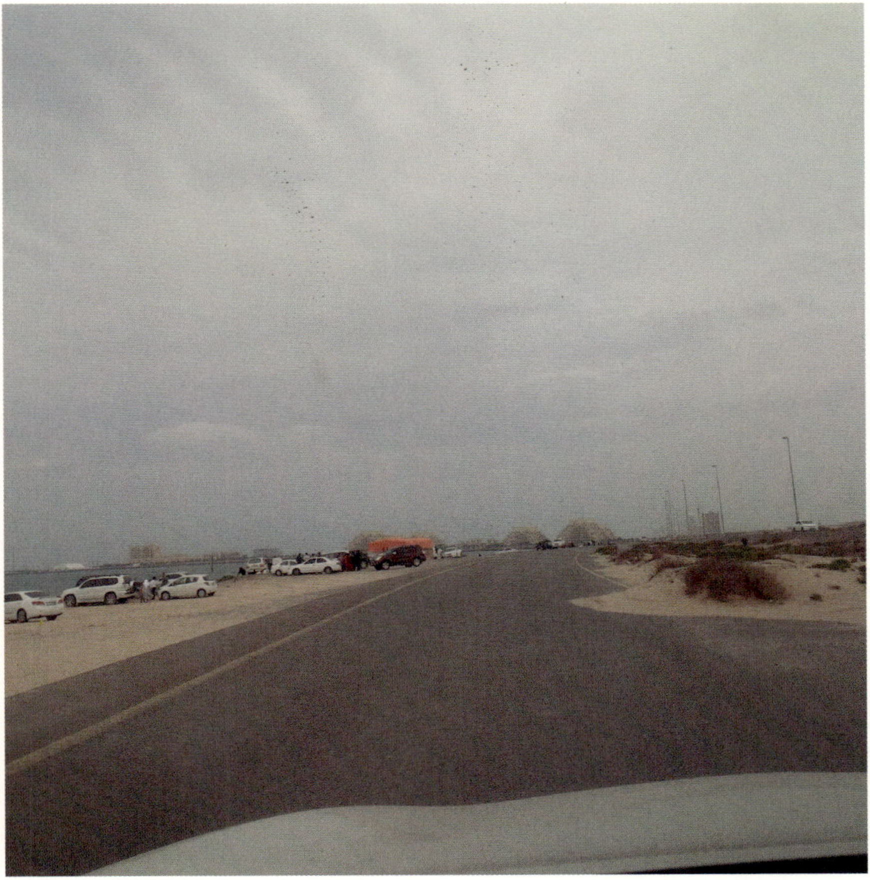

take advantage of the pro-Arab feeling in the region. When the Saudis delayed, the British went ahead and awarded the Dubai-Sharjah section of the road to their company, Halcrow. The Saudis then completed the Sharjah-Ras al-Khaimah section just as Sheikh Zayed began to ensure that the people of the Trucial States would begin to share in the region's new-found wealth.

Cross the border into Sharjah and now you're on al-Wahda Street—the name still evoking unity and brotherhood—passing through a mini-Dubai of tall apartment buildings with cheaper rent than in Dubai itself. If you keep following today's E11, you'll deviate from the road's earlier route, which passed around the edge of old Sharjah. The roadway itself suddenly takes flight, its elevated lanes are still jammed with traffic. I had a view of the road once from a cheap room in the CityMax hotel, an amazingly appropriate stroke of luck for a graduate student who had just come across the documents in the British National Archives on the road's birth fifty years before. The traffic went on all day and all night.

Only on arrival in Hamriya—a slice of Sharjah on the other side of Ajman—does one get a glimpse of the wide open road of earlier times. There are a few houses in the distance, and some exits here and there, but the sky is wide open. Then comes Umm al-Quwain, and an important clue to the road's history—the turnoff to the town itself is named King Faisal Road, after its original benefactor. You'll see the long lines of one-story shops and cafeterias that give the Northern Emirates their human scale. A stop at this cafeteria yields one of my favorite Chips Oman sandwiches, a full meal with just the right amount of spice for two dirhams and fifty fils.

But it's between Umm al-Quwain city and Ras al-Khaimah where the road turns glorious. If you've done it right, you left Dubai in the morning and only now in very late afternoon are you watching the sun beginning to set over the Gulf to your left. You're forced to slow down; the speed limit is 80, not the usual 120. A mysterious airplane sits on an abandoned tarmac, just before you pass the (in)famous Barracuda. Nobody quite knows how it got there, but it inspired a reporter for *The National* to conduct what turned out to be a fruitless search. There is an architecturally one-of-a-kind ADNOC station at the roadside near the neighborhood of al-Rafaah, its roof arched like birds' wings.

But mostly, it's just beautiful coastline that draws weekend crowds. Nearly everywhere along the E11, the original road has either been diverted, expanded, or simply lost. But here it survives, first in a small bridge —abandoned between two newer ones—and then in a single lane of pavement that unintentionally helps those crowds drive down to the waterside before turning into a dead end, cut off by the new roadway.

After that it's straight ahead again to Ras al-Khaimah itself. Go as far as you can, through the oldest part of the city, and at the end the road suddenly curves around to the old Corniche, with the Gulf now right in front of you. At sunset, this Corniche is the place to see and be seen and a hive of activity. Impromptu cricket and football on the beach, selfies on the rock jetties and the sidewalk, *karak* tea at the cafeterias, and car-washing in the parking lot. Traffic moves slowly, but nobody is really trying to go anywhere; the shouts and honks are greetings, not warnings. For a moment or two, I can imagine this is the good old days people talk about. Perhaps it is, but the roadway, the Corniche, and the beach are all modern inventions, built in part to help prevent flooding; in the UAE even the coastlines are always changing. And yet, whenever I'm on that corniche, I can't help feeling like I've recovered a bit of what many remember from their own pasts.

Sawt al-Arab, or 'Voice of the Arabs', was a prominent Egyptian transnational radio station. From the mid 1950s to the early 1970s, it was the main medium through which Gamal Abdel Nasser's messages promoting pan-Arabian unity were broadcast.

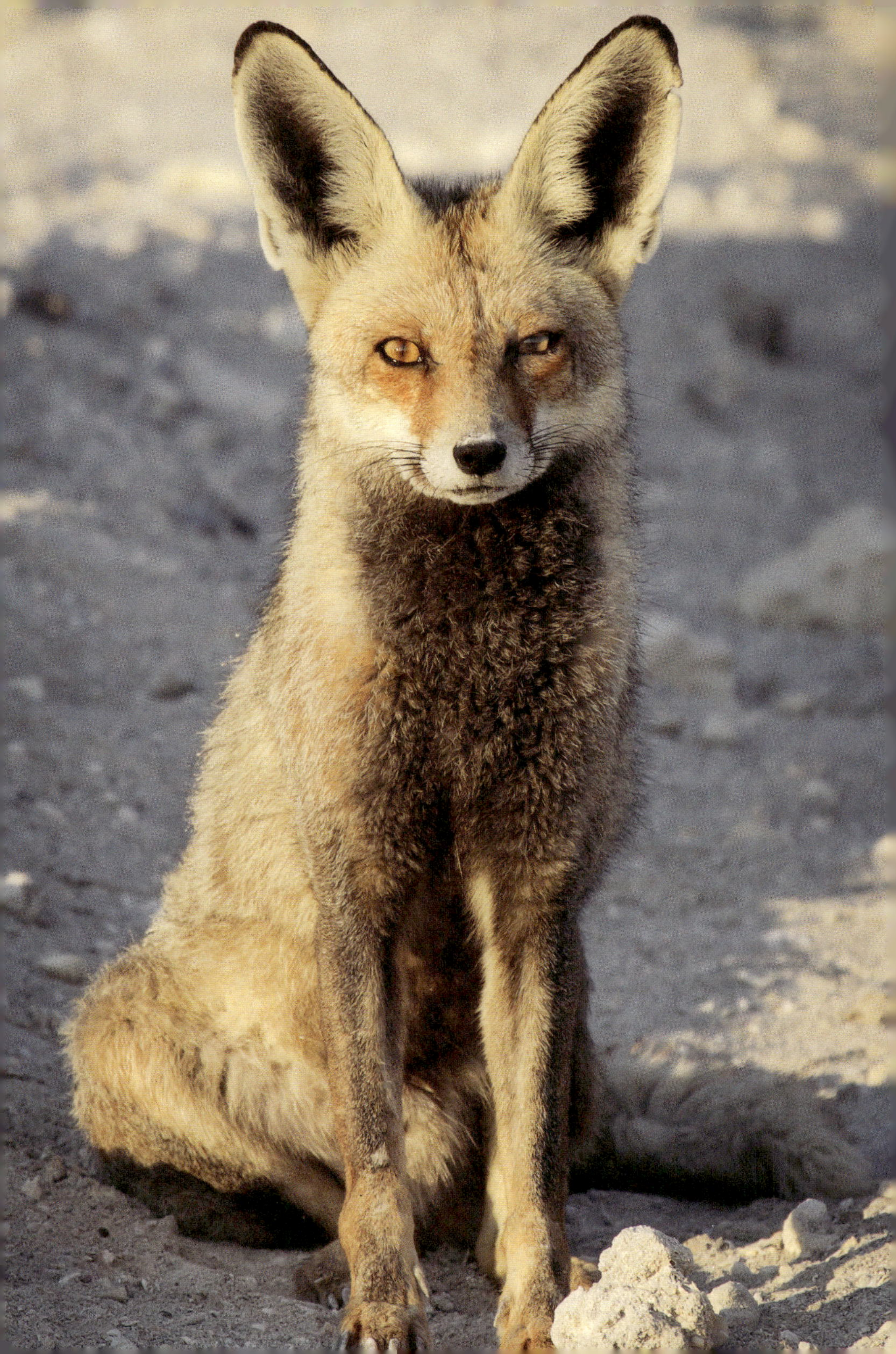

ARABIAN FOX

ROB GUBIANI

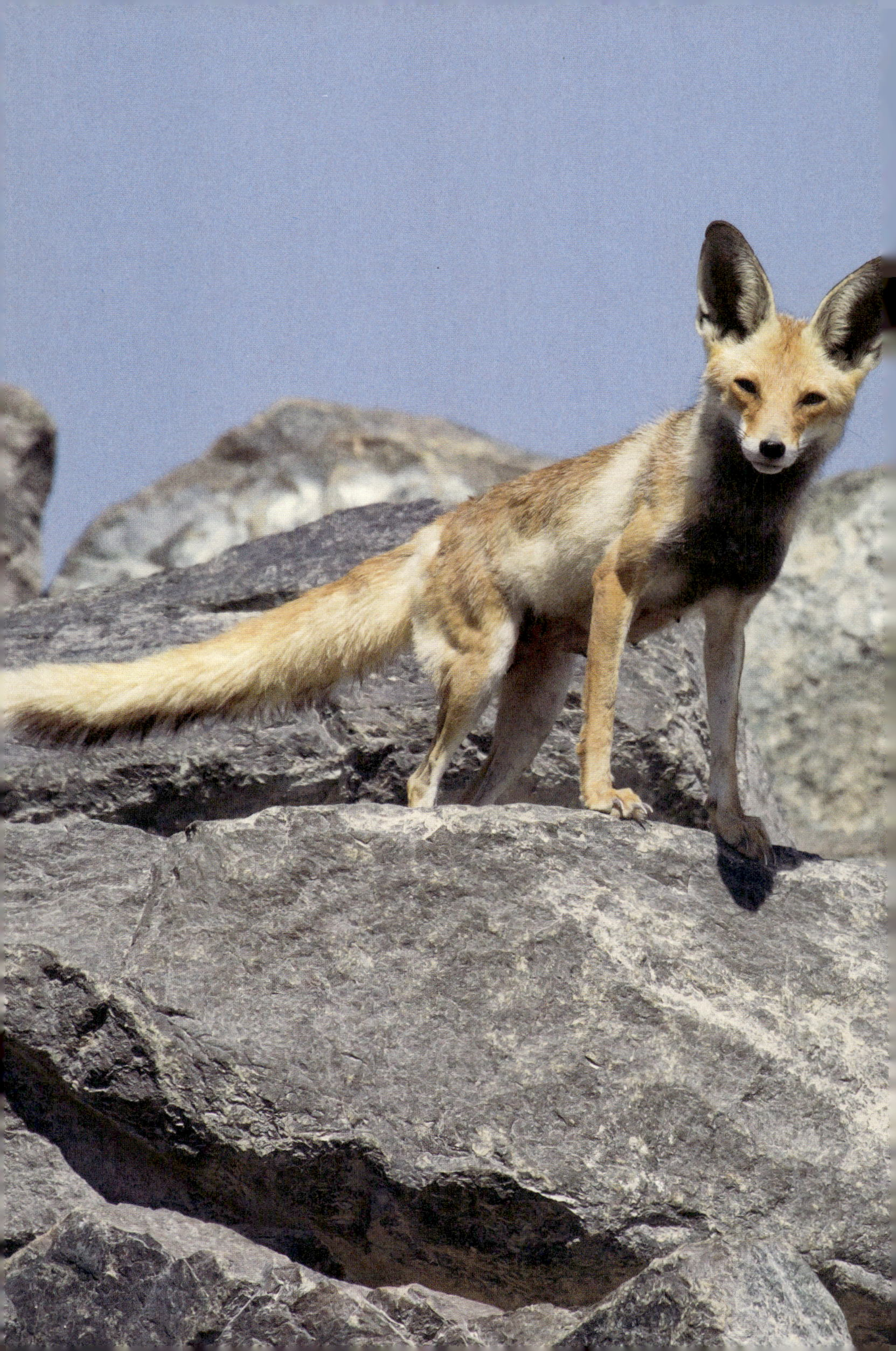

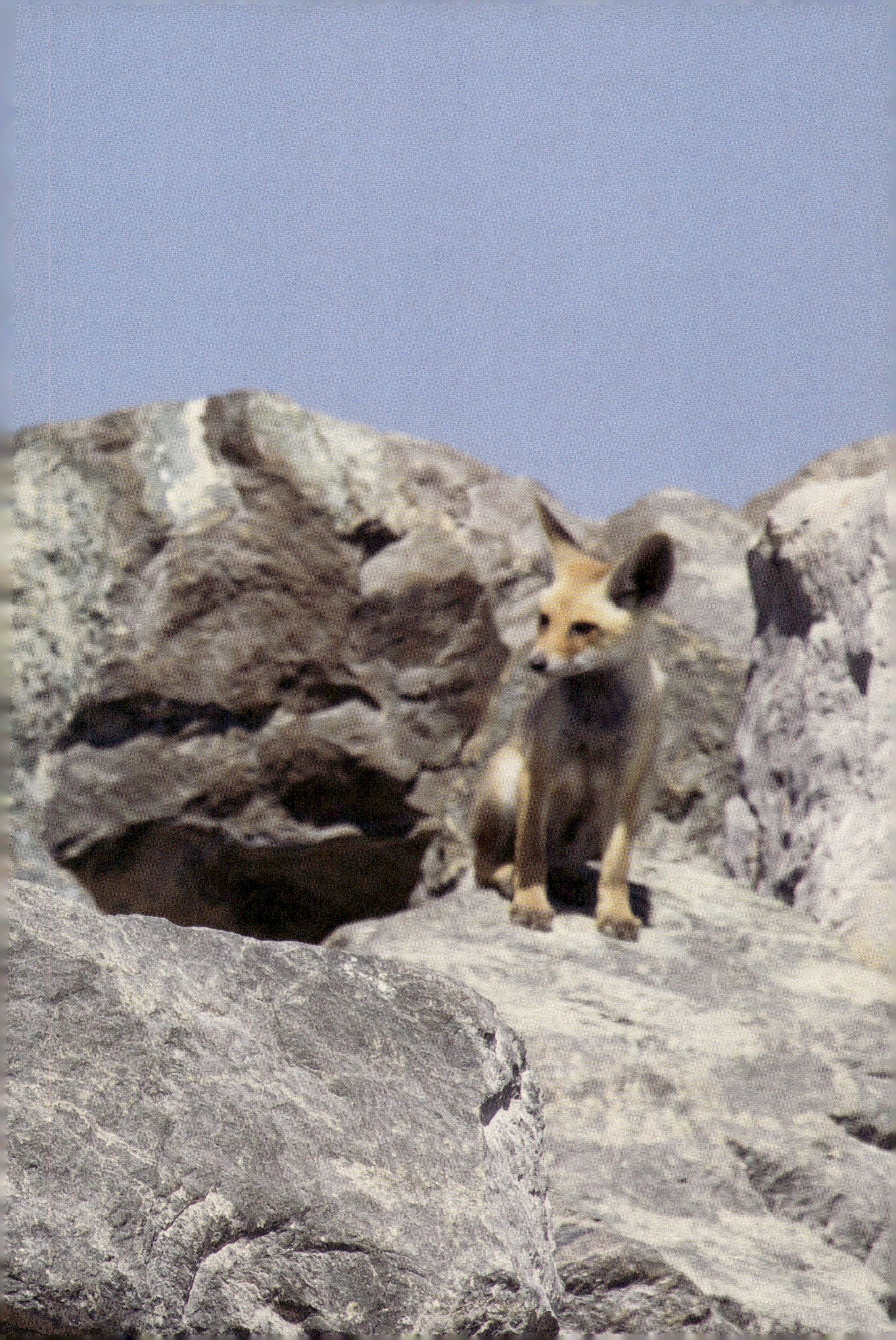

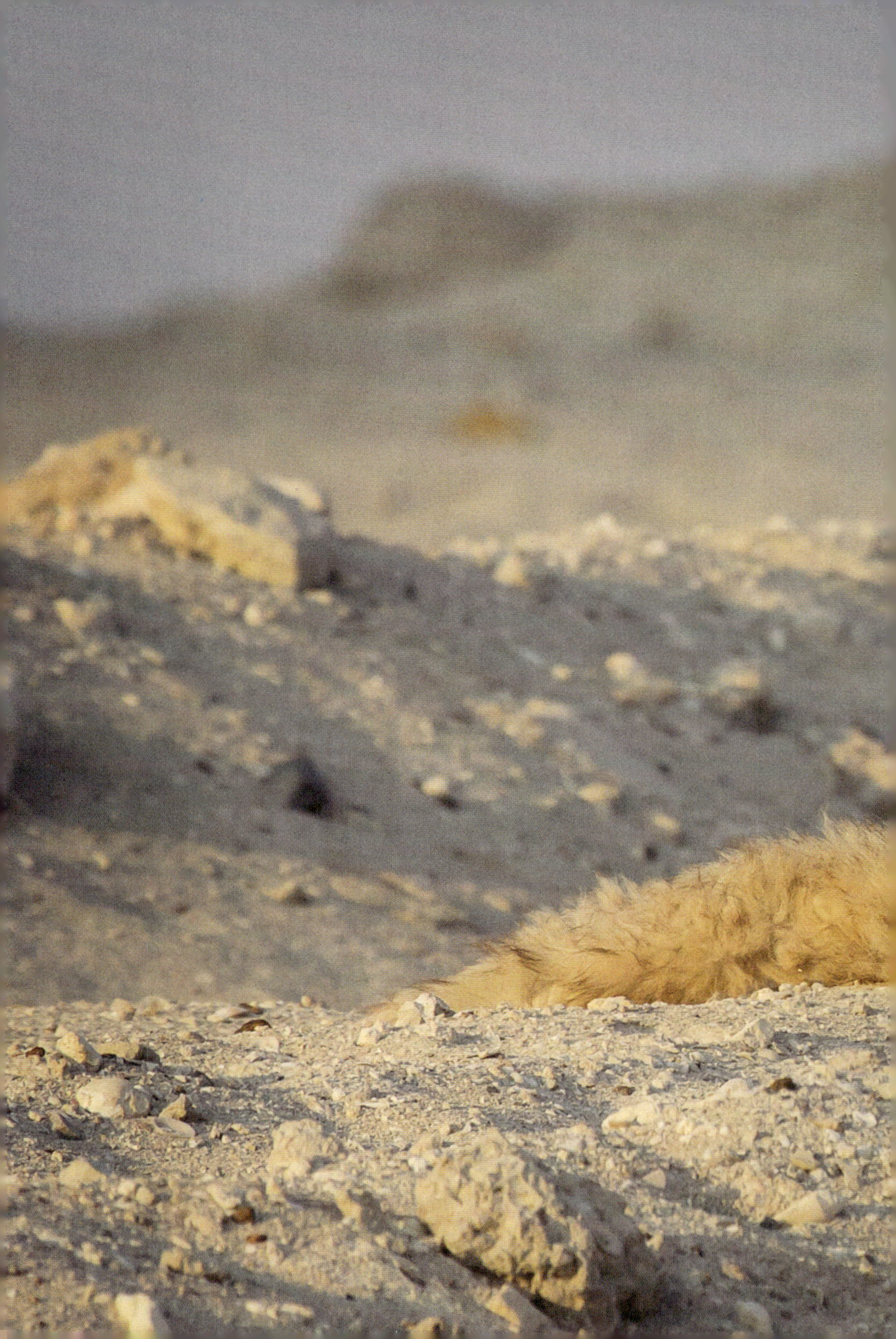

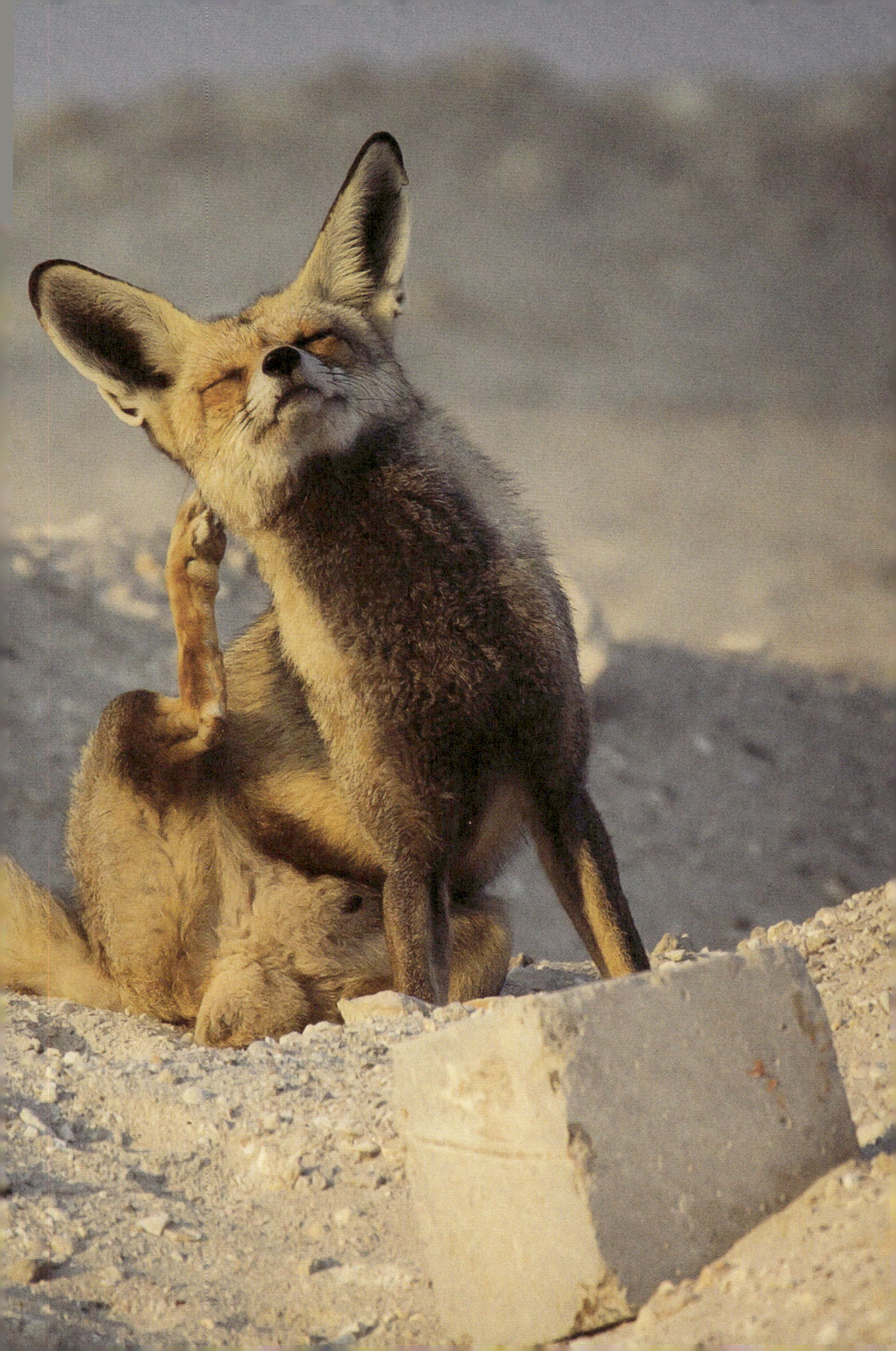

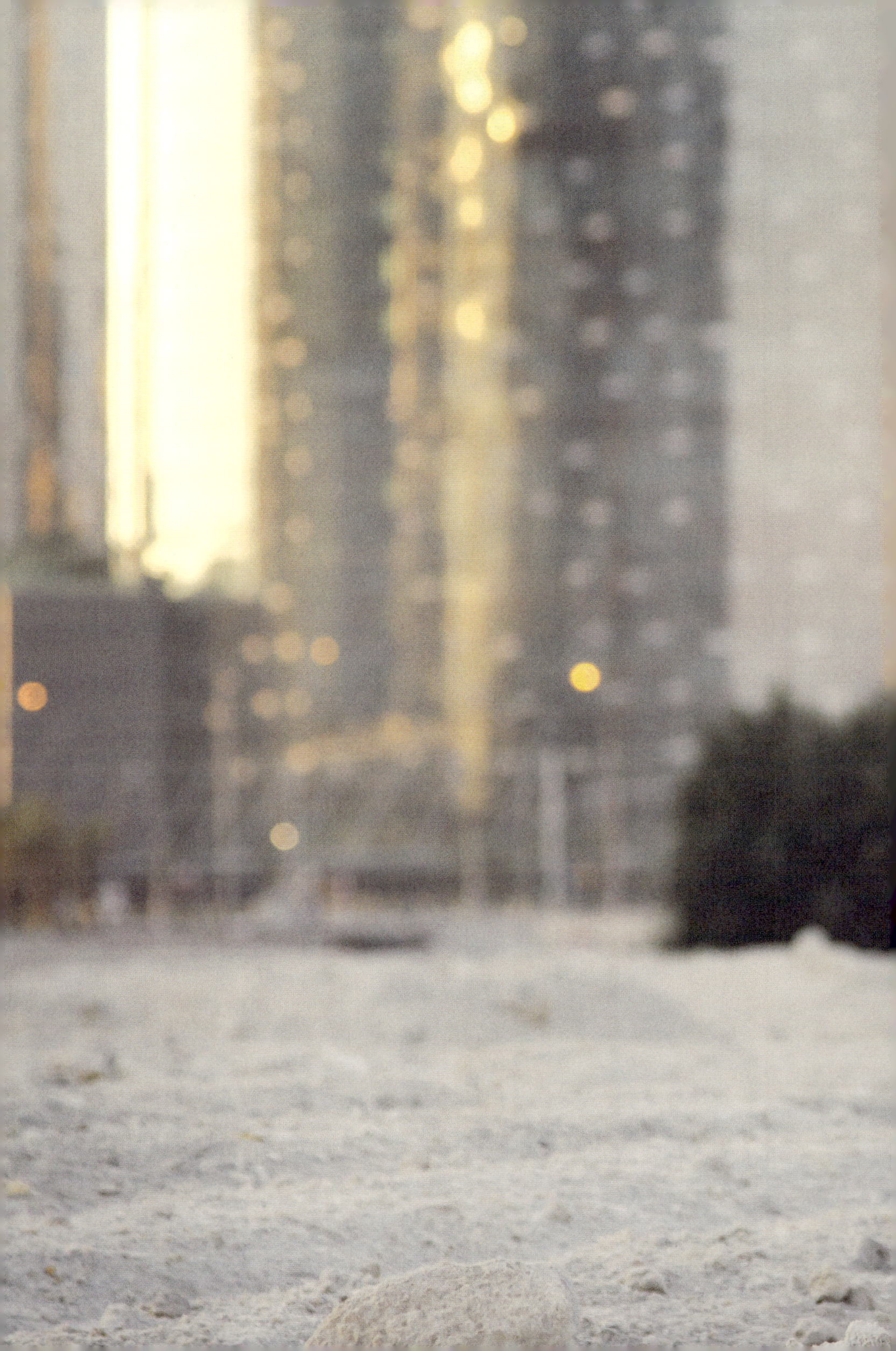

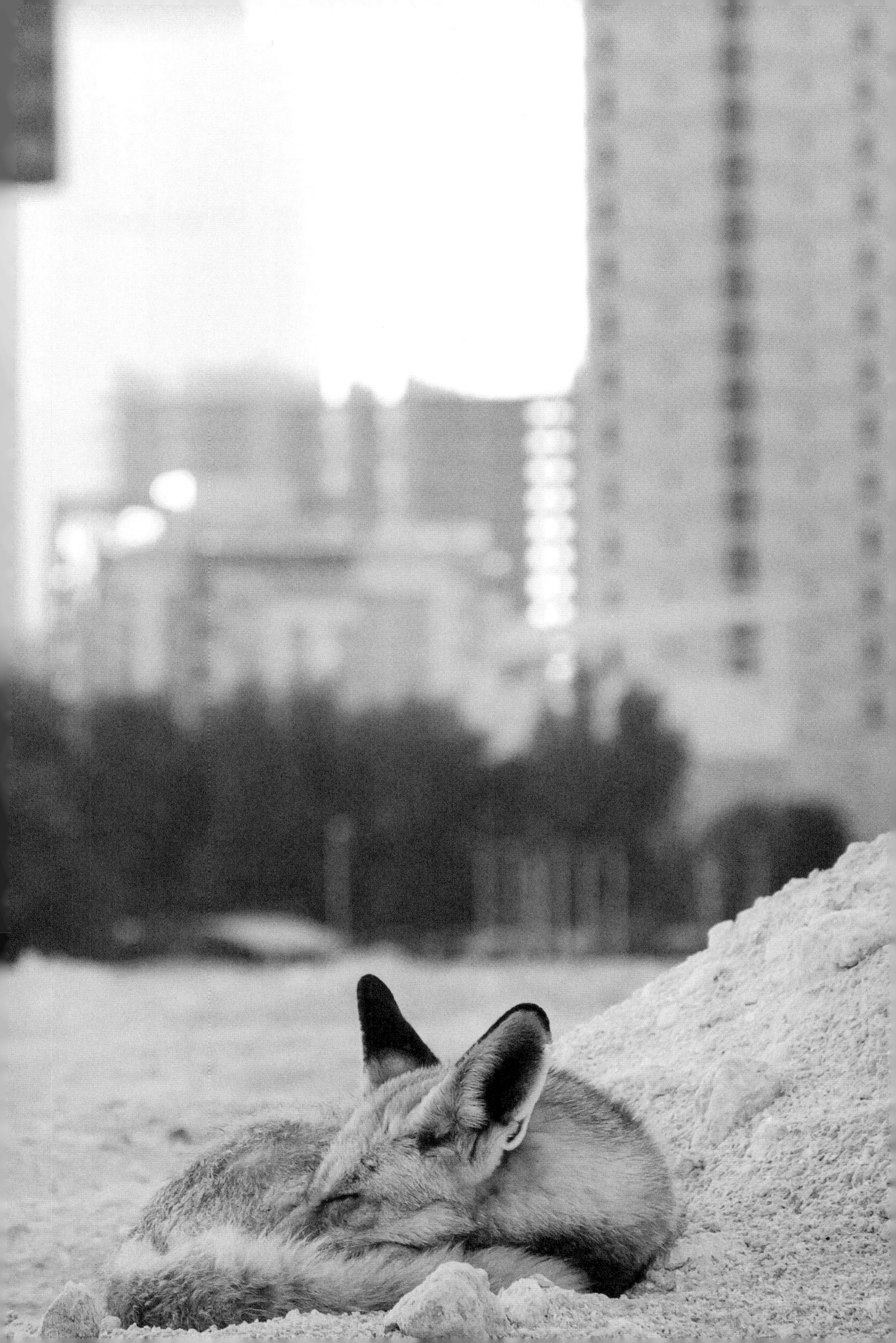

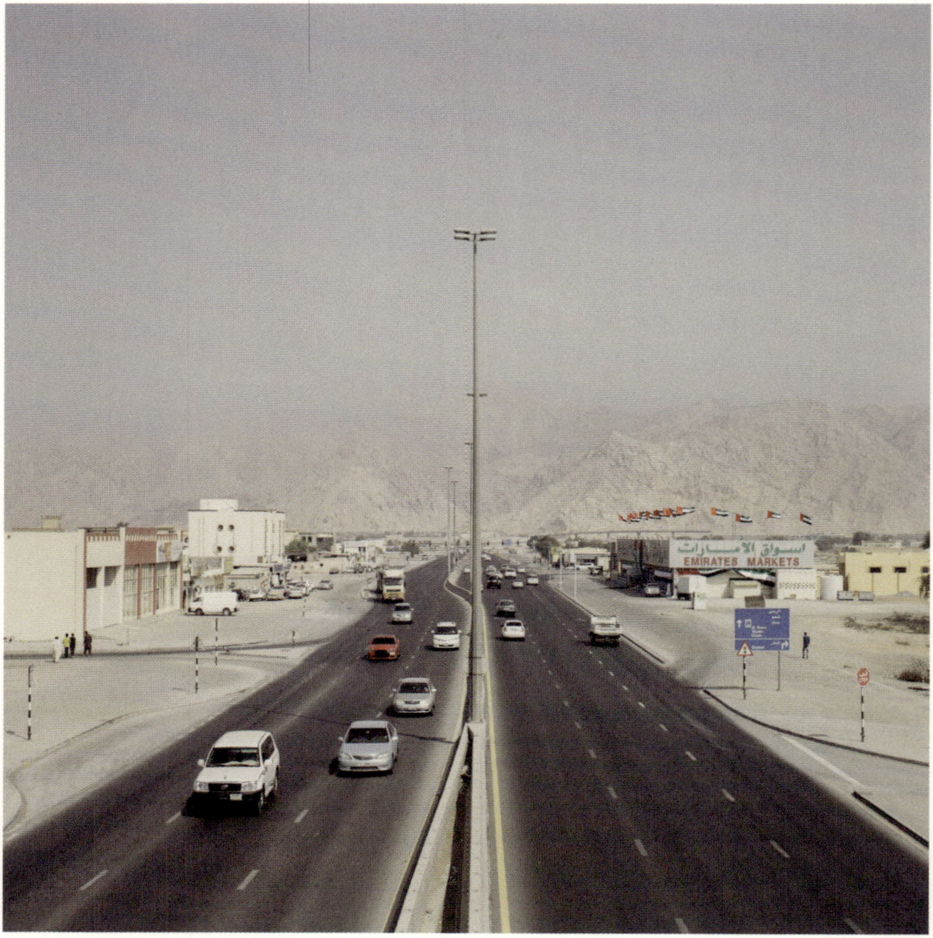
اسواق الامارات
EMIRATES MARKETS

SHA'AM

RAZAN AL ZAYANI

The fresh and salty scent of the sea lingers all over Sha'am, on the sands of the open beach, in the small farms dotted across the coast, in the open courtyards of the Emirati houses, and sometimes en route to the Hajjar mountains that hug Sha'am ever so tightly. This sleepy village situated in the northernmost tip of the UAE just before the border with Oman doesn't receive too many tourists, most pass by the town without giving it a second thought, eager to get to their weekend getaway in Musandam.

The road to Sha'am is constantly in flux, one drives out of the frenzied city highways of Dubai, onto Sharjah, then Ajman until the road finally opens up to the red-rich desert sands of Umm Al Quwain and Ras Al Khaimah. This desert road has changed in recent years, with bulldozers, new side roads, and ongoing construction visible and present on both sides of the highway. They are signs of changes to come, ones which will slowly encroach on the sleepy village of Sha'am.

For now, Sha'am conjures up a nostalgia for a simpler time and space. Little shops, restaurants and mini grocery stores line the main road, a visual cacophony of neon lights, plastic seating arrangements, inflatable beach paraphernalia, and ever so occasionally a goat or two passing by, further completing the landscape. Young teenagers zip past on derelict scooters, weaving in and out of the main street, the mountains opening up to them above and the open sea revealing itself to them below.

The beach is the focal point of the community; it is where families, fishermen, expats and locals alike gather daily in the late afternoon to spend time outdoors. Fishing trucks drive up right to the water on one side of the beach, Emiratis and Bangladeshis working side by side to load the day's catch. Some casually jog up and down the beach, stopping every so often for small chat with other village residents. On the far side of the beach is a women-only section, where the women swim, relax and picnic while their children splash and play in the azure waters. The communal convergence of the sea as a source of sustenance and joy, for so many, fosters an unspoken mutual understanding of its importance. The residents that aren't fishermen, commute and work outside of the town, some even driving to Dubai and back everyday, are constantly reminded that change is coming. But for now, things will hopefully remain as they are.

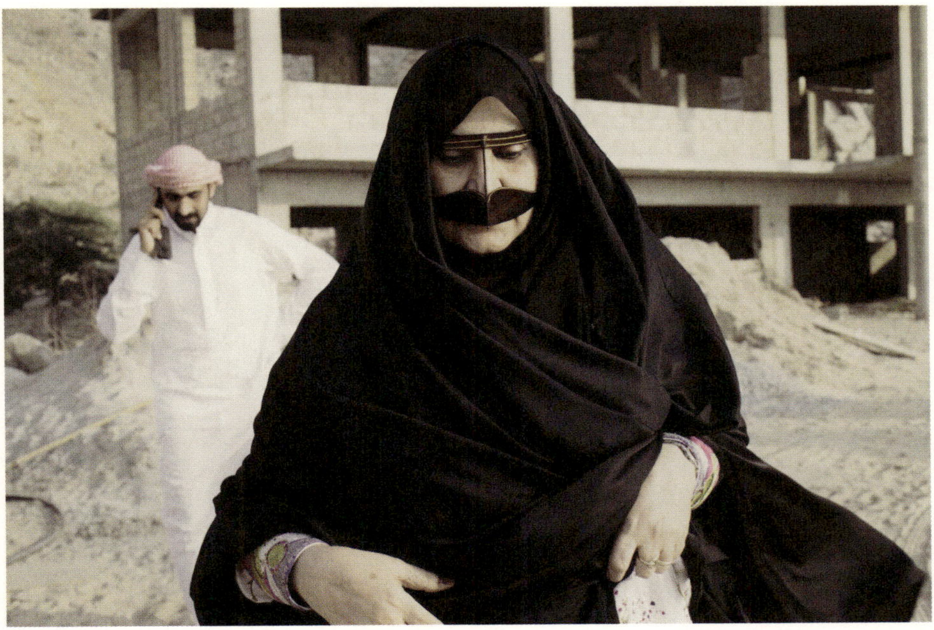

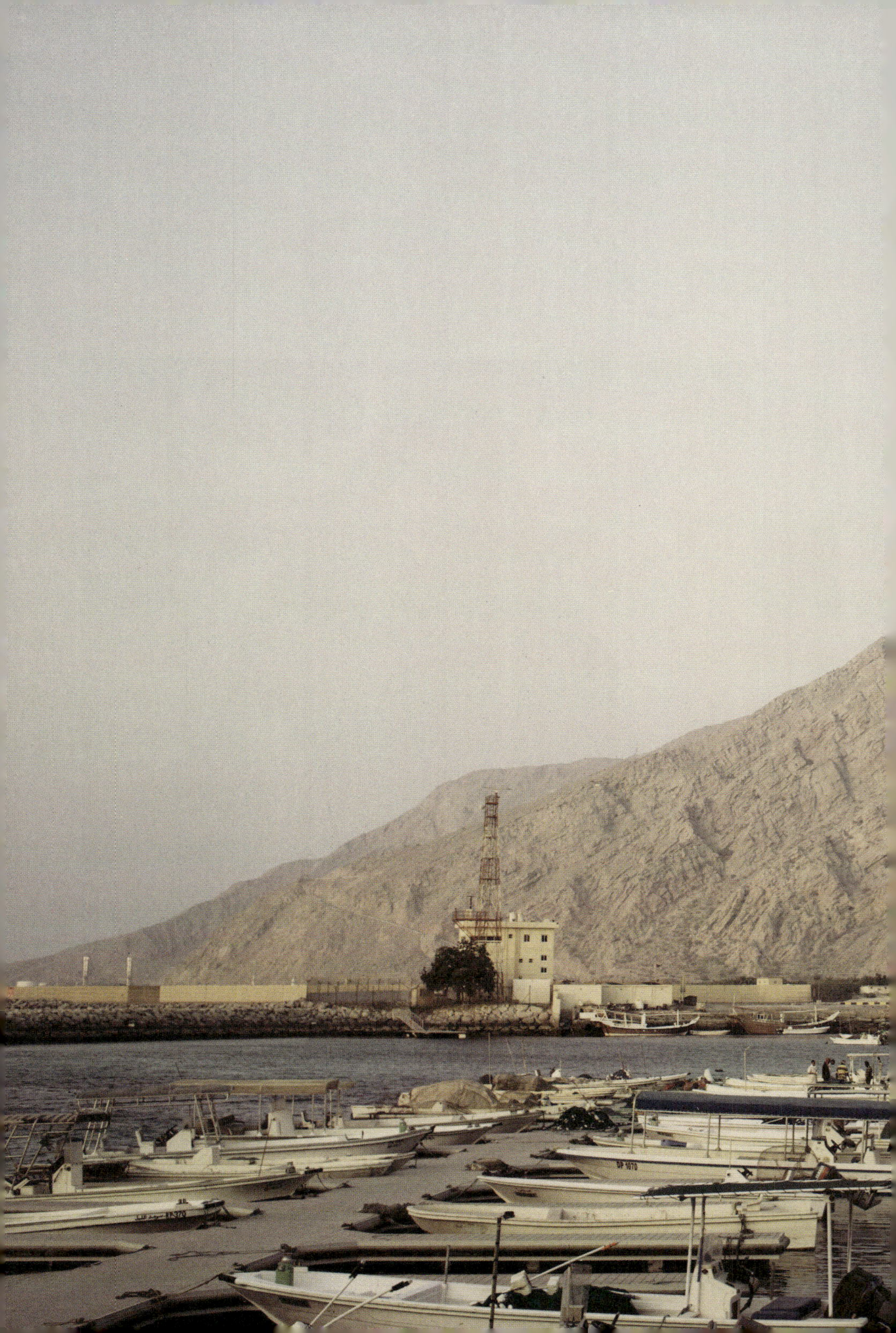

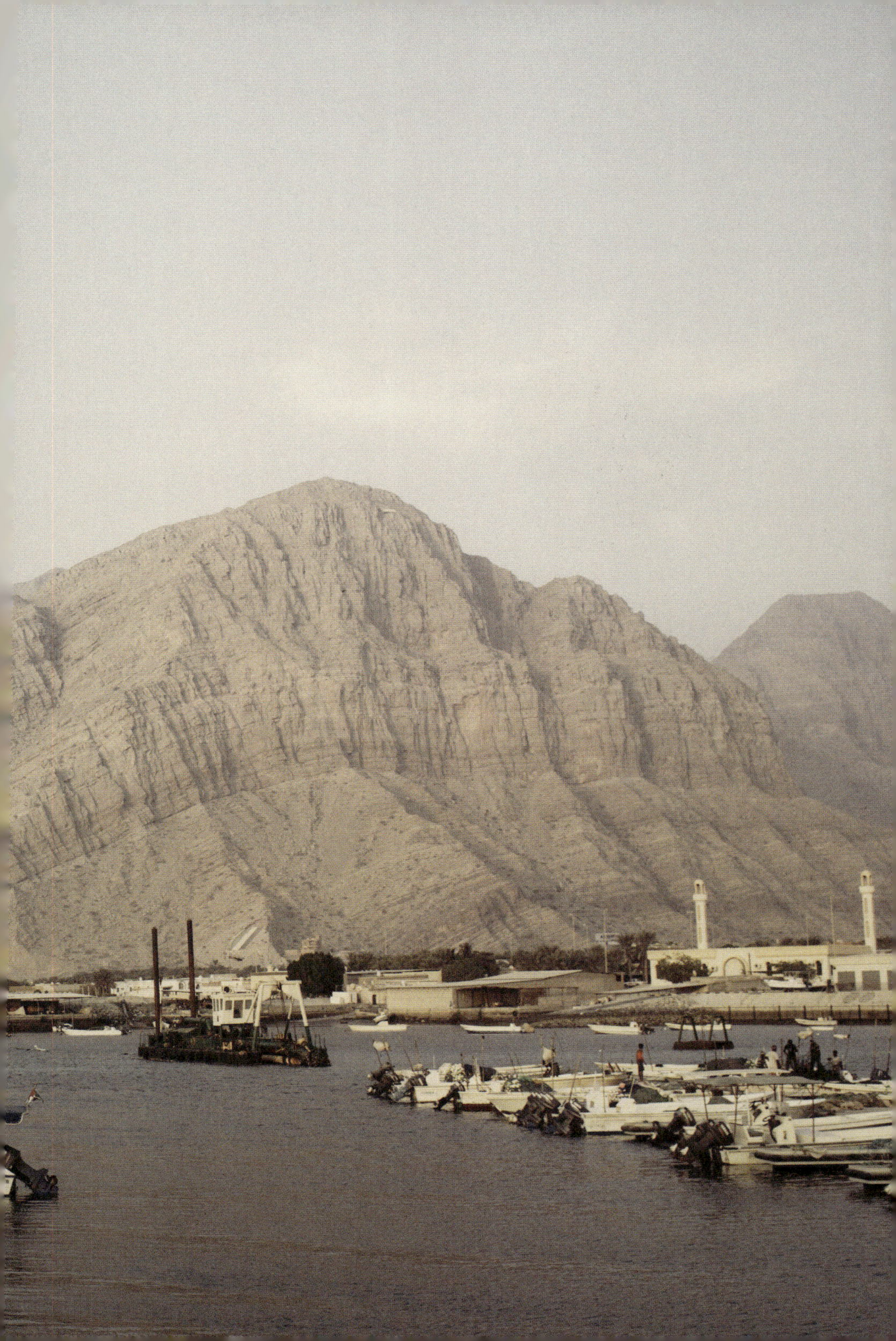

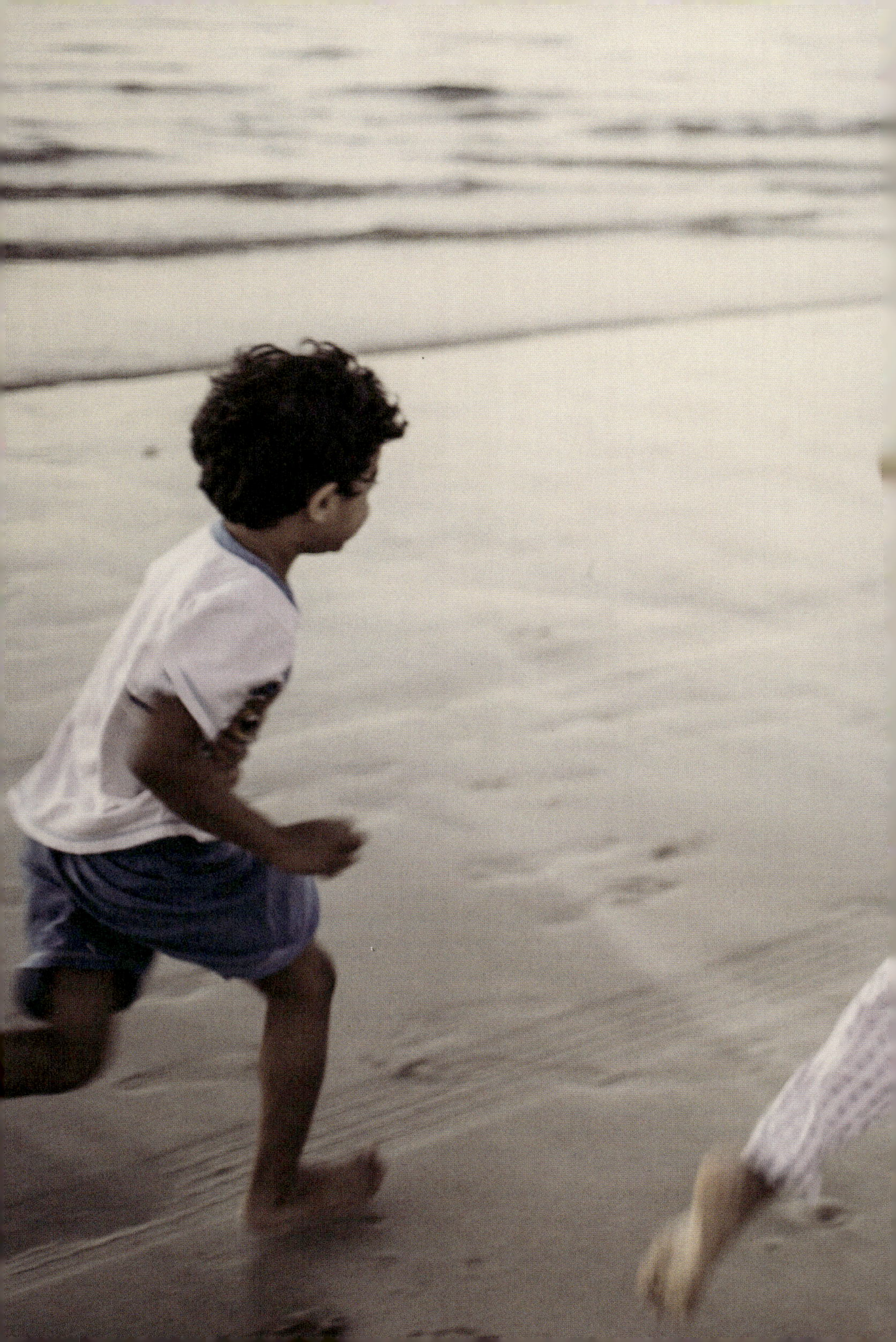

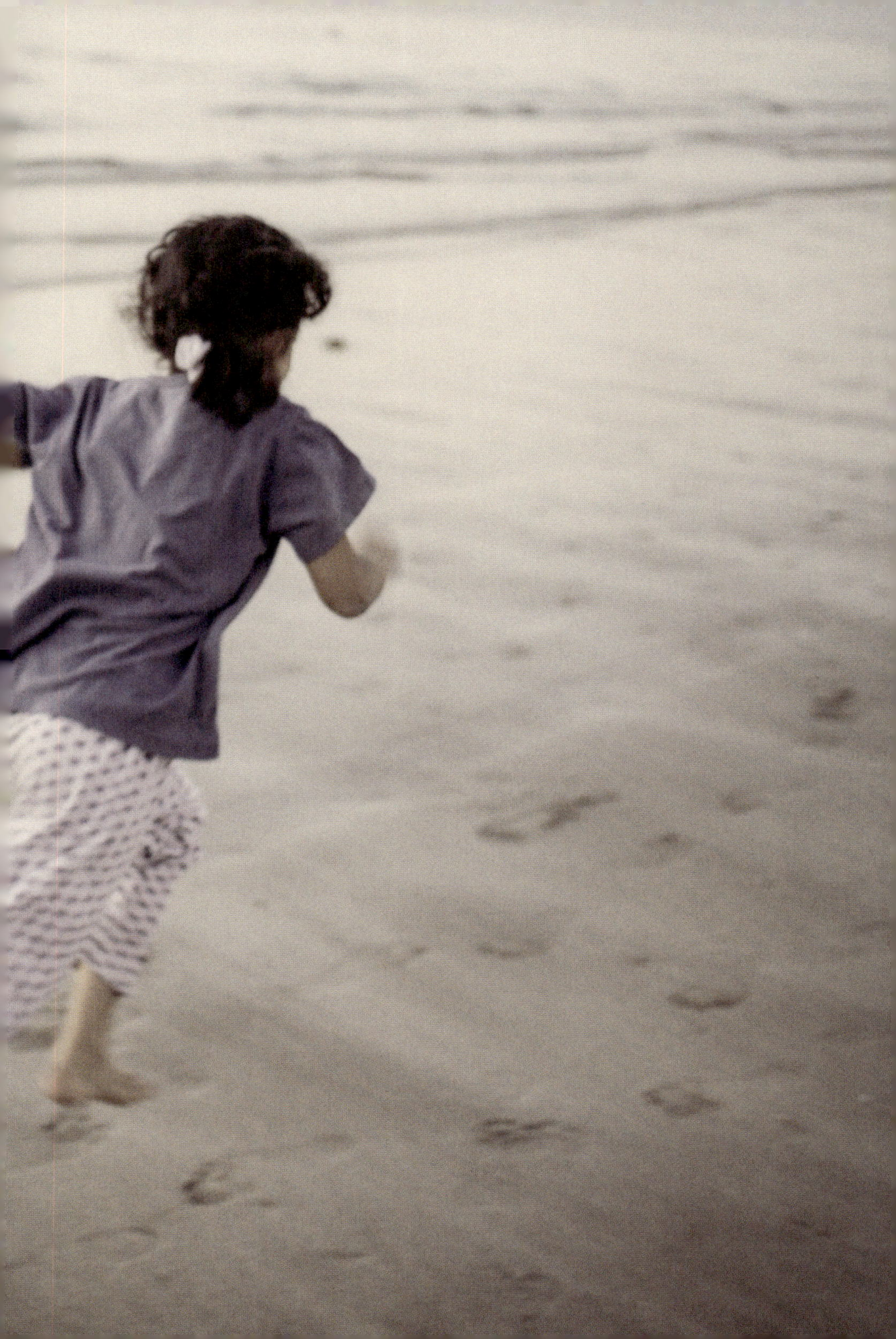

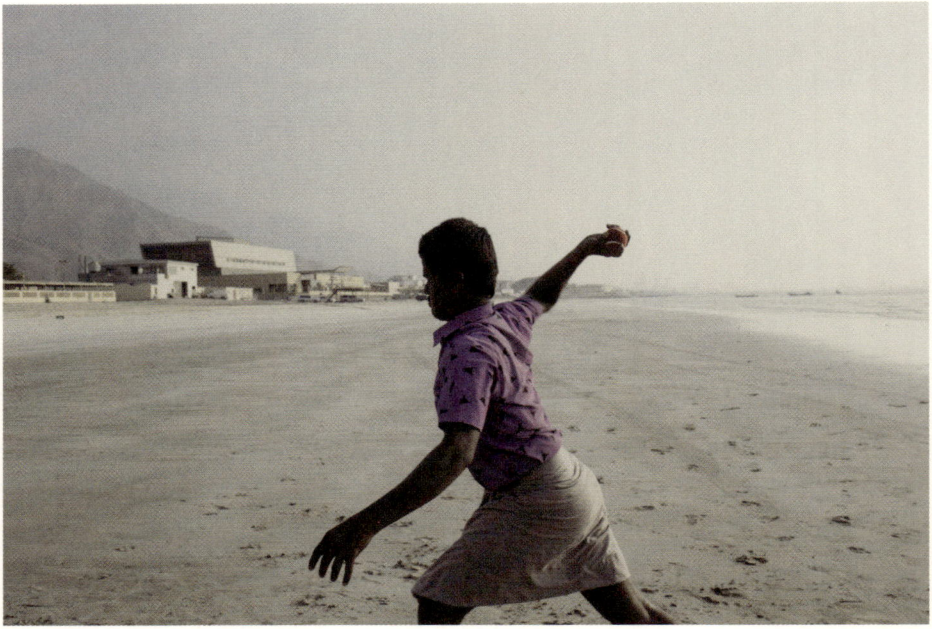

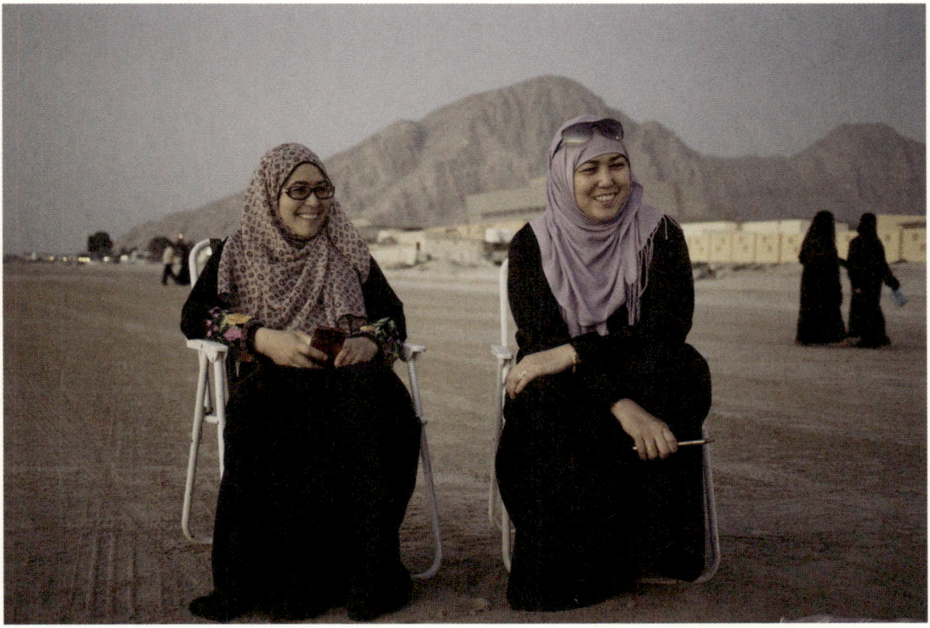

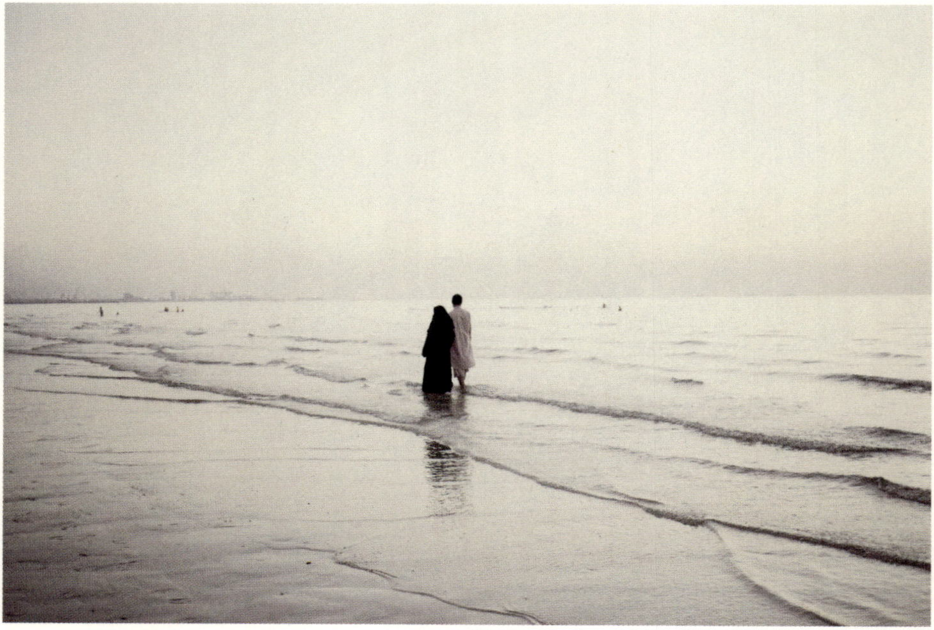

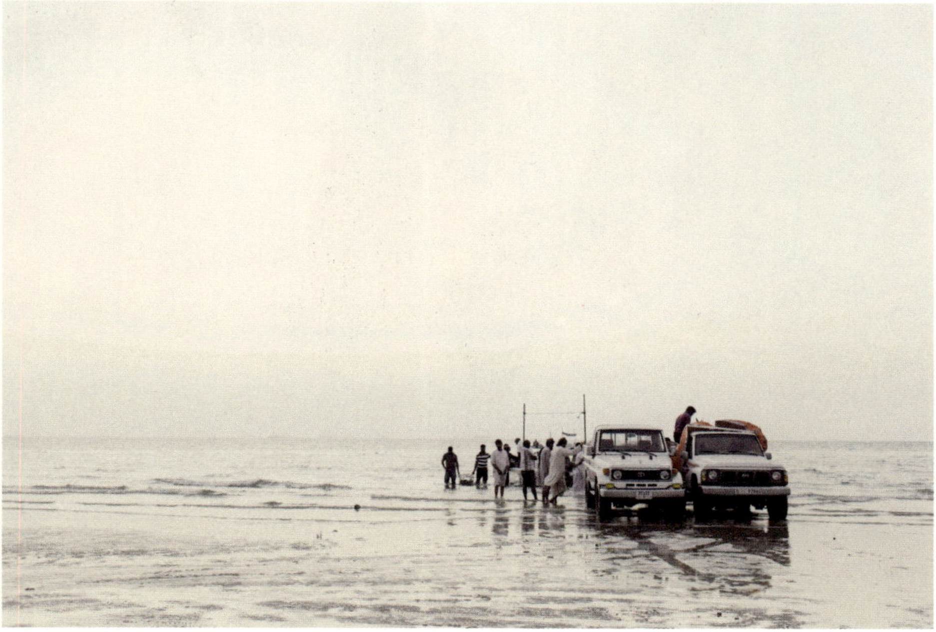

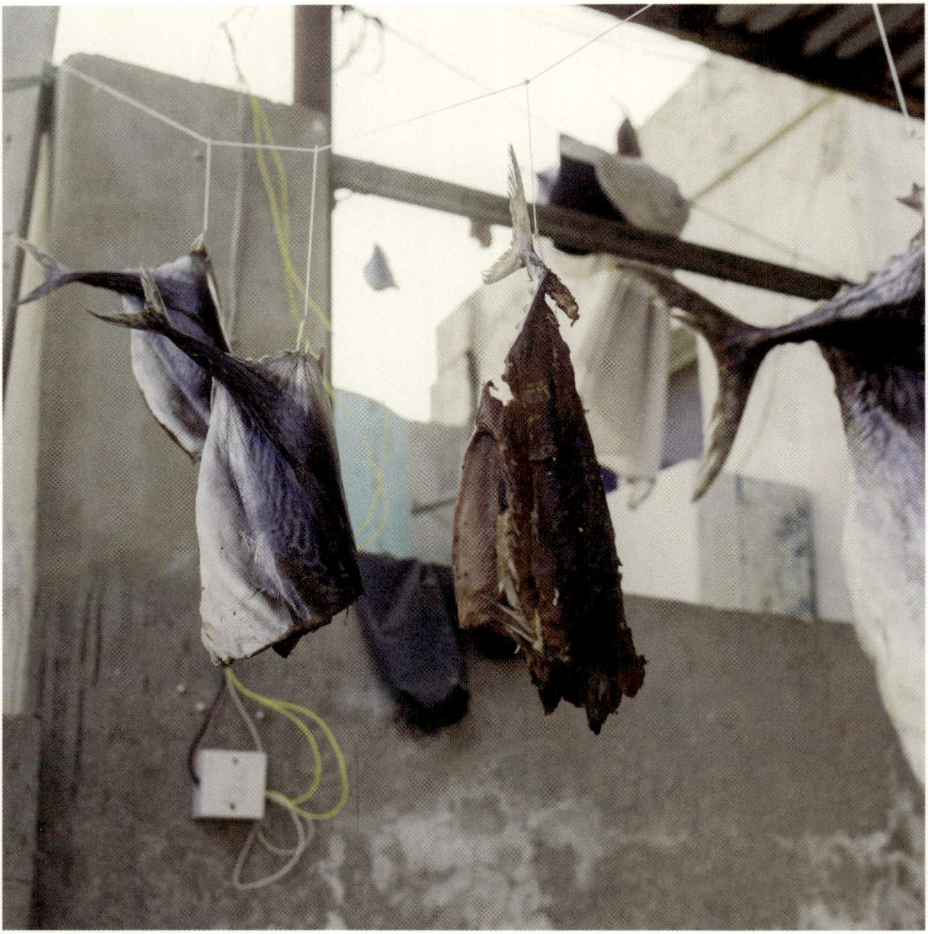

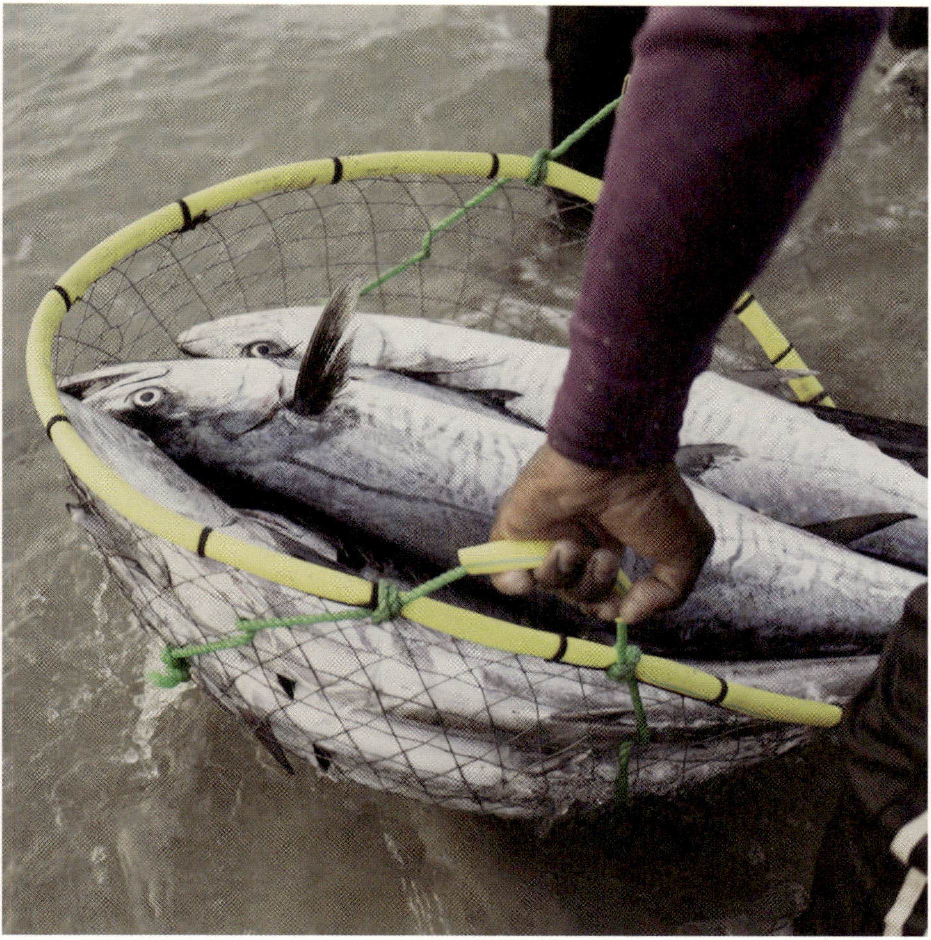

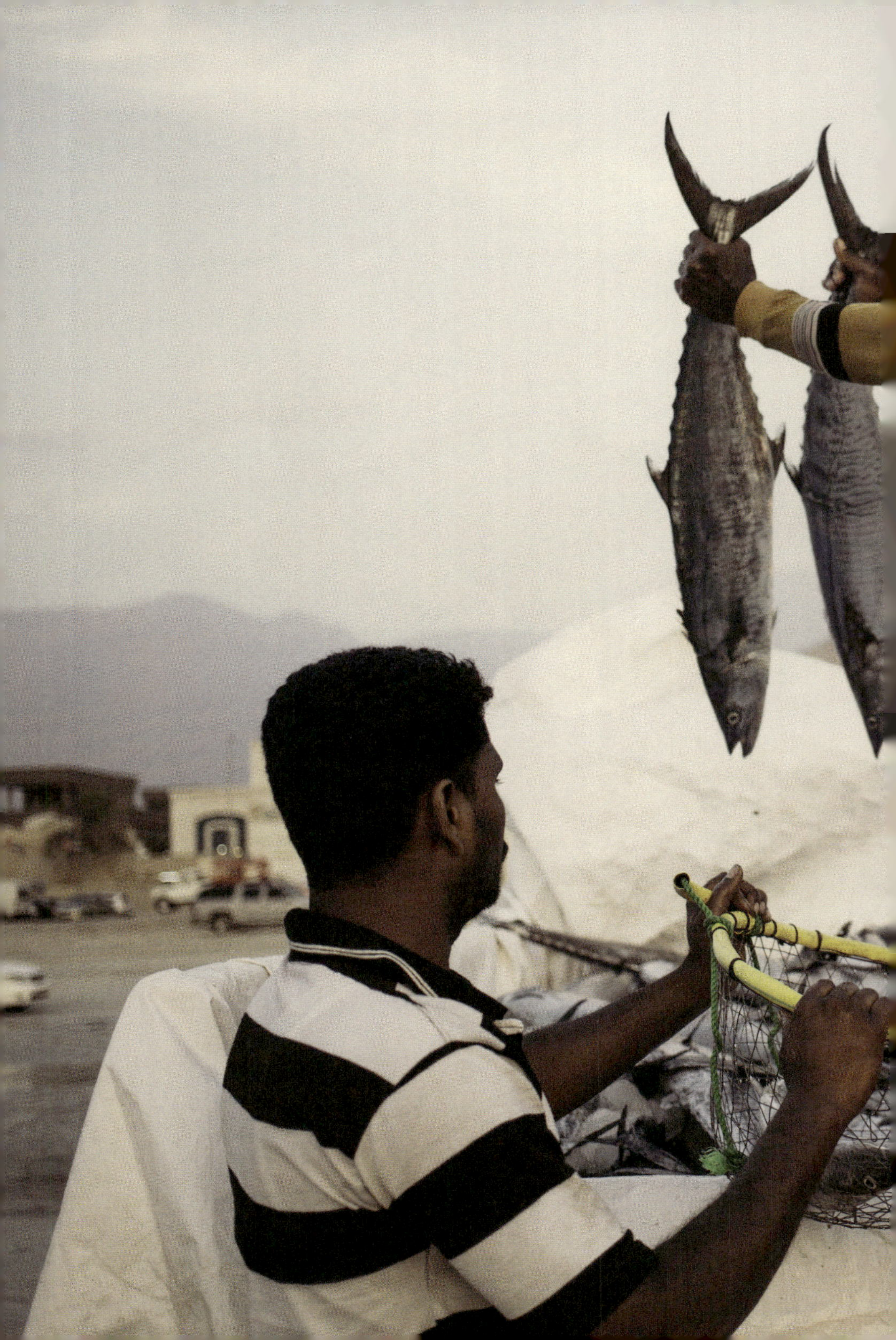

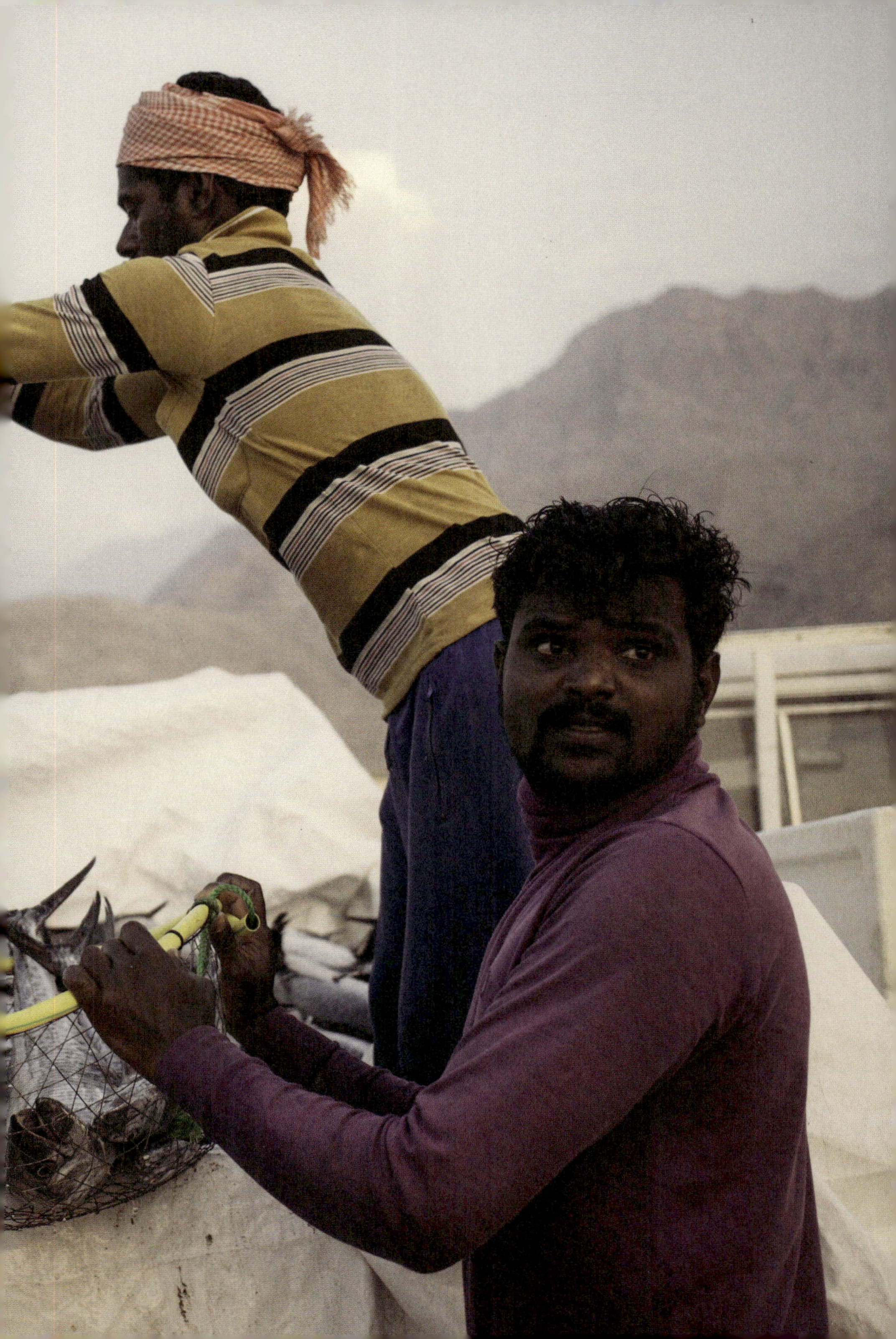

NOTES FROM ADDRESS BOOKS

CROSSROADS OF CIVILISATIONS MUSEUM

COLLECTION OF HISTORIC ARTEFACTS, RARE MANUSCRIPTS AND ARMORY.

AL KHALEEJ ROAD, SHEIKH HASHER AL MAKTOUM HOUSE

+971 4 393 4440

THEMUSEUM.AE

AL JADAF SHIPYARD

ONE OF THE FEW SPOTS TO SEE TRADITIONAL DHOWS BEING BUILT AMONG OTHERS.

WATER TAXI STATION CLOSE BY.

OFF AL KHAIL ROAD, BEFORE BUSINESS BAY CROSSING

DUBAI WORLD TRADE CENTRE FALCON LOUNGE

33RD FLOOR OF DUBAI WORLD TRADE CENTER, SHEIKH ZAYED ROAD

+971 4 309 7979

AL NASR LEISURELAND

SPORTS AND ENTERTAINMENT FACILITIES SINCE 1979.

OUD METHA, BEHIND AMERICAN HOSPITAL

+971 4 337 1234

COMPTOIR 102

CONCEPT STORE AND CAFÉ IN REPURPOSED VILLA.

JUMEIRAH BEACH ROAD OPPOSITE OLD DUBAI ZOO, JUMEIRAH 1

+971 4 385 4555

COMPTOIR102.COM

AL MASKOOF AL IRAQI RESTAURANT

ABU HAIL, OPPOSITE AL MAMZAR SHOPPING CENTER

+971 4 2972282

DAMPA SEAFOOD GRILL: IN THE PHILIPPINES, A DAMPA IS A PLACE WHERE ONE CAN GO TO EAT GRILLED SEAFOOD CAUGHT FRESH FROM THE SEA. THE RESTAURANT IS KNOWN FOR ITS 'BOODLE FIGHT' SEAFOOD SHARING PLATTERS.

PORT SAEED TOWER B CLOCK TOWER R/A, DEIRA CITY CENTRE

+971 4 299 0884'

HYATT REGENCY, DEIRA – AL DAWAAR

DUBAI'S ONLY REVOLVING RESTAURANT AND LOUNGE WITH PANORAMIC VIEWS OF DEIRA AND THE COAST

+971 4 209 6914

MAGRUDY'S JUMEIRAH

JUMEIRAH BEACH ROAD, JUMEIRAH I

+971 4 344 4193

BOOKWORLD KINOKUNIYA

DUBAI'S LARGEST BOOKSTORE LOCATED IN A MALL OF MANY OTHER SUPERLATIVES.

THE DUBAI MALL, 2ND FLOOR OPPOSITE METRO LINK

BOOK WORLD

THIS SECOND-HAND BOOKSHOP IN SATWA IS A LOCAL FAVORITE FOR BACK ISSUES OF PERIODICALS AND LUCKY FINDS. THE SHOP ALSO DOUBLES AS LIBRARY AND CUSTOMERS CAN TRADE IN THEIR BOOKS.

AL HUDAIBA STREET (PLANT STREET), SATWA

+971 4 349 1914

THE OLD LIBRARY DUBAI

A NONPROFIT ORGANISATION, RUN ENTIRELY BY VOLUNTEERS, THE LIBRARY IS THE OLDEST OF ITS KIND IN THE UAE. FOUNDED IN 1969, THE LIBRARY HAS HAD MANY HOMES THROUGHOUT THE CITY OVER THE YEARS. SINCE IT MOVED TO BARSHA IN 2006, THE LIBRARY HAS BEEN PART OF THE DUBAI COMMUNITY THEATRE AND ART CENTRE.

DUCTAC COMPLEX, MALL OF THE EMIRATES

+971 4 341 4777

THE COURTYARD PLAYHOUSE

DUBAI'S FIRST AND ONLY DEDICATED, PURPOSE DESIGNED IMPROVISATION THEATRE. THE PLAYHOUSE SPECIALIZES IN JOHNSTONIAN INSPIRED IMPROVISATION, STAND-UP COMEDY AND ACTING.

THE COURTYARD, STREET 4B, AL QOUZ

+971 50 781 2269

DUBAI CAMEL RACING CLUB AT AL MARMOOM HERITAGE VILLAGE

COMMUNITY SPORTS CLUB THAT FOCUSES ON CAMEL RACING SPORTS.

AL AIN-DUBAI ROAD, AL MARMOOM

+971 4 832 6526

DUBAI CYCLING COURSE

A 50-KILOMETRES LOOP FOLLOWED BY A SECTION COMMONLY KNOWN AS "THE STICK" WHICH RUNS APPROXIMATELY 15-20 KILOMETRES STRAIGHT ALONG AL QUDRA ROAD SET AMONG DUBAI'S SAND DUNES AND ORYX PATHS. DRIVING EAST OUT OF DUBAI, NEAR ARABIAN RANCHES AND STUDIO CITY – YOU CAN ARRIVE AT THE CAR PARK AND CHANGING FACILITY. ANOTHER ACCESS POINT IS THE BICYCLE STORE OFFERING RENTAL SERVICES AND MECHANICS, A COFFEE SHOP AND MEDICAL CENTRE.

ARRIVE BETWEEN 5AM AND 7AM TO BEAT THE HEAT.

AL QUDRA LAKES

AL QUDRA LAKE IS A MAN-MADE LAKE IN THE MIDDLE OF THE SAIH AL SALAM DESERT IN DUBAI. THE LAKE, SPREAD OVER 10 HECTARES, IS HOME TO MORE THAN ONE HUNDRED SPECIES OF BIRDS INCLUDING MANY MIGRATORY BIRDS.

LIWA OASIS, GHARBIA REGION, ABU DHABI

LIWA SITS AT THE ENTRANCE TO THE FAMED RUB AL KHALI, OR THE EMPTY QUARTER, THE WORLD'S LARGEST SINGLE EXPANSE OF DESERT. LIWA IS FAMOUS FOR ITS LARGE DATE PALM PLANTATION CONSISTING OF MORE THAN 100,000 TREES. THIS DATE PALM OASIS HAS BEEN FORMALLY RECOGNISED BY THE UNITED NATIONS' FOOD AND AGRICULTURE ORGANISATION FOR ITS IMPORTANCE AS REPOSITORIES OF GENETIC RESOURCES, BIODIVERSITY AND CULTURAL HERITAGE.

VISIT JANUARY'S TEL MOREEB FESTIVAL, AL DHAFRAH FESTIVAL IN DECEMBER OR JULY'S LIWA DATE FESTIVAL.

HILLI ARCHEOLOGICAL PARK, ABU DHABI

THE VILLAGE OF AL HILI, ABOUT 12 KILOMETRES NORTH OF AL AIN CITY, HAS BECOME INTERNATIONALLY KNOWN FOR ITS ARCHAEOLOGICAL EXCAVATIONS WHICH WERE CONDUCTED STARTING IN THE LATE 1960'S. TEAMS FROM UNIVERSITIES AROUND THE WORLD HAVE DISCOVERED REMAINS OF A SETTLEMENT AND TOMBS DATING BACK TO THE THIRD MILLENNIUM BC.

AL AIN OASIS, ABU DHABI

CONTAINING OVER 147,000 PALM TREES, 550 FARMS, AND INHABITED FOR OVER 4,000 YEARS, AL AIN OASIS, WHICH HAS BEEN LISTED BY UNESCO AS A WORLD HERITAGE SITE. THE OASIS, COVERS MORE THAN 1,200 HECTARES. THE HERITAGE SITE, WHICH CONTAINS THE MAIN OASIS, ALSO FEATURES A NUMBER OF OTHER ATTRACTIONS, SUCH AS THE SHAIKH ZAYED PALACE MUSEUM, THE ECO CENTRE, THE OASIS GARDEN, AND THE WEST GATE EXHIBITION.

MLEIHA ARCHEOLOGICAL CENTER

THE CENTER IS LOCATED 50 KILOMETRES EAST OF THE CITY OF SHARJAH, WEST OF THE LOWER RANGE OF THE HIJAR MOUNTAINS. THE CENTRE DETAILS EXCAVATIONS AND DISCOVERIES MADE OVER THE PAST 40 YEARS AT MILEIHA, PARTICULARLY THE IMPORTANT FAYA NORTH EAST FIND, WHICH POINTS TO THE SPREAD OF HUMANITY FROM AFRICA ACROSS THE RED SEA TO THE GULF PENINSULA AND ONWARD TO POPULATE THE WORLD THROUGH IRAN, INDIA, EUROPE AND ASIA. TOURS ARE OFFERED FROM THE CENTRE TO NEARBY ARCHAEOLOGICAL SITES.

FRIDAY MARKET MASAFI

ON THE DUBAI-FUJAIRAH ROAD APPORACHING THE VILLAGE OF MASAFI WHICH SITS ON THE EDGE OF THE HAJAR MOUNTAINS IN FUJAIRAH. OPEN 7 DAYS A WEEK. FRESH AND LOCALLY GROWN FRUITS AND VEGETABLES, RUGS, POTTERIES AND SOUVENIRS.

SOUK AL ARSAH SHARJAH

SOUK AL ARSAH (COURTYARD SOUK) IS ONE OF THE OLDEST MARKETS IN THE UAE. HISTORICALLY, IT HAS BEEN A MEETING POINT FOR TRADERS. IT WAS REBUILT IN THE 90S AND IS CENTRALLY LOCATED IN THE ARTS AND HERITAGE DISTRICT IN THE HEART OF SHARJAH. ITS SMALL STORES SELL REGIONAL AND LOCAL ANTIQUES AND HANDICRAFTS.

BIOGRAPHIES

EBTISAM ABDULAZIZ IS A CONCEPTUAL ARTIST WHO WORKS AND LIVES IN WASHINGTON, D.C. SHE WORKS WITH GEOMETRY AND MATHEMATICS TO ADDRESS ISSUES OF BELONGING AND IDENTITY THROUGH INSTALLATIONS, PERFORMANCE ART, AND OTHER MEDIA.

GAAR ADAMS IS A WRITER AND PHOTOGRAPHER BASED IN ABU DHABI. HIS WORK AT THE INTERSECTION OF ART, CULTURE, AND THE ENVIRONMENT IN THE MIDDLE EAST AND SOUTH ASIA HAS APPEARED IN THE ATLANTIC, VICE, ROLLING STONE, FOREIGN POLICY, NPR, SLATE, AND ELSEWHERE.

FARAH AL QASIMI IS AN ARTIST WORKING IN PHOTOGRAPHY, VIDEO, SOUND AND PERFORMANCE. SHE RECEIVED AN MFA IN PHOTOGRAPHY FROM THE YALE SCHOOL OF ART IN 2017. HER PRACTICE IS FOCUSED ON LOCATING THE FANTASTIC IN THE EVERYDAY. FARAH ALSO EXPLORES HOW CONSUMER CULTURE SEDUCES PEOPLE, PARTICULARLY WOMEN, WITH PROMISES OF BEAUTY OR SELF-IMPROVEMENT.

RAZAN ALZAYANI IS A FREELANCE PHOTO AND VIDEO JOURNALIST IN DUBAI. HER WORK HAS BEEN FEATURED BY THE BBC, THE GUARDIAN, THE WASHINGTON POST, BLOOMBERG AND THE INDEPENDENT, AND MANY OTHER PUBLICATIONS.

ALEX ATACK IS A FREELANCE PHOTOGRAPHER BASED IN BRISTOL, ENGLAND. HE GREW UP IN THE UAE AND THE UK, AND GRADUATED FROM FALMOUTH UNIVERSITY IN 2014. SINCE THEN, HE HAS WORKED AROUND THE WORLD ON ASSIGNMENTS FOR CLIENTS SUCH AS THE NEW YORK TIMES, THE GUARDIAN, AND MONOCLE.

LAYAN ATTARI LAYAN'S PRACTICE INVOLVES EXPLORATIONS WITHIN DESIGN, ILLUSTRATION, AND DOCUMENTARY PHOTOGRAPHY. HER VISUAL IMAGERY IS DEFINED BY HER PLURALISTIC UPBRINGING IN SHARJAH AND DRIVING ON SHEIKH MOHAMMED BIN ZAYED ROAD EVERY DAY.

JOOBIN BEKHRAD IS AN AWARD-WINNING WRITER AND THE AUTHOR OF NUMEROUS BOOKS OF PROSE AND POETRY. HIS WRITINGS CAN ALSO BE FOUND IN SUCH PUBLICATIONS AS THE NEW YORK TIMES, FORBES, THE ECONOMIST, THE BBC, AND COLUMBIA UNIVERSITY'S COLUMBIA JOURNAL, WHOSE GUEST EDITOR HE SERVED AS IN LATE 2016.

FAYSAL BIBI (PH.D) WORKS ON THE EVOLUTION OF MAMMALS AND THE EFFECTS OF CLIMATE CHANGE ON ECOSYSTEMS OF THE PAST. HE LED PALEONTOLOGICAL RESEARCH IN THE UAE FOR OVER 10 YEARS AND HAS BEEN INVOLVED IN FIELDWORK ACROSS THE WORLD. HE HAS BEEN A RESEARCH SCIENTIST AT THE MUSEUM FUR NATURKUNDE IN BERLIN SINCE 2014.

BEVERLY CASTRO TO BEVERLY AND HER FAMILY, DUBAI IS MORE THAN JUST THE GLITZY SKYSCRAPERS AND FUTURISTIC DEVELOPMENTS. APART FROM THE BEACH AND THE SUN, THEY ENJOY DRIVING TO THE ROCKY MOUNTAINS AND THE DESERT DUNES WHERE ONCE IN A WHILE, THEY'D GET AMAZED AT THESE FLOURISHING NATURE SANCTUARIES THAT WOULD OTHERWISE SEEM TO BE DRY AND HOT CORNERS FOR HALF OF THE YEAR.

LEN CHAPMAN TRAVELLED THE WORLD AS A SEA-GOING ENGINEER BEFORE COMING ASHORE TO WORK IN SEA PORTS. HE JOINED A 3-MAN

START-UP TEAM FOR NEWLY BUILT PORT RASHID, DUBAI, IN MARCH 1971, INTENDING TO STAY A YEAR. HE STAYED 32 YEARS AND WITNESSED DUBAI UNDERGO CHANGES THAT, BACK THEN, SEEMED A NATURAL PART OF EVERYDAY LIFE.

CRISTIANA DE MARCHI IS AN ITALIAN-LEBANESE ARTIST, CURATOR, AND POET LIVING AND WORKING IN DUBAI AND BEIRUT. SHE CONDUCTS PERSONAL ARTISTIC AND LITERARY RESEARCH BESIDES PUBLISHING ARTICLES AND ESSAYS IN CATALOGUES AND MAGAZINES DEVOTED TO CONTEMPORARY ART.

VIKRAM DIVECHA IS AN ARTIST CURRENTLY BASED BETWEEN DUBAI AND NEW YORK.HIS WORK OFTEN ADDRESSES TIME, VALUE AND LABOR AND HIS PRACTICE HAS DEVELOPED AROUND WHAT HE CALLS 'FOUND PROCESSES'—THOSE FORCES AND CAPACITIES AT WORK WITHIN STATE, SOCIAL, ECONOMIC, AND INDUSTRIAL SPHERES. HIS SOCIAL ENGAGEMENTS TRANSLATE INTO PUBLIC ART, SCULPTURAL INSTALLATIONS, VIDEO, AND DRAWINGS.

YASSER ELSHESHTAWY IS AN INDEPENDENT WRITER, RESEARCHER AND CURATOR. HE WAS A PROFESSOR OF ARCHITECTURE AT UNITED ARAB EMIRATES UNIVERSITY, AL AIN, WHERE, IN ADDITION TO TEACHING, HE ALSO RAN THE URBAN RESEARCH LAB. HE WAS APPOINTED AS THE CURATOR FOR THE UAE PAVILION AT THE 15TH VENICE ARCHITECTURE BIENNALE IN 2016. HIS SCHOLARSHIP FOCUSES ON URBANIZATION IN DEVELOPING SOCIETIES, INFORMAL URBANISM, URBAN HISTORY AND ENVIRONMENT-BEHAVIOR STUDIES, WITH A PARTICULAR FOCUS ON MIDDLE EASTERN CITIES. ELSHESHTAWY IS CURRENTLY WORKING ON A BOOK ON THE ARAB GULF CITY TITLED: "TEMPORARY CITIES."

LAMYA GARGASH IS AN EMIRATI ARTIST WHO LIVES AND WORKS IN DUBAI. CONCERNED WITH THE RELICS OF AN EVER SELF-RENEWING ARCHITECTURE, SHE DOCUMENTS THE FORGOTTEN SPACES IN PUBLIC AND PRIVATE REALMS IN EMIRATI SOCIETY. DURING THE COURSE OF HER CAREER, LAMYA HAS WON A NUMBER OF AWARDS FOR HER WORK IN FILM AND PHOTOGRAPHY.

ROB GUBIANI IS AN AUSTRALIAN WILDLIFE AND LANDSCAPE PHOTOGRAPHER WHO LIVES IN THE UAE. HE HAS PUBLISHED HIS WORKS IN A NUMBER OF MAGAZINES, NEWSPAPERS AND SCIENTIFIC JOURNALS INCLUDING NATIONAL GEOGRAPHIC AND ACCLAIM MAGAZINE.

SOUAD HERVÉ IS A FRENCH-ALGERIAN PHOTOGRAPHER. HER TRAVELS BROUGHT HER TO DUBAI WHERE SHE STAYED FOR A FEW YEARS WORKING AS AN OFFICIAL PHOTOGRAPHER FOR DUBAI CULTURE. INTRIGUED BY THE EERIE AND HISTORICAL SCENERY OF BERLIN, SOUAD RELOCATED TO THE GERMAN CITY TO PURSUE HER PHOTOGRAPHY PROJECTS THERE.

GEORGE KATODRYTIS IS AN ARCHITECT INVOLVED IN PRACTICE, TEACHING AND RESEARCH. HE IS CURRENTLY PROFESSOR AND HEAD OF THE DEPARTMENT OF ARCHITECTURE AT THE COLLEGE OF ARCHITECTURE, ART AND DESIGN AT THE AMERICAN UNIVERSITY OF SHARJAH. HE STUDIED AND TAUGHT AT THE ARCHITECTURAL ASSOCIATION IN LONDON AND HAS BEEN A VISITING PROFESSOR

AT VARIOUS SCHOOLS AROUND THE WORLD. HE BUILT A NUMBER OF PROJECTS IN EUROPE AND THE MIDDLE EAST AND ALSO PUBLISHED WIDELY ON CONTEMPORARY ARCHITECTURE, URBANISM, CULTURAL THEORY, AND DIGITAL MEDIA. HIS WORK ADDRESSES THE 'CITY', PARTICULARLY AS IT IS EVOLVING IN THE 21ST CENTURY.

MOHAMMED KAZEM IS AN EMIRATI ARTIST AND CURATOR LIVING AND WORKING IN DUBAI. HE HAS DEVELOPED AN ARTISTIC PRACTICE THAT ENCOMPASSES VIDEO, PHOTOGRAPHY, AND PERFORMANCE TO FIND NEW WAYS OF APPREHENDING HIS ENVIRONMENT AND EXPERIENCES.

SULAYMAN KHALAF (PH.D) IS A SOCIOCULTURAL ANTHROPOLOGIST WHO SPECIALIZES IN GULF ARAB SOCIETIES AND CULTURE, AND TRIBAL/PEASANT COMMUNITIES IN NORTHEASTERN SYRIA. HIS BA AND MA ARE FROM AUB, AND HIS PHD IS FROM UCLA. HE HAS WORKED FOR THE ABU DHABI AUTHORITY FOR TOURISM AND CULTURE AND AS A PROFESSOR OF ANTHROPOLOGY AT KUWAIT UNIVERSITY, UAE UNIVERSITY, SHARJAH UNIVERSITY, AND UNIVERSITY OF BAHRAIN. HE HAS ALSO BEEN A VISITING SCHOLAR AT HARVARD AND A VISITING PROFESSOR AT STOCKHOLM UNIVERSITY. HIS RESEARCH INTERESTS IN THE GULF REGION ARE IN THE AREAS OF GLOBALIZATION, HERITAGE, NATION BUILDING, AND NATIONAL IDENTITY.

MATTHEW MACLEAN RECEIVED HIS PHD IN HISTORY AND MIDDLE EASTERN AND ISLAMIC STUDIES FROM NEW YORK UNIVERSITY IN 2017. HE HAS LIVED IN AL AIN, DUBAI, ABU DHABI, AND RAS AL KHAIMAH, WHERE HE SPENT A YEAR AS A VISITING SCHOLAR AT THE SHEIKH SAUD BIN SAQR AL QASIMI FOUNDATION FOR POLICY RESEARCH.

AHMAD MAKIA IS A GEOGRAPHER FROM DUBAI WHO WRITES ABOUT WET MATTERS, GULF LANDSCAPES, AND SEX. HE CO-FOUNDED 'THE STATE', A PUBLISHING PLATFORM THAT FOCUSES ON SOUTH-SOUTH ORIENTATIONS, THE DIGITAL HUMANITIES, AND NARRATIVES FROM THE GULF REGION. HE USED TO MAKE BOOKS WITH FRIENDS BUT NOW PRODUCES THEM FOR CONTEMPORARY ART INSTITUTES.

BEATRIZ ITZEL CRUZ MEGCHUN (PH.D.) IS AN ACADEMIC, CONSULTANT, AND RESEARCHER WHOSE WORK FOCUSES ON THE USE OF DESIGN AS A STRATEGIC INSTRUMENT AT THE NATIONAL AND BUSINESS LEVEL. HER RECENT RESEARCH CONCERNS UNDERSTANDING SPATIAL FORMS OF INCLUSION AND EXCLUSION IN MULTI-CULTURAL LOCATIONS. SHE IS CURRENTLY THE ASSISTANT PROFESSOR OF DESIGN AT THE PAMPLIN SCHOOL OF BUSINESS, UNIVERSITY OF PORTLAND.

KEVIN MITCHELL IS A PROFESSOR OF ARCHITECTURE AT THE COLLEGE OF ARCHITECTURE, ART AND DESIGN AT THE AMERICAN UNIVERSITY OF SHARJAH. HE CURRENTLY SERVES AS THE VICE PROVOST FOR UNDERGRADUATE AFFAIRS AND INSTRUCTION.

MARYAM MUDHAFFAR IS AN EMIRATI ARCHITECT AND ARCHITECTURAL HISTORIAN. SHE COMPLETED HER BACHELORS OF ARCHITECTURE FROM THE AMERICAN UNIVERSITY OF SHARJAH, AND HER MASTERS IN ARCHITECTURAL HISTORY FROM THE BARTLETT AT UCL IN LONDON, WHERE SHE FOCUSED ON ISSUES OF REPRESENTATION, MATERIAL CULTURE, GENDER STUDIES, AND PLACE-BASED MEMORIES.

ANNA NIELSEN IS A DANISH PHOTOJOURNALIST CURRENTLY LIVING IN THE UAE, WHERE SHE WORKS AS A FULL-TIME PHOTOGRAPHER. SHE

WORKS ON ASSIGNMENTS AND COMMISSIONS FOR PUBLICATIONS, INCLUDING HARPERS BAZAR, THE NATIONAL, BROWNBOOK, MONOCLE, AND ARTJOURNAL.

SALLY PROSSER IS A TRAVEL AND FOOD BLOGGER FROM THE UK, SHE HAS LIVED IN DUBAI FOR ALMOST TWO DECADES, WITNESSING THE TRANSFORMATION OF THE CITY FIRSTHAND. SHE IS THE AUTHOR OF THE AWARD-WINNING BLOG MYCUSTURDPIE.COM.

TODD REISZ IS AN ARCHITECT AND WRITER FOCUSING ON THE CITIES OF THE GULF REGION, FROM BOTH HISTORICAL AND CONTEMPORARY PERSPECTIVES. AMONG OTHER WORKS HE IS THE EDITOR OF 'AL MANAKH 2: GULF CONTINUED', WHICH ANALYZES THE RECENT DEVELOPMENTS OF CITIES IN SAUDI ARABIA, KUWAIT, QATAR, BAHRAIN, AND THE UAE. HE TEACHES AT HARVARD UNIVERSITY'S GRADUATE SCHOOL OF DESIGN.

JUAN ROLDÁN (M. ARCH AND MS SC) IS AN ARCHITECT AND DESIGNER TEACHING AND RESEARCHING AT THE AMERICAN UNIVERSITY OF SHARJAH. HIS RESEARCH IS FOCUSED ON THE DOMESTICATED PUBLIC REALM AND PUBLIC INTERIORS.

KUBA RYNIEWICZ IS A PHOTOGRAPHER AND CREATIVE PRODUCER BASED IN THE NORTH-EAST OF ENGLAND. HIS WORK CHALLENGES TRADITIONAL PORTRAITURE AND TRAVEL CHRONICLE TO NARRATE UNHEARD STORIES IN THE CONTEXT OF LANDSCAPE, HISTORY, FASHION, AND CULTURE. HIS WORK HAS APPEARED IN FANTASTIC MAN, APARTAMENTO, THE PLANT, WIRE, PIN-UP, WIRED (JAPAN), AMONG OTHERS.

MAHYA SOLTANI BORN IN TEHRAN, AND RAISED BETWEEN TEHRAN AND DUBAI, MAHYA IS AN IRANIAN DESIGNER AND VISUAL ARTIST CURRENTLY RESIDING IN BROOKLYN, NEW YORK. AFTER PRACTICING AS A DESIGNER AND ART DIRECTOR IN DUBAI FOR FOUR YEARS, MAHYA MOVED TO THE UNITED STATES TO PURSUE HER MFA IN DESIGN ENTREPRENEURSHIP AT SCHOOL OF VISUAL ARTS IN NEW YORK. HER PRACTICE AS AN ARTIST ENGAGES TIME AS A TOOL FOR CHALLENGING EXPECTATIONS AND PERCEPTIONS WHILE DELINEATING THE EXISTENCE OF ALTERNATE REALITIES.

NJ STALLARD IS A WRITER, EDITOR, AND POET. AS AN EDITOR, SHE HAS WORKED ON NUMEROUS PUBLICATIONS AND HER WRITING HAS BEEN FEATURED IN THE GUARDIAN, VICE, TANK MAGAZINE, ANOTHER, PN REVIEW AND OTHERS. PREVIOUSLY BASED IN BEIRUT, DUBAI, AND ISTANBUL, SHE IS CURRENTLY STUDYING POETRY AT THE UNIVERSITY OF MANCHESTER'S CENTRE FOR NEW WRITING.

ANNA ZACHARIAS IS A CANADIAN JOURNALIST AND AUTHOR OF 'PEOPLE OF RAS AL-KHAIMAH'. SHE JOINED THE NATIONAL NEWSPAPER, IN 2008, AS ITS RAS AL-KHAIMAH CORRESPONDENT. BASED IN ABU DHABI FROM 2011 TO 2014, SHE WORKED AS A SENIOR FEATURES WRITER AND WROTE THE NATIONAL'S CAMEL BLOG, A YEAR AT THE CAMEL RACES.

SHARMEEN INAYAT GREW UP IN DUBAI, KARACHI, SAN FRANCISCO AND NAIROBI, AND VARIABLY CLAIMS ORIGINS IN EACH. SHE IS ENGAGED IN SPATIAL PRACTICE AND RESEARCH WITH REGIONAL AND INTERNATIONAL ORGANIZATIONS. HER INDEPENDENT WORK EXPLORES HUMAN GEOGRAPHY WITH A FOCUS ON URBAN MIGRANT EXPERIENCES.

Cover Photo and Stock Photography pp. 13, 97, 181, 239: Sharmeen Inayat.
End Papers: *Survey Sketch of the Port of Dubai* part of a larger set of drawings completed by H. F. Walter on behest of the British Royal Navy, 1910.
Fonts used: Garamond Premier Pro, Gotham HTF, Akzidenz-Grotesk Numbers.

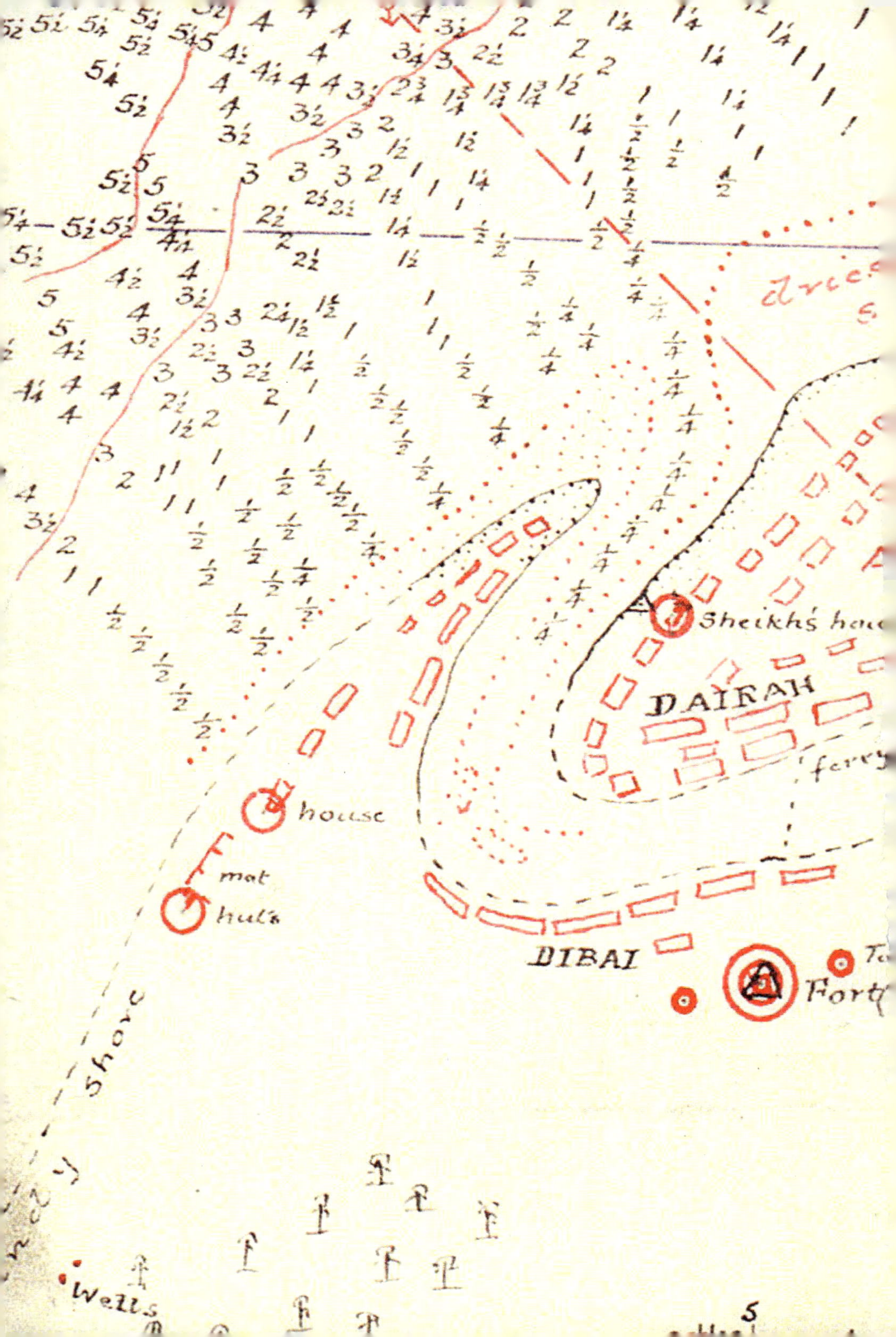
DAIRAH
Sheikh's hou
ferry
house
mat
huts
DIBAI
Fort
Shore
Wells